They Fought in
the Creature Features

Other Interview Books by Tom Weaver and from McFarland

Attack of the Monster Movie Makers: Interviews with 20 Genre Giants (2014)

Earth vs. the Sci-Fi Filmmakers: 20 Interviews (2014)

I Talked with a Zombie: Interviews with 23 Veterans of Horror and Sci-Fi Films and Television (2014)

I Was a Monster Movie Maker: Conversations with 22 SF and Horror Filmmakers (2011)

Science Fiction Confidential: Interviews with 23 Monster Stars and Filmmakers (2010)

A Sci-Fi Swarm and Horror Horde: Interviews with 62 Filmmakers (2010)

Eye on Science Fiction: 20 Interviews with Classic SF and Horror Filmmakers (2007)

Science Fiction and Fantasy Film Flashbacks: Conversations with 24 Actors, Writers, Producers and Directors from the Golden Age (2004)

It Came from Horrorwood: Inteviews with Moviemakers in the SF and Horror Tradition (2004)

Return of the B Science Fiction and Horror Heroes: The Mutant Melding of Two Volumes of Classic Interviews (2000) (A combined edition of the two earlier Weaver titles *Interviews with B Science Fiction and Horror Movie Makers* and *Science Fiction Stars and Horror Heroes*)

Other McFarland Books by Tom Weaver

Poverty Row HORRORS! Monogram, PRC and Republic Horror Films of the Forties (1993)

John Carradine: The Films (2008)

By Tom Weaver with Michael Brunas and John Brunas

Universal Horrors: The Studio's Classic Films, 1931–1946, 2d ed. (McFarland, 2007)

By Tom Weaver, David Schecter and Steve Kronenberg

The Creature Chronicles: Exploring the Black Lagoon Trilogy (McFarland, 2014)

They Fought in the Creature Features

Interviews with 23 Classic Horror, Science Fiction and Serial Stars

TOM WEAVER

McFarland & Company, Inc., Publishers
Jefferson, North Carolina

> *The present work is a reprint of the library bound edition of* They Fought in the Creature Features: Interviews with 23 Classic Horror, Science Fiction and Serial Stars, *first published in 1995 by McFarland.*

Library of Congress Cataloguing-in-Publication Data

Weaver, Tom, 1958–
   They fought in the creature features : interviews with 23 classic horror, science fiction and serial stars / by Tom Weaver.
      p.   cm.
   Includes filmographies and index.

   ISBN 978-0-7864-9575-7 (softcover : acid free paper) ♾
   ISBN 978-1-4766-1686-5 (ebook)

   1. Horror films—History and criticism.   2. Science fiction films—History and criticism.   3. Motion picture serials—History and criticism.   4. Motion picture actors and actresses—United States—Interviews.   I. Weaver, Tom, 1958–
PN1995.9.H6T47   2014
791.43'616—dc20   94-48609

British Library cataloguing data are available

© 1995 Tom Weaver. All rights reserved

No part of this book may be reproduced or transmitted in any form or by any means, electronic or mechanical, including photocopying or recording, or by any information storage and retrieval system, without permission in writing from the publisher.

Front cover image: the Metaluna Mutant may have the upper pincer at the moment but will not prevail in its battle with *This Island Earth* star Rex Reason, one of the 1950s' top movie monster-fighters, 1955 Universal

Printed in the United States of America

McFarland & Company, Inc., Publishers
  Box 611, Jefferson, North Carolina 28640
    www.mcfarlandpub.com

Amidst the many real-life people thanked
in the *Preface* on page ix, there are 13 "fictional"
names—characters in some of the SF and horror titles mentioned
in this book. If you're one of those remarkable people who can
pick out these 13 names, *and* provide the titles of the
flicks in which they appear, then this book
is very appreciatively dedicated to *you*.

Table of Contents

Acknowledgments viii
Preface ix

Julie Adams 1
John Agar 13
Richard Anderson 25
John Archer 37
Jeanne Bates 51
Billy Benedict 61
Turhan Bey 73
Lloyd Bridges 85
Ricou Browning 97
Robert Cornthwaite 111
Louise Currie 131
Richard Denning 145
Anne Francis 161
Mark Goddard 173
June Lockhart 187
Eugene Lourie 201
Jeff Morrow 211
Lori Nelson 221
Rex Reason 233
William Schallert 245
Don Taylor 263
George Wallace 277
Jane Wyatt 289

Index 303

Acknowledgments

Abridged versions of the interviews in this book were originally published in the following magazines:

Julie Adams: "Creature Love," *Starlog* #167, June, 1991
John Agar: "Creature Crusher," *Starlog* #164, March, 1991
Richard Anderson: "Tales of the Forbidden Planet," *Starlog* #156, July, 1990
John Archer: "Lunar Destiny," *Starlog* #202, May, 1994
Jeanne Bates: "The Phantom's Lady," *Comics Scene* #44, July, 1994
Billy Benedict: "Captain Marvel's Pal," *Starlog* #199, February, 1994
Turhan Bey: "Stardom at Bey," *Fangoria* #105, August, 1991
Lloyd Bridges: "Man of the Seas," *Starlog* #182, September, 1992
Ricou Browning: "Creature Man," *Starlog* #167, June, 1991
Robert Cornthwaite: "Friend of the Thing," *Starlog* #178, May, 1992
Louise Currie: "Cliffhanger Queen," *Comics Scene* #21, October, 1991
Richard Denning: "Creature Hunter," *Starlog* #164, March, 1991
Anne Francis: "Woman of the Forbidden Planet," *Starlog* #186, January, 1993
Mark Goddard: "Space Duty," *Starlog* #190, May, 1993
June Lockhart: "Outrageous Original," *Starlog* #198, January, 1994
Eugene Lourie: "Director of Dinosaurs," *Starlog* #193, August, 1993
Jeff Morrow: "Jeff Morrow—The Man from Metaluna," *Starlog* #118, May, 1987
Lori Nelson: "Creature Lady," *Starlog* #167, June, 1991
Rex Reason: "Memories of Metaluna," *Starlog* #140, March, 1989
William Schallert: "Character Star," *Starlog* #184, November, 1992
Don Taylor: "Director of Men-Apes," *Starlog* #165, April, 1991
George Wallace: "Call Him Commando Cody," *Comics Scene* #20, August, 1991
Jane Wyatt: "Mother Knows Best," *Starlog* #161, December, 1990

Preface

This companion volume to my earlier *Interviews with Science Fiction and Horror Movie Makers* (1988), *Science Fiction Stars and Horror Heroes* (1991) and *Attack of the Monster Movie Makers* (1994) could not have been written without the generous assistance of many of the same people who have helped me in the past. Sincere thanks go to Mark Martucci, Greg Luce, Tom Johnson, Kyra Zelas, Buddy Barnett, Ron Borst, Paul and Donna Parla, Louise Carey, David Skal, Will Murray, Captain Jim Maddison, Frank Coghlan, Jr., Eric Jacobs, Alex Gordon, Don Leifert, Isabel Lewis, Dan Scapperotti, the nice folks at Photofest, Fred Olen Ray, David Schow, *Fangoria*'s Tony Timpone and Mike Gingold, *Starlog*'s Dave McDonnell, Mitch MacAfee, John Foster, Quintillus Aurelius, Joe and Jeff Indusi, Carl Maia, Alex Lugones, Captain George LeMay, Dennis Daniel, Carl and Debbie Del Vecchio, Miklos Sangre, Glenn Damato, John Antosiewicz, Greg Mank, Tal Chotali, Gary and Sue Svehla (and the rest of the FANEX gang), Cal Meacham, Ruth Brunas, Rich Scrivani, Phyllis Allenby, Joe Dante, Jon and Julie Weaver, Erin Ray Fresco, Bandit and Tigger, Joe Kane and all the friendly people at Manhattan's Lincoln Center.

Research associates Mike and John Brunas did their usual, terrific job helping me whip this into shape, and John Cocchi and Jack Dukesbery furnished their always-invaluable assistance with the many filmographies. Thanks, too, to all of my new interviewees; and *special* thanks to the additional interviewees who were promised slots in this book, but (because of lack of space) had to be bumped. Needless to say, they'll all be on proud display in (gulp!) my fifth interviews book with McFarland.

Tom Weaver
North Tarrytown, New York

The Creature scared people, but there was also a sort of sweetness about it. In the real classics, there always is that feeling of compassion for the monster. I think maybe it touches something in ourselves, maybe the darker parts of ourselves, that long to be loved and think they really can't ever be loved. It strikes a chord within us.

Julie Adams

They Fought in the Creature Features

IT'S BEEN ALMOST 40 years since Julie Adams was caught in the web-fingered clutches of the Gill Man, and she has not quite managed to wriggle free yet. It is the type of highly visible role that dogs an actress, even a talented one who has proven her dramatic worth in dozens of movies and enough television to fill that back lot Black Lagoon where the Creature, gulping like a lovesick schoolboy, suffered its initial attack of love-at-first-sight.

"Once I was working in Chicago in a play, *Father's Day* by Oliver Hailey, and I was peeved when I got this review that said, 'Julie Adams shows more depth than one would have suspected from the star of *Creature from the Black Lagoon*.' No matter what you do, you can act your heart out, but people will always say, 'Oh, Julie Adams—*Creature from the Black Lagoon*.'" Adams laughs, long and loud, but you have to wonder whether it isn't one of those crying-on-the-inside situations. She insists, convincingly, that it's not. "Oh, no, no, no. One must take all these things with humor. After all, it's amazing that the film connected with that many people. To be so closely connected with it is fine, just fine."

But like Lori Nelson, leading lady of *Revenge of the Creature*, Adams did squirm just a mite when she was first assigned to *Creature from the Black Lagoon*. "But then my attitude was, oh, all right. I was a contract player at Universal: Sometimes I did *this*, sometimes *that*, sometimes the other. I was working in four or five movies a year at that time, so it didn't seem like any big deal. I just went right along with it. I never really fought the studio much about things. And then I wound up having *such* a good time on the picture that there's no *way* I can say now that I was unhappy about it."

Still active and glamorous today, Julie Adams is probably Waterloo, Iowa's, greatest gift to the motion picture industry. Although born in the Hawkeye State, Betty May Adams grew up in Arkansas and made her acting debut in a third grade play. "I was in *Hansel and Gretel* and some milk spilled, and I ad-libbed and saved the day. This gave me a flush of power—in the third grade—and I think that's where it all began *[laughs]*! Then I was taking things like expression lessons when I lived in a town called Blytheville, Arkansas—a town of about 10,000 people—because I somehow knew that I wanted to be an actress. I went a couple of years to junior college, to please everybody, and then I came to California to try to be an actress. Nobody found me *[laughs]*, I had to go and find *them*!"

Working three days a week as a secretary to support herself, Adams concentrated the remainder of her time on taking speech lessons (to lose her Midwestern accent) and making the rounds at the various studios' casting departments. Her first movie role was playing a starlet, appropriately enough,

Previous page: Beauty (Julie Adams) consorts with the Beast ("Creature" Ben Chapman) in a between-takes pose. (Photofest)

Adams realizes that the Creature (Ben Chapman) just "longed to be loved," but doesn't seem too keen on the idea in publicity shots.

in a Paramount film called *Red, Hot and Blue* (1949), followed by a leading role in a 58-minute Lippert Western, *The Dalton Gang* (1949) with Don "Red" Barry. Over a period of five weeks, she appeared in six more quickie Lippert Westerns, co-starring with memorable(?) Western favorites(??) Jimmy "Shamrock" Ellison, Russell "Lucky" Hayden and Fuzzy Knight. "It was crazy! There were two leading men, Jimmy Ellison and Russell Hayden, and also a large cast of character actors, and we were all in all of the films. I was The Girl in all of them, so I had three outfits. I had a riding outfit, a stagecoach 'dress-up' outfit and a 'farm girl' outfit. We'd shoot all the farmhouse scenes for all six movies at once, then all the stagecoach scenes. I had a hard time remembering who I was. 'Am I the farm girl this time, or the cow girl?' It was very funny!"

Adams' first big show business break was at Universal, when she appeared in a screen test opposite All American footballer Leon Hart, a Detroit Lions end. It was Hart who was being considered by the studio, but the gridiron star flopped while Universal executives flipped over Adams. The studio changed her first name, possibly to cover up her prior history of low-caliber Westerns, and put her to work on the Universal lot. She co-starred in 21 Universal films over the next several years, including *Bright Victory* (1951) and *Bend of the River* (1952)—as well as the usual mixed bag of lesser-known, less respectable titles like the awful *Finders Keepers* (1951) and desultory Technicolor Westerns like *The Man from the Alamo* and *The Stand at Apache River* (both 1953).

She also had to put up with the harmless but tacky publicity ploys of the day, including having her legs, "the most perfectly symmetrical in the world," win an award, with the result that Universal insured them for $125,000. Of course, they were nowhere to be seen in the period dramas in which Universal kept placing her, so the studio obligingly gave her a bathing suit lead in *Creature from the Black Lagoon*. Richard Carlson was the nominal hero, but the *real* stars of *Creature* were Adams (in a white one-piece swimsuit that fit her far better than the title of "marine researcher") and a scaly foam rubber costume fabricated in the Universal makeup department.

"Bud Westmore and Jack Kevan made the Gill Man outfit in the lab. Bud particularly was a great friend of mine, I was extremely fond of Bud, and I liked Jack as well. Whenever I would go by, I would see them making their magic—pouring the foam rubber, working with molds, painting and fixing the costume and so on. They were quite marvelous, and in a way it was sort of an unrecognized art when you think of these things [like the Creature] that have become part of our culture. And it really *has* become part of everybody's psyche—people recognize it immediately.

"The first Creature suit was made in a certain way that was all wrong. Most of us knew it was wrong, but it was designed more to the taste of one of the executives at the studio, who wanted the Creature to look like the Oscar statuette. It was almost like a body suit; it just didn't have any menace or any kind of excitement about it. And when it was tested on film, it became clear that that was *not* going to be it! The day they tested it in the tank at Universal, I tried out the Aqualung—I swam around in the tank for about twenty-five minutes, and it was so wonderful. So the picture was closed down while Bud Westmore and Jack Kevan and whoever else made the monster suit that they'd had in mind in the first place. And because we had nothing to do until the new monster suit was made and approved, 'Scotty' Welbourne, who did the underwater photography, and Ricou Browning the man who played the Creature, and I, we lugged tanks from the studio and we went to Catalina and went diving. I had a wonderful time learning how to use what was then relatively new equipment."

Adams enjoyed working with Carlson as well as the other male leads, Richard Denning and Antonio Moreno. "It was a very, very pleasant movie, and we all laughed a lot. You *had* to! We were down on the beach on the edge of the water one day, doing the scene where the Creature has killed one of the natives. We were looking down at the body and there was this moment where we were all very still. Richard Carlson was in his bathing trunks and he had his face mask on his forehead, and in just the way people take off their hats for the dead, he reached up and took off his face mask. He doffed it so seriously that we all started to laugh, and it took us a long time to come back together again. It was just too absurd *[laughs]*! And then we had this wonderful guy who did the clapboard for the different shots, an old vaudevillian. The day that Whit Bissell's face was all bloodied up by the Creature, this fellow clapped the board and then he said to Whit *[out of the corner of her mouth]*, 'How ya fixed for blades?' *[laughs]*."

Director Jack Arnold, Adams reminisces, "I liked a lot. He's an extremely nice man and very easy to work with. In those days, we just sort of made movies—do you know what I mean *[laughs]*? We just got on with it, we just went forward. But Jack was extremely efficient. Pictures survive when they have an emotional impact, and I think that so often that is due to the director. That's really his job, because when a picture is finished shooting, basically it's just all this exposed film. The director had to have a picture of it in his mind, to know what's telling and what isn't. Jack really put together a film that touched people."

And William Alland, the too-often unsung producer of so many seminal fifties SF films, "was relatively quiet, soft-spoken, but seemed very efficient and very pleasant always. Now that I have two sons in production (one's in post-production and the other is a first assistant director), I've suddenly discovered that there really is an awful lot that actors don't know about. A producer works with the real nuts and bolts of the production and the actors know only what concerns them. I have to assume that William Alland was a good producer because *Creature from the Black Lagoon* came out looking so well, which is quite remarkable considering the fact that we didn't go on location. People are always quite astonished that we made it on the back lot."

While Jack Arnold put his cast and Creature (Ben Chapman) through their paces at Universal, director James C. Havens headed up the Florida-based second unit photographing underwater scenes at Wakulla Springs. "They ran some rushes of the Florida second unit stuff for us while we were doing *Creature,* and they were so wonderful. Especially the dive that Ricou Browning made, kidnapping the girl [Ginger Stanley] who was doubling me. A fifty foot

Beauty meets the Beast: Julie Adams and the *Creature from the Black Lagoon*.

dive! And after a fifty foot dive, you can't just come back up, you have to get air. So hidden behind some of the rocks at the bottom were breathing hoses, and they could breathe off of those—it forces the air through the side of your mouth. It was very exciting."

Less exciting was the morning when Adams found herself in a studio tank that no one had remembered to heat beforehand. "The day we shot on the stage where they had the Creature's underwater grotto, we were in this huge tank of water. They had forgotten to heat the tank, and the water was ... *so*

... *cold. S-s-s-so c-c-c-cold!* It was sort of a disastrous morning all in all. It was freezing cold, and I was trying not to shiver as I was lying limp in this poor guy's [the Creature's] arms. And he could barely see, so as he carried me, he scraped my head on a plaster rock and skinned my head *[laughs]*! It was not the best morning of the picture!"

Even though she insists that she enjoyed working in *Creature*, Adams also admits that, "I didn't really want to be in the sequels, to tell you the truth. So I was happy that they didn't come to me anyway." Is *Creature from the Black Lagoon* a film that gets much play in her home video recorder? "No, never. But that's not saying anything against *Creature*, it's just that I'm really not one for watching my old movies. I never really like my work very much, I think about how I'd like to do it over—I'm very critical. I like to see something until I learn what I *can* learn from it, and then I put it away. I just don't believe in looking back."

Like both of the Creature's later female leads, Lori Nelson and Leigh Snowden, Adams also marked time as leading lady to another one of Universal's more unlikely leading men, Francis the Talking Mule. The gimmick that initially sparked the series had worn fairly thin by the time of *Francis Joins the WACs* (1954)—not that Adams missed much by failing to appear in the series during its dubious "prime." "*Francis Joins the WACs*? Well *[laughs]*, what can we say? I enjoyed working with [series star] Donald O'Connor more than Francis! They had a little tiny wire under the lip of the mule, and from the side they would pull on the wire, move it around, to make him 'talk.'" Better roles lay ahead in pictures like the 1955 soaper *One Desire* (as the wicked wife of Rock Hudson, dying in flames at picture's end), the war actioner *Away All Boats* (1956) and the rackets exposé *Slaughter on Tenth Avenue* (1957). An added dividend of appearing in *The Looters* (1955) was meeting leading man Ray Danton, who "punched" her in the film and married her in real life in February 1955.

In 1958 she left Universal ("My contract was up and I was married and I had a baby, and I was just not as interested in working for a while"). But she soon made a comeback, appearing in movies and also on television, where her first regular role was opposite Jock Mahoney on CBS's short-lived *Yancy Derringer*. In 1962 she took the science fiction plunge again, playing a scientist in Columbia's *The Underwater City*, a soggy title-tells-all science-fact drama. Adams admits frankly that she has forgotten everything that happened to her on that forgettable picture, and from what she remembers of the one time she saw the film, "I'm very glad it hasn't been run on TV a lot." Columbia, who distributed the color film in black and white, apparently shared her misgivings.

The Allied Artists haunted house comedy *Tickle Me* (1965) was not much better, but what Elvis Presley leading lady could forget *that* experience? "He was such a gentleman, and surprisingly shy. There was a scene in the picture most outlandish mixed marriage. So what is it about the Creature that accounts for its ongoing popularity? Julie Adams, the love of its million-year life, thinks she knows.

"The Creature scared people, but there was also a sort of sweetness about it. In the real classics, there always is that feeling of compassion for the monster. I think maybe it touches something in ourselves, maybe the darker parts of ourselves, that long to be loved and think they really *can't* ever be loved. It strikes a chord within us. That's what *Creature from the Black Lagoon* did."

JULIE ADAMS FILMOGRAPHY

As Betty Adams:

Red, Hot and Blue (Paramount, 1949)
The Dalton Gang (The Outlaw Gang) (Lippert, 1949)
Crooked River (Blazing Guns) (Lippert, 1950)
Hostile Country (Outlaw Fury) (Lippert, 1950)
West of the Brazos (Rangeland Empire) (Lippert, 1950)
Colorado Ranger (Guns of Justice) (Lippert, 1950)
Fast on the Draw (Sudden Death) (Lippert, 1950)
Marshal of Heldorado (The Last Bullet) (Lippert, 1950)

As Julia Adams:

Hollywood Story (Universal, 1951)
Bright Victory (Universal, 1951)
Finders Keepers (Universal, 1951)
Bend of the River (Universal, 1952)
Horizons West (Universal, 1952)
The Treasure of Lost Canyon (Universal, 1952)
The Lawless Breed (The Texas Man) (Universal, 1952)
The Mississippi Gambler (Universal, 1953)
The Man from the Alamo (Universal, 1953)
The Stand at Apache River (Universal, 1953)
The World's Most Beautiful Girls (Universal short, 1953)
Wings of the Hawk (Universal, 1953)
Creature from the Black Lagoon (Universal, 1954)
Francis Joins the WACs (Universal, 1954)

As Julie Adams:

The Looters (Universal, 1955)
One Desire (Universal, 1955)
The Private War of Major Benson (Universal, 1955)
Six Bridges to Cross (Universal, 1955)
Four Girls in Town (Universal, 1956)
Away All Boats (Universal, 1956)
Slim Carter (Universal, 1957)
Slaughter on Tenth Avenue (Universal, 1957)
Tarawa Beachhead (Columbia, 1958)
The Gunfight at Dodge City (United Artists, 1959)
Raymie (Allied Artists, 1960)
The Underwater City (Columbia, 1962)
Tickle Me (Allied Artists, 1965)
Valley of Mystery (Universal, 1967)
The Last Movie (Universal, 1971)
McQ (Warner Bros., 1974)
Psychic Killer (The Kirlian Force) (Avco Embassy, 1975)
The McCullochs (The Wild McCullochs) (AIP, 1975)
The Killer Inside Me (Warner Bros., 1976)
Goodbye Franklin High (Cal-Am, 1978)
The Fifth Floor (Film Ventures International, 1980)
Champions (Embassy, 1984)

... *cold. S-s-s-so c-c-c-cold!* It was sort of a disastrous morning all in all. It was freezing cold, and I was trying not to shiver as I was lying limp in this poor guy's [the Creature's] arms. And he could barely see, so as he carried me, he scraped my head on a plaster rock and skinned my head *[laughs]*! It was not the best morning of the picture!"

Even though she insists that she enjoyed working in *Creature,* Adams also admits that, "I didn't really want to be in the sequels, to tell you the truth. So I was happy that they didn't come to me anyway." Is *Creature from the Black Lagoon* a film that gets much play in her home video recorder? "No, never. But that's not saying anything against *Creature,* it's just that I'm really not one for watching my old movies. I never really like my work very much, I think about how I'd like to do it over—I'm very critical. I like to see something until I learn what I *can* learn from it, and then I put it away. I just don't believe in looking back."

Like both of the Creature's later female leads, Lori Nelson and Leigh Snowden, Adams also marked time as leading lady to another one of Universal's more unlikely leading men, Francis the Talking Mule. The gimmick that initially sparked the series had worn fairly thin by the time of *Francis Joins the WACs* (1954)—not that Adams missed much by failing to appear in the series during its dubious "prime." "*Francis Joins the WACs?* Well *[laughs],* what can we say? I enjoyed working with [series star] Donald O'Connor more than Francis! They had a little tiny wire under the lip of the mule, and from the side they would pull on the wire, move it around, to make him 'talk.'" Better roles lay ahead in pictures like the 1955 soaper *One Desire* (as the wicked wife of Rock Hudson, dying in flames at picture's end), the war actioner *Away All Boats* (1956) and the rackets exposé *Slaughter on Tenth Avenue* (1957). An added dividend of appearing in *The Looters* (1955) was meeting leading man Ray Danton, who "punched" her in the film and married her in real life in February 1955.

In 1958 she left Universal ("My contract was up and I was married and I had a baby, and I was just not as interested in working for a while"). But she soon made a comeback, appearing in movies and also on television, where her first regular role was opposite Jock Mahoney on CBS's short-lived *Yancy Derringer.* In 1962 she took the science fiction plunge again, playing a scientist in Columbia's *The Underwater City,* a soggy title-tells-all science-fact drama. Adams admits frankly that she has forgotten everything that happened to her on that forgettable picture, and from what she remembers of the one time she saw the film, "I'm very glad it hasn't been run on TV a lot." Columbia, who distributed the color film in black and white, apparently shared her misgivings.

The Allied Artists haunted house comedy *Tickle Me* (1965) was not much better, but what Elvis Presley leading lady could forget *that* experience? "He was such a gentleman, and surprisingly shy. There was a scene in the picture

where I pursued him around a desk and kissed him. All his friends from Memphis were standing around — all 'the guys' — and I suddenly felt like I was at a party where we were playing post office, and the boy was very bashful! But I was quite in awe of him because he would do a musical number in one take, and that was wonderful. And the most fun he had in the picture was when he and all his friends from Memphis staged a fight scene and tore up a barroom! They had great fun doing that!"

In the late sixties, she was a regular on the afternoon soap *General Hospital* and in 1971 she landed her best-remembered television role, as spouse to the star of *The Jimmy Stewart Show*. Curiously, one of the people she beat out in winning the role was Stewart's real-life wife, Gloria. "How did *I* get the role instead of her? That I don't really know *[laughs]*! I think Gloria is the most charming and delightful woman that I know, but that doesn't mean that you're necessarily an actress! But she is such a wonderful person and she has a real glamour about her that I've always loved — a really Class-A person."

Psychic Killer (1975) was a gruesome shocker bogged down by some cluckish moments of unwanted comedy relief. An obvious melding of *Psycho* and *The Exorcist*, it starred Jim Hutton as a one-time mental patient who uses newly acquired mystical powers to take "out-of-body" revenge on those he feels have wronged him. Horror film fans were delighted to find how chic Adams still looked, and probably a bit surprised by the mild bedroom scene she shared with co-star Paul Burke. "I enjoyed working on *Psychic Killer*. Ray Danton, who was by then my ex-husband, directed it; he was a wonderful director. I had some fun scenes to play, and I found it *not un*interesting to work on." The film was shot on actual locations (including a vacant house in Glendale and an unused jail), and Adams gave the best performance in it, prompting *Variety* to comment, "Adams does fine things with her part, making it one of the rare honorable outings for an actress in films this year."

One of her last pictures to date, *Black Roses* (1988), was also genre-related, with Adams as a small town resident opposed to the arrival of a visiting rock group. "We're of the opinion that their music is demonic. When the group finally does come to town, they seem very tame and we're all reassured. Then, of course, it turns out that they really *are* demonic! They turn into all kinds of nasty things."

Even today, Julie Adams laughs, she's "pressing on, pressing on," working on the stage and, more noticeably, in a semi-recurring role on the hit television series *Murder, She Wrote*, which she describes as "lots of fun." Now and forever, though, she will be mainly remembered by fans of *Creature from the Black Lagoon* as the girl in the brief shorts who almost became half of filmland's

Opposite: **Adams remembers just enough about** *The Underwater City* **to be grateful that the film does not crop up on television much. Helping her out of a tight spot is William Lundigan.**

most outlandish mixed marriage. So what is it about the Creature that accounts for its ongoing popularity? Julie Adams, the love of its million-year life, thinks she knows.

"The Creature scared people, but there was also a sort of sweetness about it. In the real classics, there always is that feeling of compassion for the monster. I think maybe it touches something in ourselves, maybe the darker parts of ourselves, that long to be loved and think they really *can't* ever be loved. It strikes a chord within us. That's what *Creature from the Black Lagoon* did."

JULIE ADAMS FILMOGRAPHY

As Betty Adams:

Red, Hot and Blue (Paramount, 1949)
The Dalton Gang (The Outlaw Gang) (Lippert, 1949)
Crooked River (Blazing Guns) (Lippert, 1950)
Hostile Country (Outlaw Fury) (Lippert, 1950)
West of the Brazos (Rangeland Empire) (Lippert, 1950)
Colorado Ranger (Guns of Justice) (Lippert, 1950)
Fast on the Draw (Sudden Death) (Lippert, 1950)
Marshal of Heldorado (The Last Bullet) (Lippert, 1950)

As Julia Adams:

Hollywood Story (Universal, 1951)
Bright Victory (Universal, 1951)
Finders Keepers (Universal, 1951)
Bend of the River (Universal, 1952)
Horizons West (Universal, 1952)
The Treasure of Lost Canyon (Universal, 1952)
The Lawless Breed (The Texas Man) (Universal, 1952)
The Mississippi Gambler (Universal, 1953)
The Man from the Alamo (Universal, 1953)
The Stand at Apache River (Universal, 1953)
The World's Most Beautiful Girls (Universal short, 1953)

Wings of the Hawk (Universal, 1953)
Creature from the Black Lagoon (Universal, 1954)
Francis Joins the WACs (Universal, 1954)

As Julie Adams:

The Looters (Universal, 1955)
One Desire (Universal, 1955)
The Private War of Major Benson (Universal, 1955)
Six Bridges to Cross (Universal, 1955)
Four Girls in Town (Universal, 1956)
Away All Boats (Universal, 1956)
Slim Carter (Universal, 1957)
Slaughter on Tenth Avenue (Universal, 1957)
Tarawa Beachhead (Columbia, 1958)
The Gunfight at Dodge City (United Artists, 1959)
Raymie (Allied Artists, 1960)
The Underwater City (Columbia, 1962)
Tickle Me (Allied Artists, 1965)
Valley of Mystery (Universal, 1967)
The Last Movie (Universal, 1971)
McQ (Warner Bros., 1974)
Psychic Killer (The Kirlian Force) (Avco Embassy, 1975)
The McCullochs (The Wild McCullochs) (AIP, 1975)
The Killer Inside Me (Warner Bros., 1976)
Goodbye Franklin High (Cal-Am, 1978)
The Fifth Floor (Film Ventures International, 1980)
Champions (Embassy, 1984)

Adams' scene was deleted from the final cut of *For Heaven's Sake* (20th Century–Fox, 1950). Her framed photograph hangs on the wall of Richard Denning's office in *The Glass Web* (Universal, 1953). She is seen in filmclips from *Creature from the Black Lagoon* in *Fade to Black* (American Cinema, 1980) and *It Came from Hollywood* (Paramount, 1982). *Black Roses* (1988) and *Backtrack* (1989) went directly to videocassette.

Acting is something that I love to do, but it's a part of me that's often dormant. So when I get an opportunity to go on a set, it's like somebody pushing a button that's been idle for a long time. And right away, I'm ready to get going at it.

John Agar

They Fought in the Creature Features

IF ONE INDIVIDUAL were to be chosen as a human emblem for the science fiction movie boom of the 1950s and 1960s, that person would be John Agar. Typecast in the genre at the height of its popularity, he has appeared in more of that era's science fiction productions than any other actor, from favorites like *Revenge of the Creature* and *Tarantula* to notorious worst-film contenders like *The Brain from Planet Arous, Attack of the Puppet People* and *Curse of the Swamp Creature.*

Agar fought against this typecasting in the fifties, even walking away from a contract with a major studio (Universal-International) who saw him as their resident science fiction star. But Hollywood being what it is, he found himself back in the genre, time and again. If there was ever any bitterness on his part, it has apparently disappeared; he trades on the reputation now when he can, turning up with some regularity in newer science fiction films and thrillers and even appearing at science fiction conventions like Gary and Sue Svehla's Baltimore-based FANEX con. "If people want to see me, if they're interested in me, I'm more than happy to cooperate and get involved in things like that. Because the way I look at it, in essence the fan is really your boss, and they're the ones paying your salary *[laughs]*. But it does amaze me that there are people who like those sci-fi things we did thirty years ago and longer. *Tarantula*—the doggone thing is running on pay TV!"

Tall, lanky and always affable, Agar (now sporting a short white beard) is more than happy to swing down memory lane, pleased that the river of time has yet to sweep him downstream; the one question he is unable to answer, though, is just why people are still interested in John Agar. "For the life of me, I don't know! Last August [1989], I received a call from North Carolina, from a movie producer down there, Rick Brophy. A young man by the name of James Cummins wrote a script called *Winstrom*—it's a fantasy, a big-budget film, and they want me to play the third lead in it. That's why I've got the beard. Originally they had Dennis Quaid and Meg Ryan playing the two leads, and I think they were going to do it through Fox. But then Fox wanted to take control and these people down in North Carolina didn't want 'em to, so I guess Fox is out. I don't know what the particulars are now, but they insist that *I* am to be in the movie.

"Today, unless you're box office and your name is current, if you go in for a part, you read for the producer or the director. What amazed me was, these people in North Carolina wanted me to read the script and let them know if *I* wanted to do it *[laughs]!* That's something I just don't see that often anymore!"

Although *Winstrom* was never made, a steady string of recent movies have featured Agar in juicy supporting parts. The best known of this new bunch, *Miracle Mile,* did not set the 1989 box office on fire but got good word of

Previous page: **John Agar, science fiction's favorite leading man.**

mouth and enjoyed a second lease on life via pay television and videocassette. A sleeper about a group of Los Angeles nocturnal denizens reacting to news of an imminent nuclear strike, it featured Agar as Ivan Peters, grandfather of a coffee shop waitress (Mare Winningham) whose boyfriend (Anthony Edwards) inadvertently gets wind of the impending Armageddon. While Winningham and Edwards race to work out an escape plan, Agar and his wife, reconciling after years of separation, serenely drive to a restaurant for one last pleasant evening before The End comes. "*Miracle Mile,* I thought, was very well done. The writer/director Steve DeJarnatt—a very talented man—it took him *ten years* to get that picture into production, from the time when he first wrote the script. It was almost two years from the time they started to shoot before it was released. And then when they did release it, they released it at exactly the same time as *Batman, Ghostbusters II, Road House*—and it got lost."

Agar worked two weeks on the picture. "The two kids in it, Anthony Edwards and Mare Winningham, did a marvelous job. And then there was a gal from Texas, name of Lou Hancock, who played my wife, and I thought she also was wonderful in what she did. But, as I said, it got lost when it came out—partly, I think, because the subject matter of the film turned a lot of people off. But it's an exciting picture."

After years of battling monsters—the Creature from the Black Lagoon, the Mole People and Zontar, the Thing from Venus, to name a select few—Agar played a hermit who wanted to *become* a monster in director Clive Barker's *Nightbreed,* a 1990 release. "That was a strange situation. They had shot most of *Nightbreed* in England, and then they got to looking at the picture and in some ways it didn't make sense. The Nightbreed—some could be killed with gunfire, but some you could shoot and it wouldn't affect 'em at all. Some were affected by fire, and then with others, fire wouldn't affect them *[laughs].* There was no explanation about any of this. So I think what happened was, somebody said, 'We better explain this thing,' so I came in and I did a scene with David Cronenberg, the Canadian director—this was his first big role in a movie. They had me tied in a chair with Christmas tree wires and bulbs while he tortures me. I was tied up for an hour and a half to two hours, sitting in that chair with that stuff wrapped around me—and then it took 'em 15 or 20 minutes to get it all off of me, they had it so tangled up *[laughs]!*"

An icon of sorts to fans of the older science fiction films, Agar liked working with modern genre giants Clive Barker and David Cronenberg, although he admits that he just barely got to know them in the one day it took to shoot his scenes. "Barker seemed to be a very nice man, and Cronenberg, too. Cronenberg chose to underplay his part; that was his choice, and Barker went with him. I think he underplayed it too much—too much for *my* taste, anyway. But that's a matter of opinion." Speaking of opinions, what did Agar think of the finished film? Not surprisingly, he reached the same conclusion as did the ticket-buying public, which stayed away in droves.

"Back when we made it, the only thing I saw were the scenes that I was in—I didn't read the script or anything. So I wanted to see what it was like. So I saw it—watched the whole thing. *[Shakes his head.]* Uhn-uh. I pass. Didn't like the movie. They didn't go enough for story—it was just shock value.

"In all movies, I think the audience has the right to use their imagination. Today's pictures are just too graphic—they don't allow you to do that. Me, I won't go—rarely do I see a movie. I have cable, but I don't have any of the movie channels. There's a time and place for everything—we all go to the bathroom, but we don't need to photograph it."

A veteran of 50 films, Agar has been in the business since the late forties, when he signed a contract with Hollywood legend David O. Selznick. He never made a film for Selznick, but was lent to other producers and appeared in three of the decade's great action films—*Fort Apache, She Wore a Yellow Ribbon* and *Sands of Iwo Jima*—all opposite John Wayne. As a youth, however, acting—and career goals in general—were the farthest thing from John Agar's mind. "What would I have done if I hadn't gone into acting? To tell the truth, when I was growing up, I really, really hadn't any idea *[laughs]*! I used to play golf pretty well, and I might have gone in that direction—although I probably would have starved to death, the way Ben Hogan and guys like him played in those days."

The oldest of four children of a Chicago meat packer, Agar grew up during the Depression, although by dint of hard work his family remained upper-middle class. "My dad used to go down to that stockyard and try to keep his meat packing company going. He had angina, and all this pressure put on him caused his early demise—he died before he reached his 41st birthday, and he left my mom loaded with four kids at the age of 38. I was 14—this was 1935." After the death of his father, the Agars relocated to California, where in 1945 John found himself in the headlines when he became engaged to "America's Sweetheart," former child star Shirley Temple. Temple, who divorced Agar in 1949, wrote about the marriage in her 1988 book *Child Star: An Autobiography,* but Agar insists he has not read it.

"Another book, *Shirley Temple: America's Princess,* was written by a lady in Massachusetts; she had asked some questions of me about our marriage, and I told her flat out, 'What is personal in Shirley's life and personal in my life is nobody's business. And I'm not going to tell you anything.' When we were separated, we made an agreement, Shirley and I, that we would not say anything against each other. I kept that promise. I will continue to keep it. I'm never gonna say anything detrimental—that's the way it is." Has Shirley Temple held to that promise? "She broke the agreement as soon as we went into court," Agar deadpans. "But that's *her* problem, not mine."

While they were still husband and wife, the Agars appeared in two films together, the first of which, *Fort Apache* (1948), was Agar's debut as well as

Pressbook ad for *Revenge of the Creature*

the first film in director John Ford's famous Cavalry Trilogy. "To me, John Ford was the epitome of screen directors. The first time I met Ford, he was on the same lot as David Selznick, who was my boss at the time—this was at RKO-Pathé over in Culver City. I went in his office and he had me standing at attention and turning right face, left face, about face. He said, 'Were you in the service?' and I said, 'Yes, sir. The Army Air Corps, sir.' 'Oh,' he said. 'You mean, off we go into the wild blue yonder—crash!' I said, 'Yes, sir. Were you in the service, Mr. Ford?' He said, 'Yep. The Navy.' I said, 'Oh, you mean, anchors aweigh—sink, huh?'

"So every time he would do something, I always considered he was kidding—and I'd kid him back! Duke, Hank Fonda, Ward Bond, Victor McLaglen, George O'Brien [the Ford regulars]—all these guys would say, 'We've known him for twenty-five, thirty years and we *never* know when he's kidding and when he's not.' But I always considered that he was kidding, and there's only one time I can remember that he really got mad at me *[laughs]*! He appeared tough, but I think Ford was a pussycat." Did Agar have first-picture nerves working with this giant of motion picture directors? "Listen, I was scared for the first twenty years," he laughs.

"You'd rehearse the scene before you'd shoot it, and John Ford wouldn't say a word to you. If you did the scene the way he thought it should be done, he still wouldn't say anything. And if you didn't do what he wanted, he would suggest *[softly]*, 'Why don't you do *this?*' 'Why don't you do *that?*' Allan Dwan *[Sands of Iwo Jima]* was the same way. So was Jack Arnold *[Revenge of the Creature, Tarantula]*. Those were people who knew what they wanted. In fact, John Ford never went to rushes, and he never allowed actors to go. If everything was technically okay, Ford knew exactly what was on film. He would go to the rough cut—that'd be the first time he'd see it. The only people who went to his rushes were the craft people. And the editor had only one way to cut that film—Ford's way—because that's all the film he had."

After a strong start, Agar's film career lost its momentum in the early fifties; in December 1950, he made his fantasy film debut playing the Scarlet Falcon in Columbia's *The Magic Carpet,* a Supercinecolor Arabian Nights programmer produced by low-budget legend Sam Katzman. "The Queen of Comedy, Lucille Ball, had a three-picture contract with Harry Cohn, who was the head of Columbia Pictures. She had made two pictures already [for $85,000 per film], and Cohn was trying to get out of having to make the third one. So he thought to himself, 'Well, I'll give her to Sam Katzman. He's making this movie called *The Magic Carpet.* She'll turn it down and I'll be out from under.' And Lucille Ball said, 'I'd *love* to do *The Magic Carpet!*' That movie took eighteen, maybe twenty days to shoot, and I don't think she worked over six—we were sitting there figuring out how much she was getting paid an hour! She was terrific, a lovely, wonderful lady."

Agar swashed and buckled his way through the film, dallied with harem

Gill Man (Tom Hennesy) towers, humans (Agar and Lori Nelson) cower. Publicity photo from *Revenge of the Creature*.

beauties and even rode on the titular conveyance. "They had it on a platform, and then they had wires to make it take off. We were on a stage, and I was thirty feet in the air on this thing! Because of my body weight, I had to lean forward to keep it moving—otherwise it would jerk along, and they wanted a smooth ride. So we tried it and it jerked, and they said, 'You've got to lean forward *further*.' I did, and the thing tipped—you should have seen me hanging onto those wires, looking thirty feet down! *That* got my attention!"

Agar freelanced for a few years, showing up in the science fiction comedy *The Rocket Man* (scripted by Lenny Bruce) as well as in the Caribbean-made voodoo adventure *The Golden Mistress*. In 1954 Agar signed with Universal-International, who were impressed with his work in *The Golden Mistress*. "I went under contract, and that was when I started into science fiction. I started out with *Revenge of the Creature*, the second Creature movie. We went to Florida, to Marineland, to shoot certain scenes, and that was lots of fun. There's one scene in there where Lori Nelson and I are swimming in a river, and that was done at Universal Studios in California. But besides that, all the underwater stuff was done in Florida. When the Creature grabbed Lori and carried her out of the Lobster House and I dove off the pier after them, that was in Florida, too. I remember there was a strong current in that river—when I dove in, it swept me quite a ways."

Swimming in the Marineland tank alongside its resident sharks did not faze Agar, Nelson or third lead John Bromfield. "In addition to Lori, John and myself, there was also Ricou Browning [the Creature], of course, and an underwater photographer. There might have been other people in there, too; in fact, I think some of the people who worked at Marineland were in the water with us, to keep creatures from getting into shots where they weren't wanted. We weren't really concerned about the sharks; Ricou was more concerned about the turtles. He had no peripheral vision at all while in that costume, and those doggone little suckers would come along and nip at him.

"Another thing that we were worried about were the moray eels—they hide in rock crevices and then jump out at you. That's the way they catch their dinner, by grabbing a fish or whatever comes by. They really weren't trouble, because we weren't about to go near the rocks where we knew they were hiding, but you could see their heads jumping out whenever a fish would go past." Plans to shoot scenes in the tank at night were discussed but quickly scuttled. "The people who were in charge said it wouldn't be a good idea. Those sharks were so well fed that you didn't have to be concerned about 'em during the daytime, but they didn't know what would happen at night."

When *Revenge of the Creature* made a splash at the box office, Universal was quick to place Agar in two other science fiction adventures, *Tarantula* and *The Mole People*. "The only picture that I made there that was not science fiction was *Star in the Dust* [1956], a Western. Then I got talking with them over there. I said, 'Gee, every time a science fiction picture comes along, you come after me.' They were building Rock Hudson and Tony Curtis at the time, and I wanted some of those kind of roles. But science fiction and the like was what they wanted me to do. So I said, 'Thanks a lot, but I'll go out on my own.'"

He made more money as a freelancer, but the reputation as a science fiction hero stuck as Agar waged war against the *Daughter of Dr. Jekyll*, *The Brain from Planet Arous* and the *Invisible Invaders*—as well as becoming a monster himself in *Hand of Death*. He hit rock bottom in the mid-sixties when he signed up to star in American International television movie remakes of the earlier AIPs *It Conquered the World*, *Voodoo Woman* and *Suicide Battalion*. "The director of those pictures, Larry Buchanan, was a man that was very infatuated with filmmaking, and in some manner or means he had become involved with Sam Arkoff—AIP. They worked a deal where he could take some of the films that AIP had done previously, change 'em around and do 'em again for however much money. (I don't know what the price was, but believe me, it wasn't very much!) As far as I was concerned, that was just a way for me to make a little extra money—that's why I did 'em. He'd fly me down to Texas, first-class accommodations, he met my salary—I had no kicks coming. Larry really was not a film director per se. He was learning his craft as we went along. I take my hat off to the guy, though—he tried. And from what I hear *[laughs]*, he's *still* trying."

By the mid-sixties, the fifties-style science fiction films were out of vogue, and Agar busied himself in the supporting casts of various Westerns: *Stage to Thunder Rock*, *Law of the Lawless*, *Waco*, the John Wayne vehicles *Chisum*, *Big Jake* and *The Undefeated* (from which Agar's footage was ultimately cut) and more. Film work was scarce in the seventies, with the notable exception of a cameo as the mayor of New York in Dino de Laurentiis's megabuck remake of *King Kong*.

"After I'd read for the role in *King Kong* and been accepted by [director] John Guillermin, I was told to go out to Metro at ten o'clock in the morning, to meet with Dino de Laurentiis. I get there quarter to ten, something like that, I'm sitting waiting, and all of a sudden Joyce Selznick, who is a casting lady and a niece of David's, says, 'Mr. de Laurentiis is not going to be able to keep the appointment.' I'd driven all the way from Burbank. She says, 'I'll call you later today, and we'll see if we can make it tomorrow.' So I go home, she calls me and says, 'All right, he can see you at ten o'clock tomorrow.'

"So I get out there again, about quarter to ten again, and about ten-fifteen he's ready to see me. Joyce takes me over to his office, we open the door, and I'll guarantee you, from the door to where his desk was, was a good forty feet—that's how deep it was. He's sitting there, and right next to him is a young man. Joyce introduces me to him, and then she introduces me to this young man, his son. That was *it*. He never said another thing. And I turned around and walked out. 'Hello, how are you?' 'Fine. How are you, sir?' And then I was ushered out. I went out there *twice* for that *[laughs]*!"

After some slow years, the offers are coming in again, and Agar is sifting through them, accepting the ones that "stick to my standards. I don't use four-letter words on the screen—no way." The thriller *Fear* with Ally Sheedy and *Perfect Bride* with Kelly Preston apparently met his criteria. "*Fear* is the story of a young lady [Sheedy] who is psychic. I play a psychopath. I've got a young girl tied up in the back of a car, and Sheedy's trying to convey to the police

Despite his popularity as Universal's resident monster fighter, Agar pined for "straight" roles. He and Richard Boone starred in the studio's *Star in the Dust* (1956).

where we are. Eventually she does—I've taken this young lady to a barn, I've got her tied on the floor and I've got a pair of shears, rubbing 'em against her face. Four cops break in, but instead of giving up, I go over to the workbench and get a gun, and they shoot me."

That's when the fun started. "The special effects people had squibs on me, and when the first one went off, I was going to hit the workbench with the lower part of my buttocks and throw myself up in the air. Then when the second squib went off, I was going to put my elbow on the workbench, roll off and fall to the ground. Well, I went up and my elbow missed, I hit hard—and I cracked my ribs. I wouldn't tell 'em—I wouldn't say a word. I was too embarrassed *[laughs]!* But I suffered for about three weeks after that."

Fear, directed by Rockne O'Bannon, premiered on cable television's Showtime rather than in theaters, but this bothers the self-effacing Agar about as much as the small size of his part. "To me, the idea of just working is what's fun. I don't give a doggone what kind of parts [I get]. Walter Huston said it years ago: 'I don't care about billing. If the show is good and I'm good in it, people are going to say, "Who *was* that?" And if it's *not,* I don't want 'em to know I was in it!'" *[Laughs.]*

And *Perfect Bride?* "That stars a gal by the name of Sammi Davis—an English actress—and Kelly Preston, who was in *Twins* [1988]. I play a ninety-year-old grandpa in this one; a friend of mine, an actor by the name of John Larch, said, 'Don't worry, Agar. They got makeup, they can tone ya down.' *[Laughs.]* Sammi plays a nurse, and in her childhood, her mother was mistreated by her father. It did something to her way of thinking, and now anytime she comes in contact with anybody (especially a man) that she thinks is doing her wrong, she takes a syringe and sticks it in their neck, and they appear to die of a heart attack. Now, she is engaged to my grandson. Kelly Preston is my granddaughter, and she becomes suspicious of Sammi. Everything was done on location, we shot over in West L.A., just off of Washington Boulevard. I had a good time doing it." (*Perfect Bride* also went directly to TV and videocassette.)

The careers of B movie stars do not often have happy endings, but John Agar is delighted to find that he has become an exception to that rule. "Acting is something that I love to do, but it's a part of me that's often dormant. So when I get an opportunity to go on a set, it's like somebody's pushing a button that's been idle for a long time. And right away, I'm ready to get going at it. It's fun for me to be able to get back into it, because it's a part of my life that I've really enjoyed."

JOHN AGAR FILMOGRAPHY

Fort Apache (RKO, 1948)
Adventure in Baltimore (RKO, 1949)
She Wore a Yellow Ribbon (RKO, 1949)
Sands of Iwo Jima (Republic, 1949)
I Married a Communist (The Woman on Pier 13) (RKO, 1949)
Breakthrough (Warner Bros., 1950)
Along the Great Divide (Warner Bros., 1951)
The Magic Carpet (Columbia, 1951)
Woman of the North Country (Republic, 1952)
Man of Conflict (Atlas, 1953)
The Rocket Man (20th Century-Fox, 1954)
The Golden Mistress (United Artists, 1954)
Shield for Murder (United Artists, 1954)
Bait (Columbia, 1954)

Revenge of the Creature (Universal, 1955)
The Lonesome Trail (Lippert, 1955)
Hold Back Tomorrow (Universal, 1955)
Tarantula (Universal, 1955)
Flesh and the Spur (AIP, 1956)
Star in the Dust (Universal, 1956)
The Mole People (Universal, 1956)
Joe Butterfly (Universal, 1957)
Daughter of Dr. Jekyll (Allied Artists, 1957)
Ride a Violent Mile (20th Century–Fox, 1957)
The Brain from Planet Arous (Howco, 1958)
Jet Attack (AIP, 1958)
Frontier Gun (20th Century–Fox, 1958)
Attack of the Puppet People (AIP, 1958)
Invisible Invaders (United Artists, 1959)
Raymie (Allied Artists, 1960)
Journey to the Seventh Planet (AIP, 1961)
Lisette (Fall Girl) (Medallion, 1961)
Hand of Death (20th Century–Fox, 1961)
Of Love and Desire (20th Century–Fox, 1963)
Cavalry Command (Parade, 1963)
The Young and the Brave (MGM, 1963)
Law of the Lawless (Paramount, 1964)
Stage to Thunder Rock (Paramount, 1964)
Young Fury (Paramount, 1965)
Women of the Prehistoric Planet (Realart, 1965)
Johnny Reno (Paramount, 1966)
Waco (Paramount, 1966)
The St. Valentine's Day Massacre (20th Century–Fox, 1967)
Chisum (Warner Bros., 1970)
Big Jake (National General, 1971)
How's Your Love Life? (Cal-Tex, 1971)
The Amazing Mr. No Legs (Cinema Artists, c. 1975)
King Kong (Paramount, 1976)
Miracle Mile (Hemdale, 1989)
Nightbreed (20th Century–Fox, 1990)

Agar's scenes were cut from *The Undefeated* (20th Century–Fox, 1969). Scenes of Agar in *The Brain from Planet Arous* and *Attack of the Puppet People* are seen in the compilation *It Came from Hollywood* (Paramount, 1982).

*When I was four, I saw my first picture in New York City....
Movies were my dream, and I always figured that was
the world that* could be, *not the world I was* in.

Richard Anderson

26 They Fought in the Creature Features

RICHARD ANDERSON has been an actor for a long time, and like most actors, his career has gone through phases. In the 1950s he was one of the busier young supporting actors toiling at MGM, turning up in over two dozen movies and working alongside "more stars than there are in Heaven" (to quote the studio's most famous publicity line). In the 1960s, he turned to television with a workaholic's zeal, guest starring on every series imaginable. But it was in the 1970s that Anderson landed the role for which he is best known today, that of Oscar Goldman on television's *The Six Million Dollar Man*.

During his stint at Metro, Anderson was one of several up-and-coming young actors with a berth aboard the United Planets cruiser *C-57-D* in MGM's space adventure *Forbidden Planet*. Anderson was sixth-billed as Olonzo Quinn, chief engineer, klystron modulator repairman and Id-monster casualty, in the 1956 science fiction landmark.

Anderson has the sort of easygoing demeanor that immediately sets an interviewer at ease, and the way he does the softshoe around an occasional question tips you off that he is a believer in the old if-you-can't-say-something-nice credo. But, as they say in the Ozarks, he shucks right down to the cob when asked about *Forbidden Planet*.

"That was a B movie, made under the B unit. Nicholas Nayfack was the producer and Fred Wilcox the director, and a program picture was all it was," Anderson reminisces, sitting near the pool of his Beverly Hills home, one good scream away from the infamous Charles Manson murder house. "Everything was categorized—MGM even signed their actors that way. An actor had to have specific qualifications: He had to *look* a certain way, *be* a certain age, have a certain demeanor, or they wouldn't be interested. They'd say, 'This is not a Metro actor.' The same with their pictures. They rarely made Westerns; most of their films were what Western actors called 'carpet movies,' where you get to act in living rooms. So they made mostly mysteries and intriguing international movies and particularly movies with great emotional depth. Those were all formulas—everything was formula, and that included *Forbidden Planet*. They had A movies and B movies—this was a B movie. However, the thing that was interesting about Metro was, they made the B movie just as well as they made the A movie technically. That's what made *Forbidden Planet* exceptional."

It's been almost 40 years since Anderson roamed the deck of the *C-57-D* or trod the surface of Altair-4, but certain recollections of *Forbidden Planet* remain vivid in his mind ("We shot those scenes on Stage 30 at MGM," he says with a twinkle, showing off an excellent memory, of which he is rightly proud). In fact, one of the actor's pastimes during his Metro years was to hang around the studio's special effects and miniatures departments. "Oh, I used to go down

Previous page: Richard Anderson in a recent shot.

there a lot. They had a miniatures department you wouldn't believe — they had it down to a science. Metro was funding those people even when they weren't working [on a movie]; if you worked in special effects there and there was nothing to do, you would stay there and tinker around and experiment with new things. It was an extraordinary operation."

Memories of his fellow space pioneers are equally respectful, particularly those of talented veteran Walter Pidgeon. "My God, that guy was a splendid actor, I thought one of the best of them all. Anne Francis, Leslie Nielsen — there were some very good actors in that picture." Told that some of the actors in *Forbidden Planet* have shown a tendency to put the picture down any time it was mentioned, Anderson is taken slightly aback; he laughs out loud when he finds out that Earl Holliman says it was his worst movie. "Earl said that? Well, I'd better leave *that* alone!" he smiles, ducking the issue neatly. But for many actors, then and now, science fiction does tend to be viewed as a bottom-of-the-barrel genre.

"Control of the picture business was in the hands of five men, and what they decided to make was what the audiences saw," the actor explains. "They saw pictures in very simple terms: love stories, high adventures, 'scary' pictures, thrillers (like Hitchcock) and so on. And if anybody could come up with something new and it worked, they'd jump on it and make ten of 'em. But there were no new plots; everything was the same. The men became old and bored . . . and rich. Louis Mayer summed it up the best; at one point an interviewer asked him, 'Mr. Mayer, don't you want to try to make your pictures better? They're all formula.' And Mayer said, 'Let me tell you something. We make 52 pictures a year, and *none* of them has to be any good.' Think about it. That's how the business was run. They tried to make 'em better and they *wanted* to make 'em better and they competed against each other, but none of 'em had to be any good because the studios had a lock on the theaters. So with *Forbidden Planet* — they made it, but it didn't set the world on fire.

"When live TV came along, new ideas came along. Writers in New York had control of ideas, and they came out with a whole array of themes. All this rich, 'different,' literate stuff that the movies wouldn't dare do because it wouldn't 'sell' — the moviemakers thought the average mind was twelve years old. Television was the breeding ground for new ideas, and out of this 'golden age,' this literate time, came new experiments in how to make pictures. Science fiction was one of them. Science fiction was never 'big' before the fifties. I grew up on science fiction, but when I was a kid, you know what it was? The serials. When I was ten years old, I used to go to every Saturday matinee for ten cents, and we saw *Dick Tracy, Flash Gordon,* all of them." Anderson does not need to be reminded that the reverberations of these old chapterplays continue to be felt today. "Spielberg and Lucas sat on a beach in Hawaii and said, 'Let's get a bunch of those old serials and see what they were made of.' And they were right, because those serials were as good as the movies — and they were

MGM's ability to make classy-looking B movies was what made *Forbidden Planet* "exceptional," according to Anderson. *Left-to-right:* Jack Kelly, Warren Stevens, Morgan Jones (background), Leslie Nielsen, Anderson.

fifteen minutes. In *Indiana Jones and the Last Crusade* [1989], there's a scene where speedboats are racing between two ocean liners which are drifting together—that was a *Dick Tracy* cliffhanger. That kind of action and excitement, that's what movies are, and I happen to personally love those best: high adventure."

Returning to the subject of *Forbidden Planet*, Anderson adds that while the movie was in production, no one seemed to realize that its screenplay was a science fiction retelling of Shakespeare's immortal *The Tempest*. "The only one who could tell you if that was intentional would be the guy that wrote the screenplay. Everybody puts a lot of interpretations into these older films; maybe the guy was reading Shakespeare and figured he could reshape it into science fiction material. And when it got into Metro, obviously they decided to make it because it was an interesting idea. What they probably liked best about it was the robot.

"We shot all the scenes of the planet surface on a soundstage—nobody went anywhere. Audiences didn't know any better back then; you can't do that sort of thing anymore," Anderson continues. "I also remember that I liked the director, Fred Wilcox. He was a gifted man. He did the Lassie movies and had a great deal of talent—sensitive and a very, very fine director."

Overall, Anderson seems pleased with *Forbidden Planet* and with the fact that it is one of the movies for which he is best known, even though Chief Quinn was the lead-off victim for an Altair-4 monster that allowed the character only a handful of short scenes before tearing him limb from off-camera limb. "*Forbidden Planet* was very well made technically, and it had a very good idea. It dealt with the id and the superego and the ego, and the story was kind of interesting. But it was basically a science fiction film, although very, very well done in terms of the miniatures department, special effects and so on."

Anderson made his film debut in 1949, but the desire to become a movie actor had already been with him for nearly his entire life. "When I was four, I saw my first picture in New York City, where I lived with my parents, and it had a tremendous effect upon me. I didn't like New York City as far as I can remember—it's not a place for bringing up kids who like the outdoors, as I do. Movies were the escape—I was allowed to go to matinees with my brother. Movies were my dream, and I always figured that was the world that could be, not the world I was in. Of course, that can run into trouble later on in life *[laughs]*, but at the time that's what I was interested in. And I never lost that ambition to be in the movies, for I felt there was where my life was going to change for the better. Of course, it turned out that it wasn't all sunglasses and autographs, but at that time I decided I wanted to be a movie actor."

Anderson appeared in high school plays, served a hitch in the army and, upon his discharge, began doing summer stock, radio work, a movie bit part (as a wounded soldier in *Twelve O'Clock High* [1949]) and the other minor jobs required of your basic struggling thespian. "Then came live television," Anderson continues, recalling his Big Break. "There was a show called *Lights, Camera, Action,* which was an hour show on NBC in the winter of 1949. What it was, was a screen test—instead of making a movie screen test, you did it on live TV. This TV screen test was seen by everybody in town, because television was very new and interesting, and everybody watched it. I was doing comedy scenes, which I haven't done since *[laughs]*. I was on *Lights, Camera, Action* three times, and judged by many, many very well known celebrities in the business, particularly directors—one of which was Preston Sturges. I was seen by the Metro people, I was seen by Billy Wilder at Paramount—I got offers from a lot of people. And I finally went to the Metro studios—I made a screen test, a scene from *The Cowboy and the Lady* opposite Sally Forrest, and I signed a seven-year contract. It was kind of a dream come true; I had been a messenger boy with the publicity department there for a time, after I had gotten out of the army. So coming back to Metro was a kind of double victory."

Anderson looked forward to playing leading roles at MGM, but the studio saw him as a good, dependable supporting player. "The pressures of staying in the business demanded that you work, that you stay on the screen. So I chose to stay on the screen. I've seen a lot of them come and go because many of 'em just want to do a certain thing. But when that fades out or when you've had your chance at it, that's it—it's over. The average life expectancy of an actor was at that time seven years, and I don't think it's too different now. So my strategy was to *work*."

And work he did, in 25 Metro movies over a six-year period, although his roles did not improve much as the years went by. "What happened was unfortunate, and it had nothing to do with me or with them. The studio system broke down, and consequently it was no longer as good a business as it had once been. That was the end of their whole system of developing actors — putting them in supporting parts with leading people, then second parts, and then giving them a shot at something. In all the time I was there, they didn't groom any actors for stardom in that fashion, with the exception maybe of Debbie Reynolds, who was in their musicals. I decided that the best thing to do was to gain experience, so I played *everything* — if they assigned me to a part, I'd just go play it. Consequently, I became an actor that they knew they could use, and they kept picking up my option for that reason. They realized I was good business, that I could always do a reliable job. That's how I learned the business. And it came in handy later on, when I got into television, where you *had* to work fast. Most of the people who worked in those films don't work TV because it's a different technique. When they got into television, where you shoot fast, many of the Metro people weren't accustomed to that kind of shooting."

Dore Schary was in charge at MGM throughout most of the years that Anderson was under contract, but early on he had an opportunity to meet Louis B. Mayer, onetime junk dealer, cofounder of MGM and executive ruffian extraordinaire. "Ruffian? That kind of takes it out of context. There's a new book out on Sam Goldwyn where I think you'll find the same type of stories that you hear about Mayer, Harry Cohn and so on. These were men who simply got hold of an industry that was no industry at the time, just a fledgling toy. They took it and made it into something when no one else touched it. I would say that these men were a combination of a lot of things. First of all, they loved more than anything else being American, and they wanted everybody to know that they were respectable and successful Americans. Secondly, they saw a great opportunity to make money. It was a new business and therefore there were no rules; as George Washington said when he became the first president, 'I trod on ground that has never been walked on before.' They set the rules, they determined how the business was going to be operated, and they hired people that were talented. And the third thing was, they simply loved the idea of making good pictures. They were rough, but look at their backgrounds, and remember that it was a rough business in those days because everybody was after it. They were instinctive players. I met Mayer, and he was quite a man. He was an idea man — no, *more* than that, he was a *talent* man. He had an instinct for talent, and an instinct for doing it big and doing it right."

Anderson (and most of those other heavenly stars) left MGM in the mid-fifties, when the studio system broke down entirely, and Anderson began to freelance. With a juicy role in Stanley Kubrick's 1957 film *Paths of Glory* (Anderson was the first person cast, and served as dialogue coach), he was off to a strong start. "When the picture was agreed upon, United Artists did not like the idea of the men being executed at the end; they stipulated that the three soldiers must not die — they should be saved. But Kubrick was absolutely adamant: to make the picture work, those men had to be killed. Kubrick sent UA a copy of the final script, and in this script the men did die. *Nobody read it at UA.* So Kubrick went ahead and shot it his way. Of course, when UA saw the finished picture, they saw that the men did die, but all Kubrick had to do was to say, 'Look here, it's in the final script which was approved.' But nobody even asked after they saw it, because they realized how powerful it was."

Among the several movies Anderson made during the late fifties were *The Search for Bridey Murphy* and *Curse of the Faceless Man*, two minor pictures of the sort that he now refers to as "things I did on my way to something else." *Search*, based on the then-current reincarnation fad, had an interesting low-key approach but it was a wholly uncinematic subject. "I remember *Search* because I looked forward to working with Louis Hayward — I remembered him from when I was a boy and I saw him in *The Man in the Iron Mask* [1939]," says Anderson. He also recalls meeting Morey Bernstein, the real-life amateur hypnotist who regressed housewife Virginia Tighe and sparked the entire fad. "It's interesting when the actors meet the real people; I don't know why, but it's usually quiet, and no one has much to say. You shape parts to your personality — or at least most actors do — and then to meet the actual person...! For instance, on *The Six Million Dollar Man*, we met the man who was the real-life Six Million Dollar Man. We all greeted him and put our arms around him; Lee Majors and I have pictures of ourselves with him; suddenly he's gone and you never see him again *[laughs]!*" By the time *Search* came out, professional debunkers had done a number on the Bridey Murphy story, and the Paramount picture died a lingering death at the box office.

Anderson's much-vaunted memory (conveniently?) lets him down when the subject turns to *Curse of the Faceless Man*, the only one of his fifty feature films in which he is top-billed. The story of an Etruscan slave turned into living stone during the eruption of Vesuvius and reanimated in our modern world, it was strictly drive-in fodder, with Anderson ill at ease as the stereotypic hero/ scientist. "That was another one I was doing just on my way to somewhere else; that trained me for television. Seven days shooting," he deadpans. "The director, Edward L. Cahn, was at Metro, in the shorts department, along with Fred Zinnemann, and I think he won an Academy Award for ... something."

It was at this same time that Anderson dove headfirst into television work, doing guest spots in every series under the sun (as well as working as a regular in such sixties shows as *Bus Stop, The Lieutenant* and *Perry Mason*. He was no stranger to horror and science fiction shows, either: *Thriller, The Alfred Hitchcock Hour, The Man from U.N.C.L.E., The Invaders, The Wild Wild West,*

Curse of the Faceless Man has slipped from Anderson's memory despite being his one-and-only starring film. *Left-to-right:* Elaine Edwards, Anderson, Jan Arvan, Gar Moore.

Land of the Giants and more. In the classic final episodes of *The Fugitive*, Anderson played brother-in-law to peripatetic escapee David Janssen, and when the moving finger of suspicion began to point to Anderson as the killer of Janssen's wife (rather than the One-Armed Man), Las Vegas oddsmakers started taking bets on his guilt or innocence.

Anderson was also a regular during the last season of *Perry Mason*, and in the last episode the actor (playing Police Lieutenant Drum) interrogates witnesses to a murder in a television studio—said witnesses being played by the *Perry Mason* crew. "The last day of that last episode, we had a courtroom scene. Every week they needed a different judge, and they brought in some day player. The fellow playing the judge this last week approaches me and says, 'Mr. Anderson, I've enjoyed watching you play this role the last year.' I didn't know who this guy was, but I could feel that he was something beyond just a day player—I knew I was into something, I knew something was coming. I said, 'Well, thank you very much.' We talked back and forth a little, he started to walk away and then he said, 'Oh, by the way, my name is Erle Stanley Gardner.' They had put him on the last day as the judge."

The number of movie roles dwindled when Anderson plunged into television, but he still managed to pop up in two of John Frankenheimer's most celebrated films, *Seven Days in May* and *Seconds*. "John is an exciting, eclectic kind of man. He has tremendous enthusiasm and he has an excitement about himself and his work—you can see it in his movies like *The Manchurian Candidate*. He exudes a great deal of energy. I think John mainly enjoys taking a piece of material that is in its simple stage and making something out of it—taking a simple plot and embellishing it.

"Motion pictures for the most part come from books—find a best-seller and make it. Both of those Frankenheimer films I was in were based on books. *Seven Days in May* was an intriguing political story. *Seven Days*, *The Best Man* [1964]—all those pictures are kind of limited in the sense that they're, well, not talking heads, but not what you'd call high adventure." *Seven Days*, scripted by Rod Serling, was a speculative suspenser about a covert military plot to overthrow the U.S. government. "An interesting idea.... It's happening this morning, right now, you know," Anderson remarks while, half a world away, all hell is breaking loose on the first day of riots in Tiananmen Square.

Asked about reported friction between stars Burt Lancaster and Kirk Douglas on the film's set, Anderson waxes philosophic. "Well, on the set, people are always trying to do their best. I'm not trying to sound like the ambassador for American films, but when people are trying to do their best, tempers run high, emotions go up, and also people are nervous. And in many cases *scared*—the best of 'em get scared. That's understandable. You have a concept, somebody else has a concept, that's what the director is there for. It's a highly volatile game, and when you get two visceral guys like that together, sure, there could be fireworks. I think Burt had just come off *The Leopard* [1963] for Visconti, probably was a bit frayed from the experience over there, and maybe he came in tired. But they have since worked on the stage together, they did *Tough Guys* [1986], so I don't think there was anything serious there. But they're guys that say what they think, that open their mouths and talk."

Anderson's other film for Frankenheimer was the offbeat *Seconds*, the story of a secret organization which (for a fee) will physically rejuvenate any individual and present him or her with a new identity. Anderson, playing the surgeon who transforms middle-aged businessman John Randolph into virile Rock Hudson, shared the world's opinion. "*Seconds* was intriguing but weird ... strange. It became a cult movie. It didn't go over too well at the box office, but it wasn't a high budget movie. People say that was Rock Hudson's best performance. Well, at least it was different *[laughs]*."

One of the most famous scenes in *Seconds* featured Anderson wielding a scalpel in the surgical operation on John Randolph, with close-ups showing the blade slicing through the skin. "We used a double for John Randolph for the actual close-up stuff, and a doctor stood in for me and made the incisions," says Anderson. "The double had makeup skin above his own skin. The doctor made the incision, and the double didn't move. When it was over, I remember Frankenheimer saying to the double, 'You okay, Bill?' They took the makeup off, and the doctor had let him have it—he went a bit too deep. It was not the surgeon's fault, but he had never done that before and he didn't know how far down to go. The double was all right, but the interesting part was, the surgeon felt absolutely, terribly embarrassed!"

Anderson's claim to fame in the early seventies was playing Burt Reynolds' boss in the successful television police drama *Dan August*, but genre fans probably remember him better as Dr. Malcolm Richards, superpowered, ageless, vampiric foe of Darren McGavin's Carl Kolchak in the 1972 television movie *The Night Strangler*. "Richard Matheson saw the Underground City in Seattle and got the idea for the story: a doctor living beneath the city since 1868 who has to come up every twenty-one years to get some blood," explains Anderson. For his scenes in this top-rated television movie, Anderson worked at the Bradbury Building in Los Angeles and at a huge old mansion on the Pacific Coast. Stuntman Dick Ziker played the title role in action scenes where the fiend's face was unseen, but Anderson took over in a finale set in the Underground City. Makeup ace William Tuttle transformed him into a hideous hundred-year-old man for the film's climax.

Running in slow motion became the newest self-defeating pastime for America's youth as soon as Lee Majors's *Six Million Dollar Man* began inching his way across picture tubes tuned to ABC in 1973. A series sparked by the success of three 90-minute *SMDM* television movies was soon a hit, and Anderson settled into a comfortable niche as Oscar Goldman, bionic Steve Austin's (Majors) government boss. Anderson is casual in discussing his relationship with Majors and the depth of his emotional involvement with the show: "When Lee's lips stopped moving, I'd talk, and when *my* lips stopped, *he'd* talk. That was how it worked. We never discussed it, never talked about our characters, never discussed the show. Mostly we talked about football and someplace to go for a beer."

A spinoff series, *The Bionic Woman*, premiered in 1976, with Lindsay Wagner as a distaff bionic hero, and Anderson suddenly found himself a regular on *two* series simultaneously. Again Anderson is self-effacing concerning his minor distinction in television history: "A fast driver and a good memory is what's needed," he grins. On a single day, between pickup shots and other miscellaneous business, he worked on seven different episodes of the two series (*"That* I'll never forget!").

After a few years of double-barreled bionic action, however, both series began running out of gas. A bionic boy (played by Vincent Van Patten) debuted on *SMDM*, but according to Anderson, "That idea didn't work

Championing the cause of justice on 1970s television: Boss man Oscar Goldman (Anderson) and bionic Steve Austin (Lee Majors) in ABC's *Six Million Dollar Man*.

because kids started jumping off of roofs and fences." Bionic dog Maximilian (max.: one million — get it?) became a regular on *Bionic Woman* but failed to bolster faltering ratings. Both shows petered out in 1978. But bionic fever spread once again in the late eighties when NBC aired two movie follow-ups: *The Return of the Six Million Dollar Man and the Bionic Woman* (1987) and *Bionic Showdown: The Six Million Dollar Man and the Bionic Woman* (1989).

Anderson returned as boss Goldman and wore a second hat as well, that of producer. "And I learned more than I learned about anything in the film business before," he confides. "It's a very exciting side of the business." (A third made-for-television feature, *Bionic Ever After?*, co-starring and produced by Anderson, aired in 1994.)

You would think that maybe Anderson might be entertaining a notion to start kicking back and smelling the roses; after 45 years in the business, he must be lighting his cigars with residual checks. Tanned and easygoing and still handsome in his mid-sixties, Anderson fakes a look of confusion. "Retirement? What does that word *mean?* It doesn't seem to make any sense!"

RICHARD ANDERSON FILMOGRAPHY

Twelve O'Clock High (20th Century–Fox, 1949)
The Vanishing Westerner (Republic, 1950)
The Magnificent Yankee (MGM, 1950)
Grounds for Marriage (MGM, 1950)
A Life of Her Own (MGM, 1950)
The Unknown Man (MGM, 1951)
Go for Broke! (MGM, 1951)
Payment on Demand (RKO, 1951)
Cause for Alarm (MGM, 1951)
Rich, Young and Pretty (MGM, 1951)
No Questions Asked (MGM, 1951)
The People Against O'Hara (MGM, 1951)
Across the Wide Missouri (MGM, 1951)
Just This Once (MGM, 1952)
Scaramouche (MGM, 1952)
Holiday for Sinners (MGM, 1952)
Fearless Fagan (MGM, 1952)
The Story of Three Loves (MGM, 1953)
I Love Melvin (MGM, 1953)
Dream Wife (MGM, 1953)
Escape from Fort Bravo (MGM, 1953)
Give a Girl a Break (MGM, 1953)
Betrayed (MGM, 1954)
The Student Prince (MGM, 1954)
Hit the Deck (MGM, 1955)
It's a Dog's Life (MGM, 1955)
Forbidden Planet (MGM, 1956)
A Cry in the Night (Warner Bros., 1956)
The Search for Bridey Murphy (Paramount, 1956)
Three Brave Men (20th Century–Fox, 1957)
The Buster Keaton Story (Paramount, 1957)
Paths of Glory (United Artists, 1957)
The Long, Hot Summer (20th Century–Fox, 1958)
Curse of the Faceless Man (United Artists, 1958)
Compulsion (20th Century–Fox, 1959)
The Gunfight at Dodge City (United Artists, 1959)
The Wackiest Ship in the Army (Columbia, 1960)
A Gathering of Eagles (Universal, 1963)
Johnny Cool (United Artists, 1963)
Seven Days in May (Paramount, 1964)
Kitten with a Whip (Universal, 1964)
Seconds (Paramount, 1966)
Ride to Hangman's Tree (Universal, 1967)
Macho Callahan (Embassy, 1970)
Tora! Tora! Tora! (20th Century–Fox, 1970)
Doctors' Wives (Columbia, 1971)
The Honkers (United Artists, 1972)
Play It as It Lays (Universal, 1972)
Black Eye (Warner Bros., 1974)
The Glass Shield (Miramax, 1995)

Anderson is also seen in *The Metro-Goldwyn-Mayer Story* (1951), a 56-minute compilation of clips from then-current MGM movies.

*I didn't give the business up,
it gave me up.*

John Archer

WITH NEARLY 60 SCREEN ROLES to his credit, in addition to a long list of television parts, John Archer has played an assortment of characters in a wide range of genres. In horror and science fiction, however, the curly-haired six-footer generally played the good-natured but no-nonsense leading man who goes toe-to-toe with the forces of the unknown, whether it be zombies and Bela Lugosi on Poverty Row or the mysteries of the universe in George Pal's movie milestone *Destination Moon* (1950). As radio's Lamont Cranston (aka *The Shadow*), he knew *precisely* what evil lurked in the hearts of men.

The actor was born Ralph Bowman in Osceola, Nebraska (a suburb of Lincoln), on May 8, 1915. His family moved to California when he was five, and Bowman went to school at Hollywood High and the University of Southern California. He first set his sights on a job *behind* the cameras, taking a cinematography course at USC, but quickly learned just how tough it was to crack open those imposing studio gates, even in a low-paying entry-level position. "Times were tough then and I couldn't get a job for fifteen bucks a week in *any* area down there," Archer reminisces. "In fact, I had to leave USC in my junior year—I ran out of loot. So I finally went to work for an aerial photographer in Los Angeles for sixty bucks a month—I worked in an office, seeing clients and so forth. He went to New York and from there he sent me a wire, saying that some relatives of his from Texas were going to be in town; would I show them around and so forth? I *did* show them around Beverly Hills, and we stopped for lunch at a place at Wilshire and Fairfax. While we were dining, the hostess came over and said that there was a director in the room that wanted to ask me a few questions. His name was Ben Bard and he owned this little legitimate theater next door. He was having lunch with an actor, Jack Carson, and an agent, Frank Stemple. I made an appointment to see Bard the next day.

"Bard said, 'You've got all the qualities, all the attributes to do some acting. Have you ever thought of it?' I told him, 'No, I'm too self-conscious. I couldn't stand up next to my desk in school and read out of a book!' He said, 'Well, why don't you give it a shot?' and I said okay, and I did. In three months, I got my first job at Universal, and in six months, I started making a living at it!" Still using his real name, Bowman made his screen debut in *Flaming Frontiers* (1938), a Universal serial with cowboy star Johnny Mack Brown; "We shot an episode a day, practically." Other movie roles followed (including the serial *Dick Tracy Returns*), as well as parts in stage productions at the Ben Bard Playhouse, where Bowman worked alongside fellow newcomers Jack Carson, Alan Ladd, Turhan Bey and Byron Barr (aka Gig Young).

Another turning point for the young actor was competing in the unique talent quest program *Jesse Lasky's Gateway to Hollywood*, a CBS radio show

Previous page: While the science fiction fans of 1950 climbed the walls in anticipation of *Destination Moon*, star John Archer did, too—on the movie's "weightless" sets. (Photofest)

whose contestants vied to win a *nom de screen* coupled with a contract with a movie studio. "John Archer" was the name for which Bowman and other aspirants from all over the United States (including Hugh Beaumont) competed for 13 weeks, with Bowman eventually winning the screen moniker as well as a contract with RKO. ("I went from being a Bowman to an Archer!") His first film with the new name was RKO's *Career* (1939), a low-budget small-town drama starring Anne Shirley, Archer and "Alice Eden" (formerly Rowena Cook), another *Gateway to Hollywood* winner. *Variety*'s Barn wrote of the contest winners: "In Archer, the *Gateway to Hollywood* has uncovered a lad with possibilities for development. He's a smooth looker, of clean-cut face and build, and with a bit of grooming has a chance to be heard from. With Miss Eden, it's another thing."

Archer's "grooming" continued, not only at RKO but at Republic, Monogram and other small companies as well. With horror films back in vogue after a late-thirties hiatus, Monogram producers Lindsley Parsons and Sam Katzman concocted cut-rate thrillers to capitalize on the new demand; Archer worked opposite black funnyman Mantan Moreland in Parsons's *King of the Zombies* (1941) and with horror king Bela Lugosi in Katzman's *Bowery at Midnight* (1942). "I enjoyed Monogram," admits Archer. "They were fast B pictures, but the people were all good. Working at Monogram, the techniques were all the same [as at larger studios], except that they would just shoot a *lot* faster. They didn't rehearse as much, and they'd shoot the whole picture in a week. In a larger studio, it would take three or four weeks to do a B picture. For instance, if you were in a B picture, actors didn't say 'God damn it!' or whatever if they flubbed a line. They just kept going, and created their own scene *[laughs]*, and the director would let 'em go as long as they wanted. Actually, that was good experience for *us*, too."

King of the Zombies, a horror comedy, was a mixed-up 67 minutes of low-cost fun, with heroes Archer and Dick Purcell encountering voodoo master Henry Victor on a mysterious jungle island near Cuba. Purcell is "zombified" early on, fifth-billed Archer handles most of the exposition, and comic Mantan Moreland, playing Archer's valet, shares his funniest scenes with Victor's band of zombies (typical dialogue: "If it was in me, I sure would be pale now!"). Besides doing his shtick in the movie, Moreland carried on and kidded between takes as well, and found a willing audience in Archer. "I liked having Mantan Moreland to work with—he was a funny little guy who just cracked me up. In fact, I thought he'd be a wonderful guy for Jack Carson to have as a sidekick on his radio show, like [Jack] Benny had Rochester. We kicked that around for a while, Jack Carson and [agent] Frank Stemple and I, but it didn't work out. They looked into it, and they realized the guy had tremendous talent and would have been very funny on the radio. But maybe it was the fact that they didn't want to get into something that would mimic Benny and Rochester."

Other *King of the Zombies* memories are less vivid, although Archer remembers Jean Yarbrough as "a good director—as a matter of fact, years later he directed a test I made for *The Egg and I* [1947] for Universal. (Fred MacMurray became available, so that stopped all conversation on the subject of me being in it!) I'm sure I saw *King of the Zombies,* and I probably enjoyed the film, but you must realize that they were still B pictures, and you could tell the difference."

While Archer's recollection of *Bowery at Midnight* is dim, the name Sam Katzman is one that the actor has not forgotten. "I worked with Sam several times after that; I think the last time was at Columbia, when he was producing a picture with Randolph Scott called *Decision at Sundown* [1957]. I'd worked for him in the interim, in a couple other pictures, too. He was a sweetheart, really, but he was a rebel. He was kind of a 'different' type of guy—a cigar-chompin' type of producer. Inwardly, he was a real nice man, but he didn't show it too often. I liked him." Bela Lugosi, the star of *Bowery at Midnight,* played a university professor who "moonlights" as a master criminal. Archer, playing one of Lugosi's students, is having trouble researching a term paper on the thoughts that cross a man's mind just before he dies; when Archer inadvertently learns about Bela's secret life of crime, the evil Lugosi gladly provides Archer with the opportunity to research the subject firsthand. Like other actors who worked opposite Lugosi, Archer concurs that "he wasn't around to have fun or to converse with, or even to rehearse with too much, until you got on the set. Then he would rehearse, and you'd do the scene. Maybe he was a shy man, I don't know—I have nothing derogatory to say about the guy, except that he was a loner."

Between *Zombies* and *Bowery,* Archer married actress Marjorie Lord, his costar in a stage production of *The Male Animal* (their daughter, born in 1947, is actress Anne Archer). Archer and Lord appeared together in *Sherlock Holmes in Washington* (1943), third entrant in Universal's series of Holmes adventures. Most audiences loved the Basil Rathbone–Nigel Bruce B series, but some critics (and finicky fans of the original Arthur Conan Doyle stories) decried the studio's decision to update the characters to the World War II era. "Those Sherlock Holmes fans—by God, they are rabid. They want everything to be just the way it was," says Archer. "But Universal was producing pictures to make money, and this was a question of making a buck. I'm sure that was their feeling—'Let's update it or change it in some way, and see if we can make a little bit more money.' *That's* when all of the diehards got on them."

"I enjoyed that movie, even though the part was minimal," Archer continues. "Basil Rathbone and Nigel Bruce were both consummate pros, and a pleasure and a delight to work with. They were wonderful people to be around, and very helpful. They each had a subtle sense of humor, which was always kind of fun. Marjorie and I had a scene together where I said good-bye to her, and I did the usual thing, I patted her on the butt, 'See ya later'—you know

College student Archer gets some sage advice from Professor Bela Lugosi — an actor Archer remembers as a loner — in Poverty Row's *Bowery at Midnight*.

what I mean. And the director [Roy William Neill] said, 'Cut, cut! Oh, come on, John, what are you *doing?*' You can do those kinds of things in the movies today, but not *then [laughs]*."

Archer acted in a better grade of picture when he went under contract to 20th Century-Fox, but even there, he admits, "I realized that all the young actors out of New York were getting the good parts and more money. That's when I elected to go to New York, because New York in those days was the front door to Hollywood. *Hollywood* was the back door!" In New York he looked for stage and radio roles, and briefly considered jettisoning the name John Archer. "When I went to New York, I thought to myself, 'Well, I'll give up this John Archer thing,' because I thought it might have an onus, being a contest winner. I thought, well, shucks, if *that's* the case, let's dump Archer and go back to Ralph Bowman. That's when the radio people said, 'No, no — the John Archer name still means something. It still has a little marquee value because it's had so much exploitation. We *like* that.' So I said, 'I don't care what you call me, as long as you call me!'" he laughs.

And call they did: Archer quickly became one of the airwaves' foremost voices. "I was doing a *lot* of radio, going from studio to studio — soap operas in the morning, regular radio shows at night. There was a call for an interview for *The Shadow*, which I accepted just as I accepted any other interview. It didn't mean that much to me—I didn't know anything about *The Shadow*, really, except the name. I went in on my lunch hour and the director Bob Steel was just leaving for *his* lunch. I explained to him that I'd rushed over to have a quick interview with him (I was working), and he said, 'Well, come on in, John, we'll give you a shot.' He did, and he liked the way I read, he liked the laugh and whatever else was necessary. He said, 'Looks pretty good, John. We'll get in touch.' And they did, and I was the Shadow in 1944 and '45."

Archer took over in the role of the veteran sleuth at the beginning of the Mutual series' 14th year, following in the phonic footsteps of former Shadows Bill Johnstone, Bret Morrison and Orson Welles. His first installment, "The Ebony Goddess," was heard on September 24, 1944; his 30th and last, "The River of Eternal Woe," on April 15, 1945. (He also made guest appearances as the Shadow on a quiz program titled *Quick as a Flash*.) Archer's "Margo Lane" was actress Judith Allen. "She was married to Gus Sonnenberg, a wrestler," he adds. "She had a slight movie career before she came to New York and they cast her in that role.

"Myself, I did not have a specific approach for that [Shadow] role. I just treated it as any other job in radio, and that's what it was. I just wanted to go in and do a good job—and get my check *[laughs]!* I guess I did all right, but I'm not the judge of that." A number of the Archer *Shadow*s were scripted by Alfred Bester, but Archer never crossed paths with the noted science fiction author ("That's not unusual, though—you didn't see writers very often back then"). In addition to the radio roles, Archer also found work on the Great White Way; his Broadway bow was in *The Odds on Mrs. Oakley* (1944). He eventually left *The Shadow*—and New York—"to go to Ellitch's Gardens in Denver to be their leading man down there for the summer. Ellitch's Gardens was one of the best-known summer theaters in the country—I think it still *is*. We did ten plays, one every week for ten weeks. Then I came back *loaded* with scripts (I got over a dozen scripts for new Broadway plays while I was down there), and I selected a musical called *The Day Before Spring,* by Fritz Loewe and Alan Lerner. It was a semisuccess. It wasn't *too* great—Bill Johnson, Irene Manning and I were the leads. But it was a departure. I'm sorry I took it, really, because I had to turn down *Dream Girl* and a couple of other beautiful shows that turned out to be big hits. But it was an experience, and it didn't hurt me in the long run."

Archer's New York gambit paid off—in a way. "I was brought back to Hollywood at a good salary, at a good studio [Universal-International]—but I sat around for six months while they didn't cast me in *any*thing! They just loaned me out for one picture of Walter Wanger's, a picture with Bob Cummings and Susan Hayward called *The Lost Moment* [1947]." His other late-forties roles were in a pair of Warner Bros. features for director Raoul Walsh:

Colorado Territory (a Western remake of Walsh's earlier *High Sierra*) and the James Cagney classic *White Heat*.

Archer got star billing for the first time in the first of the fifties science fiction classics, producer George Pal's landmark *Destination Moon*. Based on a screenplay by science fiction novelist Robert Heinlein and screenwriter Rip Van Ronkel, the Technicolor space adventure was the first-ever Hollywood film to treat the subject seriously, with Archer starring as an aircraft industrialist "sold" on the idea of space travel by former army general Tom Powers and research scientist Warner Anderson (the nation that militarily controls the Moon controls the Earth as well). With additional financing furnished by other industrialists, an atomic rocket is constructed in the Mojave Desert, but insidious foreign-inspired propaganda turns the tide of public (and government) opinion against the project. Caution is tossed to the winds as Archer, Powers and Anderson—joined by electronics technician Dick Wesson—decide to make a hasty predawn liftoff in the untested spaceship *Luna* before the enemies of the project can use the law to bar the launching.

"I guess my agent got me an interview with George Pal, and I was signed," Archer surmises about the beginnings of his involvement. "I knew going into it who he was (everybody had tried to fill me in); he was one of the *best* in the [puppet animation] field originally. George Pal was a marvelous man, very thoughtful, very inventive. He wasn't on the set a *lot,* but he *was* there from time to time; he wanted to come down (I don't blame him!), and we were always happy to see him because he was such a pleasant man. He surrounded himself with such great talent; the writer, Robert Heinlein, was there a lot, and so was the man who designed the moonscapes, [space painter] Chesley Bonestell. They did some beautiful work. I thought they were highly intellectual and intelligent and interesting men. It was a pleasure to be with them, just to listen to them *talk*. Even though a lot of it was quite technical, it was understandable, and that's when you began to *believe* that these things were in the works, that they were going to happen. I really enjoyed those men very much, and I thought their talents were exceptional. And Lionel Lindon, the cameraman—*he* was exceptionally good. We were all kind of good friends, and we enjoyed working the movie."

The Irving Pichel–directed feature went into production November 14, 1949, at General Service Studio, where spaceship sets were ingeniously (and economically) constructed. "The spaceship set was a brilliant mechanism," Archer says. "They had this set that would turn over [like a rolling drum]. It was a fascinating set to be in. If you were required to walk on the wall, the set would be turning so that the wall was under your feet. We were just doing what we had to do, and the *set* was rotating. And we reacted as we went along. I thought that was very interesting. For scenes where we were floating around weightless in the cabin, they had tracks up in the ceiling area, and motors would just move us out to wherever it was we were supposed to be."

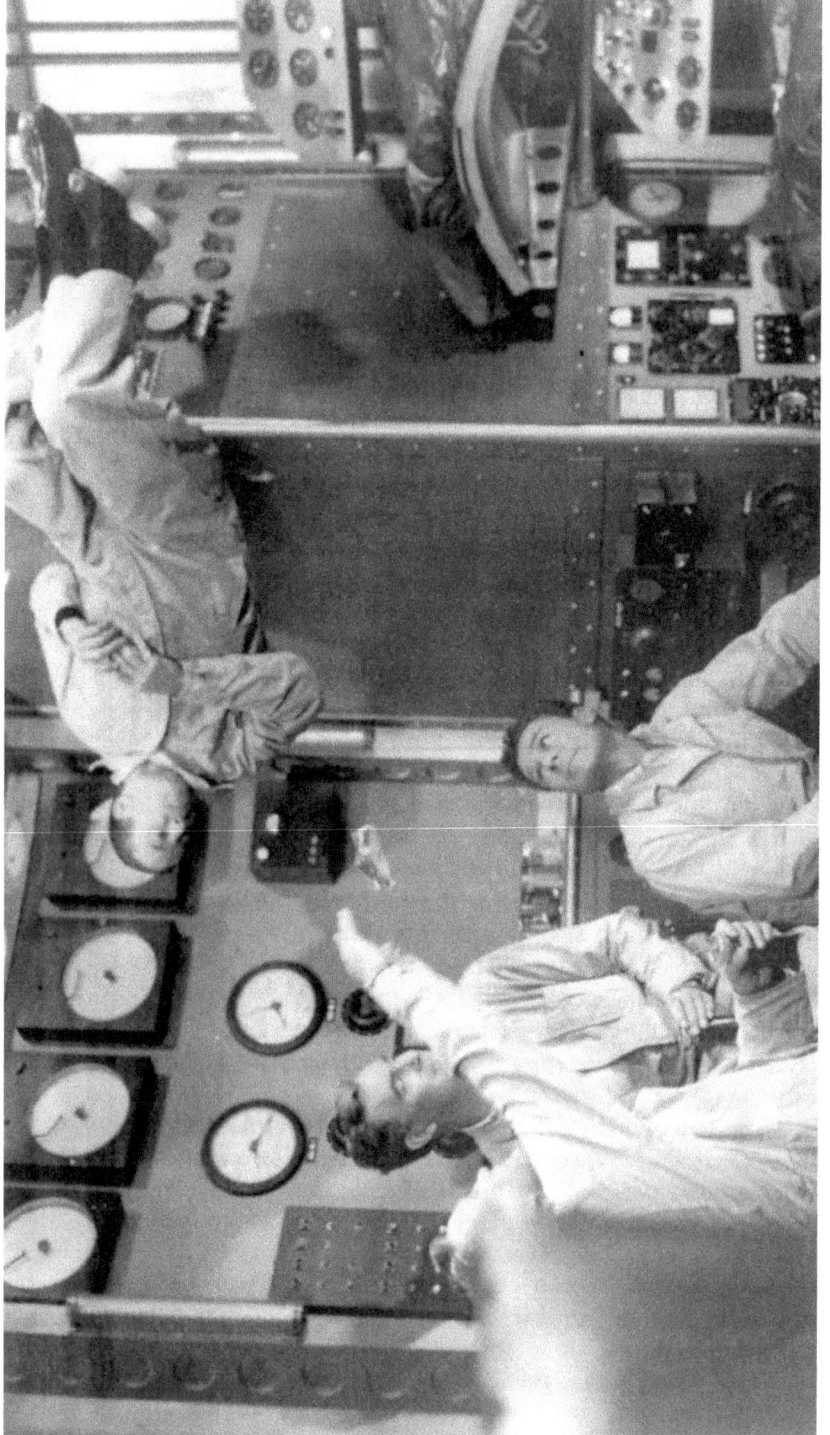

In the film's famous takeoff scene, the pressure of G forces distorts the faces of the pioneer astronauts—a special effect Archer remembers well. "That, I thought, was very interesting. Before shooting that scene, they put a wire and a piece of tape on each cheek and then they covered it with makeup. As the intensity increased, someone would be underneath us, out of camera range, pulling on these patches with the wire, which would force our faces back into that position. And, naturally, we cooperated as much as possible.

"In another scene, when we went outside the ship into space, Warner Anderson's character lost contact with the ship and floated off into space. I had to take a tank of oxygen and propel myself *to* him, and bring him back to the ship. Again, all that was done on a stage, with wires, and it was very exciting. That scene had a great, gorgeous background of brilliant stars—that was a backdrop that Bonestell had done. It was just breathtaking, the sight of it."

As for the moonscape set (representing the crater Harpalus), Archer recalls: "That was just a big, cracked-up thing, *unlike* what was actually found when they landed on the Moon. But this was their idea of it, big craggy areas and little valleys and hills. It was *very* effective. The problem with all those cracks was that they made our footing insecure and we had to look *down* too much, 'cause otherwise we'd have fallen on our faces! Remember, we were inside space suits, and our vision was hampered—we could only see so far with the helmets on. By the way, in those space suits, and under those lights, the actors got about as hot as you can get. Oh, it was insufferable *[laughs]*! But, oh, who cared? You did the work, it was no big deal."

Director Pichel (who directed Archer again a year later, in the Technicolor Western *Santa Fe*) is described by Archer as "a very easygoing, swell guy. He had an actor's approach because he *was* an actor—in fact, he appeared in *Santa Fe*. Very protective of his actors, very understanding—and very *good*. He could give you a lot. From being an actor, he knew the kind of stuff that we wanted *from* him, and we appreciated that." Pichel's set was constantly being invaded by press, scientists and other curious kibitzers, but according to Archer, the barrage of visitors did not seem to hinder production. "We knew these people were there—all the top guys from the top schools and laboratories were coming on, but we didn't know who they were and we didn't pay that much attention. They didn't seem to be interfering with anything, and you wouldn't even know they were there until you were told later." An occasional visitor would take a look around and comment that Pal was producing a *fantasy* film—an observation that would annoy the producer, who took great pains with what he called his "documentary of the future." "I can sympathize with

Opposite: "Weightless" Dick Wesson is about to catch a light snack on *Destination Moon*'s "rolling drum" spaceship set. Left-right: Tom Powers, Warner Anderson, Wesson, Archer.

George," Archer adds. "I'd have gotten pissed off and kicked 'em off the set [*laughs*]!"

To insure that the average Joe could relate to the futuristic goings-on in *Destination Moon,* a Woody Woodpecker cartoon simplistically described the principles of space travel, and actor Dick Wesson accompanied the space party as the low-comic Brooklynite radar-radio operator ("Go ahead, Oith!"). "I thought it distracted a *little* bit, but that's the way it was written, that's the way they wanted it and that's the way it was directed, so I guess that was supposed to have some kind of comic relief," Archer comments. "But, you're right, I don't know if it came off that well. By the way, Dick Wesson and I were good friends—the Wesson Brothers, Dick and his brother Gene, did a lot of vaudeville work around the country. Dick and his wife and my then-wife Marjorie and I used to do a lot of socializing."

More disastrous than Wesson's unfunny interludes was independent producer Robert Lippert's decision to cash in on the avalanche of publicity surrounding *Destination Moon*: Lippert knocked off a half-alike space travel movie and rushed it into release ahead of Pal's feature. Archer remembers the race for (theater) space well: "The Lippert picture with Lloyd Bridges, *Rocketship X-M*—they did that one in a hurry, because we were taking our time on *Destination Moon*. Ours was in color and it was just going to be great (and it *was*), so Lippert jumped the gun with that other movie and got it out a couple of weeks ahead of ours—and it *did* kind of steal our thunder a little bit. *Destination Moon* was getting a lot of attention [from newspapers, magazines, etc.] during production, and by coming out first, they stole a little of that for themselves. But there was nothing we could do about it."

One thing they *could* have done was rush through the balance of *Moon* when they saw Lippert's picture preparing for liftoff, but according to Archer, the pace of production did not change even when the imitation loomed. "No, that was never manifested at *all* during the shooting. We were on a schedule and Irving Pichel was doing a fine job *keeping* on schedule. We were never pressed at any time. If an audience saw our picture, and then walked next door to another theater and saw this *other* one, they'd say, 'Oh, my God—somebody's goofy *some*where.' What *[Rocketship X-M]* did was cut corners. We tried *not* to cut corners."

Almost a half century later, Archer is still able to look back on *Destination Moon* with pride: "I loved the movie and I *knew* that it was possible to someday get to the Moon. And later on, during the making of subsequent pictures, America *was* in space, making these wonderful orbits around the world in their spacecraft. And we on the set would always have a radio tuned in somewhere and we'd listen to this stuff, because a lot of us were interested in it. And then [in 1969], when a man finally *did* walk on the moon, I was amazed and awestruck at how little [the landing procedure in] *Destination Moon* differed from the actual landing." The $586,000 feature grossed $5.5 million

Archer dated Mari Blanchard in real life, and married and shot her in *reel* life — in the low-budget *She Devil*.

for distributor Eagle-Lion and won the 1950 Academy Award for special effects.

Archer worked throughout the fifties, on television and in movies big and small; his only other science fiction credit, *She Devil* (1957), has slipped from his memory other than the fact that it was made around the time that the divorced actor was dating the film's star, gorgeous Mari Blanchard. Television jobs included two stints on Ivan Tors' *Science Fiction Theatre* ("The episodes

I didn't think so much of—I don't think *Tors* did, either—but what the heck, we were all making a living") and Rod Serling's *The Twilight Zone* (in the classic episode "Will the Real Martian Please Stand Up"). "Rod Serling was on the set a few times, and he was a very interesting, fast-witted guy. Well, he had to be, because he wrote all those things overnight, practically. He was a nice man." Movie work ran the gamut from *The Big Trees* with Kirk Douglas to *Rock Around the Clock* with Bill Haley and His Comets and *Blue Hawaii* with Elvis Presley ("a great guy and a wonderful gentleman)."

Another sixties movie role was as the father of teenager Sara Lane in William Castle's 1965 suspenser *I Saw What You Did*, starring Joan Crawford. "Joan did all of her stuff in a hurry and got out, and everybody else came to work then," Archer laughs. "I only saw her at the wrap party! I don't remember much else about that one, except that I've never known a picture to get so much exposure. I still get residuals from that, and I wonder where it in the heck it is they're still showing this thing *[laughs]*."

Archer's final feature to date was the Don Knotts comedy *How to Frame a Figg* (1971) and his last television role was in the "wonderful" *Rich Man, Poor Man*. "I didn't give the business up, *it* gave *me* up. I had a nice career and I felt that I should move along, so I went into something else which I enjoyed very much; in the sixties, I went into the trucking business with my brother, and we built that sucker up to quite an important arena in Los Angeles. I'd always go back and do a TV show if anybody hollered, but then I lost my agent and I just became disenchanted."

But John Archer isn't crabbing. Remarried (since 1956), he has four children (two by Marjorie Lord, two by second wife Ann), a new grandchild to visit and "some wonderful memories" of a long career in all media. If anybody wants to holler for him to do a television show *now*, their lungs had better be in shape: for the past four years, he's been living in the state of Washington, where one of his sons works for an engineering firm. "I'm also involved with the Radio Enthusiasts of Puget Sound. We had our first convention last June and it's a nice group, people who are just *nuts* about old-time radio, and naturally I'm part of it."

Obviously, fans of radio have not forgotten John Archer, the redoubtable Shadow—but will Universal, which is presently planning a big-screen version of the mysterious sleuth's exploits? Perhaps more pertinently, would Archer be tempted at this point by an offer of work? "You know, I've thought about that. For two or three years they've been talking about the movie, and I thought it was probably shelved. But *if* they do it, I *might* qualify as the Inspector—I'm the right age now. (They might want someone younger.) But, yeah, I'd like to be in it, and it couldn't *hurt* in a little exploitation way to say, 'Archer was the original Shadow.' Well, *one* of them!"

JOHN ARCHER FILMOGRAPHY

As Ralph Bowman:

Flaming Frontiers (Universal serial, 1938)
Letter of Introduction (Universal, 1938)
Overland Stage Raiders (Republic, 1938)
Dick Tracy Returns (Republic serial, 1938)
Spring Madness (MGM, 1938)
Barnyard Follies (Republic, 1940)
Cheers for Miss Bishop (United Artists, 1941)

As John Archer:

Career (RKO, 1939)
Curtain Call (RKO, 1940)
City of Missing Girls (Select, 1941)
Mountain Moonlight (Republic, 1941)
The People vs. Dr. Kildare (MGM, 1941)
King of the Zombies (Monogram, 1941)
Scattergood Baines (RKO, 1941)
Paper Bullets (Gangs Incorporated) (PRC, 1941)
Highway West (Warner Bros., 1941)
Sucker List (MGM short, 1941)
Hi, Neighbor (Republic, 1942)
Bowery at Midnight (Monogram, 1942)
Mrs. Wiggs of the Cabbage Patch (Paramount, 1942)
Scattergood Survives a Murder (RKO, 1942)
Police Bullets (Monogram, 1942)
Shantytown (Republic, 1943)
The Purple V (Republic, 1943)
Crash Dive (20th Century-Fox, 1943)
Guadalcanal Diary (20th Century-Fox, 1943)
Hello Frisco, Hello (20th Century-Fox, 1943)
Sherlock Holmes in Washington (Universal, 1943)
The Eve of St. Mark (20th Century-Fox, 1944)
Roger Touhy, Gangster (20th Century-Fox, 1944)
No Exceptions (20th Century-Fox/Office of War Information short, 1944)
I'll Remember April (Universal, 1945)
The Lost Moment (Universal, 1947)
Colorado Territory (Warner Bros., 1949)
White Heat (Warner Bros., 1949)
Destination Moon (Eagle-Lion, 1950)
The Great Jewel Robber (Warner Bros., 1950)
High Lonesome (Eagle-Lion, 1950)
My Favorite Spy (Paramount, 1951)
Best of the Badmen (RKO, 1951)
Santa Fe (Columbia, 1951)
Rodeo (Monogram, 1951)
The Big Trees (Warner Bros., 1952)
Sea Tiger (Monogram, 1952)
A Yank in Indo-China (Columbia, 1952)
Sound Off (Columbia, 1952)
The Stars Are Singing (Paramount, 1953)
Dragon's Gold (United Artists, 1954)
No Man's Woman (Republic, 1955)
Emergency Hospital (United Artists, 1956)
Rock Around the Clock (Columbia, 1956)
Three Brave Men (20th Century-Fox, 1957)
Affair in Reno (Republic, 1957)
She Devil (20th Century-Fox, 1957)
Decision at Sundown (Columbia, 1957)
Ten Thousand Bedrooms (MGM, 1957)
City of Fear (Columbia, 1959)
Blue Hawaii (Paramount, 1961)
Apache Rifles (20th Century-Fox, 1964)
I Saw What You Did (Universal, 1965)
How to Frame a Figg (Universal, 1971)

*A painter can go and paint,
and a musician can practice by himself,
but an actor has to have an audience.*

Jeanne Bates

HER ACTING CAREER BEGAN not with a bang but with a scream—something she has been doing regularly since. That's not all Jeanne Bates is known for: In addition to her radio and screen shrieks, in movies ranging from Bela Lugosi's *The Return of the Vampire* to the recent cannibal horror/comedy *Mom*, she has performed in dramas, Westerns and comedies, sung onstage, and played a regular role on television's *Ben Casey*. Serial and comic strip fans may first recognize her name from the credits of Columbia's jungle adventure *The Phantom* (1943).

Born in Berkeley, California, Bates began her acting career while a student at San Mateo Junior College, appearing on radio soap operas in San Francisco. She played the lead in an airwave mystery series, Lew X. Lansworth's *Whodunit* (Bates's scream was the show's signature), which became so successful that it (and Bates) moved to Hollywood in 1941. Bates and Lansworth married in 1943.

By the time the two were married, Bates was already under contract to Columbia Pictures, although she had no delusions that the studio intended to build her into one of their big stars. "I was just one more Columbia starlet," says Bates, now in her sixth decade of movies. "Max Arnow was the head casting man, and he took me in to meet Mr. [Harry] Cohn, the head of Columbia. Mr. Cohn looked up at me for a couple seconds, and then went *right back* to what he was doing *[laughs]*. But even though I knew they had no 'big plans' for me, I did do about twenty-two films in the short time I was there. There was a very nice man in charge of Columbia's B unit and he liked me a lot, and he put me into some films."

Bates's debut was in a Boston Blackie mystery with Chester Morris, followed by a Charles Starrett Western on which she learned one of her earliest moviemaking lessons. "I love horses, but I never could afford to take riding lessons or anything. So the day I had to ride the horse, I practiced and practiced. But after practicing with the horse all morning long, when they said 'action,' the horse went one way when we were supposed to go the *other* way! I had no control over the horse whatsoever. So early on I learned not to say that I could do things I couldn't, because it's too dangerous." Other early roles included a precredits bit as a woman stalked by a vampire (Bela Lugosi's stand-in) in 1943 in *The Return of the Vampire* (screaming that scream again), comedy two-reelers, an Office of War Information short (*It's Murder*) and other bottom-of-the-bill features.

One of her first costarring roles was in Columbia's *The Phantom* (1943), based on the King Features syndicated comic strip. It took four writers to adapt Lee Falk's popular strip into the 15-episode adventure, which featured cowboy actor Tom Tyler as Godfrey Prescott and his masked alter ego, the Phantom. If the premise sounded glamorously exotic, the production, needless to say, was

Previous page: Jeanne Bates (seen here in a Columbia glamour pose) never kidded herself that the studio had star-making roles in store for her.

anything but. "We shot that at a studio called Darmour on Santa Monica [Boulevard], a really old, *old* studio. It must have been there in silent times. I think they had only *one* stage and the dressing rooms and it was all kind of out in the open — if it rained, forget it, folks — you'd be drowned between leaving the dressing room and getting to the soundstage *[laughs].*" Exteriors were shot "across from the Valley, in the hills up there, where Charles Manson killed all those people. Then there was another scene we shot at Malibu Lake, where all the natives climbed into the canoe — and the canoe sank! They had all these extras getting into this canoe and I thought to myself, 'They're not all gonna get in there, it's gonna sink.' And sure enough, it went down with all these guys trying to get into it. And, of course, the camera kept rolling as the boat and all these guys went down. It was *very* funny."

In the serial, directed by veteran soundstage speedster B. Reeves Eason, Professor Davidson (Frank Shannon) and his daughter Diana (Bates) arrive in Africa searching for the Lost City of Zoloz and its hidden treasures. Other self-interested parties with designs on the city and its riches include a local crook (Joe Devlin) as well as an international baddie (Kenneth MacDonald) who intends to build a secret air base there. Bates's fiancé (Tom Tyler) takes on his second identity (the Phantom) and, together with his dog Devil (played by Ace, the Wonder Dog), battles the villains throughout 15 "pulse-pounding" chapters before restoring peace to the jungles.

"Tom Tyler was very nice," Bates says of the *Phantom* himself. "Later on in life, he got some disease — elephantiasis or some other terrible thing! He was a nice man, very quiet and he did his job. And I was very impressed with the man who played my father [Frank Shannon, *Flash Gordon*'s Dr. Zarkov]. There was one scene where they were opening a treasure chest, and his hand got caught on a hinge and it cut the [webbing] of his hand, between the thumb and the forefinger. And he didn't stop. I would have screamed and yelled and hollered and so forth, but this actor, bleeding to death, went through this scene without a murmur. Only *after* the shot was completed did he say, 'Well, I've been cut.' And I thought that was wonderful, because he *was* an older man. I was very impressed with that.

"There was another incident where the heavies grabbed us and they were taking us up a ladder. Supposedly the Phantom was down below, being eaten by a gorilla — or whatever! The heavies went up this ladder, and it was nailed into the wall of this mountain. When I started going up — I remember that my boots were too big and my pants were too tight [for climbing] — the ladder started coming away from the wall. One of the actors at the top saw it happening and he grabbed it, so I finally got up. (They don't stop, you know — they keep shooting.) Then we were supposed to go over to the edge and look down to see the Phantom being eaten by the monster. Well, at the end of the shot, I couldn't *move*. I was frozen. My husband had been a reporter when the Bay Bridge was being built and he said that people would freeze — that's how they'd fall off the bridge and drown. Well, from that day on, I can't get up on a height without freezing, and I think it was all from that—it was kind of a traumatic experience."

Bates recalls working "three or four weeks" on the 15-chapter (30-reel) *Phantom,* including a period of a couple of days "when production was closed down because somebody caught cold or whatever, because it was freezing. It was *very* cold—they were shooting this in the winter, and we were in pith helmets and short sleeves. And every time we spoke, you could see our breath. On one of the first days of shooting, we were way up in the mountains, and they went downtown to Los Angeles to get 'natives'—extras. They bus-loaded these guys up there ... and then they stripped 'em. And as I said, it was freezing cold. They were stripping 'em down to loincloths and painting their bodies brown to look like natives, and these guys were shivering to death. There was an Indian man who was in the picture, and he said that how you keep from catching cold is to keep standing, do not sit down. So I've always remembered that—I don't know whether it works or not, but it seemed to work then!"

B. Reeves Eason, who was better at directing action than actors (his second-unit credits include the chariot race in the silent *Ben-Hur,* the burning of Atlanta in *Gone with the Wind* and the charge in Errol Flynn's *The Charge of the Light Brigade*), "was an old-time director, from way back. He had a nickname, 'Breezy.' I don't remember him too well, but he was one of those rugged guys, I guess like John Ford, that kind of guy. He *never* stopped the camera." Bates, who never read the *Phantom* strip, also did not see her serial when it was originally released "because they showed at Saturday matinees, for the little kids. But I now have *The Phantom* on tape, all fifteen episodes, given to me on two tapes by a man out in Burbank. I've seen one tape, and *[laughs]* I haven't gone on to the other one yet!"

Elevated to B stardom, Bates played one of the leads in Columbia's 1944 horror movie *The Soul of a Monster,* about a dying surgeon (George Macready) whose foolhardy wife (Bates) prays that the Devil will save his life. A satanic emissary (Rose Hobart) appears and saves Macready, who is now a different man, cruel and mysterious. Bates has fond memories of her *Soul* costars, particularly "Rose Hobart—the poor thing. There was a scene where I was supposed to slap her. Well, I would grit my teeth and try and try and try. I'd get up to that point in the scene and I just couldn't do it. Instead of a slap, it would just be a pat—and a pat—and a *pat,* no good for the scene. And I guess the *pats* were just driving her up the wall, because finally she said, 'Will you please—will you *p-l-e-a-s-e*—just slap me!' And to tell the truth, I don't remember now if I was ever able to really hit her or not, but I know she pleaded with me to do it, just to get it over with!"

It was after her stint at Columbia that Bates had one of her best forties film roles, as the long-suffering wife of mad illusionist Erich von Stroheim in PRC's horror melodrama *The Mask of Diijon* (1946), directed by Lew Landers.

Serial star Bates stands ready for action with Tom Tyler and Wonder Dog Ace in Columbia's *The Phantom*.

"He was wonderful, von Stroheim," says Bates. "My husband had told me about him—I was fairly young at the time and I didn't know too much about von Stroheim. I guess von Stroheim did the picture just because he wanted the bucks. And he got his girlfriend [Denise Vernac] in the picture, too, so *she* got paid! I don't know how much he got paid, but I guess it was a goodly sum. This was shot just after the war [in November 1945] and he was on his way

Sinking canoes, rickety ladders and freezing location work were just a few of the *Phantom* pitfalls braved by Bates.

back to France, to Paris, and he had trunkloads of makeup and wigs and all kinds of things for the actors who had been deprived of all that stuff during the war. What impressed me was the fact that he would listen to what I had to say [in the scenes]. Most actors would ask you a question and you'd be answering them, and their eyes would drift off to see who was coming in or who was going out. I was very impressed with the fact that he would listen to anything I had to say *[laughs]*. I liked him very much, he was a very nice man."

Although *Diijon* is directed with more style than the average Lew Landers movie, Bates doesn't recall master director von Stroheim ever whispering in Landers' ear. "No, as far as I know, von Stroheim just was an actor. I think it was the cameraman, Jack Greenhalgh, who created the mood in *Mask of Diijon*, more (probably) than Lew, and it was absolutely wonderful. It was his lighting. In the close-ups, there was such a mood, and I think that was Jack, who I remember very well. At Columbia I didn't photograph that well, and here I thought I did—*very* well. (My husband once told me, 'It's too bad you don't photograph better,' which was a great help, I must tell you *[laughs]*!) At Columbia they just threw a bunch of light on you and that was that. Greenhalgh created a mood, and he probably was responsible for a lot of the [artistic] touches. With von Stroheim, I just remember one scene he wanted to take over—it was a scene where he was perspiring and he was crying, so there was a lot of water coming down. When I saw it in the rushes, it was very funny, and *he* laughed, too."

In the fifties she worked on television as well as in features, including a role that has completely faded from memory, as Peter Coe's wife in the jungle adventure *Sabaka* (1953) with Boris Karloff. She also worked regularly as a nurse—in the movies, that is—first in the supernatural *Back from the Dead* (1957), as midwife to ghost-possessed mom-to-be Peggie Castle, and again in *The Strangler* (1964), where mad mama's boy Victor Buono murders Bates for saving his ailing mother's (Ellen Corby) life. ("It was kind of spooky lying on that gurney, being hauled out like I was dead. I remember thinking, 'My God, how horrible that this could happen to a person!'") She wore white on television as well, playing the compassionate Miss Wills on the hospital drama *Ben Casey* (1961–66).

Other television roles included Rod Serling's *Twilight Zone* (in the classic "It's a Good Life" episode) and two visits to *One Step Beyond*, hosted by John Newland. "I knew Newland from radio," says Bates, who appeared twice on *Beyond*, the first time as Mrs. Abraham Lincoln in "The Day the World Wept." "I thought that was quite good—I liked doing that one. I remember that the makeup on the actor who played Lincoln, Barry Atwater, took *hours*. I did some research, of course, on Mary Todd Lincoln, but they wanted her to come across as a kind of dreary lady so I got that black wig—and, come on, folks, that ain't gonna make you look glamorous." In the sixties she also went back to her first love, stage work, appearing in "legitimate" productions (including several musicals) in the Los Angeles area as well as on the road.

Film work in the seventies included the satirical *Suppose They Gave a War and Nobody Came?* (1970) and one of her most unusual feature credits, David Lynch's experimental *Eraserhead* (1978). "That was quite an experience. One of the ladies in it, Judith Anna Roberts, who plays the girl in the room across the hall [from star John Nance] — she belonged to Theater West, which was a theater group that I belonged to, and she recommended me for *Eraserhead*. I then went on an interview for David, who was an art student, and he said, no, I was much too pretty. And I said, 'No, no, you don't understand. I can be pretty and I can be awful.' So I sold myself on how awful I could look *[laughs]*. And it worked! Also, the man that played my husband, Allen Joseph, was from Theater West, so Judith got us a *couple* of jobs.

"We worked at the Doheny mansion that the AFI [American Film Institute] used to rent for a dollar a year. David didn't shoot in the mansion itself, we shot in the stables — upstairs in the stables, they had living quarters for the grooms and so forth. It was great working for David. I think I only worked a week or so, and he insisted on paying us. Then I saw him a couple of years later, in the bank, and I asked him how it was going, and he hadn't finished it yet because he ran out of money. Finally he got somebody to finance it and he finished it."

The nightmare-like student film (Lynch's feature debut) reportedly took a year to shoot and another year to edit; Bates and her husband had the opportunity to catch an early cut of the cult-movie-to-be. "My husband, Lew, who was a writer, and I went to see it, the first showing, and Lew said to David, 'Don't you think it's a little long?' And it was like stabbing David in the heart. Since then, they've cut it — that first [cut] was forever, it went on and on and on. But *Eraserhead* was what got him his start — it's still showing today, and, needless to say, *Eraserhead* got him *The Elephant Man* [1980]."

Eraserhead also led to more film work for Bates, including the title role in the cannibal horror film *Mom* (1991). In the direct-to-home-video feature, Bates is the unsuspecting landlady of an unearthly flesh eater (Brion James) who bites her, turning her into a fellow carnivore (with fangs and yellow contact lenses). "Both the casting director of *Mom* and Pat Rand, who directed it, were ardently in love with *Eraserhead*, so that was part of the reason I got it. And also because I could scream good *[laughs]*!"

Primarily shot in a rented house in downtown Los Angeles, *Mom* was Bates' first brush with modern monster makeup. "They had to make a plastic mask of my face, and not knowing what that was like, I said, 'Sure, go ahead.' Well, I'm kind of claustrophobic, and when you're under that thing for forty-five minutes, you can get a little antsy. *That* wasn't too pleasant! I wore rubber appliances that were supposed to swell up, and I had hoses on my back that they pumped air through, to make the appliances inflate. (I didn't think they

Bates is still active in movies, on television and on the stage.

swelled up that much—I didn't think it looked *that* disastrous!) To put the makeup on, it took about two hours. So we started putting the makeup on at around five o'clock, and I didn't work until twelve-thirty the next morning. And carrying this stuff around with you, this whole appliance, it was excruciating."

"Mom's" victims included prostitute Stella Stevens as well as a homeless man from L.A.'s mean streets. "I believe they got an actual street person—his name was Bates, too, I remember. They hired a whole bunch of street people because they wanted to have people lying on the street for their shots. They fed them 'lunch' at 11 P.M. and after that, these street people decided they'd been there long enough and they all left! So all the ADs had to lie on the street with newspapers over 'em, because all the street people they'd hired got tired and left."

Despite the discomfort of the makeup, Bates enjoyed the experience of making *Mom* ("It was one of the first really good parts I'd had in a long, long time, and I liked doing it very much"), not to mention the fact that it led to another horror role, as the senior sorceress of a coven of modern-day witches in director Brian Yuzna's *Initiation: Silent Night, Deadly Night 4* (1990). "Oh, *that* disaster!" the actress scoffs. "I felt so sorry for that young actress [Neith Hunter] with all of those bugs crawling all over her—ai yi yi! That was a cheapie, shot at night. I got that from *Mom*, because I showed the tape of *Mom* to Brian Yuzna and he loved it. And Brian's little boy was in it, too—he was the little boy that we were going to kill."

Other roles in newer movies have included director Lawrence Kasdan's *Grand Canyon* (1991) as well as *Die Hard 2* (1990), as Bonnie Bedelia's sassy fellow plane passenger. Bates also still works on television (*The Commish*), in commercials and onstage (most recently in Jean Giradoux's *Ondine* in Los Angeles), so apparently retirement is not on the horizon. "But, you know, you're *semi*retired whether you want to be or not, when you get to be a mature lady!"

According to Bates (widowed since 1981), the important thing is simply to keep working, which is why, after a half-century in the business, she still belongs to acting workshops and does the occasional freebie play on the side. "I'm not ready to die yet!"

JEANNE BATES FILMOGRAPHY

The Return of the Vampire (Columbia, 1943)
The Chance of a Lifetime (Columbia, 1943)
The Phantom (Columbia serial, 1943)
The Black Parachute (Columbia, 1944)
Shadows in the Night (Columbia, 1944)
She's a Soldier, Too (Columbia, 1944)
Sundown Valley (Columbia, 1944)
The Racket Man (Columbia, 1944)
The Soul of a Monster (Columbia, 1944)
Tonight and Every Night (Columbia, 1945)
Sergeant Mike (Columbia, 1945)
The Mask of Diijon (PRC, 1946)
Death of a Salesman (Columbia, 1951)
Trouble In-Laws (Columbia short, 1951)
Paula (The Silent Voice) (Columbia, 1952)
The Hindu (Sabaka) (United Artists, 1953)
Marty (United Artists, 1955)
Trooper Hook (United Artists, 1957)
Back from the Dead (20th Century–Fox, 1957)
Blood Arrow (20th Century–Fox, 1958)
Vice Raid (United Artists, 1959)
The Strangler (Allied Artists, 1964)
Suppose They Gave a War and Nobody Came? (Cinerama, 1970)
Eraserhead (AFI/Libra, 1978)
Die Hard 2 (20th Century–Fox, 1990)
Grand Canyon (20th Century–Fox, 1991)
Wild Orchid 2: Two Shades of Blue (Triumph, 1992)
Dream Lover (Gramercy Pictures, 1994)

Jitters, the monkey, I'll never forget. One day he jumped out of a tree and landed on the top of my head ... turned his tail around ... and you know what happened next. All over me!

Billy Benedict

BILLY BENEDICT HAS A MODEST ATTITUDE about his acting career. He considers each of his 200 or so movie roles "just work" and the fabled stars he worked alongside only "coworkers"; the casual way he puts each role in its proper place, as a very small part of a very big picture, it is tough to disagree with him. But when he talks too modestly about his career as a whole, he is in for a fight. During Hollywood's Golden Age, and for decades afterward, he managed to keep his face in front of cameras, either in features or on television, and make it one of the most recognizable ones in the business; that is no small achievement. Fans probably remember him best as one of the East Side Kids (or the Little Tough Guys, or the Bowery Boys; he was part of all three "splinter groups"), but serial and science fiction aficionados know him, too, primarily for his costarring role in Republic's 12-chapter *Adventures of Captain Marvel* (1941).

"There wasn't much difference between working at one of the big studios and working at places like Republic and Monogram," Benedict, now 76, recalls in his Hollywood home, "not as far as the work itself was concerned, anyway. At Republic, you moved a little faster *[laughs]*, and got a lot more done in a shorter length of time, but, really, it was all work any way that you look at it. Some of the schedules were short and others were longer, even at Republic and Monogram. Working fast or working slow, *I* had no preference—or, I should say, it didn't make any difference. It was work. In those years, we were young and it was a buck, and that was the important thing. I think *Adventures of Captain Marvel* was twenty-eight days, but that was early in the morning till late at night."

Like Red Ryder, Brenda Starr and other comic strip luminaries Benedict worked opposite, Captain Marvel too leapt from the printed page onto the silver screen, but the comic book Marvel was not one Benedict had kept up with. "No, I didn't read *Captain Marvel*, but *Brenda Starr* I looked at occasionally and *Red Ryder*, also. And *Tim Tyler's Luck* I'd read as a comic strip when I was younger; it was an exciting thing for me to read. But making *[Adventures of Captain Marvel]* was an enjoyable experience. Tom Tyler, who played Captain Marvel, was an exceptionally nice man and a very good actor, but he was very quiet on the set. He knew what he was doing and he always knew his dialogue very well—not that he had much of it in *that* thing *[laughs]*."

Curiously, Benedict himself did not have a word of dialogue in *Captain Marvel*'s first chapter *(Curse of the Scorpion)*, despite lots of screen time, but he found his voice again in subsequent episodes. His character, Whitey, was the sidekick to Billy Batson (Frank Coghlan, Jr.), a boyish newscaster who accompanies the Malcolm Archaeological Expedition on a trek into the barren wilderness of Siam. There the scientists discover the Golden Scorpion, an atom-smashing apparatus devised by the ancients, which has the power to turn

Previous page: Benedict (on the right) warily watches for the monkey's next move. (From *Perils of Nyoka*)

Benedict (holding hat) sizes up the bevy of suspects (George Pembroke, Robert Strange, John Davidson, Harry Worth) in *Adventures of Captain Marvel.*

base metals into gold. Motivated by greed and the lust for power, one of the scientists takes on the new identity of the masked Scorpion, an archvillain whose master plan includes laying evil hands on the Golden Scorpion and using it to rule the world. Batson, Whitey and Betty (Louise Currie), a secretary, are the youthful trio who battle the masked evildoer, with considerable help from Batson's alter ego, the superpowered, high-flying Captain Marvel (Tyler).

"Louise Currie was a lovely gal and it was nice working with her," Benedict continues. "I had met Frank Coghlan before we did *Captain Marvel* together, but we didn't become well acquainted until we did it; we've been friends ever since. [Stuntman] Dave Sharpe, who doubled for Frank and for Tom Tyler, was an exceptional man with tremendous talent, and as far as I'm concerned, he was one of the best stuntmen the business ever had. Dave's career went way, way back, almost as many years as Frank's; he did some comedies for Hal Roach and then he did some Westerns. Dave, unfortunately, had a voice that had rather a high pitch to it, and it was not really compatible as far as motion pictures were concerned. He was one hell of a guy, that's for sure.

"It was amazing what Dave did as Captain Marvel. For his takeoffs, he worked off a trampoline a lot of times, and the way it's cut together, it's pretty difficult to tell who was who. Dave had certain idiosyncracies [of movement] that if you *knew* him, it was easy to tell whether or not it's him doing a stunt in a picture or not. If I'm not mistaken, he even doubled for *me* once, in [the 1942 serial] *Perils of Nyoka*." Asked if he could have played Billy Batson as well as Coghlan did, Benedict scoffs. "No, I don't think so. For one thing, *physically* I was not right for it, I wasn't what the comic strip ordered."

As for directors John English *(Adventures of Captain Marvel)* and William Witney *(Marvel, Perils of Nyoka)*, "I liked them very much; in fact, I saw Bill Witney up in Lone Pine [California] last year, at a convention, and I'll probably see him again this year. And Jack English [who died in 1969] was a delightful man, too — just the opposite of Bill Witney in dress and speech and everything. But they were very compatible, and it was a pleasure to work with them."

Benedict has lost count of how many movies he has been in; with the awshucks attitude he brought to many of his screen characters, he responds to the question with an embarrassed "Oh, gosh, no, I really couldn't tell you." He *does* know that he was born in Haskell, Oklahoma, on April 16, 1917. ("There are a lot of books that list me as being born in 1906; I'm aware of 'em, but there's not much you can do about 'em!") Asked what led him to a career in the picture business, the best the Panhandle State native can muster is a matter-of-fact "it just *happened*. One reason was the economic situation. I came out here to Hollywood during the Depression when jobs were hard to come by, and I figured that if I could do something in movies, I might make a couple of bucks. I graduated from high school in Tulsa — I had been active in the drama department there, and I also had been studying dancing. My older sister and I just decided that we would come to California — get out of the Dust Bowl — and we did, in 1934."

Benedict's sister did not go into showbiz, but Benedict did — and right away. "I had originally been a dancer [on the stage in Oklahoma], dancing at different spots — it was a rough go. I decided I'd attempt to do the same thing here in Hollywood, but I very quickly found out that dancers were a dime a dozen. So then I figured to try it as an actor. I went to the old Fox studio on Western Avenue to see a man by the name of Jim Ryan — he was the casting director. There was a lady there who was his secretary, Mary Yost, and she happened to be the aunt of a fellow from Tulsa whom I knew *[laughs]*. So we got in a conversation, and she said, 'Well, if anything comes up, I'll kind of jack up Mr. Ryan, and see if we can do anything.' About two weeks later I got a call from her, to come down and see Ryan. I went down and there was an interview. I went in, met Mr. Ryan and a director, George Marshall, and a producer (whose name I've forgotten). We talked for a while, and as a result of that, I got a part in *$10 Raise* [1935] with Edward Everett Horton. That was the first picture that I did."

Benedict went onto the Fox payroll as a "featured player," playing roles there at the studio (soon redubbed 20th Century–Fox) as well as at other lots;

his thirties credits include the classics *After the Thin Man, Bringing Up Baby,* and Universal's *The Road Back,* directed by James Whale. His first serial experience came at the same studio, when he costarred in their 12-chapter *Tim Tyler's Luck* (1937). "Frank Thomas was the star, and I liked working with him very much. Both his mother and father were in show business; in fact, his father and I became very well acquainted when we were both under contract at RKO." Benedict also would go to see his own pictures, as well as the serials in which he had acted, in the theaters. "I enjoyed going to the movies — I always have — and it was a big thrill for me to see myself on the screen. I even went to some of the kiddie matinees when I wanted to see a chapter of one of the serials I'd done. I'd sit with the kids — and I even got recognized occasionally!"

Characteristically, he never considered the possibility of stardom ("I really wasn't thinking about it"), for characteristic reasons ("Just to keep working, that was the important thing"). He insists that he did not have an in at the various casting offices, although he never seemed to lack for work; counting serials and shorts as well as features, he was in an amazing total of 80 titles between 1940 and 1944 alone. Many of them might have been one-day gigs, but others, like some of the serials and the East Side Kids pictures, had him in costarring roles. "How did I keep so busy? Again, I don't know — my ability, my talent (if I had any!), or whatever. Evidently they liked what I did, so they put me to work. It happened and I enjoyed it."

Benedict worked in serials not only at Republic but also at Universal and Columbia, and he shares the widely held belief that Republic's were by far the best of the bunch. "Oh, yes, they were, very much so. Republic had the ability to get a crew together that knew what the hell was going on. They made the moves — they could almost second-guess what the director would want. They went very smoothly, and they were a great, great crew to work with — fantastic."

Perils of Nyoka gave him another sidekick role, this time to two-fisted Clayton Moore and Kay Aldridge (Nyoka), in a tale no less exotic than *Captain Marvel*'s. This scientific expedition takes our heroes to the deserts of northern Africa, where they search for the Lost Tablets of Hippocrates but find instead a villainous high priestess (Lorna Gray), her trained killer ape and hordes of angry tribesmen. "We shot that at Iverson's Ranch — the same place we went for Westerns and everything else Republic wanted to do," chuckles Benedict. "Clayton Moore and Kay Aldridge were both a lot of fun, and Jitters, the monkey, I'll never forget. One day he jumped out of a tree and landed on the top of my head ... turned his tail around ... and you know what happened next. All over me!" As for a favorite serial, Benedict cannot choose between *Marvel* and *Nyoka*. "I like both of 'em very much, and I enjoyed working in them. I've collected some of my serials on videocassette and I do dig 'em out occasionally and look at them. They're still pretty good.

Perils of Nyoka protagonists Benedict, Forbes Murray, Kay Aldridge, George Pembroke, Clayton Moore and Robert Strange await their next skirmish.

"I did a lot of my own stunts on *Perils of Nyoka*. But on some of the stuff I did down at Monogram, there were a couple of times where, after I had done my stunt, I wished that they had gotten a stuntman. I'm talking about the pictures with the Bowery Boys now. And there were also a couple of stunts they wanted me to do, which I did kiss off."

The early East Side Kids flicks were produced by Sam Katzman, the Hollywood moviemaker with the well-earned reputation of never meeting a corner he couldn't cut or a penny he couldn't pinch. "He also produced one of the serials I was in, *Brenda Starr, Reporter* [1945]," Benedict recalls of "Jungle Sam." "The Republic serials were by far much better directed, much better written, and the overall picture was much better [than *Brenda Starr*]. With Sam Katzman, they were on a strict budget, and they got by just as cheap as they could, and didn't worry too much about a lot of things that they *should* have. But Joan Woodbury, who played Brenda Starr, was a lovely gal and it was a lot of fun."

Returning to the subject of the East Side Kids, Benedict remembers, "Sam Katzman had latched onto all the Dead End Kids and signed 'em up. I had worked for Sam when he was an independent producer, years before, and he kind of liked me. He asked me to come down and go to work in one of these pictures. I said, 'Sam, you can't pay my salary.' And he said, 'Well, just try me.' So he got on the phone and called my agent, and I got the money I wanted.

"Katzman would hang around with his cane and beat the floor when things weren't going well. (Maybe some times he'd even try to beat you [*laughs*].) I got along very well with Sam, and made a lot of movies with him." In the mid-forties the popular low-budget series got a much-needed facelift; budgets and shooting schedules were upped and the band of slaphappy hooligans was redubbed the Bowery Boys. "Sam Katzman and [series lead] Leo Gorcey couldn't get along, so Leo and his agent, Jan Grippo, made a deal together and started producing the pictures themselves. Now we were the Bowery Boys," says Benedict.

Not surprisingly, Benedict adds, Leo Gorcey and his "boys" were in real life nothing like the roughnecks they played—publicity to the contrary. "When they were away from the set, they were altogether different than when they were on. But they had to keep up appearances for publicity's sake. I got along with all of 'em very well." Various adventures found the slum kids pitted against horror-type actors in haunted houses and similar settings, giving Benedict an opportunity to see stars of this genre at work. "Glenn Strange [*Master Minds*, 1949] was a good actor and a nice guy. Bela Lugosi [*Ghosts on the Loose*, 1943] was in those, too, of course, and there again, he was a very pleasant individual. Before we did [*Spook Busters*, 1946], I had worked with Charlie Middleton at Republic—he was the villain in *Nyoka*—and he was a hell of an actor, that's for sure. So was Lionel Atwill [*Junior "G" Men of the Air*, 1942]. Both of those gentlemen were exceptionally good professional people.

"When I first started doing the East Side Kids pictures, we did 'em in three days and three nights. Later they got up to about four days, and then when the Bowery Boys came along, they went all the way up to five or six days. Toward the end, they were taking ten days, which no one had intended to happen, but it did." On his departure from the series (his last was *Crazy Over Horses*, 1951), he hesitantly admits, "I had just had enough. I suddenly decided I'd had enough of 'em, and it was getting a little rough doing 'em—emotionally—so I kissed 'em goodbye, and that was it. It got to be too much of a hassle. There was a lot of infighting going on with everybody concerned and I said, to hell with it, I don't need this."

By the early fifties, of course, Benedict was already acting on television in addition to tackling minor movie roles; one of his small-screen roles was as a baddie in the poorly produced (and short-lived) *Dick Tracy* with Ralph Byrd ("nice man"). *The Magnetic Monster,* a 1953 science fiction entry, had Benedict in the small part of a hardware store employee whose entire inventory has inexplicably become magnetized—the result of the presence of a deadly radioactive element hidden in an apartment above. "That was for [writer/director] Curt Siodmak, and it was made as an independent by Ivan Tors, before he moved on to his TV series. I found Siodmak very easy to work with; he might have

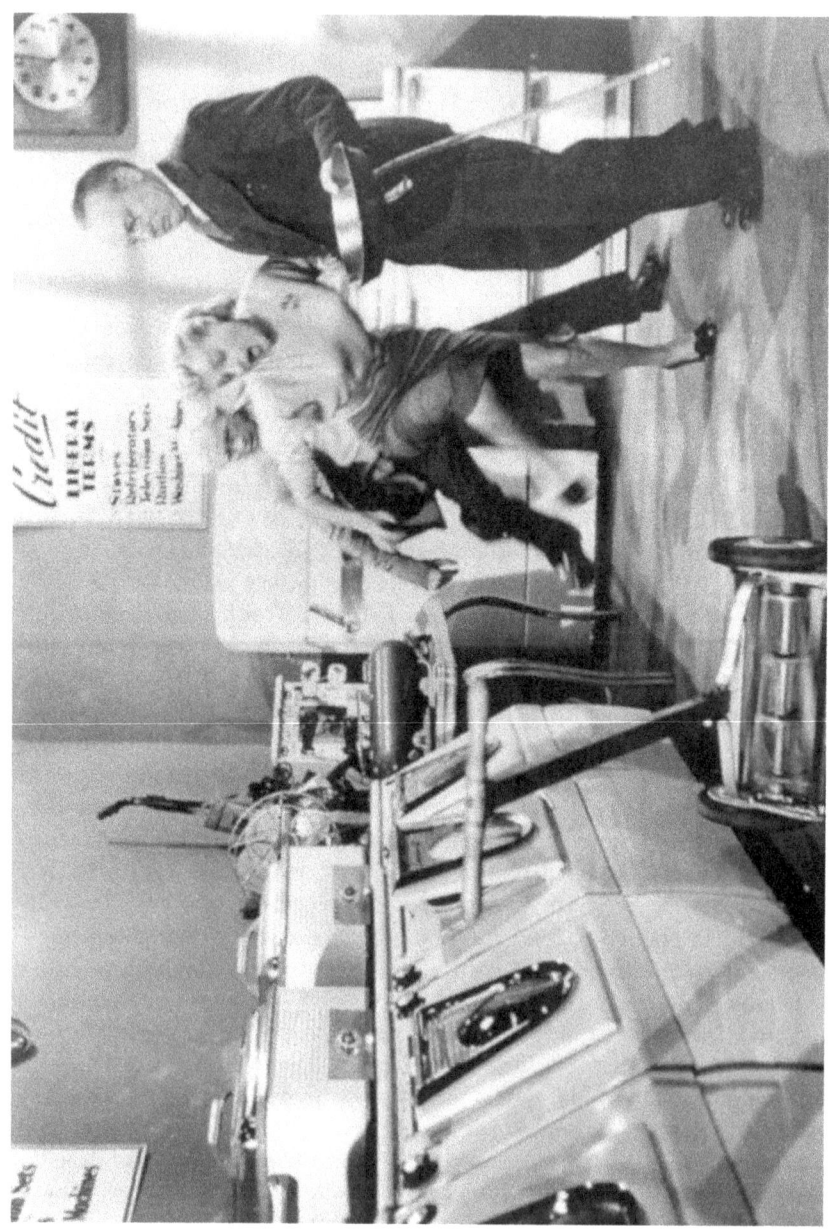

been a little hard to understand, but he was very pleasant with me. He was the man who had written *Donovan's Brain*, and he was a delightful man as far as I was concerned. That job went about three days, I think." On the opposite pole from *Magnetic Monster* (quality wise) was the Ed Wood concoction *Bride of the Monster* (1956), which Benedict recalls with a laugh and a "God Almighty! People get a laugh out of Wood's movies nowadays, they poke fun at 'em—and they *should*. He was a real hustler and a promoter. I don't know how many pictures he did, or attempted to do; I met him somewhere, don't ask me where, and he took a shine to me and wanted me to work in the picture. We started to work, and then the Guild shut it down because there was no money up front for the actors! (We finally *did* get paid.)"

Other television work has included *I Dream of Jeannie, Mission: Impossible, The Twilight Zone, Land of the Giants* and *The Incredible Hulk*; one of his last features (to date) is *Homebodies* (1974), which has a cast of veterans (Ian Wolfe, Ruth McDevitt, Peter Brocco, Douglas Fowley, more) and a horror/comic plot about oldsters resorting to murder to protect their condemned building. "*Homebodies* was directed by a man by the name of Larry Yust, with whom I'd worked before. That was one of the few commercial films that he made—the others that he had made were educational films. He was a good director—in fact, a very good director—and a nice man. I saw the movie, and it shakes you up a little bit, that's for sure!"

Billy Benedict, the man of many movies (and, generally, few words) describes himself today as "sort of kind of retired. I occasionally do a commercial. If something comes along, fine; if not, I go about my own business—I go fishin' *[laughs]*! And this is about as active as I want to be." Looking back over an almost-60-year career, he remarks, "All I can say is that it's been a lot of fun. If I had it to do all over again, I suppose I would do it the same way." Regrets? He's had a few; but then again, too few to mention. One of his only good *dramatic* parts was in William Wellman's *The Ox-Bow Incident* (1943); he would have liked to have played more roles like that. Other than that, he's been in plenty of other types of roles, in practically every sort of movie. In fact, there might be only one thing that Billy Benedict, the hoofer from Oklahoma who came to Hollywood with his eye on a dancing career, might have enjoyed doing in a movie, but never had the chance:

"Strange as it seems, I've never once danced in a picture!"

Opposite: Years before *The Lawnmower Man*, Benedict, Elizabeth Root and Byron Foulger were attacked in *The Magnetic Monster*.

70   They Fought in the Creature Features

BILLY BENEDICT FILMOGRAPHY

$10 Raise (Fox, 1935)
The Farmer Takes a Wife (Fox, 1935)
Steamboat 'Round the Bend (Fox, 1935)
Doubting Thomas (Fox, 1935)
Ladies Love Danger (Fox, 1935)
College Scandal (Paramount, 1935)
Silk Hat Kid (Fox, 1935)
Way Down East (Fox, 1935)
Your Uncle Dudley (Fox, 1935)
Show Them No Mercy (Fox, 1935)
Three Kids and a Queen (Universal, 1935)
Welcome Home (20th Century–Fox, 1935)
Can This Be Dixie? (Fox, 1936)
Meet Nero Wolfe (Columbia, 1936)
The Country Doctor (20th Century–Fox, 1936)
Theodora Goes Wild (Columbia, 1936)
Adventure in Manhattan (Columbia, 1936)
Crack-Up (20th Century–Fox, 1936)
After the Thin Man (MGM, 1936)
Ramona (20th Century–Fox, 1936)
M'Liss (RKO, 1936)
The Witness Chair (RKO, 1936)
Libeled Lady (MGM, 1936)
Captain January (20th Century–Fox, 1936)
A Son Comes Home (Paramount, 1936)
They Wanted to Marry (RKO, 1937)
The Last Gangster (MGM, 1937)
Jim Hanvey—Detective (Republic, 1937)
Rhythm in the Clouds (Republic, 1937)
That I May Live (20th Century–Fox, 1937)
Love in a Bungalow (Universal, 1937)
Tim Tyler's Luck (Universal serial, 1937)
Laughing at Trouble (20th Century–Fox, 1937)
A Dangerous Adventure (Columbia, 1937)
The Road Back (Universal, 1937)
Tramp Trouble (RKO short, 1937)
Flying Fists (Victory, 1937)
There's Always a Woman (Columbia, 1938)
Hold That Co-ed (20th Century–Fox, 1938)
Bringing Up Baby (RKO, 1938)
Say It in French (Paramount, 1938)
Walking Down Broadway (20th Century–Fox, 1938)
Young Fugitives (Universal, 1938)
King of the Newsboys (Republic, 1938)
Hold That Kiss (MGM, 1938)
No Time to Marry (Columbia, 1938)
Little Tough Guys in Society (Universal, 1938)
I Met My Love Again (United Artists, 1938)
Pack Up Your Troubles (20th Century–Fox, 1939)
Newsboys' Home (Universal, 1939)
Timber Stampede (RKO, 1939)
Code of the Streets (Universal, 1939)
Call a Messenger (Universal, 1939)
Man of Conquest (Republic, 1939)
Hollywood Hobbies (MGM short, 1939)
The Bowery Boy (Republic, 1940)
Legion of the Lawless (RKO, 1940)
My Little Chickadee (Universal, 1940)
Adventures of Red Ryder (Republic serial, 1940)
Lucky Partners (RKO, 1940)
Rhythm on the River (Paramount, 1940)
Grand Ole Opry (Republic, 1940)
Second Chorus (Paramount, 1940)
Prairie Law (RKO, 1940)
Stage to Chino (RKO, 1940)
The Great McGinty (Paramount, 1940)
Young People (20th Century–Fox, 1940)
Melody Ranch (Republic, 1940)
Give Us Wings (Universal, 1940)
Chicken Feed (RKO short, 1940)
And One Was Beautiful (MGM, 1940)
Citadel of Crime (Republic, 1941)
In Old Cheyenne (Republic, 1941)
The Richest Man in Town (Columbia, 1941)
Jesse James at Bay (Republic, 1941)
She Knew All the Answers (Columbia, 1941)

Unholy Partners (MGM, 1941)
The Man Who Lost Himself (Universal, 1941)
Variety Reels (*Meet the Stars* series) (Republic short, 1941)
Mr. District Attorney (Republic, 1941)
Bad Man of Deadwood (Republic, 1941)
Great Guns (20th Century–Fox, 1941)
Adventures of Captain Marvel (Return of Captain Marvel) (Republic serial, 1941)
The Great Mr. Nobody (Warner Bros., 1941)
The Mad Doctor (A Date with Destiny) (Paramount, 1941)
Tuxedo Junction (Republic, 1941)
Time Out for Rhythm (Columbia, 1941)
Confessions of Boston Blackie (Columbia, 1941)
Dressed to Kill (20th Century–Fox, 1941)
Home in Wyomin' (Republic, 1942)
Talk of the Town (Columbia, 1942)
A Night to Remember (Columbia, 1942)
Valley of Hunted Men (Republic, 1942)
Right to the Heart (20th Century–Fox, 1942)
A Tragedy at Midnight (Republic, 1942)
On the Sunny Side (20th Century–Fox, 1942)
Junior "G" Men of the Air (Universal serial, 1942)
Get Hep to Love (Universal, 1942)
Perils of Nyoka (Nyoka and the Tigermen) (Republic serial, 1942)
Rings on Her Fingers (20th Century–Fox, 1942)
Lady in a Jam (Universal, 1942)
The Glass Key (Paramount, 1942)
Wildcat (Paramount, 1942)
Two Yanks in Trinidad (Columbia, 1942)
Mrs. Wiggs of the Cabbage Patch (Paramount, 1942)
Almost Married (Universal, 1942)
Heart of the Golden West (Republic, 1942)
Affairs of Jimmy Valentine (Unforgotten Crime) (Republic, 1942)
Thank Your Lucky Stars (Warner Bros., 1943)
Clancy Street Boys (Monogram, 1943)
Aerial Gunner (Paramount, 1943)
Hangmen Also Die! (United Artists, 1943)
Mr. Muggs Steps Out (Monogram, 1943)
Whispering Footsteps (Republic, 1943)
Adventures of the Flying Cadets (Universal serial, 1943)
Ghosts on the Loose (Monogram, 1943)
The Ox-Bow Incident (Strange Incident) (20th Century–Fox, 1943)
Moonlight in Vermont (Universal, 1943)
Nobody's Darling (Republic, 1943)
All by Myself (Universal, 1943)
Million Dollar Kid (Monogram, 1944)
The Lady and the Monster (Republic, 1944)
Janie (Warner Bros., 1944)
The Whistler (Columbia, 1944)
My Gal Loves Music (Universal, 1944)
Follow the Leader (Monogram, 1944)
Goodnight Sweetheart (Republic, 1944)
The Merry Monahans (Universal, 1944)
Block Busters (Monogram, 1944)
That's My Baby (Republic, 1944)
They Live in Fear (Columbia, 1944)
Cover Girl (Columbia, 1944)
Follow the Boys (Universal, 1944)
Bowery Champs (Monogram, 1944)
Night Club Girl (Universal, 1944)
Brenda Starr, Reporter (Columbia serial, 1945)
The Story of G.I. Joe (G.I. Joe) (United Artists, 1945)
Docks of New York (Monogram, 1945)
Mr. Muggs Rides Again (Monogram, 1945)
Patrick the Great (Universal, 1945)
Come Out Fighting (Monogram, 1945)
Road to Utopia (Paramount, 1945)
Hollywood and Vine (PRC, 1945)
A Boy, a Girl and a Dog (Film Classics, 1946)
The Gentleman Misbehaves (Columbia, 1946)

No Leave, No Love (MGM, 1946)
One More Tomorrow (Warner Bros., 1946)
Live Wires (Monogram, 1946)
In Fast Company (Monogram, 1946)
Without Reservations (RKO, 1946)
Bowery Bombshell (Monogram, 1946)
Spook Busters (Monogram, 1946)
Mr. Hex (Monogram, 1946)
Gay Blades (Tournament Tempo) (Republic, 1946)
Do You Love Me? (20th Century–Fox, 1946)
Never Say Goodbye (Warner Bros., 1946)
The Kid from Brooklyn (RKO, 1946)
Hard Boiled Mahoney (Monogram, 1947)
The Hucksters (MGM, 1947)
Fun on a Weekend (United Artists, 1947)
Bowery Buckaroos (Monogram, 1947)
The Pilgrim Lady (Republic, 1947)
News Hounds (Monogram, 1947)
Merton of the Movies (MGM, 1947)
Jinx Money (Monogram, 1948)
Smugglers' Cove (Monogram, 1948)
Angels' Alley (Monogram, 1948)
Trouble Makers (Monogram, 1948)
Secret Service Investigator (Republic, 1948)
Night Wind (20th Century–Fox, 1948)
Fighting Fools (Monogram, 1949)
Hold That Baby! (Monogram, 1949)
Master Minds (Monogram, 1949)
Riders of the Pony Express (Kayson/Screencraft, 1949)
Angels in Disguise (Monogram, 1949)
Blonde Dynamite (Monogram, 1950)
Lucky Losers (Monogram, 1950)
Triple Trouble (Monogram, 1950)
Blues Busters (Monogram, 1950)
Bowery Battalion (Monogram, 1951)
Ghost Chasers (Monogram, 1951)
Let's Go Navy! (Monogram, 1951)
Crazy Over Horses (Monogram, 1951)
The Magnetic Monster (United Artists, 1953)
Bride of the Monster (Banner, 1956)
The Killing (United Artists, 1956)
Rally 'Round the Flag, Boys! (20th Century–Fox, 1958)
Last Train from Gun Hill (Paramount, 1959)
Lover Come Back (Universal, 1961)
Dear Heart (Warner Bros., 1964)
Harlow (Paramount, 1965)
Zebra in the Kitchen (MGM, 1965)
The Hallelujah Trail (United Artists, 1965)
Frankie and Johnny (United Artists, 1966)
What Am I Bid? (Emerson, 1967)
Funny Girl (Columbia, 1968)
Big Daddy (Paradise Road) (Syzygy/United, 1969)
Hello, Dolly (20th Century–Fox, 1969)
The Dirt Gang (AIP, 1972)
The Sting (Universal, 1973)
Homebodies (Avco Embassy, 1974)
Farewell, My Lovely (Avco Embassy, 1975)
Won Ton Ton, the Dog Who Saved Hollywood (Paramount, 1976)
Born Again (Avco Embassy, 1978)

Benedict's footage was deleted from *Metropolitan* (20th Century–Fox, 1935). He also acted in the unreleased *Rogue's Gallery* (Paramount, 1968).

Oh, horror films are wonderful.

Turhan Bey

TALL, DARK AND EXOTICALLY HANDSOME, Turhan Bey was emblematic of the breed of foreign-born leading men that flourished briefly in Hollywood during the World War II years. But Bey's home studio was Universal, the company whose most famous players had names like Dracula, Frankenstein and Kharis; unlike other Hollywood players who had lovely leading ladies in picture after picture, Bey occasionally found himself opposite such unglamorous costars as the Mummy, the Mad Ghoul and Boris Karloff. Surely the suave star of forties classics like *Ali Baba and the Forty Thieves* and Katharine Hepburn's *Dragon Seed* saw these B horror films as a decided comedown.

"No, I liked the horror films. I wish I could have kept it up," Turhan Bey declares emphatically. "I *always* liked horror films and I always liked playing heavies, when they were interesting. There are some heavies that are just mean, but I was lucky, I always played heavies that had some kind of a hidden cause to be mean. But dislike horror films? Oh, no, no! I *loved* them! I loved to see them and I loved to play in them."

It has been years since Turhan Bey has acted; even his "newest" film, a 1953 Sam Katzman quickie called *Prisoners of the Casbah,* is long gone into the limbo of forgotten celluloid. But Bey's memories of his movie days are still vivid. On an extended visit to Hollywood from his native Austria, seated poolside at his Beverly Hills hotel, he is only too happy to reminisce candidly about the highs (and lows) of his unique acting career.

Turhan Selahettin Schultavey (the "Bey" is actually a title) was born in Vienna, son of a Turkish father and a Czech mother. After his mother sold her lucrative glass manufacturing business in Czechoslovakia, the family moved to Paris, where they met a friendly American lawyer who recommended they visit California and gave Bey a letter of introduction to film director Arthur Lubin. The Beys left Paris because "my mother had the feeling there was going to be a war—and nobody else shared that opinion. But she had a wonderful sixth sense for those things, and she made us come to America."

Migrating to America in the late thirties, Bey spent his first several months in the States in Littleton, New Hampshire, where he lived with his mother and grandmother and studied English. The three later traveled west to California and presented the letter of introduction to Arthur Lubin, who proceeded to show them Hollywood. After that, Bey's decision to become an actor was not long in coming. "The fact that I had to perfect my English made me go to [acting teacher] Ben Bard's dramatic school. After a while, Ben Bard needed for one of his plays an actor to play a character that would fit me very well. And when the play was seen by two Warner Brothers talent scouts, I had my first role at Warner Brothers."

Bey earned $500 a week for his film debut, a supporting role in Warners' comedy-mystery *Footsteps in the Dark* (1941) with Errol Flynn. After making

Previous page: Turhan Bey in a characteristic forties pose.

a second Warners film, *Shadows on the Stairs* (1941), "I made a film at Universal and they liked what I did. At that time, they had a great many roles for people of my looks, which were Oriental ... could-be-Chinese, could-be-Japanese, all of which I played. And Universal signed me up." At first, the roles were not great, and neither were the movies: Bey had character names like Luchau, Muto, Chundra and Juma, and the pictures had titles like *Drums of the Congo* and *Raiders of the Desert*. (In the screen credits of *Raiders*, a typo makes him Tur*b*an Bey.) Excelling in minor villainous characters, he was the perfect choice to play the baddie in Universal's *The Mummy's Tomb*.

Second in Universal's series of Kharis films, *Tomb* moved the action from Egypt to America, as the Mummy (Lon Chaney) stalks and kills members of the expedition that desecrated his final resting place in the previous movie *(The Mummy's Hand)*. Chaperoning Kharis on his first trip abroad, Turhan's Mehemet Bey gave the Mummy his nightly wake-up call and brewed those eye-opening cups of tana fluid before sending him out on his murderous missions. "I felt terribly sorry for this excellent actor Lon Chaney, who had to wrap himself up every day, even in the greatest heat, in that fabulous costume of his. Except to speak with his body, he couldn't do anything. The costume was held together with a zipper in the back, so it wasn't all too difficult to get in and out of it — they didn't have to wrap all those bandages around him. Only one eye was showing through the mask, and there was a small slit for him to breathe through his nose and through his mouth. But that was all."

The Mummy was Chaney's least favorite monster role, and on the set of a later Kharis film, *The Mummy's Ghost,* the actor told a United Press visitor that people were crazy to spend their money to see Mummy films. On the set of *Mummy's Tomb,* however, Bey says that Chaney kept his dissatisfaction strictly to himself. "He was a real professional. He would never show anybody that. He may have felt that he couldn't do any acting [as the Mummy], but when you watch the way he moved, the rhythm of his various movements, he *did* do some acting with his body, as his father did."

Engagingly disingenuous, Bey insists — as he has in the past — that *The Mummy's Tomb* is perhaps his favorite among his own films. "I guess it's my favorite because it was a part closest to my own nationality — it was a young Egyptian who believed in something which we could not comprehend with our five senses. As I said before, I do like people who are in contradiction with all laws of human decency because of some reason, some inexplicable belief that they have. I don't mean that I would like to have people like that around me in life *[laughs]*, but I like to portray them. If I could have picked my own roles, I would have played these kinds of heavies, people who have a mental quirk or who, for some reason or another, are acting against the positive side of the plot of the picture. I like heavies with a cause, so I think *The Mummy's Tomb* was one of my favorite roles — really. But, to be perfectly honest with you, I

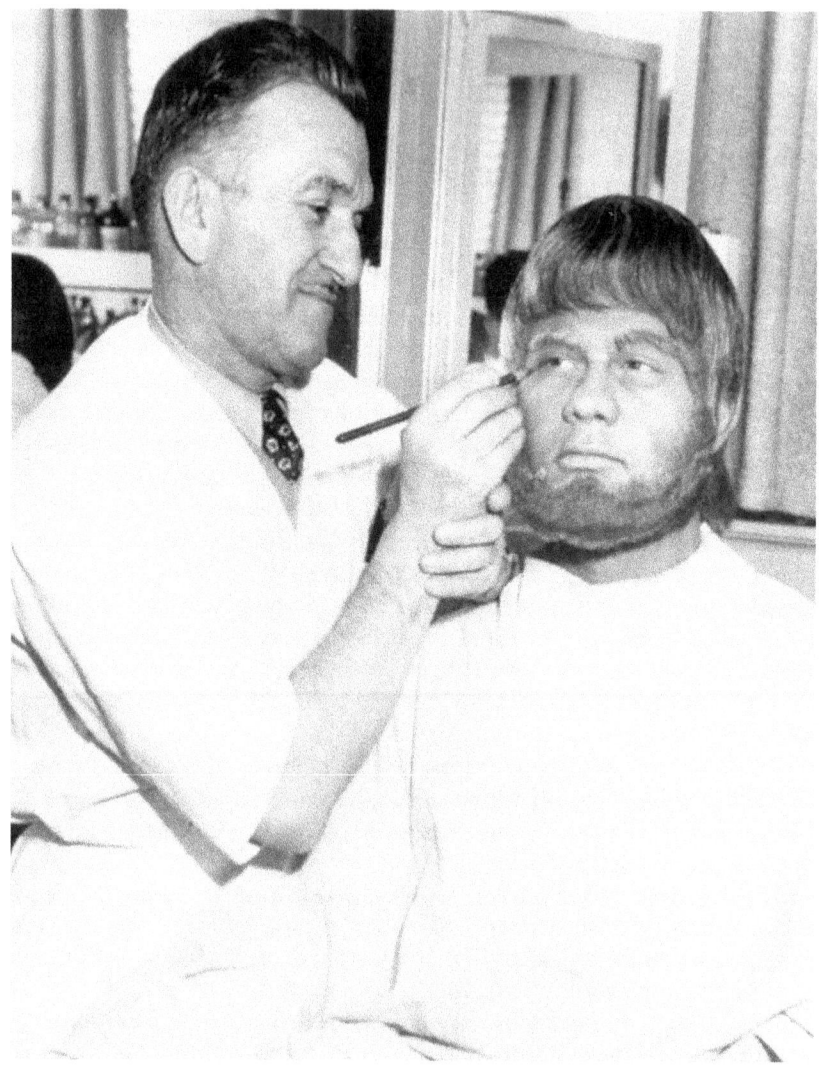

Jack P. Pierce makes up Turhan Bey for his role as the ape-like Aesop in Universal's *Night in Paradise*.

never saw the movie. For many of my films, I saw the rushes but never saw them finished. In fact, I never even kept a still picture of myself."

The films for which Turhan Bey remains best known are the Arabian Nights costumers Universal churned out in the early forties. Often paired with fellow camel jockeys Jon Hall, Sabu and, of course, Universal's Queen of Technicolor, Maria Montez, Bey costarred in the garish escapist romps *Arabian*

Nights, *White Savage*, *Ali Baba and the Forty Thieves* and *Sudan*. Today the movies themselves are regarded as kitsch, and Maria Montez has become the darling of the high camp set. Bey insists, however, that the people involved in the making of these films did not have their tongues in their cheeks.

"I didn't have that attitude, nor did the people I worked with. I took them very seriously; I think that's the only way to do anything, except when you play in a comedy. If you don't take these costume pictures seriously, they become a comedy, too." Bey—who, until this question, never heard of the word *camp*—is mildly distressed that the films have this sort of reputation today. "It would be terrible if you were to do something and to think that, in ten years, it would be ridiculous. You can't do that, you have to take it seriously. By the way, I saw *Ali Baba and the Forty Thieves* in Austria—nobody laughed at it; they enjoyed it. We wouldn't have made them if we thought they were 'camp.'" And as for the notorious Maria Montez, Bey is taken aback to hear that she's gone down in the Hollywood history books as a highly difficult and temperamental actress. "I enjoyed working with her very much. We were very dear friends. She wasn't always on time, but the difficulty with Maria was that she was brought up in a very Catholic and a very strict family surrounding, and some of the studio language isn't always the best *[laughs]*. So when somebody talked like that in front of her, she was shocked, and told him what she thought of him!"

By this time, of course, the six-foot-one Bey was known as one of Tinseltown's most eligible bachelors, frequently photographed arm in arm with Hollywood lovelies and endlessly profiled in movie magazines that dubbed him "Mystery Man," "Ladies' Knight" and, inevitably, "The Terrific Turk." Returning to horror, Bey furnished the closing narration for Universal's *Captive Wild Woman* before finally getting an opportunity to play hero, protecting Evelyn Ankers from the clammy clutches of *The Mad Ghoul*. Bey remembers remarkably little about the film, except that he enjoyed working with costars Ankers and veteran movie baddie George Zucco. "Zucco was one of the finest gentlemen I have ever worked with, and the last person in the world I would suspect to play horror parts. Except for his fantastic, menacing eyes and his voice, which he could manage so well, there was nothing horrible about him at all." And Ankers, reigning screen queen of the Universal lot, was "a very pleasant, wonderful girl with whom I had lunch once. We were talking about romance and things like that, and she said to me, 'Turhan, you're the kind of a man I'd like to have an affair with, but I'd hate to be married to.' *[Laughs]* That was her definition of Turhan Bey!"

The Ghoul himself, boyish leading man David Bruce, was "the sort of pleasant young man that was under contract to Universal at the time, a fellow who tried to make life as agreeable as possible for everybody. I think that at Universal, that was the tendency. We all got along fine and I don't remember ever having a serious clash with anybody. Not even an *un*serious clash." Bey's upbeat memories also extend to the people behind the camera at Universal, like prolific B producer Ben Pivar and *Mad Ghoul* director James Hogan. "Hogan was very matter-of-fact, but an excellent craftsman. And a craftsman was what you had to be when you directed B pictures. You could be an artist at the same time, but mainly you had to be a craftsman, because you had X number of scenes to shoot every day and you had to keep on schedule. And Ben Pivar was a wonderful man. The great thing about Universal at that time was that most of the producers were musicians — they loved music or wrote music or conducted it. And musicians are wonderful people."

On loan from Universal, Bey made his best-known film, MGM's *Dragon Seed* (1944) with Katharine Hepburn, a massive (145 minutes) production quite different from the ten-day B's that the Universal factory pumped out like automobiles from a Detroit plant. "*Dragon Seed* was different in the respect that it was very exciting to me. MGM was the studio of really big stars, so just to walk in there and to see Gable, Stewart, Spencer Tracy, Katharine Hepburn —! Maybe it was only the fact that it was different from Universal, but it excited me very much and I was very happy to be there. But as far as the work was concerned, I must admit that I almost preferred the way Universal worked, because it was faster and less time-consuming. *Dragon Seed* was very time-consuming. But maybe if it had been another MGM picture, I would have enjoyed it just as much."

Unlike the programmer-style *Mummy's Tomb* and *Mad Ghoul,* Bey's next Universal film, *The Climax,* was a comparatively major horror production. Prompted by the success of the studio's 1943 hit *Phantom of the Opera,* producer/director George Waggner dressed up this new opera-house horror film in Technicolor and lavish sets, filled it with songs and production values — and then forgot to put in the horror. "George Waggner was a wonderful, sensitive man, one of the most enthusiastic people I'd ever known," Bey reminisces. "I think you could have given him a Mickey Mouse picture to do — no offense to Mickey Mouse *[laughs]* — and he would have put just as much of his efforts and excitement and enthusiasm into that. I had one big row with him, and it was my own fault. There was a scene where he needed the camera to stay very long on me, for a dissolve, and I had to hold still. Then suddenly I said, 'This is too long for me. I just can't stand it anymore.' Poor George, he had to do something much different from what he had planned. That was our only row and it was my own doing."

Starring in *The Climax,* Boris Karloff was the sinister Dr. Hohner, full-time physician and part-time nut job, fiercely determined to thwart the Royal Theatre's plans to revive an opera that originally starred his sweetheart — whom he himself has since murdered. Susanna Foster, who played the female lead in both *Phantom of the Opera* and *The Climax,* scarcely enjoyed the experience of acting opposite Karloff ("Working with Karloff was like working with a slab of ice," Foster insists), but Bey begs to differ.

"He was an Englishman, and Englishmen are not as outgoing as Americans are on the set—he retired to his dressing room when he wasn't needed on the set. But, my God, he was a very pleasant, wonderful partner whom you could rely on to give you every cue—so disciplined! I didn't know Susie felt that way about him. I know I sound like Pollyanna in Hollywood, as if I loved everybody, but it's true, I've never encountered anybody whom I disliked. Boris I liked particularly, but he was a very shy man who I don't think associated really in what I would call a palsy-walsy form with anybody on the set." As for his own romantic role in the film (as Foster's chivalrous fiancé), "I enjoyed that part very much. It wasn't a very large role, but it was very interesting and quite different from what I had done before. I don't know how it went over with the public, but to me it was a great pleasure playing it." Critics lambasted *The Climax*; Arthur Lubin tells people that the film's failure hurt George Waggner's Universal career. "Certainly not that I noticed," Bey shrugs. "The only picture that ever hurt *me* was a picture that Arthur Lubin directed *[laughs]*."

The picture in question, *Night in Paradise,* was a gaudy fantasy placing the fabled storyteller Aesop (Bey) in the royal court of King Croesus (Thomas Gomez), circa 560 B.C. After appearing sleek and unruffled opposite such heavily greasepainted ghastlies as the Mummy and the Mad Ghoul, it was now Bey's turn to climb into Jack P. Pierce's makeup chair to be transformed into the apelike Aesop. "It was at least an hour that Jack Pierce spent on me. It wasn't as difficult as it might look; the wig was easy, but the beard had to be done very carefully, each hair on its own, not just a beard pasted on. I really am proud to say that I got along very well with Jack Pierce, because Jack was not a man who took a liking to everybody. Oh, no, not at all! He never was temperamental or anything, but to get him to laugh, you had to be very close. This I had the pleasure of being with him. He was definitely the specialist in horror makeups. He was never rude, but I never saw him really warm up to anybody, and some people were a little scared of him. And nobody ever dared to come late to Jack Pierce—even the big stars. When Jack said, 'Be here at five-thirty,' you had to *be* there *[laughs]!*"

Bey's romantic vis-à-vis in *Night in Paradise* was leading lady Merle Oberon; with his usual disarming candor, Bey admits, "I enjoyed working with her very much, but I doubt that she enjoyed working with me! This was at a time, unfortunately, when I was often very late on the set. Thomas Gomez, whom I loved, gave me hell every time I came late—he was very, very strict with me *[laughs]!* But I appreciated that; he was right, and he openly told me his mind. Merle Oberon behaved wonderfully, never said anything, but I know she was an absolute professional and she was always on time. There were several times when I was about an hour late. That's unforgivable, and I regret it tremendously now."

Night in Paradise was a tepid, almost vulgar fantasy, destined to die a slow

Bey (seated) cooked up a spiritualistic scam in the suspense film *The Amazing Mr. X.* Bey is flanked by Cathy O'Donnell and Lynn Bari; the ectoplasmic intruder is Donald Curtis.

death at the box office. "After the second week I knew it going to be a terrific flop, and I think everybody else knew it, too," Bey says. "So you can imagine that *that* was a little depressing. I think the thing that made me a little dubious about what [director] Arthur Lubin was doing was that he treated us more or less like robots. When we came to the set, everything was already there; our movements were already laid out for us. Nobody could say, 'Look, couldn't I do it *this* way?' or 'I would feel much better doing it a different way.' To make a change was impossible, because everything was already set up. I had never encountered this before; in all the B pictures that I worked on, nobody ever did this."

The postwar years were a time of decline for Turhan Bey; a hitch in the army interrupted his career momentum, and many long-established leading men, missing from the Hollywood scene in the early forties, were now back from the fighting and competing for the worthwhile roles. "When I came back from the army, Universal had been sold to an entirely new group of people. The first part they offered was impossible for me. I said to the producer, 'Look, couldn't we rewrite this a little bit?' and he said *[flatly]*, 'Out of the question!' So I went on suspension, and they said, 'Not only do you go on suspension, but we also will sell your contract.' I said, 'All the better!' So after that, I had two or three very happy years with Eagle-Lion, the studio they sold me to." Asked for concluding comments on Universal, Bey offers, "Very pleasant; very constructive; the end, unfortunately, a big flop, but c'est la vie." Special memories? "Yes, of all my friends there. It was a studio of cooperation, where the biggest producer never was too tired to talk to you or to listen to your problems." And regrets? "Well, yes. I should have been a little more serious about my work, but I was very young and maybe I can be forgiven for that. I don't think I did *bad* work; I could have done better, I think."

Just like those at Universal, the films in which the Eagle-Lion studios placed Bey were often fluff and nonsense, but there was at least one diamond in the rough, the moody suspense film *The Amazing Mr. X,* with Bey as a phony spiritualist cooking up a plan to murder widow Lynn Bari for her money. "The memory that I have of this film is that it was a fantastic role with wonderful people to work with, and a lovely death scene which I completely loused up. Absolutely. It was one of those days where I just didn't know what acting was, and it was one of the best scenes that any actor could wish for. When I saw it, I said to myself, 'Turhan, you've got to start all over again.' But any actor will tell you that there are days when you just are not fit to work. I just wish all of my roles would have been as interesting as that one. *Amazing Mr. X* was a picture I wish we had had a little more time to do."

By the late forties, with the war over, Bey was called upon to return to Europe to handle business and property matters. "I told my agent I was going to Europe and I'd be back in three months, because in three months I had a picture lined up. Well, I stayed three *years.* Then, once I came back, I waited for (I think) six months before I got a picture at Columbia, a Sam Katzman picture with Cesar Romero called *Prisoners of the Casbah.*" It was not long afterward, of course, that Turhan Bey threw in the towel acting-wise, returning home to Austria and later turning his attention to fashion (and nude) photography. "I've always been a photographer, even before I became an actor. And now that's all I'm doing, so I'm extremely happy. That doesn't mean that I wouldn't *like* to act again, but only the things I like to do."

Is Turhan Bey happy with the course his Hollywood career took? "No, I'm not happy about it. It was a very short career, and because of my own doing, it never got me to where every actor would like to be, which means being recognized as an actor. Of course, the kinds of films I made were not *[laughs] — not* the films that are nominated for Oscars or other kinds of awards, but you can't think about things like that. Like everything else, it could have been better."

And any closing comment for the contingent of horror film fans that have always looked upon Turhan Bey as one of their favorites?

"Yes, that I'm honored if they regard me as a favorite. I've done very few horror films, but I would like to have done many more. Of course, in all genres,

"I should have been a little more serious about my work [in films], but I was very young and maybe I can be forgiven for that." Turhan Bey in 1991.

there are good and bad. But basically, from *The Exorcist* down to *The Mummy's Tomb,* I enjoy seeing them, and I certainly would enjoy doing them again. Oh, horror films are *wonderful!*"

TURHAN BEY FILMOGRAPHY

Footsteps in the Dark (Warner Bros., 1941)
Shadows on the Stairs (Warner Bros., 1941)
The Gay Falcon (RKO, 1941)
Raiders of the Desert (Universal, 1941)
Burma Convoy (Universal, 1941)
A Yank on the Burma Road (MGM, 1942)
The Falcon Takes Over (RKO, 1942)
Bombay Clipper (Universal, 1942)
Destination Unknown (Universal, 1942)

Danger in the Pacific (Universal, 1942)
Arabian Nights (Universal, 1942)
Unseen Enemy (Universal, 1942)
Junior "G" Men of the Air (Universal serial, 1942)
The Mummy's Tomb (Universal, 1942)
Drums of the Congo (Universal, 1942)
The Adventures of Smilin' Jack (Universal serial, 1943)
Captive Wild Woman (voice only; Universal, 1943)
The Mad Ghoul (Universal, 1943)
White Savage (Universal, 1943)
Background to Danger (Warner Bros., 1943)
Ali Baba and the Forty Thieves (Universal, 1944)
Follow the Boys (Universal, 1944)
Dragon Seed (MGM, 1944)
Bowery to Broadway (Universal, 1944)
The Climax (Universal, 1944)
Sudan (Universal, 1945)
Frisco Sal (Universal, 1945)
Night in Paradise (Universal, 1946)
Out of the Blue (Eagle-Lion, 1947)
Adventures of Casanova (Eagle-Lion, 1948)
The Amazing Mr. X (The Spiritualist) (Eagle-Lion, 1948)
Parole, Inc. (Eagle-Lion, 1949)
Song of India (Columbia, 1949)
Prisoners of the Casbah (Columbia, 1953)
Stolen Identity (producer, Helen Ainsworth Corp., 1953)

Postscript: Bey has recently returned to acting after a 40 year hiatus, appearing on TV's *seaQuest* and *Babylon 5* and in direct-to-video *Possessed by the Night* (1994) and *The Skateboard Kid 2* (1995).

I don't remember that Rocketship X-M *did my career much good. It was considered a B picture, and you never make much of an impression on the industry if you're in a B picture.*

Lloyd Bridges

LLOYD BRIDGES—YOU CAN SAY *that* again. He bridges nearly all the media, having established himself time and again, and he spans the generation gap as well. He started out on stage in the 1930s, playing classical roles in college, in summer theaters and even on Broadway. In the forties he concentrated on his screen career, playing first in minor roles and later in solid supporting parts in some top Hollywood features. Baby boomers remember that in the fifties he became a household name thanks to *Sea Hunt*, then the most-watched syndicated television show in the United States. More recently, a whole new generation has come to know him for his befuddled roles in the zany spoofs *Airplane!*, *Hot Shots!* and now *Honey, I Blew Up the Kid*.

"They don't *really* blow the baby to pieces," Bridges is quick to correct. "What happens is, the baby gets ahold of something that increases his size, something that blows him up all out of proportion. He leaves the house, and is on his way to Las Vegas. And now it's a mad chase to get to him before he gets to Las Vegas, where the neon lights are going to make him God-knows-how-much taller than he is already."

As Disney's sequel to the hugely successful *Honey, I Shrunk the Kids* gears up for release, Bridges takes a break from the activity in his bustling Los Angeles home and talks about the real star of his upcoming feature: "The star of the whole thing is the wonderful special effects; it's just amazing what these effects men can come up with today," he affirms. "We worked some pretty late hours on the picture, but the cast was all very nice and it was a pleasure working with them. It was pleasant working with [star] Rick Moranis, who is a very nice man as well as a talented man. And I could say the same thing about the director, Randal Kleiser. He's someone who really knows his business. He's done quite a few of this kind of picture before, so it wasn't anything new for him."

Science fiction is also nothing new to Bridges, who has worked more than just occasionally in the genre. The star of many land, underwater and outer space adventures was born Lloyd Vernet Bridges, Jr., in San Leandro, California, and grew up in various Northern California towns. His father, who was in the hotel business in California, wanted him to become a lawyer, but young Lloyd's interests turned to acting while at the University of California at Los Angeles. (Dorothy Simpson, Bridges' wife of more than 50 years, was one of his UCLA classmates, and appeared opposite him in a romantic play called *March Hares*.)

"Working on the stage was my main ambition when I left college," he reminisces. "I did a lot of Shakespeare and Greek drama—as a matter of fact, I played the lead in *Oedipus* at UCLA, and played Hamlet and Romeo and all those things. That's what I was interested in when I went to New York to seek my fortune, but all I got was an extra part in [the 1937 Broadway produc-

---

Previous page: Bridges over troubled waters: a posed shot for television's syndicated hit *Sea Hunt*.

tion of] *Othello* with Walter Huston and Brian Aherne. But later on I did an adaptation of *Othello* and played Iago and directed it.

"A bunch of us New York actors couldn't get a job, and we started what *I* think was one of the first off-Broadway theaters. We found this old iron foundry and made it into a theater and put on about five plays. We were pretty well received — the big-time critics came down and reviewed us, and were very kind to us. It was there that the owners of a place called Green Mansions saw us and hired us. And so I was acting and directing and producing and *everything* there at Green Mansions, which was up in the Catskills. Sidney Buchman, who was the right-hand man to Harry Cohn at Columbia at the time, saw me in quite a few different things, and he felt that I had talent. He arranged for a screen test with Columbia, and my wife helped me — she played the gal in the test that I made. As a result of the test, I got started in pictures."

Although Bridges grew to miss stage work during the long motion picture and television career that ensued, he is quick to admit that "I did get kind of disenchanted with the stage because, on a couple of the plays that I was in, the atmosphere wasn't as good as I'd have liked it to be. And if a play 'runs,' if it's a success, you [the cast] are on top of one another for a year or two. There's a lot of backbiting that sometimes goes on. But it all depends on what kind of company you're in. Some of 'em were just wonderful, a lot of fun." Of course, once Bridges became established in pictures, there was a second consideration as well. "The other gamble that you have to think about is whether you want to take several months out of your life to do a play — and give up the possibility of doing a picture that might come up and mean a lot more money *[laughs]*. But the stage is still exciting, and certainly a great way to get started. When you've got a base like the theater, it always puts you in good stead working in pictures."

His stage background notwithstanding, Bridges's screen career got off to a fairly slow start at Columbia. Although the studio had him working constantly (almost 50 films in just four years, beginning in 1941 with *The Lone Wolf Takes a Chance*), they cast him in mainly minor roles in small, now-forgotten pictures: *I Was a Prisoner on Devil's Island, The Medico of Painted Springs, Two Latins from Manhattan, Sing for Your Supper,* even a two-reeler with the Three Stooges. ("Columbia got their money's worth out of me, you can believe that!") He played his first "fantastic" film role in the company's supernatural comedy *Here Comes Mr. Jordan* (1941), as the pilot of a Heaven-bound airplane, and made his horror film debut in Universal's *Strange Confession* (1945), an entry in the studio's heavy-handed Inner Sanctum series. Of the film's star Lon Chaney, Jr., Bridges recalls, "I enjoyed working with him very much. Of course, I'd been a great admirer of his father's. [Chaney, Jr.] was very sweet, very nice. The picture might not have been too much to brag about, but he was a very pleasant man to work with."

By this mid-forties period, Bridges was gone from Columbia and freelancing, landing two of this best early roles in *A Walk in the Sun* (1945), a thoughtful character study of men in war, and *Home of the Brave* (1949), with Bridges as the longtime chum of a black soldier (James Edwards) coping with racism during World War II. Then it was on to science fiction, as Bridges starred in the first postwar outer space adventure, *Rocketship X-M*.

Years before the expression "race to space" denoted the competition between the United States and the Soviet Union, two Hollywood moviemakers were locked in a competition of their own. Producer George Pal was taking pains with his production of *Destination Moon*: spending well over a half-million dollars on the film, working with scientists and space travel experts, creating an avalanche of advance publicity. B movie maven Robert L. Lippert decided that his company could quickly knock out a half-alike film, beat Pal to the finish line and take advantage of his rival's initiative and costly promotion. Lippert's film was *Rocketship X-M*.

"I don't know how much artistic value Lippert gave to a piece," Bridges recalls, "but he *was* crazy about motion pictures, and had seen just about every one that was ever made. Most of the things he did were the so-called B pictures of the day, but he made his impression on the business, I think. With *Rocketship X-M*, we *did* beat our competitor, *Destination Moon*. And they paid a *lot* more for their production. We kind of took advantage of the publicity that they were putting out—people weren't quite sure whether they were seeing *that* picture or *our* picture."

Lifting off from the Government Proving Grounds in White Sands, New Mexico, the multistage *RXM (Rocketship Expedition Moon)* was the first manned rocket into space, with a lunar landing and exploration planned. But a storm of meteors sends the rocket off in a new direction at incredible velocity, toward Mars. Taking advantage of the opportunity, the crew of five—pilot Bridges, designer John Emery, chemist Osa Massen, navigator Hugh O'Brian and engineer Noah Beery, Jr.—land and (in red-tinted scenes) scout the planet's barren surface, finding evidence of a long-ago civilization destroyed by atomic war. Savage Martian cave dwellers attack, killing Emery and Beery and wounding O'Brian. The survivors escape aboard the *RXM*, but a fuel shortage spells disaster. After shortwaving a full report to base, Bridges and Massen declare their newfound love for one another as the rocket plunges to a devastating crash landing on Earth.

"I begged the director not to shoot that love scene, when we're plummeting to the Earth and we pour out our hearts to one another," Bridges asserts. "I told him, 'You know, at a time like that, it just doesn't make sense.' It seemed so wrong to me to destroy the illusion; I was sure people would laugh at it. But he insisted, and who knows whether he was right or not."

The director, Kurt Neumann, is best recalled today for his science fiction films such as *Rocketship X-M*, *Kronos* and *The Fly*, but Bridges mostly remembers him as "a man who believed we had to do it fast *[laughs]*. We had

Lloyd Bridges got a taste of approaching "star"dom playing the top role in 1950's science fiction classic *Rocketship X-M*.

a very short schedule, I think maybe ten days or something like that. When we went out on location to film the scenes of Mars, we went out to Death Valley, and we had to put on our wardrobe and makeup en route, in the *plane*, so that as soon as the plane landed, we were ready to go to work right away.

"Everything went smoothly and fast [in the Death Valley scenes]. It *had* to—or else they'd just skip the scene. I always felt that we should never have

Bridges' various story and directorial suggestions regarding *Rocketship X-M* were all treated with equal respect: Every last one was ignored! (Hugh O'Brian, Osa Massen and Bridges pictured.)

seen any of the Martians, they should have been just shadows. Imagination is stronger than actually seeing. (Not many of my suggestions were taken, as you may have noticed!) But I did think that the red tinting of the Martian scenes was a good idea, and Death Valley turned out to be a good location for us. It looked a bit like what we later found out that the Moon was like."

The *Rocketship X-M* spaceship interiors, Bridges continues, were shot "in the studio. I don't know how much of that [aeronautical equipment] was real; it was before its time, so I guess they figured they could be pretty freethinking about it. They were a bit crude, all of the *Rocketship X-M* effects, when you look at 'em today."

Bridges also remembers the cast of *Rocketship X-M* as a "very congenial" group of actors. "Osa Massen we don't see much of lately, but for quite a while we kept in touch. She was a very sweet person; she had been an editor for some time before she became an actress. She had a fascinating kind of personality, I thought, and she was a beautiful girl. In fact, Hugh O'Brian was very much in love with her—I guess we *all* were *[laughs]!* John Emery was quite the Shakespearean actor, always spouting Shakespeare, and as a matter of fact, a lot of people felt he was very much like John Barrymore. I remember that he kind of patterned himself after Barrymore to a certain extent; he always had some sort of Barrymore-like comment to make about everything. I think he was trying to figure out how he found himself in the desert, among the rocks, making *Rocketship X-M*, when he should have been in the theater doing Shakespeare!"

While many actors squawk about latter-day tampering with vintage films, Bridges has a casual reaction to news that new special effects scenes for *Rocketship X-M* were shot in the seventies. "Well, if it improved the film, I guess it doesn't matter," he says with a shrug. "It's the same kind of thing people are saying about colorization. With some of the classics, I think colorization would be a mistake. But for something like *Sea Hunt*, I think colorization would be an improvement. The first two *Sea Hunt* pilots that we did were in color, but because of the fact that they were going to cost a few thousand bucks more [per episode] to make 'em in color, the producers decided they didn't want to take the gamble."

Bridges adds quickly that the people behind *Rocketship X-M* had no idea that it would become any sort of classic. "I'm not sure that it has—*has* it? Well, because it was one of the first films of its sort, I guess it might have. I don't remember that it did my career much good. It was considered a B picture, and you never make much of an impression on the industry if you're in a B picture. Not even if you're in a good one." Does he consider *Rocketship X-M* "a good one"? "I like it, except that last love scene continues to bother me. I just can't imagine that any two people would be that calm about it all."

Another strong role came via producer Stanley Kramer's *High Noon* (1952), with Bridges as a conniving deputy who threatens not to back up town marshal Gary Cooper when outlaws invade their quiet Western town. But after *High Noon* came allegations that Bridges had been at one time involved with the Communist Party. After an FBI clearance, he resumed work, but once again he was in the clutches of the B moviemakers. Robert Lippert, producer of *Rocketship X-M*, was one who kept Bridges gainfully employed.

"Lippert was a lot of fun, a real promoter, a jolly, rotund kind of guy. I did several pictures for him; I especially remember one called *The Tall Texan* [1953] with Marie Windsor, Lee J. Cobb and Luther Adler. We were often rewriting that script the night before we were going to shoot, and Lee Cobb and Luther Adler, I guess because of their background in the Group Theater, were pretty adept at coming up with lines. So they were writing themselves into a lot more scenes *[laughs]*. We told 'em that was great, that we appreciated being able to take advantage of the tremendous talent they both had, but that we had better change the title to *The Short Texans [laughs]*."

Other producers who hired Bridges included England's Hammer Films and low-budget Hollywood maverick Roger Corman. Hammer's made-in-Spain *Deadly Game* (1954), according to Bridges, "was a lot of fun because it was a pleasure working with the English actors—they're always so good." And Corman, who directed Bridges in AIP's *Apache Woman*, "didn't know too much about directing at the time, and *[laughs]* I sort of pulled him through the whole thing. And I felt that I never got any thanks from him at all. He was one of the few guys I've worked with that I felt was very selfish—someone who wanted good results but didn't care how he got 'em."

Bridges's most enduring claim to fame remains *Sea Hunt* (1958–61), the Ivan Tors teleseries that grew in popularity until it became the country's most successful syndicated show. The series' one regular was Bridges as Mike Nelson, a one-time navy frogman who specialized in freelance underwater investigation. "When I first met Ivan Tors, I found out that he had seen a film of mine called *16 Fathoms Deep* [1948], where I played a sponge diver—'hardhat' diving gear. The whole interview, he didn't even ask me if I knew how to swim *[laughs]*. But he was a wonderful man. He was very smitten with all the latest things that science had to offer, and he incorporated most of that stuff in our shows.

"We started out filming the underwater stuff for *Sea Hunt* in the tank at Marineland out here. (They've torn it all down since.) Then we shot the topside scenes all up and down the coast nearby—Santa Monica piers, Malibu piers and so on. The underwater stuff for the first six episodes or so was done at the Marineland tank, but it got so that we recognized the same fish going by all the time *[laughs]*—we had to change the topography underwater. So we went to Nassau and shot underwater at a place called Lyford Cay. Lyford Cay turned out to be a beautiful place to do underwater photography. We'd do about eight [episodes' worth of topside scenes] and then go to Nassau and do underwater stuff for the eight."

Teaching Bridges the ins and outs of diving was done quickly, and not exactly by the book. "I had swum quite a bit in the ocean, 'cause we always had a place on the beach, but I didn't know anything about diving. So Courtney Brown [Bridges' underwater double] checked me out in a pool for one day, and the next day they threw me in the ocean *[laughs]!* That was all new and very exciting to me—it was a whole new world, as it was to everyone who saw the show." Another side benefit to having his own television series was being able to provide occasional employment to his acting sons, Beau and Jeff. "Yeah, they both got their feet wet in the business on *Sea Hunt*, and so did my daughter Lucinda."

Sea Hunt and other television tours of duty kept Bridges off the big screen throughout the late fifties and early sixties, and when he returned, it was in another subaqueous Ivan Tors adventure, *Around the World Under the Sea*. Introduced with a foreword by astronaut M. Scott Carpenter ("The sea is a tough adversary—much more hostile an environment than space"), the MGM production centered around the crew of the nuclear-powered submarine *Hydronaut* and their efforts to anchor earthquake sensors in strategic pressure points on the ocean floor. The premise may have been earthquakes but the film itself was less than earthshaking. "We did that in Miami, at Ivan Tors' studio there. David McCallum was in it, [Keenan] Wynn, the pretty English girl from *Goldfinger* [Shirley Eaton], Gary Merrill—they had a good cast for that one.

"The director was Andrew Marton, who did some of the *Sea Hunt*s, and who also directed my son Beau in (practically) his first movie, a Jon Hall thing called *Zamba* [aka *Zamba the Gorilla*, 1949]. The acting bug had bitten Beau, even that young. I remember on *Zamba* they gave us the script and I told him the story. And when Andrew Marton interviewed Beau, he asked, 'Are there any questions about the script? Is there anything that bothers you at all? Being with the gorillas and all that—does that worry you?' Beau said, 'No, but the thing that *does* bother me is when I have to parachute out of the burning plane.' He thought he'd have to do it himself—but he was ready regardless [*laughs*]!"

Another Bridges teleseries, *The Loner*, premiered on CBS in September 1965 and disappeared from the airwaves the following April. Bridges has fond memories of the short-lived program, and of writer Rod Serling. "I loved that man. It was a shame that he didn't last longer. He was a beautiful human being as well as a very talented writer—one of the most talented writers that we had in TV. I thought *The Loner* was a good show, and that it had an interesting format. It was just after the Civil War and I was an ex–Union officer trying to 'find myself'—I was very disappointed about the way the world was shaping up. I was restless, kept moving all the time, just me and my horse (a beautiful black stallion, a five-gaited American saddle bred). We had some very good scripts because Rod Serling was on top of it all."

Other Bridges series include *The Lloyd Bridges Show*, *San Francisco International Airport* and *Joe Forrester*, not to mention a host of television movies. Bridges, who explored Mars in *Rocketship X-M*, was cast as an extraterrestrial himself in ABC's movie *The Love War* (1970) with Angie Dickinson. "In that one, the idea was that, to save a lot of lives, there was going to be a war between my planet and the Earth, and it was settled with just about three of us. Angie Dickinson played a character with whom I fell in love. But she played a dirty

A series of outrageous movie comedies (such as *Hot Shots!* pictured 'ear) have made Bridges recognizable to a whole new generation of fans.

trick on me—she led me to believe that she was just a regular, normal gal, but instead she was an alien. And in the end, she shot me and I wound up in a puddle *[laughs]!*"

Above all, Lloyd Bridges just keeps on working, in movies, on television, and in seemingly every miniseries (*Roots, Movieola, East of Eden, The Blue and the Gray, George Washington* and *North and South, Book II*, just to name some). And the end, apparently, is nowhere in sight, with Bridges just recently winning yet more new fans with his portrayal of the addled Admiral Benson in *Hot Shots!* and *Hot Shots! Part Deux*, the smash-hit send-ups from the codirectors of *Airplane!* "*Hot Shots!* was a spoof on the Air Force, completely mad, a wonderful comedy, I thought. And as a matter of fact, deck scenes for the aircraft carrier in *Hot Shots!* were shot on the very spot where Marineland used to stand—where we used to film the underwater scenes for *Sea Hunt*. For *Hot Shots!* the ocean was in the distance, and so it saved a lot of expense and a lot of time; we'd have had to go back and forth on a boat to do it on a real carrier. And the navy wasn't too anxious to cooperate with us on that one, anyway—the film didn't paint a very flattering picture of the navy!"

LLOYD BRIDGES FILMOGRAPHY

Dancing Feet (Republic, 1936)
Freshman Love (Warner Bros., 1936)
The Lone Wolf Takes a Chance (Columbia, 1941)
The Royal Mounted Patrol (Columbia, 1941)
I Was a Prisoner on Devil's Island (Columbia, 1941)
Our Wife (Columbia, 1941)
Three Girls about Town (Columbia, 1941)
Sing for Your Supper (Columbia, 1941)
You Belong to Me (Columbia, 1941)
They Dare Not Love (Columbia, 1941)
The Son of Davy Crockett (Columbia, 1941)
Here Comes Mr. Jordan (Columbia, 1941)
The Medico of Painted Springs (Columbia, 1941)
Two Latins from Manhattan (Columbia, 1941)
Honolulu Lu (Columbia, 1941)
Harmon of Michigan (Columbia, 1941)
Canal Zone (Columbia, 1942)
Harvard Here I Come (Columbia, 1942)
Tramp Tramp Tramp (Columbia, 1942)
Counter Espionage (Columbia, 1942)
Cadets on Parade (Columbia, 1942)
Pardon My Gun (Columbia, 1942)
Riding through Nevada (Columbia, 1942)
Sweetheart of the Fleet (Columbia, 1942)
Alias Boston Blackie (Columbia, 1942)
A Man's World (Columbia, 1942)
Stand By All Networks (Columbia, 1942)
The Great Glover (Columbia short, 1942)
Blondie Goes to College (Columbia, 1942)
Shut My Big Mouth (Columbia, 1942)
Flight Lieutenant (He's My Old Man) (Columbia, 1942)
Atlantic Convoy (Columbia, 1942)
Talk of the Town (Columbia, 1942)
Riders of the Northland (Columbia, 1942)
Underground Agent (Columbia, 1942)
West of Tombstone (Columbia, 1942)
The Wife Takes a Flyer (A Yank in Dutch) (Columbia, 1942)
North of the Rockies (Columbia, 1942)
The Spirit of Stanford (Columbia, 1942)
The Daring Young Man (Columbia, 1942)
Commandos Strike at Dawn (Columbia, 1942)
They Stooge to Conga (Columbia short, 1943)
Sahara (Columbia, 1943)
His Wedding Scare (Columbia short, 1943)
The Heat's On (Columbia, 1943)
Passport to Suez (Columbia, 1943)
Hail to the Rangers (Illegal Rights) (Columbia, 1943)
Destroyer (Columbia, 1943)
A Rookie's Cookie (Columbia short, 1943)
Crime Doctor's Strangest Case (Columbia, 1943)
Once Upon a Time (Columbia, 1944)
Riding West (Columbia, 1944)
She's a Soldier, Too (Columbia, 1944)
Louisiana Hayride (Columbia, 1944)
The Master Race (RKO, 1944)
Saddle Leather Law (Columbia, 1944)
Mr. Whitney Had a Notion (MGM short, 1944)
A Walk in the Sun (20th Century-Fox, 1945)
Secret Agent X-9 (Universal serial, 1945)

96 They Fought in the Creature Features

Thunderbolt (narrator; Army Air Force/Monogram documentary, 1945)
Miss Susie Slagle's (Paramount, 1945)
Strange Confession (The Missing Head) (Universal, 1945)
Abilene Town (United Artists, 1946)
Canyon Passage (Universal, 1946)
Ramrod (United Artists, 1947)
The Trouble with Women (Paramount, 1947)
Unconquered (Paramount, 1947)
Secret Service Investigator (Republic, 1948)
16 Fathoms Deep (Monogram, 1948)
Moonrise (Republic, 1948)
Red Canyon (Universal, 1949)
Hideout (Republic, 1949)
Home of the Brave (United Artists, 1949)
Calamity Jane and Sam Bass (Universal, 1949)
Trapped (Eagle-Lion, 1949)
Colt .45 (Thundercloud) (Warner Bros., 1950)
Rocketship X-M (Lippert, 1950)
The White Tower (RKO, 1950)
The Sound of Fury (Try and Get Me) (United Artists, 1950)
Little Big Horn (Lippert, 1951)
Three Steps North (United Artists, 1951)
The Whistle at Eaton Falls (Columbia, 1951)
High Noon (United Artists, 1952)
Plymouth Adventure (MGM, 1952)
Last of the Comanches (Columbia, 1952)
The Tall Texan (Lippert, 1953)
City of Bad Men (20th Century–Fox, 1953)
The Kid from Left Field (20th Century–Fox, 1953)
The Limping Man (Lippert, 1953)
Deadly Game (Third Party Risk) (Lippert, 1954)
Pride of the Blue Grass (Allied Artists, 1954)
Wichita (Allied Artists, 1955)
Apache Woman (American Releasing [AIP], 1955)
Wetbacks (Bob Banner Associates/Realart/Gibraltar, 1956)
The Rainmaker (Paramount, 1956)
Ride Out for Revenge (United Artists, 1957)
The Goddess (Columbia, 1958)
Around the World Under the Sea (MGM, 1966)
Attack on the Iron Coast (United Artists, 1968)
Daring Game (Paramount, 1968)
The Happy Ending (United Artists, 1969)
To Find a Man (Sex and the Teenager; The Boy Next Door) (Columbia, 1972)
Running Wild (Deliver Us from Evil) (Golden Circle, 1973)
Scuba (narrator; Caribbean Films, 1973)
Behind the Iron Mask (The Fifth Musketeer) (Columbia, 1977)
Mission Galactica: The Cylon Attack (Universal, 1979)
Bear Island (Columbia, 1980)
Airplane! (Paramount, 1980)
Airplane II: The Sequel (Paramount, 1982)
Weekend Warriors (Hollywood Air Force) (The Movie Store, 1986)
The Wild Pair (Trans World Entertainment, 1987)
Tucker: The Man and His Dream (Paramount, 1988)
Cousins (Paramount, 1989)
Winter People (Columbia, 1989)
Joe versus the Volcano (Warner Bros., 1990)
Hot Shots! (20th Century–Fox, 1991)
Honey, I Blew Up the Kid (Buena Vista, 1992)
Hot Shots! Part Deux (20th Century–Fox, 1993)
Blown Away (MGM, 1994)

In as far as I see it, Creature from the Black Lagoon *was just another movie, just another job. I've done many things since then that I am much more proud of. But I've gotten more reaction out of the Creature thing than anything else. I guess that's life!*

Ricou Browning

They Fought in the Creature Features

IN THE MINDS OF SCIENCE FICTION film fans, there are not many actors who are tied as closely to a single role as Ricou Browning, the extraordinary swimmer who donned the scaly foam rubber suit of the *Creature from the Black Lagoon*. Browning played the role three times, in *Creature* and its two sequels, before going on to become one of the industry's most capable underwater stunt coordinators and directors of underwater sequences (as well as doing plenty of other film work topside), but the tight link between himself and the Gill Man role exists to this day. Not exactly proud but certainly not unhappy with his major claim to fame, Ricou Browning relives his Creature past (and other subaqueous adventures).

Born in Fort Pierce, Florida, in 1930, Ricou (pronounced Rico) grew up in nearby Jansen Beach and got a career start high diving and springboard diving in local water shows. By his early twenties, he was producing underwater shows at Weeki Wachee Springs and topside water shows at Rainbow Springs and other locations. A call from a coworker first alerted Browning to the fact that Universal Pictures was planning to photograph portions of their newest science fiction thriller (initially titled *Black Lagoon*) in the area.

"I was in college when that happened. A friend of mine who I used to work *with* and *for* phoned me and said that he had received a call about showing some Hollywood people a place called Wakulla Springs, which is south of Tallahassee. He couldn't make it, so he asked me if I wouldn't mind showing it to them. I said fine. So these people called me and told me when they were coming into town, and I met 'em at the airport in Tallahassee. It was Jack Arnold and the cameraman, 'Scotty' Welbourne, and a couple other people, I just don't remember who they were. Anyway, I took them to Wakulla Springs and showed 'em the area, and they loved it. 'Scotty' had his underwater camera and he asked me if I would get in the water with him and swim in front of the camera so they could get some perspective as to sizes of things with the background. I said sure, so I did. We had dinner that night, talked a little bit about the Springs, and they left.

"Later I received a call from Jack Arnold, and he said, 'We've tested a lot of people for this part, but I'd like to have you play the Creature—I like your swimming. Do you want to do it?' I said sure. So that was it."

The next stop, of course, was a trip to Universal Studios in California and the usual messy assortment of body molds, costume tests and time-consuming trial and error, with designers Jack Kevan and Tom Case doing most of the work. "It was a matter of making molds—body, face and so forth. Then, after molding the pieces, they made a latex suit, like a leotard, and they glued the pieces onto the latex. It was like a football uniform in the sense that they had thigh areas that they'd glue on, then the fin in the back, on and on—they piecemealed it together. They did it with the latex suit on *me* to begin with,

Previous page: The Man in the Foam Rubber Suit, Ricou Browning, doffs his Gill Man mask for a photo-op. (Notice the snaps along the costume's "collarbone.")

Browning tests out the Gill Man suit in the studio tank.

but then the glue started burning me badly; it went through the leotard and onto my body, and as it started setting up, it got very hot. So they made another mold of my body and then molded it onto that. The suit was foam rubber with a latex skin."

A first Creature suit, which Browning describes as "looking like a sausage," was quickly rejected. "It was kind of shaped like a man (of course) and it was just more streamlined: less scales, less fins, and the head was more like you were wearing a tight stocking over your face. A little bit more human in appearance."

Underwater test footage was shot of Browning in Universal's back lot tank, not only for showing to studio execs but also to allow Browning to gain experience swimming in the cumbersome outfit. "After the suit was finished, we would go in the water and I'd swim around. Then I would tell 'em what I needed for my purposes, and they would revamp the suit a little. Once we got it where we wanted it, we photographed it in the tank and then showed it to the studio heads, Jim Pratt and Ed Muhl, as well as the producer, William Alland."

Although the Creature's "look" had been agreed upon, numerous problems still had to be overcome, like how to get Browning to stay underwater in his buoyant foam rubber suit. "To get negatively buoyant, I had 'em make me a thing that was kind of like an armor vest. It was lead and it form fitted my upper body, from just below my neck down to just about the navel. I also had some lead plates that I wore in the Creature feet, and then I had little pockets on the back right side and left side, where I could insert a few weights, depending on whether I was in salt water or fresh water, because the buoyancy in fresh water and salt water varies. It was kind of like swimming in your overcoat.

"The most difficult part of the entire process was vision. I tried to wear little goggles, like pearl divers wear, but once you got water in the goggles, there was no way to get it out. That just didn't work. And then we tried a face mask, but that made the face of the Creature protrude too far. So we went without anything, and I just saw with my naked eyes. The eyes of the Creature mask were a couple of inches beyond my eyes, so it was kind of like looking through a keyhole. And looking through an underwater keyhole without a mask on, your vision is blurred—*very* blurred. It was very awkward seeing, and a lot of it was kind of hit and miss."

Yet another minor dilemma presented itself when Universal decided that at six feet, Browning was not tall enough to play a sufficiently menacing Gill Man in the underwater encounters with the movie's heroes and heroine. "We decided that when we did the underwater scenes, that we would scale the doubles for the 'human' actors down in size. In other words, if the stars were six feet tall, the doubles would have to be five-something. That way, I would appear much larger."

James C. Havens flew to Florida in the second week of October 1953 to direct the underwater second unit scenes with Browning and a trio of doubles. The underwater doubles for leading players Richard Carlson and Richard Denning were college students from Florida State University, and the double for Julie Adams was Ginger Stanley, a "mermaid" at Weeki Wachee. Jack Arnold—on whom praise for the direction of the underwater scenes has been heaped by science fiction film reviewers—was thousands of miles away, directing his portions of *Creature* at Universal, while Havens put Browning and the doubles through their underwater paces in Wakulla Springs.

An incredible swimmer, Browning still required underwater safety men, air hoses and a "distress signal" to ensure a speedy (and safe) production. "In order to breathe, I did what we call hose breathing. You have an oxygen tank or, coming from the surface, just an air hose. I'd stick the air hose in my mouth and breathe from it, like you would drink water from a hose in your backyard. There's kind of a little knack to it, but I learned it when I was very young, at Wakulla Springs, before they ever invented Aqualungs; we used it in the water shows at Weeki Wachee Springs. That's how the mermaids there would get air. Anyway, it was something I did very naturally, and so it came easy for me. I could insert the hose in the mouth of the Creature, then I'd have to go a couple of inches further, to get to my own mouth and then breathe.

"Let's say we were ready to do a scene: I would have a safety man with me and I'd be breathing, and when I was ready to go, I'd give the cameraman the okay sign—hand signals—and I'd keep breathing. When he would give me the signal he was rolling the camera, I would release the air hose, giving it back to the safety man, and then (if it was just a swim-through) I would swim by camera. On the other side, there'd be another safety man who'd give me a different air hose. So I had safety men in various places in order to get air."

If Browning got into trouble, a very basic signal was used to alert his coworkers. "If I got to where I was really desperate for air, I would just stop everything and go limp, and the safety man would swim in to me and give me an air hose. Or if I was in a fight scene, I would just stop fighting and not do anything, and then they would come in and give me an air hose. I had people that I had worked with underwater for years prior to this, so I had a lot of confidence in them. They were very good and it worked fairly well.

"We were shooting out in the middle of the Spring, and I had to go to the bathroom. They were going to take me ashore in a boat, but I said, no, I was gonna swim over. I swam underwater—sometimes it was easier to swim underwater in that suit than it was to swim on the surface. I swam to the ladder that was on the dock next to shore. I came up the ladder, and there was a lady and a little girl standing there. I came out, and this little girl started screaming. She started screaming and running and the mother went after her, and I went after *both* of 'em, trying to say, 'Hey, hey, it's okay, it's okay!' But me saying, 'It's okay!' didn't do a thing *[laughs]*. They took off, and that's the last I saw of 'em! But I never went out of my way to try and scare anybody, no; from then on, I made sure I kept the head off whenever I came ashore."

While the Gill Man suit is viewed by Creature fans as a marvel of design and execution, Browning is dismissive of the costume in comparing it to today's monster outfits. "Compared to what they do today as far as makeup and monsters' faces and so forth, the Creature would be considered the Model T. For instance, I had a little squeeze bulb that I held in my hand, and the tube from it ran up my arm. I could squeeze that and make the gills fluctuate in and out. I could move the lips a little by moving my chin, but the eyes I had no control over whatsoever. It was very crude compared to what they do today."

Universal apparently had great faith in *Creature from the Black Lagoon,* launching plans for a sequel even before the original's release. Lensed under the title *Return of the Creature,* the follow-up film *Revenge of the Creature* was made in midsummer 1954—a welcome turn of events for Browning, who shot the first film during a Florida cold spell. "For my part, shooting *Revenge of the Creature* in the summer made it easier. It can get quite cold in Florida, and that suit's wet continuously. So, when it's wet and cold, *you're* wet and cold. On [the original] *Creature*, everybody was trying to be nice and they kept

giving me shots of brandy. And soon, they had a drunk Creature on their hands, so I had to cut *that* out! *Revenge* was easier. In the summer, you got hot, but you could pour water down the suit, or stay in the water."

Most of Browning's scenes in *Revenge of the Creature* were shot in a tank at the Marineland Studios, on the ocean south of St. Augustine. "On *Revenge*, we'd drive every morning from St. Augustine to Marineland, and on the way, there was a public beach. Charlie McNabb, one of the safety guys, had a bright idea: 'Why don't we take the suit back with us this weekend, and we'll take you out in the ocean? You jump in and swim to shore and come up, and we'll see what happens!' I said, 'Well, that'll be fine, but some idiot will think they can shoot me, and do it!' So, no, we didn't go through with that *[laughs]!*"

Headquarters for the troupe was a Marineland motel where, Browning concedes with *Revenge* stars John Agar and Lori Nelson, cast and crew whooped it up in grand style. "We used to have water fights and God knows what at the motel, big luaus on the beach—we had a great time. The cast and the crew just got along great, and it was a fun show."

Not even the fact that Browning, Agar and Nelson had to share the Marineland tank with sharks and other potentially dangerous deep-sea critters put a damper on things. "I really didn't have time to worry about 'em, I was too busy getting the air and taking of myself. I did have one thing happen: I had gone in the water and I was sitting down on a big anchor. They had the chain around my ankle in that scene, but I could get out of it anytime I wanted. Anyway, I was sitting there and I felt something tug on my foot. I looked down and, glory, it was a big turtle—he had taken a big hunk out of the heel of the Creature's foot and he was swimming off with it. Luckily, he didn't get *me*—he got the foam rubber, and he was trying to eat it. I realized that this was my last pair of flippers—I wore the other ones out, 'cause the way you swim and hit things, you tear 'em up pretty much. This was the last pair, so I got out of the chain, swam up fast as I could and I was yelling to Jack Kevan, but he couldn't understand me. So I finally swam over there and he finally understood me: 'The turtle's got the heel of the foot!' So everybody dove in the water and they went after the turtle *[laughs]!* They did get the piece back, and then I had to come out and they had to rinse it in fresh water and glue it back on."

As far as the land scenes shot at Marineland are concerned, Browning dismisses the recent rumor that Clint Eastwood—a budding bit player at the time, seen as a lab assistant in *Revenge*—squeezed into the scaly suit for some of the landlocked action. "The [land Gill Man] was a guy by the name of Tom Hennesy (nice guy). Hennesy was in the scene in the Lobster House in Jacksonville, and the reason I remember is because he had an alligator in the bathtub *[laughs]*. We were rooming together, I walked in and found that he had

Opposite: The underwater camera crew catches Browning solo.

bought an alligator and stuck it in the tub. A cayman, actually — a South American alligator — 'cause you can't buy alligators."

The Lobster House scene, where the Gill Man (Hennesy) disrupts a jam session by crashing the party, was shot in Jacksonville, on the St. Johns River — but not without incident. "They used people from the insurance building next door as extras, and these people all came with their husbands, wives, girlfriends, whatever, all dressed in formal wear. They were shooting inside for about an hour and a half. I was sitting on top of the roof when suddenly I heard all this commotion. What had happened was, they had moved the arc lights up into the ceilings, and set off the sprinkler system. The entire bunch of people were just full of water and rust — the sprinkler system probably was never used, and was full of rusty water. So they had to wrap for the night."

Despite all the work Browning put in on the *Creature* movies, he was credited neither on-screen nor in publicity. "Universal's idea was, they didn't want people to think the Creature was human. When the second film came around, they called me again and I started to do the picture, and I said, 'Hey, I want to get credit for this, because it helps me to get other work.' We bickered and bickered — I think William Alland was involved, and Jim Pratt, and whoever else. They still didn't want to give credit, but they promised me that they'd get me publicity. So they started getting me interviews with people. And, sure enough, they really did — I must have been interviewed twenty times, by syndicated columnists, magazine writers, et cetera, et cetera. There were pictures and stories and a lot of publicity — they kept their word. But they still didn't give me credit *[laughs]*!"

While *Revenge of the Creature* was a slick-looking sequel overall, some of the underwater Gill Man scenes were slightly spoiled by the sight of a stream of bubbles floating up out of the top of the monster's head. "Well, that was unfortunate," admits Browning. "The Creature head fits over your head, and when you exhale as you're breathing inside, air goes up by your face and then goes up into the top of the head. Then it slowly goes up through that foam rubber — air is buoyant. Usually, I'd take a breath, give the air hose to the safety man, and then the safety man would grab the top of my head and squeeze it, and *I* would squeeze as much as *I* could (with those Creature hands, I couldn't do much). We were trying to squeeze all the air out of the top of the head, so that when I would go into the scene, no bubbles would be coming out. But sometimes we just didn't get 'em all out, and they'd come up out of the top during the scene."

Box office receipts for *Revenge of the Creature* called for a third Gill Man go-round, and *The Creature Walks Among Us* went into production in August 1955. By this point, however, Universal was beginning to economize in the

Opposite: **The Creature (Browning) and the Teamster from the Black Lagoon prepare for a scene.**

production of its science fiction films and the Gill Man was scaled down—quite literally—in this perfunctory sequel, in which its gills are accidentally destroyed by fire. Surgically converted into a land creature by screwy sawbones Jeff Morrow, the Gill Man was played on land by character actor Don Megowan, and Browning's underwater footage was minimal.

Returning to work at various Florida water shows, Browning got back into the swim of production a few years later as a result of an encounter with film and television producer Ivan Tors. "I worked for Ivan for about 15 years, and I wound up being president of his studios down here in Florida. He was a pretty great guy. The thing about him, more than anything else, is that once he got confidence in you as an employee of his, no matter who you were or what position you were in, he just let you go. He didn't stay on your back or anything. He and I got along famously. First I did three years of [Tors's television series] *Sea Hunt*, starting out as a stuntman. Courtney Brown doubled Lloyd Bridges, and in every show, Lloyd ran up against a heavy. Courtney did all the underwater for Lloyd and I did the underwater for all the heavies. They even started casting people that looked a little bit like me—dark hair, about the same size—because it made everything easier. Then Ivan did a show called *The Aquanauts* [aka *Malibu Run*], where I was the double for [series star] Keith Larsen, and Courtney started doubling the bad guys—that reversed our situation to where I was winning the fights and he was losing 'em! Courtney and I spent our whole career fighting each other *[laughs]!*"

In the early 1960s, Browning made another splash in the television/movie history books when he created *Flipper,* dolphin hero of two MGM feature films and four years' worth of episodic television. "That all started when I got the idea, as a publicity stunt, to go to South America and capture freshwater dolphin—they'd never been captured before. We formed an expedition over a period of a year, went to the Amazon, captured freshwater dolphin, brought them back to Silver Spring [a water park] and put them in the water there. We had 'em for about a year or so. In the process, I used to swim with them. Then I started thinking, they did a film about Lassie and a boy; why not do one with a *dolphin* and a boy? (In Grecian legends and so forth, they swam with dolphins.)

"I got together with Jack Cowden, who was a radio announcer in Ocala at the time, and we spent a couple of evenings jotting down an idea for a story. Then we thought about making the story into a book: I had the idea that if we did it into a book first, that I would have more protection if we went into making it as a movie. I flew to New York and spent about two weeks trying to peddle it as a book, and I got three or four companies interested—but none of them were interested enough to say, 'We'll do it.' So having known Ivan Tors, I got the bright idea to call him, get him to say he was considering it for a movie, then call a book company and say, 'I have someone interested in making it into a movie' to encourage *them* to make it into a *book*. Anyway, I called

Ivan and told him all about it, and I asked him if he would say that he was interested in it as a film. He said, 'Yeah, I'll say I'm considering it. But also send me a copy of it.' So I mailed him a copy, and sat back and waited to see if I'd hear anything from New York. About two weeks later, I got a call from Ivan, and he said, 'Let's make a movie,' and I said, 'What are you talkin' about?' He said, 'Let's make *Flipper*.' We did *Flipper* [1963] and after that *Flipper's New Adventure* [1964], then four years of *Flipper* on television."

A search for the right dolphin to play Flipper turned up nothing but the fact that aquarium-trained dolphins were frightened when humans joined them in the water. Browning, however, was undeterred. "During our travels, we went through the Keys and we found a guy named Milton Santini and his wife; he caught dolphins for a living and sold them to aquariums. But they had kept one dolphin, Mitzi, as a pet. When the other dolphins would arrive, they would see Mitzi feeding and they would start eating in captivity quicker than they would otherwise. I got in the water, Mitzi swam up right next to me and I put my arms on her—and as soon as that happened, we said, "This is the animal." Then we spent maybe six weeks working with the animal, trying to get her to do the things that we were going to need for the film.

"We knew nothing about [dolphin training], really, but we learned by hit and miss. I trained Mitzi down in Grassy Key, at a little motel with a natural pool coming into the center of the motel area from the sea. I had my son Ricky with me, he was nine years old at the time, and I was trying to get the animal used to a boy. And I couldn't figure out how he could ride her. I tried and tried to get something to happen, and I couldn't. But I had gotten her to retrieve a ball—several balls, as a matter of fact—and towels and whatever. And so one afternoon I got a bright idea: If I threw Ricky in the water like you'd throw a ball in the water, and say, 'Fetch!' maybe Mitzi would bring him back. I threw him in the water and I told Mitzi to fetch, and she swam over there and she grabbed a loop in his cutoff jeans and tried to pull him back. But he wasn't streamlined—it was kind of awkward. His arm fell on her back and I said, 'Hold her fin!' He held her fin—and she pulled him right to me. And from that day on, we had a boy riding a dolphin. Anyway, that was the process in which we trained her.

"After *Flipper* [the first movie], we didn't use her anymore. We got five dolphins from the Miami Seaquarium. They were new dolphins, all female—the reason we got females was that we heard that females were easier to train. We started training 'em, and the first one I was able to train was Suzy, and we used Suzy all through the *Flipper* series. I then acquired a bunch of trainers and I made a boy named Ric O'Feldman head trainer, and he trained another one called Kathy; about halfway through the series, we quit using Suzy and used Kathy. So actually there were three animals involved in all of the filming. You could do a book on it—they've only scratched the surface as to what you can do with dolphins. They're wonderful, wonderful animals."

Taking advantage of Browning's unique experience, the makers of *The Day of the Dolphin* (1973) hired him as technical adviser, but the association was short-lived. "When they got ready to film, Mike Nichols and I couldn't quite agree on things, so I left the film."

Fans of science fiction/action films also remember Browning's name from the credits of the James Bond adventure *Thunderball* (1965) as well as its 1983 remake, *Never Say Never Again*. "I got involved in *Thunderball* through Kevin McClory, who was one of the writers on it. He knew me and Ivan, and he had [Bond producer] 'Cubby' Broccoli call me. Kevin and I went over to London and we had four or five meetings and discussed what we were going to do, and they said, 'You got the job.'"

Shooting the underwater sequences in the Bahamas took three months, culminating with the harrowing aquatic free-for-all which remains the film's highpoint. "There aren't really many anecdotes I can tell you about it because it was so serious, because we had so many chances of somebody getting hurt. And we did have a few people hurt—nothing deadly or that serious, but it was a very serious shoot. In one scene Bond scuba-dives down and swims into a bomber that had crashed and sunk into the sea. We had caught a lot of sharks for this and other scenes. I was on the deck of a ship over the submerged plane and I said to one of the guys I work with, 'Big John, When Bond swims into the bomb bay, I want a shark coming down. Get a shark up in the bomb bay.' He said, 'What shark?' and I said, 'Get the biggest one.' So I was standing around on deck and John came back up and he said, 'The shark won't fit in the bomb bay. He's too big.' I said, 'Well, stick his tail in the pilot's cabin.' And John said, 'Are you kidding me?' *[Laughs.]* Well, we did it, and it worked out fine."

And series star Sean Connery? "Oh, he was a super guy, a gentleman and very professional. He's an excellent diver and did a very good job—he did all of his own stuff in close-ups, and we had doubles for the scenes where he was involved with sharks and so forth. He would have done whatever we asked him to do, but we didn't want to ask him to do stuff that was hairy." Browning's direction of the undersea segments helped *Thunderball* win the Academy Award for Special Visual Effects.

Film work has not been sparse for Browning in more recent years, either: He has been a director (*Island of the Lost*, *Salty* and more), second unit director (*Nobody's Perfekt*, *Caddyshack*, *Raise the Titanic!* and others), stunt coordinator (*The Heavenly Kid*, *Opposing Force*), stuntman (*The Six Million Dollar Man*, *The Bionic Woman*), writer (with Jack Cowden) of the 1980 science fiction film *Island Claws* and much more. "And I'm *still* directing; just recently, I finished a couple of commercials in the Bahamas."

With these credentials behind him, it is not surprising that Ricou Browning does not enjoy being primarily remembered as the Man in the Green Rubber Suit, but he's not about to make waves over it. "When we did the Creature films, no one ever thought they would remain popular; we thought, it was a movie, it's over and that's it. But it's a thing that just kind of lingers, and *[laughs]* nobody seems to forget it! Years later, I directed a feature called *Salty* [1975], about a sea lion. I put a lot of heart and soul into this film, and it was a good, G-rated family film, and it turned out real well. We were publicizing it and traveling with a Winnebago that we made for the sea lion to live in, and going to TV stations and so forth. Well, the PR people sent my résumé ahead of me to these different places. We'd go into these TV studios and I wanted to talk about *Salty,* but from my résumé they saw I had played the Creature, and all *they* wanted to talk about was the Creature! So I finally had to get the PR people to scratch that off, so I could talk about the film we just made *[laughs]!*"

Ricou Browning sets the record straight: "So you can get some kind of reality out of this picture, in as far as I see it, *Creature from the Black Lagoon* was just another movie, just another job. I've done many things since then that I am much more proud of. But I've gotten more reaction out of the Creature thing than anything else. I guess that's life *[laughs]!*"

The secret behind The Thing's *staying power?*
Gosh, I don't know. I cannot read
the public; I only know my own reactions.
When I saw it, I thought, "Ah, it's a good movie.
Thank God *it's a good movie!" Because,*
I confess, I really didn't know what *to expect!*

Robert Cornthwaite

FEW SCIENCE FICTION FILMS of the 1950s can compare to *The Thing from Another World* in the near brilliance of its writing and execution or in the opportunities it provided for some of the people involved. Apart from helping to establish the science fiction film genre in the fifties, it gave Christian Nyby an imposing initial directorial credit; made a fan favorite of star Kenneth Tobey; added to the legendary canon of producer (and de facto director) Howard Hawks; and even gave some early notoriety to James Arness, who played the space invader that terrorizes an Arctic base. But for film newcomer Robert Cornthwaite, the movie was more of a premature career peak than a stepping stone; he has been working constantly ever since, on the large and small screens as well as on the stage, but he has had few movie roles as meaty or as memorable as that of Dr. Arthur Carrington, the obsessive scientist who places the intellectual "carrot" Arness above the welfare of his fellow humans.

Born in St. Helen's, Oregon, Cornthwaite insists his first acting jobs happened "by accident, as I think it does to most actors. I have an older brother, one year older than I am, and Bill was my mentor in grammar school. He said, 'Don't let 'em get you into one of these school plays.' He had hated it, absolutely. So I took his word as gospel, and I carefully avoided it. When the school would send notes home, I wouldn't deliver 'em — I told the teachers, 'My mother doesn't want me to do that.' I don't think they really believed me, but they didn't force me to do it until the eighth grade, when I was about to graduate into high school. The teacher said, 'You can't get out of school without being in *one* play.' So I was in the Thanksgiving play, and had the deathless line, 'Thank God the ship has come!' I had this new thirteen-year-old voice, cracking all over the place most of the time, but I found that it was fine when I was on the stage *[laughs]*. And that hooked me — that was it. From then on, I was in plays wherever I could manage to be. I did my first work with professionals when I was eighteen, in a production of *Twelfth Night* up in Portland, on the Reed College campus. That was in 1935. My family moved to California in '35; as a matter of fact, the morning after we closed in *Twelfth Night,* we were on the road. (They weren't exactly waiting for me, but it coincided.) I worked on radio down here in Southern California."

Paramount showed what Cornthwaite calls "lukewarm interest" in signing him to a term contract, "but when they found I was 1-A on the draft status, that cooled that fast," he remembers. "Then there was the hiatus of almost four years in the air force [during World War II], three of which I spent overseas, which was really a great boon. They gave me the grand tour, let me tell you: We sailed from New York, around South Africa, put in at Durban and wound up in Egypt. (Of course, we didn't know where we were going till we got there.) We were flying air cover for the British Eighth Army; I was in a B-25 outfit, a radio gunner. Then they got me confused with a guy named Cornwall — leave it to the military to get things screwed up — and I wound up, off and on, with

Previous page: Robert Cornthwaite in 1992.

the RAF for the next three years, on detached service. It was a great adventure: We were all over the Mediterranean, we followed the Eighth Army west across the Sahara to Tunis, and linked up with the American forces there. Back with the British to Malta; then for the invasion of Sicily, I went *again* with the British. The Sicilian campaign, and then the Italian. Then I got into public relations — somebody found out I had worked in radio before the war, and they were setting up a new outfit called the Mediterranean Allied Air Forces, so I was in the headquarters of that, in public relations, and flying all over the place. Corsica, Sardinia — I covered the invasion of Southern France and got the Bronze Star for it. It was the adventure of my life."

Returning to Hollywood after the war resulted in what Cornthwaite calls "a terrible anticlimax. I found out that the people I knew in Hollywood radio had all gone in the four years that I was away. So I went back to radio announcing, which I had done as the bread-and-butter job: newscasting, disk jockeying, everything that came on your shift as a staff announcer. I did that, but got steadily more disenchanted with it, because there were very few acting opportunities. I did sneak off to Hollywood and used about half-a-dozen different names as an actor on network shows there, but I decided I wanted to be an actor full-time. So I just quit radio, cold.

"The agent who had handled me before the war — I told you about the Paramount deal that never came off — managed to sell me as a character actor. I was losing my hair by that time, and had always been a character actor anyhow. Within six months of quitting radio, I was doing pictures. That first year [1950], I did six movies, five of them before *The Thing*. And of course *The Thing* was a good, long period of employment, nearly five months on that."

Cornthwaite's involvement with the milestone science fiction film began with an interview at RKO with Howard Hawks and Christian Nyby (Hawks' longtime film editor), who would receive the "official" credit for direction of *The Thing*. "Then I started a picture called *Mark of the Renegade* [1951] at Universal, playing a Mexican. While I was working on that, Hawks decided he wanted to shoot a screen test, and Universal let me off to go over and shoot the screen test. It was supposed to be just a photographic test: They would shoot some film to see if I would photograph old enough for the role. They were shooting a number of tests on actors for the same part [Dr. Carrington], one after another. (Another actor up for the part was Philip Bourneuf, whom I later directed in a production of *Richard II*.) After they got me into makeup, Mr. Hawks said to me, 'We'd like to do it in sound because I want Howard Hughes to hear your voice.' So we did a test in sound, in *one* take, and I raced back to Universal, back to work. And I didn't hear anything for a few days. Then my agent brought the *[Thing]* script one day to this ramshackle place where I was living; he threw it down and said, 'Well, you've got the part.'"

RKO was at the time owned by Howard Hughes, the wealthy recluse who (disastrously) ran the studio by remote control. Cornthwaite, who never met or even saw Hughes during his acting stints at RKO, adds, "I heard rumors that he never actually set foot on the lot. He kept offices elsewhere and he met people in automobiles and things like that. Very secretive! But it was kind of funny, my Hughes connection. At the time, my mother was still living, down in Long Beach, and she was completely dependent on me—I'd go down on weekends and do the chores for her. I went down after that screen test (I still hadn't heard the results of it), and she wanted to know what had been happening during the week. I said I finished a picture at Universal, and I had a test at RKO and it sort of depended on what Howard Hughes said about it. She said, 'Howard Hughes? Is he from Texas?' I said, 'Yes, I believe so.' She said, 'Beaumont?' 'I don't know anything about Beaumont, but I've heard Houston.'

"She said, 'Well, of *course* Houston, that's where I *knew* him. How old is he?' I said, 'I haven't met him, but I guess he's probably in his late forties or around fifty now.' She said, 'No, no, no—too young. The Howard Hughes I knew would be much older than that,' and we dropped it. A couple of hours later, I was in the backyard doing something or other, and she came to the back door and said, 'But he had a *boy* named Howard, too!'

"This is the way it turned out: My mother's father was a building contractor and he had built the Southern Pacific railway stations across the South, among other things in his career. And he had done work building oil rigs for Howard Hughes, Sr., at Beaumont. Hughes would bring his little boy, six or eight years old, and my mother would mind him and play with him while the two fathers were doing business! So *she* knew him—but I never did!"

Production of *The Thing* began at RKO on October 25, 1950. On November 27, with RKO soundstage filming at an end, the company moved to the California Consumers downtown icehouse in Los Angeles. "That was where they'd shoot scenes where they had to have the breath showing; *Lost Horizon* [1937] was perhaps the first film shot in there, and then many pictures after. It's long since been destroyed. Then we did go up, just before Christmas time as I recall [December 9, 1950], to Montana, where they had built the huge set for the flying saucer sequence, and also the whole compound where the Arctic party was supposed to be—all the exteriors where the planes landed and so on. The locals made a big hoopla over us. Ken [Tobey] and Dewey [Martin] and I were adopted into the Blackfoot Tribe in a big ceremony with the chiefs, including the old chief who had signed the last treaty of peace between the Sioux nation and the United States. I couldn't believe he was still alive in 1950, but he was, a very dignified old man.

"Anyhow, we sat around doing *nothing*. We got acquainted with some of the local people, and a lady asked me, 'When are you going to start shooting?' I said, 'As soon as there's enough snow on the ground. We need eight or ten inches of virgin snowfall for what we need to shoot.' She said *[in a concerned voice]*, 'Don't they *know* that the snow doesn't *stay* on the ground here?' It was a high plateau up there at Cut Bank, Montana; that's why the U.S. built a landing strip there for the takeoff to Alaska, because the snow is blown off by the winds. I told [associate producer] Eddie Lasker, who was putting up the money for the picture, and *[laughs]* it *disturbed* him — he couldn't deal with it. He said *[sputtering]*, 'N-n-no, we, we, we've got photographs, the snow stays on the ground here, it stays on the ground here, it stays on the ground here' — sort of an *incantation,* hoping it would happen! It never did — we never got a shot with actors. They did get a few brief shots with doubles. And then they had to rebuild the set in (I think it was) Minot, North Dakota; and they were *thinking* about building a set up in the Yukon (I don't think they ever did). But they did shoot some stuff in North Dakota, apparently, which I was not involved with at all, it was all doubles. I had about six doubles in that picture before it was done."

The fruitless stay at Cut Bank lasted, according to Cornthwaite, "a week or ten days, something like that. The whole cast was up there — that is, everybody that was concerned with the flying saucer scene. We shot that eventually in Encino, California, at the RKO Ranch. That was the last thing we shot, that was in early March of 1951, and they had a date in April that they *had* to have the film ready by, for exhibition at Radio City Music Hall. Dimitri Tiomkin, who did the score, was composing the music as we went along, toward the end. I met him when we got together and rehearsed for him this flying saucer scene, so that he could compose the score for it. He had, of course, been watching the dailies and the rough cut, so that he could time his music by each frame of film. When we met and shook hands, Dimi said, in his very thick Russian accent, 'Jesus Christ, you're just a boy!' He'd been used to the old man on screen!"

For that classic scene (in which Tobey's crew, Cornthwaite and his colleagues discover the flying saucer frozen beneath the Arctic ice), "a big expanse on the Ranch in Encino was where they built a huge backdrop which blended with the sky — at least, when you had the proper lenses on, and soft focus in the background / sharp focus in the front. It was simply done with fake snow against this huge cyclorama backdrop. I got an injured eye from that: They blew a mixture of Styrofoam and shaved ice in front of the wind machines for the snow stuff, and a bit of the Styrofoam stuck in my right eyeball. We got the shot *[laughs]*, but I couldn't see out of that eye for twenty minutes afterwards, it was watering so much. That sort of stuff can happen very easily, and it's very painful. As a matter of fact, it pierced the eyeball in my case and formed what they call a pseudo-pterygium: A little bit of the eyeball structure extrudes through. It's visible now; it photographs. They could perform an operation in which they would slit the eyeball and tuck it back in; I said, 'No, thanks.'"

Wearing coats, hats and other gear beneath the California sun resulted in the expected discomfort for Cornthwaite and his fellow actors. "Well, March is not too bad, but it was no fun, I can tell you. It was sunny weather and there was not too much smog in those days in the Valley, and it was hard trying to play cold. I remember [actor] Bob Nichols was particularly good at playing cold. I thought, 'Well, Dr. Carrington, he wouldn't *allow* himself to be cold!'"

In addition to his Arctic raiment, Cornthwaite was also encumbered by a phony beard and other makeup in order to play the middle-aged Carrington. "They bleached my hair so that it would photograph gray, and I used to have to get to the studio at a quarter to five on the days when they had to touch up the bleach job," the actor recalls. "I'd go into women's hairdressing, where they did the bleaching. Janet Leigh, Gloria DeHaven and Ann Miller were shooting *Two Tickets to Broadway* [1951] at the same time, and while they were getting their hair done, *my* hairdresser was doing the bleach job on me. Ann Miller always called me 'the Professor,' because she couldn't remember my name. By the way, in the sequence where we're out around the flying saucer, *that* is my own beard, and that's the only sequence in the picture where it is. I had let it grow, thinking, 'Well, I can always shave it off, and they can paste the other one back on again.' Makeup man Lee Greenway decided that I had enough beard to work. I had to bleach it, because my beard was sort of a bright red in those days, red and black."

The excellent script of *The Thing*, credited to Charles Lederer, may also feature contributions by William Faulkner, whom Ken Tobey briefly met prior to the start of shooting. "I heard that rumor, too, but I don't know whether it was true," Cornthwaite says. "Quite possibly it was, because he did a lot of things for Hawks. At that time, he was working for several months there on the script of *The Left Hand of God,* which Hawks never made—he sold it to 20th, and Henry Hathaway directed it with Humphrey Bogart [in 1955]. Faulkner fascinated me, because I had read a great deal of his stuff. Ken was lucky; I never met Faulkner. I thought I'd better *not* meet him! I'd see Faulkner every day in the commissary, and he looked so morose, so dour. He would sit at this little table, by himself, and no one ever came *near* him except the waitress, who'd come and replenish his coffee from time to time. He looked *so* sour; I thought, 'One of these days, I may go up and say, "Mr. Faulkner, I admire your work very much," and then run like hell!' Because I thought he'd throw the sugar container at me!"

Possibly because of the overlapping dialogue in *The Thing*, another rumor started that Orson Welles had a hand in it behind the scenes, but Cornthwaite discounts that story. "I never heard *that*," he scoffs. "I never saw Welles. *I* think that *Welles* was influenced by *Hawks'* filmmaking. Hawks was, in my book, the greatest filmmaker that I ever worked with, and I've worked with some pretty good ones: George Stevens, Billy Wilder, people with reputations like that. But Hawks had such complete control over all aspects [of his films]; he was a great writer, for instance. He never, to my knowledge, had screen credit for writing, even though he rewrote the scripts constantly. But he hired, in the first place, the best writers, like Faulkner, like I.A.L. Diamond. Charlie Lederer got the credit on *The Thing,* but Ben Hecht I know worked on the screenplay. I never met Hecht, but I heard that, definitely, that he had done one treatment at least, or maybe a screenplay of it."

The question inevitably asked of every veteran of *The Thing*—"How much directing did Christian Nyby actually get to do?"—is one that Cornthwaite is well prepared for. "Here's the way I look at it: Howard Hawks was launching Chris, who had been his cutter on several pictures, as a director. But on a Hawks picture, there was only one boss; he was an absolute autocrat. There were a few—*very* few—occasions when Hawks was *not* on the set and Chris *was* the actual director. But Chris *always* deferred to Howard Hawks—and for damn good reasons. Here was a great filmmaker, and Chris was not really in the same league. But as far as I was concerned, if it was between them that Chris was the director, then Chris was the director.

"There were times when Hawks would take me aside and give me direction, *away* from the set—which I took as a great compliment. He asked me to write the last scene—*my* last scene, that monologue with the Thing at the end of the corridor, just before they electrocute him." Did he write it? "I did very little; I cut it a bit, I rearranged it a little, but I didn't write a new one. I thought, 'No, these are good writers'—I had nothing better to offer *[laughs]!* But, getting back to your question about Hawks and Nyby, whenever that comes up, I answer always that, yes, it was Howard Hawks' picture, but Chris Nyby *was* the official director, and that's how it stands as far as I'm concerned.

"At that time, I think the people that worked *behind* the camera were much more interesting to me than the people in *front.* Don Steward was the special effects man; he had worked with Hawks on other things and was one of Hawks' 'regulars.' Hawks had favorite cameramen—Russ Harlan was cameraman on *The Thing,* and he did a lot of Hawks pictures. He was an excellent cameraman with a slew of Academy Awards. And Russell had *his* own crew. It was my first time out with 'em, but here was a crew of veterans who had worked together many times, and it was a very smooth operation. It was a pleasure working with all those people. They were damn good, top of their profession."

Cornthwaite's primary concern with his playing of the costarring role was "with playing with enough age and maturity. There've been rumors that I was in my twenties at the time, but I was thirty-three, which is not a kid. But the man's supposed to be fifty-five or so. I knew that, with film, it's not like theater where you can do a bit of faking; there's got to be a kind of reality in eyes and in movement. My principal concern was with that. Also, there are a few references in there to the fact that Carrington's a Nobel Prize winner. Well, *that* kind of puts you on the spot! If I had any images in mind, I suppose they were maybe a little of [J. Robert] Oppenheimer, who was in the news at that time (not specifically any mannerisms of his); and also Enrico Fermi, the Italian who was in on the atomic bomb. Such people. That was the image in my mind: A man of some dignity, but not without a sense of humor." Dr. Carrington had a sense of humor? "I thought he was not without a sense of humor, but *[laughs]* with a pasted-on beard, it's hard to smile without cracking the foliage off your face!"

In some respects, Cornthwaite's Dr. Carrington is the heavy in *The Thing,* standing up for the alien and thereby endangering everybody else. The actor remarks, "I thought to myself, 'The man believes what he says, and therefore in his own mind, he's not the heavy at all, he's doing the right thing.' Carrington was trying to increase the world's store of knowledge, and if there are going to be other Things coming in, we damn well better be prepared to deal with 'em for what they are. I think, actually, he was *right,* but from the point of view of a kid's matinee on a Saturday, he's the heavy." If Robert Cornthwaite were trapped in that Arctic base, what would he have thought of Carrington then? "Hard to say. Because people think only in terms of their own preservation, not about any future encounters. It's tough to be objective."

In an early draft of the script, the Thing decapitates Dr. Carrington, but according to Cornthwaite, "Hawks changed that, among many things, as we went along. Here was Hawks' method: While the actors' stand-ins went in and the gaffers lighted them, the actors would retire to a table that Hawks always had on any set where he worked. We would sit around and Hawks would say something like, 'Well, now, forget what's in the script. When *this* happens (whatever the scene entailed), what would *your* reaction be?' And if you had anything to suggest, you'd throw it in. It might be accepted, it might be rejected, it might be accepted in part and modified. That is the way the scene was developed, and this is how the overlapping dialogue was set up. Then we would go onto the set, the stand-ins would step out, and we would shoot the master shot (and then of course the two-shots and the over-the-shoulders). Meanwhile, Lorrie Sherwood, the secretary, would madly type up the scene we had put together around the table so that we could match what we had done in the master when we got around to closer shots and reverses.

"In *The Thing,* Hawks had very few individual shots, and no close-ups whatsoever—that also contributed to the sense of reality, I believe. That's the way he worked. When I worked with him again on *Monkey Business* [1952], it was the same way.

"Remember my first scene in *The Thing,* the scene where George Fenneman shows Ken Tobey slides of the saucer in flight? A great chunk of that dialogue initially was in my part. Hawks took me aside—that was my first day on the picture—and he said, 'You know, when I make a picture with John Wayne or Gary Cooper, they go through the script and they say, "How about taking this line of mine, having someone *else* say it, and I just react?" That way, *they* [Wayne and Cooper] come out looking better; the other people have the dull things to say, and all Wayne and Cooper do is react to 'em. I tell you this because I don't want you to feel bad: I'm going to take this long speech

Robert Cornthwaite 119

Eduard Franz, Cornthwaite, Norbert Schiller and (squatting) Paul Frees share a tense moment during the search for the missing *Thing*.

and give it to George Fenneman.' So that's what we did. But I had learned this speech—I memorized it the night before. George got it *cold [laughs]*, there on the set, this great big chunk of technological dialogue. He was a very experienced radio announcer, but he was used to having a script in front of him. And he simply couldn't get the words out *[laughs]!* I don't know *how* many takes we took! And finally Chris, who was a very considerate man, said, 'All right, that's a wrap for today. We'll start with that in the morning.' Then, of course, in one take the next morning, George had it. But he took such a kidding throughout the picture because of this, and he was so good-natured about it."

Less harmonious was the relationship between actor Douglas Spencer, who played reporter Scotty, and director of photography Russell Harlan. "Somehow or another, I don't know how, Doug rubbed Russ Harlan the wrong way—and suddenly his key light started disappearing. There are some scenes where you can see all the actors, but there's another face there *in the dark,* and it's Doug. In some scripts—I think in the Ben Hecht script, probably—the Spencer role, Scotty, was the central role of the film, the point-of-view character. Because Hecht, of course, had been a newspaperman himself." Cornthwaite adds that none of the actors had much difficulty overlapping dialogue. "No, I think we all enjoyed doing it. Sometimes it involved a certain amount of ad-libbing beyond the line, in order for the overlap to work. You'll notice that, in spite of the overlaps, what is necessary for you to hear comes out *crystal clear*. This was part of Hawks' technique. And it's a *witty* picture, isn't it? I had no idea until we saw a rough cut of about twenty-five, thirty minutes that it *was* witty. I didn't know that; I thought we were playing kind of a straight sci-fi melodrama. The fact that it was witty was escaping me during the making of it."

The self-animated Thing hand on the lab table "was made of latex rubber, like a glove. There was a girl with very slim hands and wrists who was under the table; she put her hand up through a hole in the top of the table, into this latex rubber forearm, and she did the movements from there. There was more than one of those latex rubber things; a collector named Bob Burns, who has a museum in his home, has one of those, and another one was found by someone else, under the soundstage floor. We shot on Stage 10 at RKO (where they shot *Citizen Kane*, by the way), and someone later found it during a cleanup." Even though he was not in the scene, "I watched the entire filming of the fire scene, and it was fascinating and *scary* to be there on the set. They had two stuntmen playing the Thing, so that they could change off. They were equipped with about a minute's worth of oxygen, so once they were sealed in that suit, they had to shoot immediately. I remember one of the guys being lighted on fire, and then they didn't call *action*. He just started jumping up and down with impatience; even though there was only so much oxygen, it puts you on the qui vive. It was exciting, *very* exciting, to watch that. And the electrocution was interesting, too. The electricity shrunk the Thing, from Jim Arness to [stuntman] Teddy Mangean, who was the middle size; then little Billy Curtis, the dwarf, was the smallest Thing. Then they just had a little doll or something. Teddy Mangean was my photographic double, and he did the fall for me there at the end of the corridor. Teddy looked uncannily like me in the makeup. I was amazed when I saw him."

As for James Arness' makeup, Cornthwaite says, "They spent two months experimenting before we started production, using Jim himself. He worked for a couple of months before we started principal photography, doing the variations on makeup and wardrobe and so on—they went through all kinds of changes before they settled on the quite-human-looking monster. Jim had done a few pictures; I think John Wayne had already taken an interest in him. Jim was a big guy, six-five, and Wayne liked to work with big men. What I heard from Lee Greenway, with whom I became very friendly during the course of the picture, was that they went from pretty outlandish ideas for the Thing, making it more and more human. I think that Hawks' reasoning, or *feeling*, was that if the Thing was not recognizably *like us*, it was not apt to be taken as seriously. Or its *intelligence* would be underestimated. You know, we have a great idea, human beings do, of our own superiority; we assume that we are about the brightest things around. So therefore, anything that doesn't look human can't be bright!"

As for Arness' attitude throughout shooting (rumor has it that the future *Gunsmoke* star was thoroughly embarrassed by his role), "I think Jim has perhaps *always* been a little embarrassed about being an actor; I don't think he was ever what you would call a dedicated actor. He hates horses, for instance; he's uncomfortable on horseback, and he just hates 'em. And on that last *Gunsmoke* special, a lot of the footage of Marshal Dillon is of Jim's photographic double, because he was in pain, and because *[laughs]* it's not what he wants to be doing. He's made a wonderful career out of it, had a great success, and I'm sure he enjoys that, but I don't think he ever particularly enjoyed making movies." And maybe he enjoyed *The Thing* even less than the others? "Well, he's on-screen, what, two minutes or less out of the picture. It's kind of an embarrassment, to have the title role and not have a word to speak, and your on-screen time is minimal. Perhaps from that point of view, it was an embarrassment to him; I don't know, he never said so to me. I had very good relations with him. When we were doing that confrontation scene, in the tunnel, just before the Thing whomps Dr. Carrington, he said something complimentary about how I was doing, and he said, 'They'll have to come in for a big close-up of you here.' And I said, 'No, they won't.' He didn't understand Hawks' way of making a picture."

Arness' Thing makeup included "a foam rubber helmet covering his head; it was built up to make him look even taller, just as his boots were built up to make him taller. He was almost seven feet in height with all these additions. He wore a green [makeup] base, I think the same green or grayish-green greasepaint that was devised for *Blithe Spirit* on the stage."

Science fiction was a new genre at the time, but Cornthwaite does not recall giving any particular thoughts to its possibilities. "I was so new at the game—it was my first year in pictures—that I don't remember having *any* attitude about it. I was working every day *[laughs]*—that's all that *I* knew. *The Thing* had a good-sized budget, but they weren't spending money on actors—we were a cast of unknowns. I think I was getting the top money in the picture; I don't think Ken ever knew that, I *hope* he didn't. I think the budget was $1,300,000 and they spent $1,600,000, so it wasn't a cheapie; the average A-picture was still under a million in those days. But on the other hand, it had no stars, and frankly I wondered if anybody would come to see it." Having a cast of unknowns in *The Thing* "was, I think, deliberate on Hawks' part. I think he wanted unknown faces, to get a freshness, a reality that you don't get when it's an identifiable star. I think that's why he used all of us.

"I think I saw *The Thing* for the first time on my birthday, which is April the 28th. It opened a few days before here in Southern California, and somebody in my family formed a little family group and we all went to see it together. I remember hunkering down in the seat and thinking, 'I don't know what this is going to be like!' *[Laughs.]* But very encouraging was the fact that the audience just whooped it up and liked it enormously." Their reaction to Dr. Carrington? "The kids' reaction was to *boo! They* knew who the hero was!"

And Cornthwaite's reaction to director John Carpenter's 1982 remake: "I thought the special effects were terrific, and the fact that they went back to [John W.] Campbell's original short story was a good idea. (I remember reading the short story early on in the shooting of our *Thing* and thinking, 'Gosh, this is an awfully good idea. I wonder why they departed from it?') All the gruesome special effects in John Carpenter's film sort of became overwhelming to me. I was not interested in the people. And I thought it would have been a nice gesture on Carpenter's part to invite survivors in and say, 'Look, we're doing a completely different version, and wanted to get your good wishes,' or something of the sort. But there was never any overture to *any* of us, that I ever heard of, from Universal or from Carpenter.

"When Universal released the remake, the Fox Venice in Venice, California—a huge, old 1920s theater—showed Hawks' *The Thing* (taking advantage of the release of the new picture) and they asked several of us to attend. I was there; Ken Tobey (I hadn't seen him in years); George Fenneman, who drove me home (I just had had a fender bender in my car); Chris Nyby and his wife, who came in from Hawaii; and others. Margaret Sheridan had died a couple of months before (we were all saddened by that), and Dewey Martin didn't want to come (he's become kind of reclusive, I understand). And the fans were there in hordes."

How often does Robert Cornthwaite rewatch his "signature" film credit? "I've got a video of it that I wanted to show some of my grandnieces and grandnephews, but their parents are leery about it; they think it's too scary for them. So I haven't shown it to them. I looked at it when I got it, and I liked it again, but—*The Thing* was many years ago. I don't identify with it, in a sense. There's not anything I'm dying to see again. After a certain period of time, they belong somehow outside of me; they're not me anymore. And that's kind of a comfortable feeling, not a sense of loss at all. I've had the experience of seeing a film that I've just done, when it's fresh in my mind what I *wanted* to do, and there's an awful sense of inadequacy and of frustration. In the actor's mind, he sees the scene one way, and the camera sees something else. Inevitably this is true."

Despite the popularity of *The Thing*, it did Cornthwaite's career little or no good. "In fact, I didn't work for eleven months after that *[laughs]*! It was a box office success from the beginning, and my agent was trying to up my salary, more than double. And getting no takers. But it was just an unfortunate time: Television was coming up strong, the major studios were falling apart, they were canceling their stock companies, letting contracts run out. Actors were becoming all freelancers. It was the wrong time to be asking for more money. When *The War of the Worlds* came along, it was the first job that I had after *The Thing*. I got very good billing for a nothing part.

"It was a dull picture to make, too. We saw none of the special effects, we were simply *told* what we were looking at. There weren't even sketches, George Pal was very secretive about it. Pal was a funny man. I had the interview for *War of the Worlds*, then heard nothing — and forgot about it, as a matter of fact. One day, my agent's office called to say, 'Go to Paramount for a wardrobe fitting.' I went over, and it was for *War of the Worlds*. I had my fitting, then went down to the studio street and was still talking to a wardrobe man — there were two or three of us there in a clump. A little man was kind of circling around the group, and he kept tapping me on the shoulder, saying *[speaking with a heavy accent]*, 'I must speak to you. I must talk to you.' I said *[casually]*, 'Yes, yes, fine.' He said, 'I am in Writers Building,' and he gave me a room number. 'Yes,' I told him, 'when I am finished here, I will see you.' Fortunately, I remembered before I left the lot — and the room was George Pal's office. It was George Pal! I hadn't remembered him from the interview at all.

"He said, very concerned, with a troubled frown on his face, 'You are a *bl-lond!*' (After *The Thing*, my hair was back to its normal color, almost black; and I was clean shaven, of course, no beard.) I said, 'No, this is my natural color —' He said, 'You are a *bl-lond!* I haff a photograph, you are a *bl-lond!*' And he brought out of a drawer one of my RKO photos, which they had taken at the end of the shoot of *The Thing*, where my hair was still bleached, before they dyed it back. Well *[laughs]*, he had cast me in *War of the Worlds* because this minor scientist that I was playing entered in the same sequence with Gene Barry, their leading man, and they wanted someone that didn't have the same coloring as Barry; a leading character has got to stand out from the surroundings. So it was into the House of Westmore for another bleach job, but this time they bleached it a kind of Technicolor pink. And that's what I wore in *War of the Worlds*."

Cornthwaite-wise, *War of the Worlds* is a switch from *The Thing:* In *War*, he is one of the scientists who cannot wait to *blow up* the Martians. "Yes, that *is* funny. But I don't think that was any sort of in-joke on anyone's part. I liked [director] Byron Haskin, but Byron was in an impossible situation: He was having to direct actors in scenes in which what they're looking at, what they're reacting to, has not even been created yet. (That was all done in postproduction.) The group of scientists I belonged to also included an old silent film actor named Ivan Lebedeff. He told me a wonderful Garbo story, he worked with her on *Conquest* [1937]. We all got along like a house afire, it was fun from that point of view, but we all had so little to do; we just stood around, we were background. We had a wonderful time among ourselves, but the actual filming was deadly dull."

The movie itself? "I didn't like it, frankly. But who am I? It's become kind of a classic, too, I guess."

Another scientist role came via a very different sort of science fiction movie, Howard Hawks' rollicking *Monkey Business* (1952), about a research scientist (Cary Grant) concocting a youth potion. "I reported for work on *Monkey Business* after they had been shooting for a few days, and when I came onto the soundstage, Howard Hawks was standing talking to Cary Grant and to John Wayne, who was visiting the set. So I just went over and found a chair to sit down in — I wasn't about to break in on *that*. And Hawks — such a strange man, really — he left these two stars to come and sit with me. He said, 'Glad to have you on the picture.' He had *fought* for me, fought to get me on the picture, for this nothing part. He had told 20th, 'If Robert Cornthwaite is available, I want him,' and 20th did not want to pay my salary. The part wasn't worth it. It went to the legal department, and finally I was in the picture — just because he *insisted!*

"He asked, 'Have you read the script?' (I.A.L. Diamond wrote that script.) I said, 'Yes, I have.' He said, 'Well, you know, we're just using that as a kind of springboard. Cary has some ideas, some things he's going to do; Charlie Coburn is always so good. And Virginia [Ginger Rogers] is going to have her hair *up* in the beginning of the picture, and then she's going to let it *down*.' And I thought, 'Oh, my God, *that's* what he thinks of Ginger Rogers' contribution to the picture!'

"At this point, Marilyn Monroe walked across the stage, and every eye was on her — it was quite a sight *[laughs]*! And Hawks said, 'I think that the overdeveloped quality in the little blond girl is going to be kind of funny.' That was his estimation of Monroe *[laughs]*! She was a lot of trouble. She was *so* insecure. I remember she and I were standing, waiting for an entrance together; we were going to come into a scene between Cary Grant and Ginger Rogers, who was playing his wife. Marilyn had four words to say in the scene, and she kept saying them over and over to me. And her diaphragm was just *vibrating*, like someone in great fright or at the end of a long run. She was scared to death! But then also, very stubborn. Joe DiMaggio was courting her at the time, and he was on the set sometimes. And when he wasn't there, she would get on the phone. They'd be shooting a scene and the second assistant would say to her *[whispering frantically]*, 'Honey! Get off the phone. We're shooting!' She would look at him with those big eyes and go right on talking.

"She kept saying that she was having attacks of appendicitis because she was scared of working; she would be late, or phone in and say she couldn't work, or whatever. And Hawks just ruthlessly wrote her out of scenes, he used her photographic double in long shots, and finally he gave the studio orders: He said, 'If she has appendicitis, send her to the hospital, have her appendix out.' There was a sequence coming up that he *had* to have her in, a scene of her and Cary Grant cruising around in a little sports car. I don't know that this is *true*, but I heard that they sent her to the hospital and she had her appendix out. That was Hawks' attitude toward her.

"Jean Peters told me a story about Marilyn that was kind of revealing, too. They were both under contract there at that time, and what the studio would

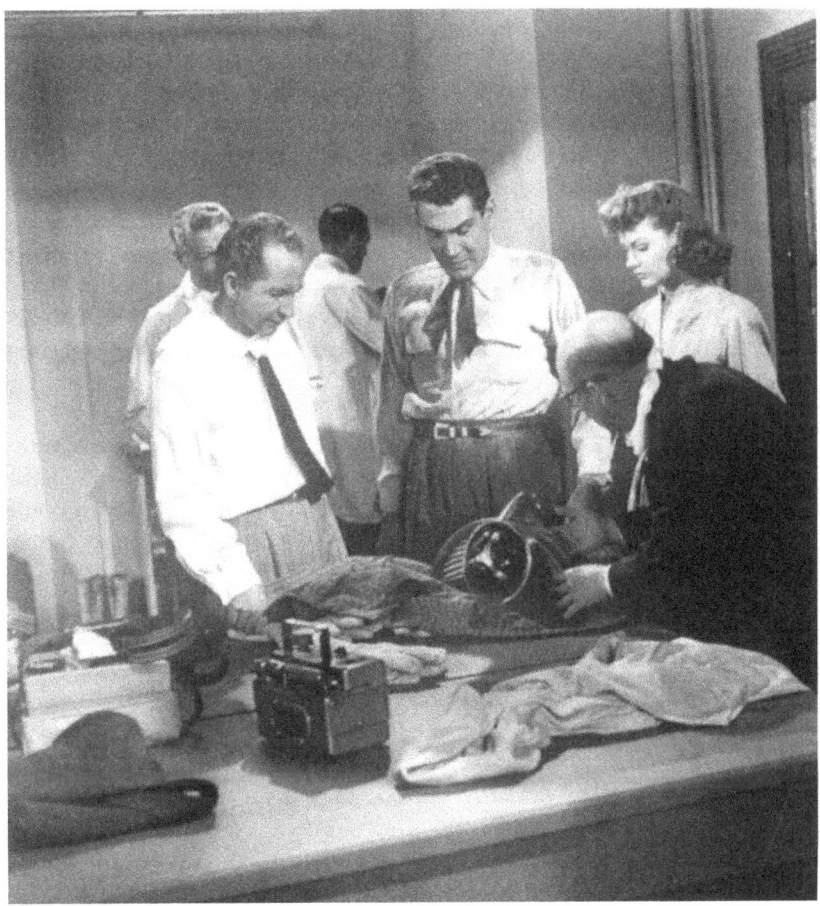

Cornthwaite was on our side (for a change) when Martians invaded in George Pal's *The War of the Worlds*. *Left-right:* Cornthwaite, Gene Barry, Alex Frazer, Ann Robinson.

do to save money was get all the girls [who were] under contract together and have a photo session — stills for publicity and magazines and whatnot — with the girls wearing all the glamorous duds that they'd wear in pictures. The wardrobe women were in attendance, and while one actress was being photographed, another would be changing; the photographer shoots, shoots, shoots, one girl after another. Marilyn and Jean Peters were in the dressing room together, changing, and Marilyn had tears in her eyes. She said, 'You other girls get to wear all the nice things. They just put me in the *sexy* things.' Now, *she* knew what she was selling, but that's the way she felt about it."

In addition to *Thing* holdover Cornthwaite, the previous film's Douglas Spencer and Bob Nichols also appeared in *Monkey Business*. "Hawks was very loyal to actors," says Cornthwaite. "He asked for me again when he did *Man's Favorite Sport?* [1964], which was a remake of his *Bringing Up Baby* [1938], and I couldn't do it. That was a great disappointment to me, but I was busy with something else. So I only worked with him the two times. I had enormous respect for him." As for Hawks' relationship with screen great Cary Grant, "I could see that Hawks had a great respect for Grant and that they loved working together. Hawks considered Grant one of the great film comedians, with his own bag of tricks, like an actor from the commedia dell'arte, a clown in a sense. And this is the way Grant looked upon himself, too, I believe. They had a long-term project which was never done, although they talked about it from time to time: They were going to make *Cinderella*. Howard Hawks was going to direct it, and Cary Grant was going to play the Wicked Stepmother *[laughs]*! It's a shame that it never got made, isn't it?

"Ginger Rogers has a talent for caricature, and she drew caricatures of everybody, cast and crew. In one set, there was a blackboard, and while Hawks was outlining a scene, she stood at the blackboard and did a very clever caricature of him — the long horse face. He was walking back and forth in front of it, he *had* to see it, but he *never* alluded to it, never gave any indication that he had seen it. So, sort of shamefacedly, she wiped it out with her hand. They went then into shooting the scene, and it was between her and Grant. They were doing a take, and in the middle of the take, Hawks walked from behind the camera, in front of the camera, and said, 'No, no, *no,* Virginia. *No-o-o-o.*' And nothing else! She stood there at attention, eyes wide open — and he walked behind the camera and said, 'All right, let's take it again,' without *ever* telling her what the 'no, no, *no*' was for. It shattered her — she was just aghast — and I thought, 'He punished her for drawing a caricature of him.' I can't be sure, but that's the way I read it. It was funny, and kind of scary."

Two of Cornthwaite's other films of this era were borderline genre, and both were for Robert Aldrich: *Kiss Me Deadly* and *What Ever Happened to Baby Jane?* "*Kiss Me Deadly* was the first time I worked for Aldrich. He told me that we had worked together when he was an assistant director on something or other, and that he had sort of liked my work. (I didn't remember it, and still cannot.) So when he made that independent, *Kiss Me Deadly,* he asked for me and I did that small part of the FBI man. Then the next thing I did for him was a major role, really about the third role in the picture although it was cut to ribbons, in a picture we made in Berlin, *Ten Seconds to Hell* [1959]. Hammer Films produced it, and they were used to making horror films. Here they were trying for a bigger market, a more ... honorable art form *[laughs]*, with this picture! And it was a very long picture, slow-paced. After Aldrich had finished his cut, Hammer hired Virginia and Andrew Stone to cut the film. And they cut it — *drastically!* The female star was Martine Carol, a French star who was very big on the Continent, and in the film,

Martine's character has a baby, which is central to the plot. They cut the baby, completely. They still left some scenes where there's a baby's crib in view *[laughs]*, but it's unexplained. And that baby was a motivating factor for many scenes; many scenes were built around it.

"I remember the first day that Martine worked on the picture, we were shooting in the Tiergarten, a big park in the center of West Berlin. It was a very cold day, the water was freezing on the lake. It was a scene with that baby—they had twins playing it, of course. The shot opened with me getting the baby out of its crib there on the lawn beside the lake, and holding it until she came up, and then giving *her* the baby. The baby was fine with me, I would hand the baby to Martine, and as soon as she took it, it would begin to cry. And it was supposed to be *her* baby *[laughs]*. Well, this was wrong, and that upset Martine greatly; we changed babies, took the other twin, and the same thing happened. Finally we got into the dialogue of the scene, two or three pages of dialogue between her and me, and *[laughs]* I could not understand a word she said, she was so upset! Eventually they dubbed her throughout the picture. Martine's English was not bad, but being upset, and with all these conditions—freezing cold, a baby that was reacting against her, her first day on the picture—it was a terrible psychological spot for her. We had a hellish time."

And in *What Ever Happened to Baby Jane?*, "I played the doctor who never arrives, like the marines who never land. Somebody else had played it—they had shot this particular scene once before, I found out later—but Aldrich called me to redo it. It was the last day of the shoot, with Bette Davis and Joan Crawford shooting close-ups for the beach scene. They had already shot it in long shots, down at Zuma, I think; for the close-ups, they rigged up a little spot of sand on the soundstage. That was my only contact with them. The two of them were very professional, and *so* conscious of what they were doing, so sure of themselves. It was kind of wonderful to see two such pros. In spite of all the publicity about their feuding (and I understand that they *really* did not like each other), they were very politely arranging a joint press conference, deciding whose house they would have it at, making these arrangements between themselves quietly and rather quickly.

"They showed the thing *[Baby Jane]* at the Directors Guild before it was in release, and we were all invited. At the time, I was going with a young lady who was kind of Hollywood-smitten, and I took her with me to see it. And as the picture ran, I thought to myself that it was the most heavy-handed, *awful* thing—I sank lower and lower in the seat. I could not think of a single good thing to say about that movie. And yet, it made nothing but money."

Like most other actors of his kind, Cornthwaite was also constantly busy on television, including (of course) the classic horror, science fiction and fantasy series like *The Twilight Zone*, *Thriller*, *Voyage to the Bottom of the Sea* and *Batman*. "One *Twilight Zone* I remember because it was with Dana

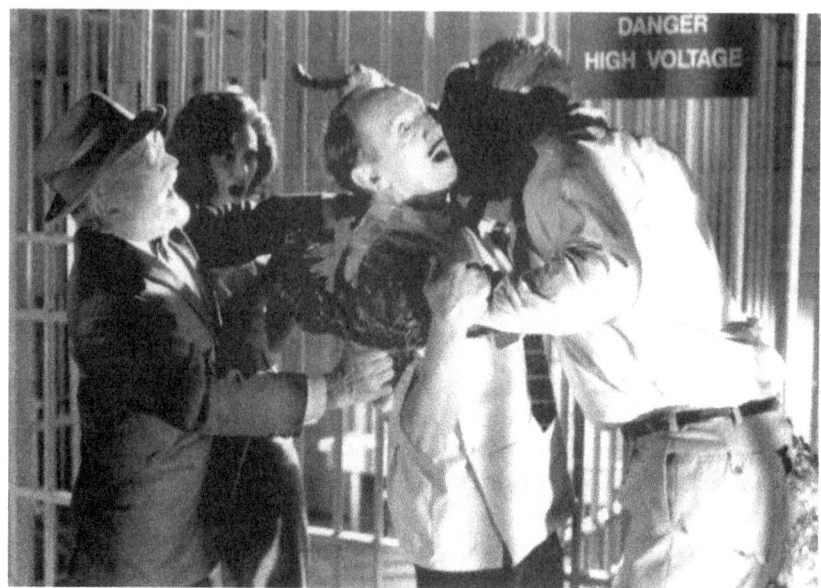

Cornthwaite and Cathy Moriarty watch as William Schallert falls prey to the ant-man in director Joe Dante's *Matinee*.

Andrews, with whom I had worked in 1936 at Pasadena Playhouse in a production of *Antony and Cleopatra*. I tried to use in that what I remembered of Wendell Wilkie's accent when he was running for president in 1940 against Roosevelt. *Thriller* I don't remember. *Voyage to the Bottom of the Sea*, that too is very vague. That kind of story is so remote from *human* values that I can't remember 'em; you do 'em, and that's it. But *Batman* had an awfully good script, and they thought this particular episode was going to be the best of them all. Art Carney was the villain [the Archer], but I really had a better role and I enjoyed doing it. But they turned it over to a director so stodgy, so unimaginative, that this good script came out as a flat piece of nothing."

He was also a regular — briefly — on the NBC spy spoof *Get Smart* with Don Adams. "I played Windish, the guy who invented all the gadgets that Agent 86, Maxwell Smart [Don Adams], used; Smart always screwed 'em up. We had shot a few of them, four or five, I guess, and Don Adams said to me, 'Do you think Windish gets angry with Agent 86 over his screwing up with the gadgets?' I said, 'Yeah, I think he gets angry, but he gets over the anger about this because he's always got *another* gadget he wants to promote.' And, after that conversation, I wasn't called for any more shows. Later I was working on something else on the Paramount lot, which is where we shot *Get Smart*, and Leonard Stern, one of the producers, came across the street toward me and said, 'Hey, Bob, I wanted to tell you that we were all very happy with what you were doing. But Don . . . he's hard to please.' I don't know what Don's ideas were, but whatever I said wasn't the right thing."

The quintessential movie scientist, Cornthwaite added two more science fiction roles to his filmography in the 1970s, *Colossus—The Forbin Project* and *Futureworld*. "I thought *Colossus* was an awfully good script, but I had very little to do in it, and it was so isolated from the other people involved that I don't remember it with any particular feeling at all. I was on it for several weeks, but in a sense it was like *War of the Worlds*: The technology was so much a part of it—special effects—we were reacting to printouts. That's a pretty *sterile* kind of thing to do *[laughs]!* But I thought it was a very clever script, and I liked Eric Braeden; he had been Hans Gudegast up until that picture. Very nice guy." And as for *Futureworld*, AIP's sequel to MGM's *Westworld*, "I had a fair part in that, I worked several weeks on it. We shot at NASA for a week or two, in Houston. Angela Greene, who played my wife in it, called me after the preview and she said, 'Honey, we are *out!*' They had cut both our parts out. We're in background and that's about it. So it was take the money and run, as it turned out."

Nowadays, says Cornthwaite, "I do theater whenever I can, always have. I prefer theater; it is far more liberating for the actor than film. Writers, directors, editors and cameramen—those are the creative people in film. Actors are of necessity farther down on the totem pole, although they don't like to think so and a lot of them don't admit it. But they're relatively unimportant. They are things being manipulated by these other people. I like theater because *I've* got the reins in *my* hands, at least once the curtain goes up."

Forty-plus years after *The Thing*, it is still the one movie most fans instantly associate him with. Is that okay with Robert Cornthwaite? "Sure, I think it's a good picture, and I'm proud of it. The secret behind its staying power? Gosh, I don't know, I cannot read the public; I only know my own reactions. When I saw it, I thought, 'Ah, it's a good movie. Thank *God* it's a good movie.' Because, I confess, I really didn't know *what* to expect!"

ROBERT CORNTHWAITE FILMOGRAPHY

Union Station (Paramount, 1950)
Gambling House (RKO, 1950)
The Thing from Another World (RKO, 1951)
Mark of the Renegade (Universal, 1951)
His Kind of Woman (RKO, 1951)
Something to Live For (Paramount, 1952)
Monkey Business (20th Century-Fox, 1952)

The War of the Worlds (Paramount, 1953)
Day of Triumph (George J. Schaefer, 1954)
Stranger on Horseback (United Artists, 1955)
Kiss Me Deadly (United Artists, 1955)
The Purple Mask (Universal, 1955)
On the Threshold of Space (20th Century-Fox, 1956)

The Leather Saint (Paramount, 1956)
The Spirit of St. Louis (Warner Bros., 1957)
Hell on Devil's Island (20th Century–Fox, 1957)
Ten Seconds to Hell (United Artists, 1959)
Day of the Outlaw (United Artists, 1959)
All Hands on Deck (20th Century–Fox, 1961)
What Ever Happened to Baby Jane? (Warner Bros., 1962)
Reptilicus (voice only; AIP, 1962)
The Ghost and Mr. Chicken (Universal, 1966)
Ride to Hangman's Tree (Universal, 1967)
Waterhole #3 (Paramount, 1967)
The Legend of Lylah Clare (MGM, 1968)
Colossus – The Forbin Project (Universal, 1970)
The Peace Killers (Transvue, 1971)
Journey Through Rosebud (GSF-Cinerama, 1972)
Futureworld (AIP, 1976)
Deal of the Century (Warner Bros., 1983)
Dr. Detroit (Universal, 1983)
Disorderlies (Warner Bros., 1987)
Who's That Girl (Warner Bros., 1987)
Time Trackers (Concorde, 1989)
Matinee (Universal, 1993)

Halloween (Compass International, 1978) features clips from *The Thing from Another World;* Cornthwaite is heard but not seen.

There has been, all through the years, a definite following for many of the films that I was in, and they've never given it up. And a lot of fans have kept up with me. Believe me when I tell you that's one of the most flattering things that can happen to an actress.

Louise Currie

A GOLDEN ANNIVERSARY is a great excuse to celebrate. The year 1989 saw classic movies like *Gone with the Wind* and *The Wizard of Oz* hitting the half-century mark while the films themselves played to capacity crowds in revival houses; 1991 was the year of *Citizen Kane,* which also went the nostalgia route via new theatrical prints and much fan ado.

Actress Louise Currie did not have a substantial part in *Citizen Kane;* she was only one of a group of reporters seen in the film's closing scene, their faces obscured by shadows, puttering around amidst an ocean of crated objets d'art at Kane's palatial Xanadu estate. Closer to the hearts of science fiction and action fans than *Citizen Kane,* however, is another Louise Currie credit, one of the best and most famous serials of all time: *Adventures of Captain Marvel* (1941). Based on the popular Whiz Comics character and transposed from comic book page to silver screen by the action experts at Republic Pictures, the classic serial also recently turned 50, and Louise Currie helps to commemorate the occasion with reminiscenes of this classic cliffhanger and of her brief but memorable career in serials and horror films.

"I can't believe it sometimes, but it seems as though *Captain Marvel* just isn't *ever* going to lose its appeal," the actress, fresh from a dip in her Beverly Hills pool, admits. "Recently a fan called me from the South; he was a schoolteacher, taught third grade, and he said that he got amazing results with his class when he got the bright idea of running *Captain Marvel* the first thing every morning. When the children would come into the room, he'd turn on one chapter. Of course, they would be all settled down and he would have their rapt attention by the time the chapter would finish, and then he'd go into the lessons—'Okay, children, what's four and four?' and so on. They couldn't *wait* to get to his class every day, and he would get perfect attendance *[laughs].* He told me he had the best luck of his teaching career when he was using *Captain Marvel* to keep the children in line."

Of course, not all of us were fortunate enough to have *Captain Marvel* included as part of our grade school curriculum, and not every actress has been able to make the kind of crowd-pleasing movies that can win her a new generation of fans 50 years after the fact. Born in Oklahoma City, Louise Currie attended Sarah Lawrence College in Bronxville, New York, became interested in acting and then attended Max Reinhardt's drama school in Hollywood. ("At the time, I was not necessarily a movie fan, but once I came to California, of course, that's what California's all about, the movie industry," Currie remembers.) Talent scouts would spot the aspiring actress in the acting workshop's stage productions and press her to make the rounds of the Hollywood studios, but Currie remained adamant about staying out of the limelight, at least temporarily.

Previous page: During her training at Max Reinhardt's Hollywood drama school, lovely Louise Currie could not have suspected that her eventual leading men would include superheroes, apes and voodoo men. (Photo from *The Masked Marvel.*)

"I said no because I felt I didn't know enough about it. I said, 'Well, if this is how it's done, I don't *want* to do it this way. If I'm going to be in pictures, I'd like to learn something *about* them first.' Several agents had asked me to sign with them, which I'd refused to do also—there again, I didn't want to start trying to get jobs if I didn't know my trade *[laughs]*! So I kept refusing until I graduated from Max Reinhardt's. At that point, I decided it was time to sign with an agent, and I went with Sue Carol. She was a very good agent and the wife of Alan Ladd, and she was developing Alan's career."

Currie's first movie (although not the first one to be released) was *The Pinto Kid* (1941), a Columbia B Western complete with post–Civil War cattle rustling, bank robberies, an attempted frame-up and wooden Western leading man Charles Starrett; *Variety* dubbed screen newcomer Currie "a neat looker." "At the end of that movie, the head of Columbia, Harry Cohn, offered me a contract. But my agent and I decided that, no, I wouldn't sign, it would maybe be more interesting to freelance. In those days, of course, the studios could build their people into stars; they had the wherewithal, the publicity and the money to do that. But we decided that I didn't want to be just a contract player at Columbia. So I went on to make about fifty movies, all freelance."

Another early role was a small but highly visible part as one of several debutantes in the song-filled mystery/comedy *You'll Find Out* (1940). Comic bandleader Kay Kyser and his motley College of Musical Knowledge were the stars of the film, and providing the menace were Hollywood's top three bogeymen, Boris Karloff, Bela Lugosi and Peter Lorre. "I appeared with Bela Lugosi three times; he was so different from the characters he played," says Currie. "He was quiet and unassuming off the screen, very studious and very sedate. Then the cameras would roll and he would be a *horrible* man *[laughs]*. Boris Karloff I remember, too, but not as specifically as Lugosi, because I played with Lugosi so much more. Karloff I'm kind of vague about; I remember talking with him, and it seemed to me that he was also quite intelligent. He was actually a very nice-looking man, too, so to find him always in such weird parts was unusual. And Peter Lorre was very small and very ... peculiar. Maybe his roles are more vivid in my mind than his actual personality, but my memory tells me he was a little weird in person."

While horror men Karloff, Lugosi and Lorre dished out their evil deeds on the set of *You'll Find Out,* a soundstage or two away, movie history was being made as 25-year-old Orson Welles gathered his Mercury Players together for their joint motion picture debut in the milestone production *Citizen Kane.* Currie and Alan Ladd were among the reporters discussing the life and times of the Hearst-like Kane (Welles) in the film's classic climax; Currie even gets to deliver the one line that perhaps best encapsulates the entire film ("If you could have found out what 'Rosebud' meant, I bet that would have explained everything").

"I remember being on that picture a long, long time, to do a sequence that seems so inconsequential," Currie says. "By the time they got through with it in the cutting room, there was not much left of the scene, but I think we were on that several months, which was amazing. It's quite a contrast to the work I *had* been doing, where I'd make a movie in ten days or something *[laughs]*. *Citizen Kane* went on and on and on and on, but it was a very educational, interesting experience. We watched Orson Welles work; his direction was remarkable, and quite unusual. He would get on the camera boom, way up, and decide how to angle his shots. He was a very demanding director; everything had to be done precisely his way. And he was not very patient unless you knew what you were doing *[laughs]*."

Of course, her minute role in *Citizen Kane* remains a footnote in Louise Currie's career; her enduring claim to fame remains *Adventures of Captain Marvel*, Republic Pictures' 12-chapter film version of the highly popular Fawcett Publications pulp hero and (according to many) the best serial ever made. "Serials were something that youngsters in those days would watch religiously, every Saturday; I remember my own son going every weekend to the movie theater in Westwood Village. That was something that all the neighborhood children did as a regular routine. When I was offered *Captain Marvel*, I thought it would be fun to try, just to see what it would be like. At that time, not being under contract, I just accepted whatever I felt might be interesting and worthwhile doing. And I ended up doing two serials, *Adventures of Captain Marvel* and *The Masked Marvel*."

The origins of Republic's Captain Marvel were markedly different from those of the comic book Marvel. In both, the caped superhero was the secret identity of Billy Batson, but in the comic book (*Whiz Comics* vol. 1, no. 2, February 1940), Batson was a newsboy who encountered the mystical wise man Shazam in a subway tunnel; invoking Shazam's name changed the wispy lad into the muscle-bound, bullet-proof Captain Marvel, champion of justice. A quintet of Republic screenwriters overhauled the comic book premise, depicting Batson (Frank Coghlan, Jr.) as a boyish radio newscaster accompanying the Malcolm Archaeological Expedition into a remote and volcanic section of Siam. There, the party discovers a secret underground tomb where Batson, exploring alone, encounters the wizened Shazam (Nigel de Brulier); the sage bestows upon Batson the ability to transform himself at will into the World's Mightiest Mortal (Tom Tyler).

Elsewhere, the remaining expedition members, accompanied by secretary Betty (Currie) and Batson's sidekick Whitey (Billy Benedict), have uncovered the tomb's greatest treasure, a large golden model of a scorpion holding in its claws five lenses. Directing sunlight through the lenses changes base metals into gold; realizing the incredible value of their find, the scientists divide the lenses and the scorpion model among themselves for safekeeping. But one of them takes on the second identity of the Scorpion, a hooded and robed supercriminal, and hatches a sinister plot to divest his former colleagues of their lenses. First in Siam, later in America, and finally once again in Siam, Batson/Captain Marvel battles the Scorpion and his henchmen, striving stoically to unmask the hooded fiend before the complete Golden Scorpion—and its destructive capabilities—are in his hands.

The plot of *Captain Marvel* was a perfect framework for action and suspense, and the Republic special effects and stunt teams operated at peak efficiency to cram the 12 episodes with unparalleled serial thrills. "The special effects men on *Captain Marvel* [Howard and Theodore Lydecker] were sensational; in fact, they were considered the best in the business at that time. They just did a fabulous job, especially with the flying dummy of Captain Marvel. I remember watching it in flight and being absolutely enthralled by the fact that they could do that. But the really interesting part was watching the stunt people work—they were brilliant. A stuntman named Dave Sharpe doubled for me—amazingly *[laughs]!* He was a smallish man but very, very versatile, and marvelous with his timing. Of course, I was there to watch them put on some of those big fight scenes we had in every chapter, but I didn't really like watching all that. I don't even like to watch fighting *today* on the screen. But they were remarkable, the way they could do it."

The hectic production pace of *Captain Marvel*—and of serials in general—presented no problem for Currie, who admits that she much preferred working that way. "Fortunately, I had enough training that I could do my scenes and not mess them up, not muff the lines. And I thought that was more stimulating and interesting than pictures like *Citizen Kane,* where you just sat on a set for endless hours, doing nothing—which to me was just a trial and a bore. So I sort of enjoyed the activity, and the fact that you could do something quickly and do it well, and have it finished—in fact, I rather liked that. (But I'm sure that most of the people that started with big A productions would never have understood that, or been able to cope with it!)

"*Captain Marvel* even had two directors [William Witney and John English], which was done, I'm sure, to save on time and budget," she continues. "The one who was not directing on a particular day could be studying what they were going to do next, or he could be off shooting on another location. I think that helped them to facilitate the thing and to make it all run faster. They were young and spirited and eager to do a good job. I believe I remember seeing the whole script at once at one point, but they were very innovative in those days and they would constantly change things *[laughs]*. You might *think* you were going to do one thing on a certain day, but they'd have you do sixteen others. So you had to be very fast and willing and ready just to go with whatever they happened to dream up."

At the conclusion of Chapter 1, the expedition members are fleeing in their cars from an angry horde of mounted natives, one of whom has mined a high chasm-spanning bridge with dynamite. The charge is detonated as the car containing Betty and Whitey is crossing the bridge, and the vehicle hurtles down into the river far below (an outstanding Lydecker miniature). Being expected to climb inside a submerged vehicle took Currie by complete, and not pleasant, surprise. "The station wagon was in the water, and I was supposed to get inside so that Captain Marvel could drag me out, rescue me. And I said to them, 'Uhn-uh. I'm not going down in that cold water, underneath a car, and wonder when I'm going to get out!' Well, that caused a little bit of discussion, but I stuck to my guns and refused to do it. It was beyond my capabilities—I studied acting, not stuntwork. So they acquiesced, and found some women's clothes for Dave Sharpe to get into. Dave ended up doing that stunt for me; once Captain Marvel carried Dave to shore, they went to a closeup of me reviving. So I was spared from doing that stunt by Dave Sharpe."

Currie's anecdote has an interesting and revealing postscript. "Years later, at a dinner party, I ran into one of the directors of *Captain Marvel*—I can't remember if it was Jack English or Bill Witney. I asked him, 'You can tell me now: How did you feel when I refused to do that stunt?' And he said, 'Well, we didn't like it, but you were absolutely in the right when you refused to do it.' *[Laughs.]* Everything was so fast and furious, you took enough chances doing a serial without doing things that were just plain dangerous like that. And the way I kept getting knocked out throughout [the serial], every time Billy Batson is about to say 'Shazam!' and change into Captain Marvel. I don't know how they thought of so many ways of destroying me. I was always getting knocked out, boards falling from the ceiling onto my head and everything—I look back at it and wonder how I did it. But at the time, you don't even realize it. That was the fun thing about doing those, the fast action—you never got bored."

Although generally regarded today as a Poverty Row studio, Republic, according to Currie, was a fun and exciting place to work. "Republic really had a lot going at that time. They were very active and had plenty of good people working there. They really were inventive, and kept doing different types of pictures: They would do extravaganzas with Vera Ralston, the ice skating star; the serials; lots of John Wayne Westerns—everything you could think of. They were always very busy and they did a good job at what they did."

Part of the fun was working alongside her youthful *Captain Marvel* costars, Frank Coghlan (Billy Batson) and Billy Benedict (Whitey). "They couldn't have been more pleasant," she states emphatically. "I still talk to them from time to time; in fact, Frank just sent me a tape of [American Movie Classics'] *The Republic Pictures Story* because I was out of town when it was shown and I couldn't record it. He really is a nice man. He and Billy were very, very cooperative and wonderful to work with. They both knew their trade and knew what they were doing, and it made working under those conditions a lot easier."

Tom Tyler, a cowboy star in a raft of B Westerns (and a supporting player in bigger productions like *Stagecoach* and *Gone with the Wind*) was ideally cast as Captain Marvel. The husky Tyler made for a unique superhero, one who combated criminals with a steely determination and showed no quarter to his defeated enemies; the serial's most notorious scene depicts Captain Marvel machine-gunning a pair of renegade natives in the back. Recalling the actor, Currie says, "Tom Tyler was very quiet and sort of reserved. Whereas Billy Benedict and Frank Coghlan were young and fun and full of enthusiasm, it seemed to me that Tom Tyler was very retiring. I don't remember talking or being with him that much, but working with him, he was very nice and very cooperative."

Currie wasn't able to see *Captain Marvel* when it was originally released for the simple reason that she was too regularly employed. "Funnily enough, I never saw any of my films; it just so happened that I worked rather constantly and rapidly. I think the one and only film that I spent any real amount of time on was *Citizen Kane*—where I had so little to do *[laughs]!* But the rest of 'em were just the opposite. So therefore, I was always working, and I really never saw them. But many years later, fans have found me and, little by little, they've sent me my films, and now I have a collection of about thirty—almost all of them I'm seeing for the first time because of all these nice fans! I would never have seen them if it weren't for all these young people."

Adventures of Captain Marvel is one that she's been able to see again in recent years, and "I really enjoy it. I think it really holds your attention, and that the cliffhanger endings are still exciting. Each chapter has a great deal of tension at the end, and I don't know how they were able to think up so many ways to be that suspenseful." Asked to rate her own performance in it, her enthusiasm wanes a bit. "Well, there was really very little performance—I was just there, being acted *upon*! There really was no acting on my part, and I don't feel that I was able to portray anything."

Her fans would, of course, disagree vehemently, and apparently so did her bosses: Two years later, she was once again selected to star in a Republic chapterplay starring a different Marvel—Tom Steele as *The Masked Marvel*. A big-city crimefighter who kept his identity a closely guarded secret, the Marvel squared off again Mura Sakima (Johnny Arthur), a Japanese spy/saboteur, in this wartime-era serial, which found Currie cast as Alice Hamilton, daughter of an insurance company executive murdered by Sakima's men. The role allowed Currie more screen time and a greater share of the action, a new arrangement she greatly preferred. "As far as my character was concerned, *Captain Marvel* was just running and screaming—or getting knocked out and being unconscious. I was more myself in *The Masked Marvel*. I had a part that was a little more normal."

Another unique serial, *The Masked Marvel* kept secret the true identity of its *hero* rather than that of its villain: Until the conclusion of Chapter 12, audiences did not know which of four young insurance investigators (Rod Bacon, Richard Clarke, David Bacon, Bill Healy) would turn out to be the

ADVENTURES OF CAPTAIN MARVEL
A REPUBLIC SERIAL

Chapter 7 HUMAN TARGETS

Marvel (actually played throughout by stuntman Steele). The cast was equally in the dark. "Funnily enough, they kept the ending so secret that, while we were shooting it, none of us knew who was going to be the Masked Marvel. They wanted it to be such a secret, such a surprise — apparently even for us. The four investigators were played by a group of very interesting young men who were all starting their careers. All of them were very attractive and talented and nice. Johnny Arthur? Well *[laughs]*, he was very ominous, wasn't he? But I'm sure the Japanese probably wouldn't have thought too much of his portrayal! And Tom Steele, just like Dave Sharpe, was really very nice, very intelligent, very capable — I can't say enough good things about both of those fellows."

Talking about the directors of her B films and serials, Currie sounds almost like a spokeswoman for the low-budget film industry. "All those young directors were very good; just like the actors, they had to know what they were doing and do it quickly and not make mistakes and not hem and haw. I think some of the big A directors ended up being regarded as good because they took four thousand shots of everything; out of that number of shots, you'd have to find *some*thing that they could piece together to make it look good."

Well directed or not, most of Currie's other films of that period lack the staying power of *Captain Marvel* and *The Masked Marvel*; titles like *Billy the Kid's Gun Justice*, *The Bashful Bachelor* and *Stardust on the Sage* have long since dropped down the memory hole. Two exceptions to that rule are the pair of horror films in which she costarred with cult horror star Bela Lugosi, *The Ape Man* and *Voodoo Man*.

"Bela Lugosi seemed to enjoy doing that kind of work, or I don't know whether he'd have done it; I think he was a fine actor. But once you start playing those kinds of roles, I suppose you're kind of stuck with it. Also, he did definitely have a heavy accent, but the kinds of parts he played, he didn't need to speak perfect English. (Sometimes he didn't need to speak!) But he was an interesting man and certainly did a brilliant job on *The Ape Man*. He took it so seriously, he really wanted it to be believable, and I think it definitely was. His wife was around, too, and she was a very lovely, educated lady. It all seemed so strange, that they had such a wonderful marriage and nice home life, and here he was portraying mad scientists and voodoo men and apes!"

A real Golden Turkey contender, Monogram's *The Ape Man* starred Lugosi as Dr. James Brewster, a famous gland expert whose rash decision to inject himself with an ape's spinal fluid has devastating consequences: Brewster is covered with hair, walks like an ape, and occasionally has the beast's killer instincts. Devout Lugosi fans hold the film in contempt; for the more open-minded, it is a camp classic of the highest order.

Opposite: Doing what a superhero does best, Captain Marvel (Tom Tyler) rescues his swooning leading lady (Currie).

One of the bad guys (George Suzanne) gets the drop on Currie (in black wig disguise) in the wartime serial *The Masked Marvel*.

Currie, who costars as a newspaper photographer caught up in the mystery, made an unfortunate decision in taking her young son to see the finished film. "After *The Ape Man* was finished, I did go to see a preview and I took my son with me—and he told me in later years that it scared him so much. He was six or seven when he saw *The Ape Man* and he had dreams for many years of the ape capturing his mother. Of course, I couldn't imagine that he'd have that kind of reaction—I was right there *with* him as he was watching it, so obviously the ape didn't 'get' me. But he vividly remembered the ape chasing his mother, and it left him with terrible dreams that had him waking up screaming for years."

Currie had a much smaller part in Lugosi's last Monogram film *Voodoo Man*, the story of a mad doctor (Lugosi) and his associates (John Carradine and George Zucco) resorting to black magic to restore life to Lugosi's dead wife. Currie, placed in a spell early on by the loony Lugosi, had little chance to contribute to the picture. "What I remember about *Voodoo Man* was walking around out in the woods with my eyes wide open, wandering around in a trance. And poor John Carradine—he played a halfwit in it. (And may I say he played it very *well*—playing a halfwit is not the easiest thing to do when you're a good actor.)"

Bela Lugosi stooped—literally *and* figuratively—to play the title role in Monogram's *The Ape Man*, with Louise Currie.

If Louise Currie had had the chance to pick her own roles, she admits horror films and cheap Westerns would not have been high on her personal list. "No *[laughs]*, that wouldn't have been what I'd have had in mind at all! I did a film with Kent Taylor that was called *Second Chance* [1947], and I enjoyed that very much—I was a lady thief, and the picture had a to-catch-a-thief kind of theme. That I enjoyed tremendously, and that would be more or less the type of role that I would enjoy. Then I did one called *The Crimson Key* [1947] and another called *Backlash* [1947], and in those last two I played heavies. Instead of just the sweet young thing, I kind of liked playing more meaty parts, and all of those three pictures I just named I enjoyed very much—they were more my type."

Within a few more years, however, Louise Currie made the decision to leave the picture business once and for all. "I had married; my husband [John Good] had been on the stage and in some very good films at Metro and Fox. But when we decided to be married, we agreed it was not an easy industry to be in if you wanted to have a happy marriage and to raise children. So we decided we would start what we called our second career. I was a decorator (I had been doing it on the side, just for fun, for my friends), and my husband was an architectural designer. So we decided we would go into business at that—which we did—and we made a pact that we would not go back to films. And, funnily enough, of course the minute you decide something like that, then you get a fabulous offer *[laughs]*! Each of us got a *very* tempting offer, and we both turned it down. And from that day on, my husband remodeled houses and architecturally made changes, I decorated them, and we'd put them on the market and sell. We've had a long career of decorating and architecture. That's been our life since then."

She has been long retired from the picture industry, but Currie seldom goes for long without hearing from fans who have never forgotten her Westerns, her horror films, her serials—and the spunky, bright-eyed leading lady that graced them. Of course, it is almost always *Adventures of Captain Marvel* that heads her fans' lists of their favorite Louise Currie films. "Apparently, people have decided that *Captain Marvel* is one of the best serials that was ever made. I'm very, very surprised, and needless to say I'm delighted, that out of all the countless serials that were made, not one but *both* of mine have happened to come out on video. (That's also made it awfully easy for me to give gifts *[laughs]*!)

"I'm just so happy that people are still enthused, that they still like what they see; after all these many years, you would think that maybe they would have another trend, a desire to see something different. But there has been, all through the years, a definite following for many of the films that I was in, and they've never given it up. And a lot of fans have kept up with *me*. Believe me when I tell you that's one of the most flattering things that can happen to an actress."

LOUISE CURRIE FILMOGRAPHY

Billy the Kid Outlawed (PRC, 1940)
Billy the Kid's Gun Justice (PRC, 1940)
The Green Hornet Strikes Again (Universal serial, 1940)
You'll Find Out (RKO, 1940)
Citizen Kane (RKO, 1941)
Dude Cowboy (RKO, 1941)
Orchids to Charlie (Elizabeth Arden-Fine Arts Studios featurette, 1941)
The Pinto Kid (Columbia, 1941)
The Reluctant Dragon (RKO, 1941)
Look Who's Laughing (RKO, 1941)

Louise Currie

Adventures of Captain Marvel (Return of Captain Marvel) (Republic serial, 1941)
Hello, Sucker (Universal, 1941)
Tillie the Toiler (Columbia, 1941)
Double Trouble (Monogram, 1941)
Bedtime Story (Columbia, 1941)
Call Out the Marines (RKO, 1942)
The Bashful Bachelor (RKO, 1942)
Stardust on the Sage (Republic, 1942)
Tireman, Spare My Tires (Columbia short, 1942)
Around the World (RKO, 1943)
The Masked Marvel (Republic serial, 1943)
A Blitz on the Fritz (Columbia short, 1943)
His Wedding Scare (Columbia short, 1943)
The Ape Man (Monogram, 1943)
Forty Thieves (United Artists, 1944)
Million Dollar Kid (Monogram, 1944)
Voodoo Man (Monogram, 1944)
Christmas Holiday (Universal, 1944)
Practically Yours (Paramount, 1944)
Sensations of 1945 (United Artists, 1944)
Love Letters (Paramount, 1945)
Wild West (Prairie Outlaws) (PRC, 1946)
Gun Town (Universal, 1946)
The Bachelor's Daughters (United Artists, 1946)
Three on a Ticket (PRC, 1947)
The Chinese Ring (Monogram, 1947)
Backlash (20th Century-Fox, 1947)
Second Chance (20th Century-Fox, 1947)
The Crimson Key (20th Century-Fox, 1947)
This Is Nylon (Nylon/Apex Film Corp., 1948)
And Baby Makes Three (Columbia, 1949)
Queen for a Day (United Artists, 1951)

When I was about to go into each of these science fiction pictures, my reaction was, "Jeez, nobody's going to believe this"—when I'd read the scripts, I had to shake my head. But there is a certain type of fan that loves this stuff. Including myself, in a way—I always enjoy watching them. It's all imagination, and that's what's great about 'em.

Richard Denning

BOUNCE THE NAME RICHARD DENNING off the average movie fan and you'll get one of a half-dozen different reactions. Many will remember him best as the strapping, athletic lead in Technicolor fluff like *Beyond the Blue Horizon* (1942) with sarong queen Dorothy Lamour. Others will recall his B-grade detective or Western films, or maybe his early television series like *Mr. and Mrs. North* and *Michael Shayne;* baby boomers might think of him first as the governor throughout 12 seasons of *Hawaii Five-O.*

But science fiction fans have a different perspective, and to us Richard Denning was perhaps *the* most decorated soldier in the 1950s war against the armies of *Its* and *Thems* that rose from the depths of the oceans or the bowels of the Earth. Whether taking on the *Creature from the Black Lagoon* or the one *With the Atom Brain*, *The Black Scorpion*, robots who made their *Target Earth* or a three-eyed mutant on the *Day the World Ended*, Richard Denning fought the good fight, sometimes single-handedly, and has survived to bring back the inside story on a lifetime of movie heroics.

Born in Poughkeepsie, New York, in 1914, Louis Albert Denninger, Jr., was the son of a garment manufacturer who relocated and set up shop in Los Angeles when Louis was 18 months old. After finishing school, Denninger enrolled at Woodbury Business College and majored in foreign trade and accounting, graduating with a master's in business administration.

"Dad wanted me to take over the business, and I thought, 'Well, why not?'—I had nothing else. But I never liked accounting, never liked the confinement of being stuck at a desk. So I started joining high school/night school little theater groups, just as a hobby. At this point I was on the road as a salesman for my dad, driving around, calling on customers, but sometimes I'd go up into the Hollywood Hills and sit in the car and work on my script for the play that night. That was my avocation."

As a whim, Denninger decided to compete in a radio contest called *Do You Want to Be an Actor?*, sure that nothing would come of it. Auditioning along with "about four hundred other young people," he read a scene from the Paramount film *The Lives of a Bengal Lancer* (1935), playing the Franchot Tone part. "The contest ran for 13 weeks, and they had a different group of people each week. And I won my week. So the 13 of us won the prize, which was a screen test at Warner Brothers. This was in the spring of '36. I went to Warner Brothers—got there at nine in the morning, went through wardrobe fitting, makeup, shot the test, and I was through by noon. All 13 of us did it—the same morning, on the same set, with the same lighting, the same everything. And we each did a different scene—you figure *that* one out. I never saw the test—naturally—because I doubt if there was ever any film in the

Previous page: An unruffled Richard Denning, showing none of the scars of battles with *The Black Scorpion*, the *Creature from the Black Lagoon* or (pictured) the *Creature with the Atom Brain.*

camera *[laughs]!* I kept asking my agent, 'Why can't I see the test?' and he said, 'It's all confidential, it's top secret.' Well, finally I got a report from him, and he said, 'Warner Brothers said that you're too much like one of their new contract players, and there'd be a conflict.' I asked, 'Who?' and he said, 'They've got this kid Errol Flynn over there.' I didn't know who Errol Flynn was, but he was under contract to Warners and that took care of that."

By now, however, Denninger had what actors refer to as "the fever," not to mention an agent who began knocking on doors on his new client's behalf. "My agent had an interview for me to go to Hal Roach Studios, where they were going to do a picture with Carole Landis called *One Million B.C.* I was to costar in it with her. I had no experience, I had never even been in a picture except my quote-unquote screen test, and they offered to sign me and I was to go right into *One Million B.C.* And I was to get $75 a week for starring in this thing. I was elated. But my agent said, 'No, I don't want you to do it.' I said, *'What?!'* I was making $25 a week at the time, working for my dad in the garment business, as a salesman and what-have-you. But the agent said, 'You're not ready for this'—which was very true. Vic Mature finally did the picture, with Carole Landis, about four years later."

Thinking ahead, Denninger's agent convinced the fledgling actor that the best course of action would be to sign with a studio. "At that time, the studios had the talent pools—they'd sign all these young people and put them through training classes and coaching. So in 1936 I finally signed a contract with Paramount.

"When I first signed at Paramount my name was still Louis Albert Denninger, Jr., and Ted Lesser, who was the head of the talent department, said, 'The first thing you gotta do is change that name.' This was during the time when John Dillinger, the gangster/killer, was popular, and Ted thought Denninger was too close to Dillinger. So we started working with numerology and everything else, trying to come up with something. I asked all my friends, 'What do you think is a good name for me?' *[Laughs.]* It ended up where Ted said, 'Well, you're *definitely* a Richard. And since Denninger is too long, we'll drop the *er*, so you're Richard Denning.' So from that day I became Richard Denning."

Home to such screen greats as Gary Cooper, W.C. Fields, Mae West, John Barrymore and others, the imposing Paramount lot on Melrose Avenue in Los Angeles became a second home to Denning, who, over the course of the next five years, appeared in almost 50 pictures there—from bits to second leads, from fluff like *College Swing* and *Seventeen* to "prestige" pictures like DeMille's *Union Pacific* and *North West Mounted Police*. Half a century after the fact, Denning concedes, "I always had a little guilt complex because I never took on Dad's business. Dad lost interest in the business when there was no point in holding on to it. He finally sold out to one of his competitors and that was that."

Toiling on the Paramount soundstages, Denning helped to support his father as well as his younger brother throughout the early days of his acting career, even though he knew his seven-year Paramount contract was not necessarily worth the paper it was written on. "Yeah, it was a seven-year contract, but that's a laugh because it's only good if Paramount wants to *use* you for seven years. They had three-month options and six-month options, and they could drop you at any time. Every time an option would come up and you were supposed to get one of their fancy raises, they'd say, 'Well, we couldn't use you that much this past term and we've been talking about having to drop you....' Of course, by this time you're panicky because you don't want to be out of a job. Then they'd say, 'Tell you what: If you're willing to work for the same money, then, okay, we'll give you another six months.' So you'd go on for maybe four years for the same money. Many of my peers thought they were going to get $800 a week or something like that, and they never got it. I remember one fellow who was signed about the same time I was — my gosh, he rented Lew Ayres' house up on the top of a hill, he threw big press parties and everything else *[laughs]*. I couldn't figure out how he could afford this, because he wasn't getting any more parts than I was. He told me *[belligerently]*, 'You gotta do this! You gotta spend it to make it!' Well, his option came up and they not only didn't take him at the same salary, they dropped him completely, and he was out of a job and that was the end of his career right then.

"I learned from my business background that you gotta save it when you're making it, 'cause when you're not making it, hopefully you'll have enough to carry you over until the next time. You don't spend it up to the hilt. I've been accused, every once in a while, like Jack Benny, of being a pennypincher, but I'm able to have a home here [in California] and to live on Hawaii, and I don't have to work. The thrift and the saving paid off and, God willing, I know that I'll never be a burden on my family. I have always been independent enough that I don't want to have to be dependent on somebody else. And now *[pointing to his wife]* I've even married a wealthy woman *[laughs]!*"

Pat Denning laughs good-naturedly at this jibe, sitting in as Denning is interviewed for the first time since the days of television shows like *Michael Shayne*. Movie fans with their elephant memories know of course that Denning's first wife was Evelyn Ankers, queen of horror films during their 1940s heyday at Universal Studios. One of filmland's most enduring unions, Richard and Evelyn married in spite of initial disapproval on the part of Ankers' mother.

"Evie's mother never wanted Evie to get married, because Evie was her meal ticket. When I met Evie she was going with Glenn Ford, and supposedly engaged to him. (Incidentally, Glenn and I belonged to the Bachelors' Club, along with Bob Stack and everybody *else* that got married later!) Glenn was somewhere in Canada telling another girlfriend that the wedding was off and that he was going to marry Evie. In the meantime, Evie's mother figured, 'This is getting too serious with Glenn,' and she started building *me* up. She talked to Danny Linden, my press agent, and he said, 'I'll get 'em together.' So one night he brought Mrs. Ankers and Evie over to the Sunset Bowling Alley, where I was competing in a tournament. They're sitting up in the grandstands watching us bowl, and Danny came down and said, 'Dick, I've got Evelyn Ankers here and she's been dying to meet you for years.' I said, 'Great!' but I was more concerned about the tournament right then. And of course Danny had told Evie, 'This Richard Denning is anxious to meet *you!*' So Evie's sitting up there watching me, and I'm ignoring her completely because I'm bowling. *I'm* thinking, 'If she's that anxious to meet me, she'll keep.' And *she's* up there thinking, 'Who does he think he is?' But she did stay, after much persuasion from Danny.

"My best friend Bob Tappan, who was an agent, was there with me that night, and Bob and I had previously arranged to have a game after the tournament — like eleven o'clock or something — and now I *am* starting to get concerned about this dame that I still haven't met. Danny says, 'Why don't you at least go on up and apologize? Or ask her to bowl or something?' I go up there, and she's dressed for dinner — really gorgeous. I said, 'Gee, how 'bout bowling with Bob and me after the tournament is over?' She's got on this big picture hat and this tight black silk dress, high heel shoes — and she said, 'I'd love it!' So she stayed on, son of a gun, she kicked off her high heel shoes, picked up the ball — and ripped her dress, right up the side. And I thought, 'What a good sport!'

"Now, her mother is very conscious of trying to break Evie and Glenn up, so she says *[in a very British accent],* 'Why don't you and Bob come up to the house, and we'll have a cup of tea?' They lived in a rented house in Beverly Hills. So we went up, and Evie and I clicked just like *that.* And about three o'clock in the morning Bob Tappan — who's been stuck with Evie's mother *[laughs]* — passes a note to me and it says, 'Get me the hell out of here, I've got to go to work!'"

Denning and Ankers began going out together, quickly became what the Hollywood columnists like to call "an item," and in September 1942, while Denning was in the midst of shooting *Quiet Please, Murder* at Fox, the pair tied the knot in an impromptu Las Vegas elopement. Part of what had attracted Denning to Ankers was the fact that she didn't like the picture business — "That was a *big* plus," Denning admits.

"Her mother pushed her into it as a girl. Evie never really liked it, but her mother was dependent on her. Her dad had left 'em when Evie was a little kid, so her mother had to raise her. Then when Evie started getting into the picture business, this was a good deal so Mama kept really promoting her heavy. But Evie couldn't stand the discipline of the picture business. She used to drive her agents right up the wall, because they'd set up an interview for her with some producer at ten o'clock, and about five minutes to ten she would say, 'Well, I guess I'd better get ready.' And she's supposed to be there in five minutes. So then it was a mad panic, and she'd dash out and get there late, and the agent and the producer would be fuming. She was a good actress, though, and if she'd liked the business, she could have gone a long way."

Sour on the Hollywood rat race in general, Ankers was even more turned off by the many horror films foisted upon her by the powers-that-be at her home studio, Universal. "Evie always wanted to do drama and, no, she *didn't* really like the horror films. But she did 'em. Evie, like all of us in the business, wanted to work, and even though you got the part that you didn't want, at least it's work." Occasionally a horror film like the Sherlock Holmes thriller *The Pearl of Death* would offer Ankers a good acting opportunity, but more often than not she found herself in minor items like *Captive Wild Woman*, *Jungle Woman* and *The Frozen Ghost*, occasionally in the company of one of her least favorite actors, Universal's "master character creator," Lon Chaney, Jr. He returned her sentiments.

"Evidently Universal gave Evie Chaney's old dressing room, and that got him shook up—he didn't like her, either. One day, writers from some of the major magazines were invited to a dinner party at Universal, where they would meet all the top Universal horror stars. Lon Chaney, who's all done up in this weird green makeup, ends up sitting next to me. I was in the service by then and I was in my uniform, my dress blues, and of course I'm kind of envious that they're all working in the picture business and I'm winning the war. And Chaney started making cracks. This was before I got into submarines, and he said, 'I see you're in uniform but you're stationed in downtown L.A.' So we started bickering back and forth.

"Now he starts pushing me. I say, 'Oh, you want to play!' I pick up my sundae and I say, 'Let's have some fun!' And I shove the sundae right in his face *[laughs]*. So Chaney reaches for his hot coffee and he shouts, 'Yeah, *let's!*' But before he can throw it, everybody's up there separating us. Afterwards I was supposed to go on the set of whatever picture it was they were making, and I didn't want to get into anything with Chaney because he was a big guy and he loved to find any excuse to get into a fight. So I just stayed on my side of the stage and he sat on the other side, and we got through the afternoon all right."

Returning to the picture business after four years in the service, Denning found it difficult to jump-start his career after the long absence. "Man, I couldn't get a job for eighteen months!" he exclaims. "By that time we'd used up all our savings, because the whole time I was in the navy I never made any money. We had to start all over again. We were in a house trailer at Paradise Cove—I have always loved the water and boats and everything else, so I set up a hundred lobster traps. I had this rowboat—I couldn't afford an outboard!— and I would row the traps out, set them in the evening and then go out and collect 'em at daybreak. We lived on lobster, and sold lobster, and were very happy. (Evie and I often would look back, years later, and realize that was the happiest time we had.) Finally, after eighteen months of unemployment, I was hired for a radio show, *My Favorite Husband,* with Lucille Ball. So I let somebody else take over the lobster business, and suddenly there were no more lobsters and the business just collapsed."

The radio situation comedy *My Favorite Husband* lasted three seasons before making the switch to television—and to a new title, *I Love Lucy.* Desi Arnaz, Lucy's real-life husband, stepped into the Denning role, but by then Denning was back on his feet career-wise, starring in B movies and also keeping busy in television.

As Denning's career picked up momentum once again, Evelyn Ankers dropped from the business—a career move partially prompted by an ugly confrontation with B movie mogul Sam Katzman, legendarily the cheapest man in Hollywood. "Oh, I tell you," Denning says, rolling his eyes, "he was Evie's demise in pictures. He produced *Last of the Redmen* [1947], which was one of Evie's last pictures, and they were on location on a hot, miserable, dusty day—they'd gotten up at four o'clock in the morning to drive up to the location. She's in a long dress, a long wig (it was a period picture), it was sweaty and miserable and everything was going wrong. And behind schedule. That would really get to Katzman—if you were five *minutes* behind schedule, you were in trouble. Everybody was tired and hungry, and of course all they had was little box lunches then. And Sam and his wife and his nephew Lennie, they're all sitting around having big ice cream sundaes. Just the Katzmans. And everybody else was watching 'em with their tongues hanging out!

"Well, they got through shooting that day, and Evie's hair was a mess. Katzman said, 'That's a wrap. Be here at daybreak in the morning.' Evie said, 'Well, what about my hair?'—she wanted to get it washed and cleaned up. Katzman said, 'Wash it!' Evie said, '*What?* You mean I gotta go home now and wash my hair and set it and everything?' And Katzman said, 'Well, you can't do it here!' And that's when Evie lost her temper—she really let him have it. She called him every name under the sun—'You cheap, tight bastard! Sitting, eating ice cream in front of all of us, never thinking to bring us anything,' on and on. And I guess the word got around that Evie was difficult after that point...."

In 1948, Denning took the science fiction plunge, into the sky-blue waters that lapped at the beaches of Film Classics' *Unknown Island.* A dinosaur movie shot in garish Cinecolor, it starred Denning, Virginia Grey, Philip Reed and Barton MacLane as adventurers who discover a lost world–type land of prehistoric beasts on an uncharted Pacific atoll. "I admired Virginia Grey very much—she was a lovely girl. Barton MacLane, Philip Reed, we all had fun." Animation buffs have given *Unknown Island* a bum rap because the film employs men in dinosaur suits rather than costly stop motion, but Denning says that "the special effects on *Unknown Island* fascinated me—split screens and black screens and all. The scenes of the men in the dinosaur suits were shot by a second unit, before we started our shooting, and the first time I saw that footage was on the process screens, as Virginia Grey and I reacted to it all. I'd pick up some of these science fiction scripts and I'd think to myself, 'This could be good if the special effects are done right.' Boy, that is the key, to have good special effects like *Unknown Island* did, or *The Black Scorpion*. For those days, I felt that they had excellent effects, and I think the men who do that sort of thing are really marvelous. In my next life I'll probably come back as a special effects man."

It was in the mid-fifties that Denning cemented his science fiction reputation, costarring with Richard Carlson in Universal-International's *Creature from the Black Lagoon*. A modestly budgeted followup to the studio's earlier *It Came from Outer Space*, *Creature* was simply meant to capitalize on the then-hot 3-D and science fiction vogues, but the picture struck a chord with monster movie fans, and the Gill Man quickly took its place alongside Frankenstein's Monster, the Mummy and other bogeymen in the pantheon of classic Universal monsters. "I was impressed with that Creature suit, first while we were filming it, and then especially when I saw the picture. It was a great suit and the man inside was good—*really* good. *Creature from the Black Lagoon* was fun. I remember on the back lot at Universal, it was like October [1953] and it was freezing cold, and we were shooting at night on the Black Lagoon set. We were out in the water and we were tired and it was late, and the prop man kept bringing us brandy to keep us from freezing to death. It worked great, and we were going just fine. And then we finally wrap it up and we go to the dressing rooms—they're nice and warm. All of a sudden *[slurring his words]* that brandy just hit like a sledgehammer! But out in the cold and the wet and wind, it didn't bother us at all!"

Adding to Denning's enjoyment of the movie was the rare opportunity to play an unsympathetic role: the expedition leader who puts the capture of the Creature above the safety of his fellow adventurers. "It was good to get to change. My wife, Pat, when she sees me in something like that, says, 'Oh, *you're* not that way. I don't know why you played that.' But I enjoyed that role in *Creature*." Still happy with his performance and impressed with the film itself, Denning dismisses the 3-D process in which it was shot. "That was a fad, and I never thought it would last. But I still think probably someday it'll be natural—you'll be able to look at 3-D movies without the glasses. They'll get it, mark my words."

Constantly busy throughout the fifties, Denning's recollection of some of his lesser pictures is hazy; *Target Earth* and *Creature with the Atom Brain* are victims of the memory hole. Pressed about *Target Earth*, a Herman Cohen production about alien robots taking over an evacuated city, Denning offers, "To get the scenes of the empty streets, we had to get out there at four in the

Dick Wessel, Barton MacLane, Philip Reed, Virginia Grey and Denning watch with horror in Film Classics' Cinecolor *Unknown Island*.

morning — in those days, there wasn't that much traffic downtown. And we'd start shooting as soon as it got daylight, before the cars started coming through." And the robots (actually only *one* robot, and made to seem like more through the miracle of film editing): "I think for those days it was good. I remember I did marvel at it — it looked phony when you were right up close, but then when you'd see it on the screen, it looked pretty good."

Creature with the Atom Brain has disappeared from Denning's memory almost completely, except for the fact that he found the makeup unconvincing (the film's legion of zombies had sutured scalps) and that director Edward L. Cahn put speed above all other considerations. "On pictures like that you really didn't even *have* a director. Those directors are just there to see that the stuff gets done — a ringmaster. They kept things glued together, and [gave] very little direction." *Atom Brain* was written by Curt Siodmak, a name Denning remembers from the Universal forties fright films that starred (as often as not) Evelyn Ankers. "That sci-fi stuff was his knack, and he was good at that. I remember when I was about to go into each of these science fiction pictures, my reaction was, 'Jeez, nobody's going to believe this' — when I'd read the scripts, I had to shake my head. But there *is* a certain type of fan that loves this stuff. Including myself, in a way — I always enjoy watching them. It's all

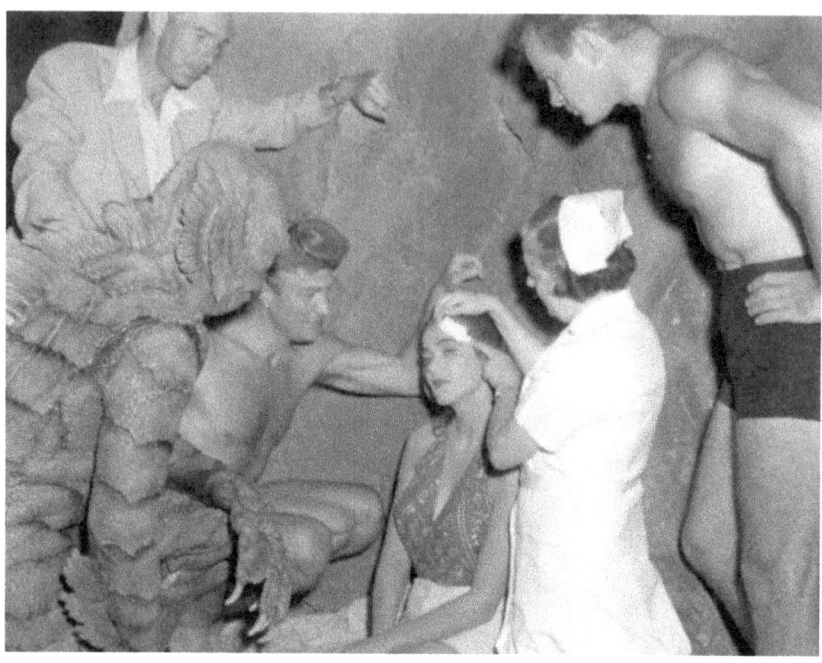

Being treated for an on-set head injury during the filming of *Creature from the Black Lagoon,* Julie Adams gets moral support from director Jack Arnold, Gill Man Ben Chapman, Denning and Richard Carlson. (Photofest)

imagination, and that's what's great about 'em. It takes a great imagination to dream that stuff up."

Another director that Denning classifies alongside Edward Cahn was Roger Corman, who starred Denning in the end-of-the-world thriller *Day the World Ended*. "Oh, he'd tell you nothing except, 'Just *do* it,'" Denning scoffs. "All he was concerned about was, 'I've got X number of pages to do today.' That was it, boom. And no matter what happened in front of the camera, it was fine — *'Print! Print!'* But the picture itself was damn good, because it was way ahead of its time."

A man more to Denning's liking was the producer of *Day the World Ended,* veteran B moviemaker and film historian Alex Gordon. "I loved Alex Gordon. Alex was probably one of the sweetest, most congenial producers that I've ever worked for, and he certainly was the greatest fan anybody could want. He knew more than you could imagine, and I just marveled at his recall and his precision. Talking about older pictures, he knew who the assistant director was, who the cameraman was, this, that and the other thing. But always very sweet and pleasant, very quiet, friendly. He must have liked Evie and me because he's been a great and constant fan and friend. I also did a film in

England for his brother Richard—*Assignment Redhead* [1962]. He was very nice, too, but Alex—I think he's the tops." Denning also enjoyed working with Corman regular Mike Connors, the baddie in Denning's *Day the World Ended* and *The Oklahoma Woman* (1956). "Mike I loved, too, we were great friends. He's a very sweet guy, and I wish we could get together more often. We did quite a few things together; I remember coming home one night from *Oklahoma Woman* and I told Evie, 'This new kid Mike Connors—I think he's really gonna make it.' Then when he did [television's] *Tightrope!* and *Mannix*, I was so glad for him. He comes to Maui every once in a while, and we get together and commiserate *[laughs]!*"

Still at AIP, Denning also appeared in Alex Gordon's *Girls in Prison* (1956) and Corman's made-in-Hawaii *Naked Paradise* (1957)—an experience that helped Denning decide to make the move to Maui upon his retirement in the sixties. By the mid-fifties, of course, Denning was well used to lightning-fast production schedules, whether they be in television (*Mr. and Mrs. North*, *Michael Shayne*, *The Flying Doctor*), the Sam Katzman B unit or at AIP. "There again, my business education: I could look at it from the producer's point of view, and knew it was costing him money. After I finished *Mr. and Mrs. North*—three shows a week, two days a show—that's when I did *An Affair to Remember* [1957], with Cary Grant and Deborah Kerr. We'd sit on the set, Cary and everybody, sitting around, rehearsing. And Cary'd say *[Denning claps his hands together]*, 'Well, I think that's enough for today,' and everybody would go home. My thought was, 'How can they *do* this? This is costing money!' In the time I spent on *An Affair to Remember*, I could have shot six feature films—and I'm only in the last half of the thing!"

Monster exterminating was a full-time job for movie heroes in the fifties, and Denning was pressed into service once again when *The Black Scorpion* menaced Mexico City in the 1957 Warner Bros. release. "Before I went down to Mexico for that picture, Evie and I had started building a new house in the Hollywood Hills. I could use the money they were going to pay me for *Black Scorpion* because I wanted to put it into the house. So I asked Evie, 'Can you handle things while I'm doing the picture?' and she said she could. (Evie could always do *any*thing.) So she took over the house, and I went down to Mexico."

In Mexico, however, taming the scorpion on film became less important than keeping leading lady Mara Corday at arm's length on the set. "Mara started to get very friendly. I'm down there over Thanksgiving—Christmas—New Year's—and she got more friendly all the time! And she was getting more and more *attractive* to me all the time!" Corday's boyfriend, actor Richard Long, was there in Mexico City as well, but not even his presence seemed to put a damper on things. "That didn't seem to bother Mara—and so I was getting less and less concerned about it *[laughs]!* Finally I got on the phone and I called Evie and told her, 'I think you better come down here.' 'Why?' she asked — she had the house project and her mom was sick and everything. I said, 'Well, there's a girl on the show and I'm afraid something's gonna happen — ' 'I'll be right down!' she said.

"So she comes down, and after all these weeks away from her I'm *ready* — you know what I mean *[laughs]*? But first we go out to dinner. Evie loved oysters, and of course in Mexico they're cheap, so she had about a dozen and a half oysters, filet mignon, champagne, the whole bit. Now we're ready to go back to the hotel — the Hotel Bamer in Mexico City — and make up for lost time. I put my arms around her and all of a sudden *[Denning pretends to be on the verge of vomiting]* — she says, 'Excuse me!' and runs off. Well, she was sick in bed for four days!" *[Laughs.]*

Mara Corday eventually proved to be the least of Denning's problems in Mexico. "We shot out in villages, and I remember one day we had box lunches out in this village, outside of Mexico City. We broke for lunch and we're having sandwiches. I went to take a bite, and the flies were so thick on the sandwich I had to blow them away before I could take a bite, and *hope* I wasn't getting too many flies! We were in the town center, and it's the town rest room — there's no sanitation. You walk in there, and you just try to find a place to step so you're not stepping on a recent pile. And the flies are all over. So I wound up after that one with intestinal amoeba and dysentery and hepatitis. All from *The Black Scorpion*." Second lead Carlos Rivas was less than sympathetic. "I was so fed up with Carlos Rivas — he'd say, 'I don't understand why you get *seek. I* don't get *seek!*' I said, 'Well, your water — ' and Rivas would say, 'I eat it all the time!' So about a year later he came up to Hollywood to do a picture, and I bumped into him. He said, 'Oh, I'm so *seek!* Your water!' I told him, 'I eat it all the time!'" *[Laughs.]*

A familiar face in science fiction films, Denning introduced himself to fans of horror movies in 1963 when he appeared in *Twice-Told Tales*, a stodgy Technicolor anthology horror film; Denning appeared in the third and final segment (*The House of the Seven Gables*) opposite the film's star, Vincent Price. "He was *[Denning hems and haws]* . . . kind of stuffy. But I never got to know him that well. I never really bothered people I worked with; if they didn't seem to be interested in getting any friendlier with me, well, then, so what? I could enjoy being a friend of the sound man or a cameraman just as much as the star — the name value never meant anything to me. That's why I wasn't that much of a fan of anybody, because I figured everybody was doing their job, just working. That was the only time I worked with Price. Beverly Garland was also in that — I still see her once in a while. A good, very efficient worker, and nice to be around."

After Denning's television series *Karen* expired in 1965, he made the decision to quit the business and move to Maui, Hawaii. "I told my agent, 'I can't believe this business anymore. I get scripts submitted to me, and I can't even figure out what they're about.' This was just when the change was starting, from the type of picture like *An Affair to Remember* to psychological things where the audience has to arrive at the conclusion of the story or something! Not long before that time, I had said to myself, 'What I need is a modern agent,' so I got one—porkpie hat, Sunset Boulevard, the whole bit. I went up to his office and he submitted his first script to me—'Oh, you're gonna love this!' he said. I read it ... I gave it to Evie ... and I said, 'What *is* it?' It was the weirdest thing. I was supposed to be a senator, and as the picture opens I'm plastering a wall, covering over something. Eventually you realize that I'm burying a woman, covering her bust with the plaster. Later I'm making violent love to a teenager on the beach—no reason, no explanation, nothing to it. I thought, 'Well, I guess the guy's a real weirdo.' Then the next scene I'm in the Senate, giving an oration, which has nothing to do with anything else. And then at the end, I'm plastering up another body in the wall! I couldn't even figure out how to play it—it was just a nut! The agent said, 'This is the new thing! This is the new era!' The business has changed so tremendously in fifty years that it's not the same in any sense of the word."

Denning was barely into his retirement when he was offered the semiregular part of Governor Philip Grey on television's *Hawaii Five-O*, starring Jack Lord. "*Five-O* was an added blessing and it worked out great. I had no idea it was gonna go twelve years, though!" Denning laughs. Evelyn Denning was offered the part of the governor's wife, but she "said no. She wanted no part of it! She had more fun when we'd go to Honolulu. I'd go there and be working on a *Five-O* and, of course, Evie would be in seventh heaven because now she was in Honolulu, which is the *big* city—she'd be in her car, shopping all over town for everything. That was much more fun for her than working *[laughs]*! She'd say, 'Somebody's gotta spend it if you're making it. I'm gonna spend it!' And she usually won, and spent more than I made! I have a knack for picking wives who like to shop!"

After the 12th season of *Hawaii Five-O*, the show's run finally came to an end and Denning remarked, "Evelyn and I are looking forward to the eighties as a new era—'retirement and pensions.' We hope it works out." But this new era was not to be: Evelyn developed cancer shortly afterward. "When Evie went through her two years with cancer, even with my Medicare and Screen Actors Guild Health Insurance, I'll bet there was still at least $75,000 left to be paid. Which, luckily, I had saved up, so it was all right." On August 28, 1985, Ankers succumbed at home.

"It was a great marriage—we were broke two or three times, but we'd always end up back on our feet again and we wound up very comfortably and raised our daughter. Evie was a wonderful wife, we had forty-three years together, and I think we got closer the last two years, when she had cancer, than we had ever been before. Our daughter Dee and Evie finally got to be close at the end as well. Evie and Dee never got along too well and they just didn't have a rapport that was what it should have been (Dee was antiestablishment).

Pat and Richard Denning in their California home, 1989.

Then when Evie got so sick, I think Dee suddenly realized, 'My gosh, I don't really know that much about Mom.' Dee finally had a reconciliation with Evie about two days before Evie died, so that was a miracle and a blessing. And she now wants to do a book on Evie and myself, and our life together."

Deeply religious, Denning thanks God for his many blessings. "I believe that with all my heart, and Pat believes it. And our relationship right now is a reward for a lot of things that we both went through. And no matter what happens, I don't feel alone because I know God is not only with me, He's with us, and God is our partner in our marriage."

Present connections with the industry: "None. I pick up *Variety* or *The Hollywood Reporter* and I might as well be reading the Chinese phone book—I hardly recognize a single name, unless it's in the obit column!"

Favorites among the movie people he's worked with: "I think Ingrid Bergman [*Adam Had Four Sons*, 1941] might be *the* favorite. She really was such an admirable person—nobody could swear in front of her. She was a lady and just a real charming person. I was also very fond of Deborah Kerr [*An Affair to Remember*], I thought she was great, and I loved Dorothy Lamour [*Beyond the Blue Horizon*]. We went through a lot together in the nine months it took to make that picture, I'll tell you."

On his days as a movie star: "I'm very greateful for a career that wasn't spectacular, but always made a living or filled in in between. I have wonderful memories of it, but I don't really miss it."

And the secret to a 45-year career in the movie business: "Get along with everybody. I never really had any trouble getting along with anybody I worked with, and I think that makes a difference. I enjoyed everything I've ever done, and when I look back I really have no regrets. It *was* a wonderful business."

RICHARD DENNING FILMOGRAPHY

On Such a Night (Paramount, 1937)
Hold 'Em Navy! (Paramount, 1937)
Daughter of Shanghai (Paramount, 1937)
Give Me a Sailor (Paramount, 1938)
The Big Broadcast of 1938 (Paramount, 1938)
The Buccaneer (Paramount, 1938)
Illegal Traffic (Paramount, 1938)
Her Jungle Love (Paramount, 1938)
Campus Confessions (Paramount, 1938)
College Swing (Paramount, 1938)
The Texans (Paramount, 1938)
King of Alcatraz (Paramount, 1938)
Say It in French (Paramount, 1938)
Touchdown Army (Paramount, 1938)
The Arkansas Traveler (Paramount, 1938)
Hotel Imperial (Paramount, 1939)
Undercover Doctor (Paramount, 1939)
King of Chinatown (Paramount, 1939)
Persons in Hiding (Paramount, 1939)
Zaza (Paramount, 1939)
Ambush (Paramount, 1939)
Union Pacific (Paramount, 1939)
Million Dollar Legs (Paramount, 1939)
The Night of Nights (Paramount, 1939)
I'm from Missouri (Paramount, 1939)
Some Like It Hot (Rhythm Romance) (Paramount, 1939)
Geronimo (Paramount, 1939)
Disputed Passage (Paramount, 1939)
Grand Jury Secrets (Paramount, 1939)
Sudden Money (Paramount, 1939)
The Gracie Allen Murder Case (Paramount, 1939)
The Star Maker (Paramount, 1939)
Our Neighbors—The Carters (Paramount, 1939)
Television Spy (Paramount, 1939)
Love Thy Neighbor (Paramount, 1940)
Emergency Squad (Paramount, 1940)
Queen of the Mob (Paramount, 1940)
The Farmer's Daughter (Paramount, 1940)
Golden Gloves (Paramount, 1940)
North West Mounted Police (Paramount, 1940)
Seventeen (Paramount, 1940)
Those Were the Days (Paramount, 1940)
Parole Fixer (Paramount, 1940)
Adam Had Four Sons (Columbia, 1941)
West Point Widow (Paramount, 1941)
Beyond the Blue Horizon (Paramount, 1942)
Ice-Capades Revue (Rhythm Hits the Ice) (Republic, 1942)
The Glass Key (Paramount, 1942)
Quiet Please, Murder (20th Century-Fox, 1942)
Black Beauty (20th Century-Fox, 1946)
The Fabulous Suzanne (Republic, 1946)
Seven Were Saved (Paramount, 1947)
Caged Fury (Paramount, 1948)
Lady at Midnight (Eagle-Lion, 1948)
Disaster (Paramount, 1948)
Unknown Island (Film Classics, 1948)
Harbor of Missing Men (Republic, 1950)
No Man of Her Own (Paramount, 1950)
Double Deal (RKO, 1950)
Flame of Stamboul (Columbia, 1951)
Secrets of Beauty (Hallmark Productions, 1951)
Insurance Investigator (Republic, 1951)
Week-End with Father (Universal, 1951)
Okinawa (Columbia, 1952)
Scarlet Angel (Universal, 1952)
Hangman's Knot (Columbia, 1952)

Target Hong Kong (Columbia, 1952)
The 49th Man (Columbia, 1953)
The Glass Web (Universal, 1953)
Jivaro (Paramount, 1954)
Creature from the Black Lagoon (Universal, 1954)
Battle of Rogue River (Columbia, 1954)
Target Earth (Allied Artists, 1954)
Air Strike (Lippert, 1955)
The Magnificent Matador (20th Century–Fox, 1955)
Creature with the Atom Brain (Columbia, 1955)
The Gun That Won the West (Columbia, 1955)
The Crooked Web (Columbia, 1955)
Day the World Ended (American Releasing [AIP], 1956)
The Oklahoma Woman (American Releasing [AIP], 1956)
Girls in Prison (AIP, 1956)
Naked Paradise (Thunder over Hawaii) (AIP, 1957)
The Buckskin Lady (United Artists, 1957)
An Affair to Remember (20th Century–Fox, 1957)
The Black Scorpion (Warner Bros., 1957)
The Lady Takes a Flyer (Universal, 1958)
Desert Hell (20th Century–Fox, 1958)
Million Dollar Manhunt (Assignment Redhead) (Tudor Pictures, 1962)
Twice-Told Tales (United Artists, 1963)
I Sailed to Tahiti with an All-Girl Crew (World Entertainment Corp., 1969)

A photograph of Denning is seen in *Night Club Scandal* (Paramount, 1937). Denning's footage was deleted from *You and Me* (Paramount, 1938). A clip of Denning and Deborah Kerr (from *An Affair to Remember*) is seen in *Sleepless in Seattle* (TriStar, 1993).

*Robby the Robot got drunk one day at noon,
and his innards were promptly replaced! ...
Drunken robots are not to be countenanced!*

Anne Francis

They Fought in the Creature Features

IT IS ONE OF THE INDELIBLE IMAGES of the 1950s: Against a backdrop of astral blackness and ringed planets, a fearsome-looking robot looms; lying unconscious in this metal monster's arms is a miniskirted girl with long ash-blond hair (and longer legs). Every science fiction fan worth his salt knows that this is the emblem for the film *Forbidden Planet*, MGM's one major contribution to the 1950s science fiction/monster movie boom, and that the fearsome mechanical man is actually the astounding Robby the Robot, poster boy for fifties science fiction. Does that make Anne Francis science fiction fans' favorite pinup girl?

"I got that part because I was under contract to MGM and I had good legs," the actress blurts out with no hesitation. "And still *do*, I might add!"

Over lunch at the Musso and Frank Grill, the popular and historic site of many a Hollywood meal and movie-related deal, Anne Francis looks back at the seminal outer space adventure with both fondness and fascinating insight. "I think that when I did the film, I *was* aware of its metaphysical implications. At that time, we did *not* have what is called today New Age thinking, which is very involved with metaphysical thinking. So for me, when I was doing *Forbidden Planet*, it seemed quite obvious that the Id was similar to what one in metaphysics would call the mass subconscious, and that what we put into this mass subconscious in our thinking comes back. Much as, in the Bible, it says, 'That which I have feared the most has come upon me.' So at that time it didn't seem dumb to me that the collective thinking could create a monster. It *still* doesn't seem dumb to me that our collective thinking is creating monsters—like nuclear bombs and everything else. The story made sense enough to me at the time."

Gulp. Lunch begins with bread, salads and that profound evaluation of *Forbidden Planet*—the sort of analysis that might sound odd coming from another fifties ingenue, but not from the cult actress whose list of credits includes *Forbidden Planet* as only *one* of many memorable titles. Born a stone's throw from Ossining, New York's, famous Sing Sing prison, Anne Francis' amazing career began when she was six months old and posing for calendar photos. Before she was five, she was a fashion model whose image appeared on the covers and pages of many national magazines; she made her television debut on an NBC Christmas show in *1939;* and she was on Broadway at age 11, playing Gertrude Lawrence as a child in the stage hit *Lady in the Dark*. Three thousand radio appearances during the 1940s earned the blue-eyed trooper the nickname the Little Queen of Soap Operas.

Eager to try acting in motion pictures, she made her first trek to Hollywood in 1946 and soon found herself under contract to MGM (where she also went to school with Elizabeth Taylor, Natalie Wood and Dean Stockwell, in the little schoolhouse on the Metro lot). "I was there under contract for one

Previous page: "Robby the Robot was the most expensive 'actor' in *[Forbidden Planet]*," says Anne Francis. "The *outer* robot, not the inner!"

year, and did two days' work in a picture called *Summer Holiday* [1948] with Walter Huston and Mickey Rooney. I went back to New York after that, into the Golden Era of Television—live TV back in New York, where they had really great writers."

She won movie roles in the East as well, appearing as a teenage prostitute in the female juvenile delinquency drama *So Young, So Bad* (1950); winning a small part in the documentary-flavored *The Whistle at Eaton Falls* (1951), made in Hanover, New Hampshire; and playing her first fantasy film role, a bit in director William Dieterle's classic *Portrait of Jennie* (1948). "I was still a kid when I did *Portrait of Jennie*, very obviously. It was just one quick scene, but I *am* glad that I shared the scene with Ethel Barrymore in a very minute way. She was very charming, very nice. And I remember William Dieterle wore white cotton editor's gloves—but I'm not certain why!"

Hollywood beckoned (and Francis reluctantly answered the call again) in the early fifties, this time landing a berth as a contract player at Darryl F. Zanuck's 20th Century-Fox. In December 1953, she played her first science fiction film lead in the Lenny Bruce–scripted science fiction comedy *The Rocket Man* (shooting title: *The Kid from Outer Space*), made at RKO by Panoramic Productions for Fox, but (like costars John Agar and Beverly Garland) she remembers little about the film. Far better and more memorable experiences awaited her once she changed studios and once again became part of the MGM "family"; for the Culver City studio, she appeared not only in *Forbidden Planet* but also in the 1955 classics *Blackboard Jungle* and *Bad Day at Black Rock*.

"*Bad Day at Black Rock* was hard," Francis recalls. "It was a very, *very* difficult show, because we were doing it in August in a place called Lone Pine, which is next to Death Valley, in the desert. The temperature was about a hundred degrees. And in those days, they used klieg lights to offset the sun. So, *with* those lights, we were working in 115, 120 degrees. We all lost a tremendous amount of weight; I mean, at the end of the day, who was hungry? You just dragged yourself back to the hotel. Spencer Tracy had a *very* hard time. They had to coax him more than once to please, *please* see it through, because it was terribly draining for him. For everyone! I mean, I was in my early twenties, so if it was hard for me, you can imagine how some of the others must have felt."

According to Francis, Tracy "would be very moody sometimes—the black Irish moods, you know. Then at other times, he'd be extremely accessible—he'd sit and work on a scene with you, and go over and over and *over* the lines. He was both an angel and—a stinker sometimes, depending what was going on in his own personal life with his physical problems and perhaps his personal emotional problems."

What might have been her least challenging MGM role has, of course, become her best known, as Francis played Altaira, the unworldly daughter of space pioneer Walter Pidgeon, in the studio's otherworldly *Forbidden Planet*. Preparing to play the naïve character with the scene-stealing legs required "no great preparation on my part; I wasn't that worldly-wise at that point myself. I remember that there were some costumes that they decided were too revealing. One was a silver lamé jumpsuit with silver boots—just absolutely gorgeous. It is rumored that [production head] Dore Schary's wife Miriam nixed it, saying that it was just too sexy, too extreme. It covered me from head to toe, along with the silver boots that matched this lamé suit. Kind of shows you how far we've come since then!"

Remembering her *Planet* costars, Francis smiles, "Walter Pidgeon loved to recite dirty limericks. He was a wonderful gentleman in every way, except for his proclivity for dirty limericks, which *were* really very, very funny—they were sort of 'the thing' back then, and none of the gentlemen on the show could match 'em. Walter and also George Sanders, who was on another film that I did [*The Scarlet Coat*, 1955], both loved dirty limericks. And Leslie Nielsen I was madly in love with. Les was a very gentle, kind, terrific guy, just as he is today. He had a great sense of humor; today it has become more extreme than it was when I worked with him in those days *[laughs]*! But Les, much like Burt Reynolds—they both have a wonderful basic outlook on life and they don't take themselves terribly seriously. Or, if they *do*, it's not noticeable on the outside."

And Robby the Robot? "Robby got drunk one day at noon, and his innards [actor Frankie Darro] were promptly replaced," she recalls, letting out another laugh. "He almost took a full nosedive, if three grips hadn't grabbed him in time. Robby was the most expensive 'actor' on the show—the outer Robby, not the inner! The facade was worth much more than any of the actors; the actors could have been replaced, but Robby would have been a terrible expense. Robby was really the star of the show, so the young man who was working him from the inside was replaced one afternoon after a five-martini lunch. Drunken robots are not to be countenanced!"

While Robby seems to be the threat to Francis on the film's poster, precautions were taken during production to protect the actress from a very different member of the cast. "They had the leopard behind glass, and made it look like I was touching the animal," she reveals. "They don't like to take chances; that's why they did it that way."

The hardest part of *Forbidden Planet*, Francis adds, was "reacting to things that weren't there. Disney's people did all of the special effects, the cartooning of the monster and all of that sort of thing. That was all postproduction. *We* were racing through the film, running away from things we had to imagine at all times. It was a matter of trying to grade our fear from one scene to another, from apprehension to *[laughs]*—to horrific extremes of facial expressions! I think that was the major challenge in the film, for all of us.

"[Producer] Nicholas Nayfack was a darling man. Fred Wilcox, the director, was fine, too, but his direction was, as I said earlier, 'Look scared. Look *more* scared.' It was not an in-depth study of character going on. I was the ingenue. It was pretty well defined, who each of us was. It was a science fiction fairy tale and I was the sleeping princess, no more, no less. I was awakened by the prince who landed in his flying saucer. I don't think anything more could be made of it; that's what the story was and there really wasn't much else to do. Yes, it's condescending, but that's what the story was. It's still going on today. Maybe women's roles have matured to a certain point, except that I think that a lot of the films are still playing the sex game. Instead of really having much growth with the women, I think their [idea of] 'feminine freedom' is that *now* one takes off more clothes. *That's* feminine freedom. I don't think there's that much more respect for women [in films] now than there was then. The attitude is that women don't have much to offer society. But that's gone on for centuries. There have been incredible women artists and composers, and folks are just becoming aware of them because more is being said about it, more is being brought forward. It's a big battle to get that information out."

Regarding *Forbidden Planet's* enduring appeal, Francis admits, "At the time, I don't think that any of us really were aware of the fact that it was going to turn into a longtime cult film, probably *much,* much stronger today than it was then." Costar Richard Anderson recalled that MGM thought of the film as a B movie, an opinion Francis doesn't dispute. "That's quite possible. But then I think at the time they also thought that *Bad Day at Black Rock* was a B movie. And *that's* become one of the big classics — which, again, I'm thrilled to have been in. So, even in those days, I think judgment was not always perfect as far as movies were concerned. *Forbidden Planet* just had a life of its own, something that none of us was aware was going to happen. I first saw the film in one of the screening rooms at the studio, and I think we were all impressed with what had been done by Disney; what they accomplished was quite phenomenal. Also, Joshua Meador's beautiful metal sculptings on the set were not nearly as appreciated as they should have been. He was a marvelous, marvelous artist who also had a lot to do with the sets and the backdrops."

Her favorite scene in the film? "Probably any scene where I kissed Les Nielsen, 'cause I had that terrible crush on him! And if Les does another *Naked Gun* movie, I think it would be wonderful fun for me to run through in the background with the lion — in the same outfit."

Looking back, Francis admits to having mixed emotions about her MGM years. "A lot of wonderful people, a lot of great crew people — but there was always the unfathomable hierarchy. I was never a very political individual; I was not able to play a lot of the games that were played in those days. I guess I was sort of a maverick in many ways. I had come out from New York, where the attitude was far more stress as far as being an actor, and looks were not really as important. Then I came out here where we were admonished to not be seen with curlers in our hair at the local market, to be made up at all times.

Jeans and tennis shoes and old shirts were not acceptable at the lot. So in many ways, it was kind of hard. Also, one would be taken to task for one's friends. I remember one day I was seen talking to a black actor at a restaurant quite close to the studio—it was a purely innocent meeting with other friends, but I was seen talking with him earnestly about a subject. And I was on the carpet the next day—I was not to be seen talking to any black actors, thank you very much. (Which I did not pay heed to.) So in many ways I didn't really fit what was expected, what the mold was supposed to be."

Freelancing after having left MGM by her own request, Francis turned up in the occasional movie but worked more steadily in television, where (among many other series) she acted on *Alfred Hitchcock Presents*, *The Alfred Hitchcock Hour*, *The Man from U.N.C.L.E.*, *The Invaders* and, perhaps most notably, *The Twilight Zone*. "Rod Serling was a wonderful man—a brilliant man, with a great sense of humor. That was back in the days when we rehearsed the show for a full week before we shot it, so we knew every shot that was going to be done. It was wonderful to be able to do that."

Her sixties film roles included the science fiction suspenser *The Satan Bug* and the melodramatic *Brainstorm* (both 1965). *The Satan Bug*, about a government search for a fanatic with a lethal supply of stolen lab-created virus, saw Francis replacing actress Joan Hackett as the female lead; just as in *Forbidden Planet* and *Bad Day at Black Rock*, she was the only woman in the cast. "I think there was some sort of altercation between Joan and the producers about how the character should be played, so I was called on a day's notice to go do it. I *liked* the script very, very much; it was an interesting script. John Sturges directed it; John had directed me in *Bad Day at Black Rock*. But John and [film editor] Ferris Webster were having meetings at lunch every day about another movie they were going to be doing, *The Hallelujah Trail* [1965]. Unfortunately, I think that *Satan Bug* kind of suffered a bit in the editing room because of this next project that they were into. I felt that *The Satan Bug* was not Ferris Webster's best job of editing: There are *long* drive-ins, *getting* out of the car, *walking* all the way up to the house, another person *opening* the door—they did not have cuts that would have kept that movie moving, and so the pace was dragged out tremendously. And it was the kind of a movie that *had* to have fast pacing. So I was very, very disappointed when I saw it. And the only thing I can consider is the fact that John and Ferris were pressed for time for this other biggie, *The Hallelujah Trail*, and that *Satan Bug* suffered. But, as I said, originally the script itself was terrific."

Brainstorm starred Jeff Hunter as a space scientist who hatches a bizarre scheme to feign insanity in order to get away with the murder of his lover's (Francis) sadistic husband (Dana Andrews). "That was directed by Bill Conrad, who is one of the brightest directors I've ever worked with in my life. He is absolutely incredible. Before a hysterical scene that I had in that film, Bill came up to me and he said, 'Now, when you get into the sobbing, I would like it

Francis (opposite George Maharis) thought *The Satan Bug*'s original script was "terrific," but that the movie suffered in editing.

to reach a peak'—and he gave me the *sound* of the highest pitch that he wanted in this sobbing scene. It was very exciting to work with somebody who had that much of an insight into the *sound* that he wanted. I had started in radio as a child, and *he* had been a radio actor for many years before he went into films and television, so he was very much involved with pitch. He also has a genius for making photographic decisions that were very unusual, on the spot. Brilliant, brilliant, brilliant director, and never really recognized as such."

In 1965 Francis also began her one-year run as a James Bond-ish private detective (complete with futuristic communicators and spy equipment) on television's *Honey West*. Based on the popular novels by Gloria Fickling and Forrest E. Fickling, the action-filled ABC half-hour series costarred John Ericson (as Honey's short-tempered partner Sam Bolt) and Irene Hervey (as her Aunt Meg). "*Honey West* was fun to do because we had such wonderful character actors on the show—I really enjoyed it for that reason. And also I loved the physical activity involved. I studied karate for the show and for about a month I worked out to get in shape for it. Actually, that came in handy many years later when I was doing a play at the Ahmanson Theater. I was going down the stairway into the bowels of the Ahmanson to get my auto—by that time, just about everyone else had cleared out—and I suddenly heard footsteps behind me. I went down one flight and I heard him; I went down a second flight and I heard him getting closer. I thought, 'Oh, baby, I'd better do something now.'

"About halfway down the next flight of stairs, as I heard the footsteps getting closer, I just whirled around and grabbed the bannister in one hand—and there was this guy. He stopped short, I looked at him and he looked at me—it felt like we were there for about a half hour, although it was probably only about three seconds. He said, 'Did I scare you?' and I said, '*No*.' And I was just waiting for him to make a move, because I knew from the karate training that, if he moved toward me, I might be hurt, but *he* would be hurt, too, because I would help him on down the stairs! So I just waited. Finally he turned around and went back up the stairs, and I went down and got in my car. *Then* I fell apart—just absolutely! But it *worked*, that instantaneous thing that just grips you, and you're prepared. I just knew instinctively that the best place for me to handle it was on the stairway with his being above me. On the flat, I would not have much of a chance."

Another part of the challenge of *Honey West* was keeping one move ahead of costar Bruce Biteabit, Honey's irascible 28-pound ocelot. "When cats get hot or tired, they start getting a little snarly. At times, it was like trying to hold a pair of cobras; each end of him was going one way or the other. From working with cats, I know that if one is happy, it bites and scratches, and if it's *un*happy, it bites and scratches. So it really doesn't make too much difference *[laughs]*! I learned pretty much to keep ahead of him when he was squirming, I do love animals, so we got along quite well. But a lot of character actors who came on the show were petrified of him." Francis was Emmy-nominated for her performance on the show ("I lost to a wonderful lady, Barbara Stanwyck—each one of us was rooting for the other"), and won a Golden Globe award. But, to everyone's surprise, the well-received and popular series was bumped by ABC at the end of its first year.

"Cancellation had nothing to do with the ratings—it was doing very well. But ABC was able to buy *The Avengers* for a lot less money than it cost to produce *Honey West*. Once they found that this genre would work, they dropped *Honey West* and brought over *The Avengers*—which did very well here. Its

Television's crime-busting *Honey West* could vamp information out of a suspect as easily as subdue him with a judo flip. Her enviable costar was Bruce Biteabit.

cancellation was a mixed blessing. I worked very hard on that show — day after day, seventeen or eighteen hours a day. I had a four-year-old daughter at the time, and I had very little opportunity to spend any 'quality time' at all with her. So in one way, the cancellation was a blessing in that I had that frustration behind me. And, for another thing, I think that if it had gone another season or two — who knows what direction anyone's life or career is going to take? I think that, when you have more than one interest in life, you can let certain areas lapse."

Another "notorious" credit for Francis was the 1968 *Funny Girl*, the Barbra Streisand–starring film bio of old-time stage comedian Fanny Brice. "The role that I was originally contracted to do was pretty much cut out of the movie, 'cut out' day by day, without shooting. So that was a very rough time for me. I don't think [director] William Wyler wanted that character in the movie to begin with, so the whole thing was unpleasant. People blamed it on Barbra; *I* did not blame it on Barbra. At that time, I had a public relations person who made a lot of statements about Barbra that were attributed to me. I *never* blamed Barbra, because I had absolutely no idea [why the cutting happened]; it may have been timing, the show may have been too long. But the role originally as written in the script was a wonderful, wonderful role—including a drunk scene which I *did* play, but they took it out of the film. It just turned into a whole mess."

In the seventies and eighties, her career took on yet more diversity, with Francis trying directing ("I didn't *try*—I *did* direct!") and turning her hand to writing. Her short film *Gemini Rising* (1970), about rodeo riders, has been seen on PBS, and her "spiritual exposé" *Voices from Home: An Inner Journey* was published in 1982. "Through my lifetime, I have had a lot of unusual experiences that would border on psychic and spiritual and such, and I have met many people along the way who were interested in such things. That's why I wrote the book, to share my experiences, so that other people who may have been going through similar things would not think they were *crazy*. (At least, I don't think *I* am!) Unfortunately, the publishers went bankrupt within a couple of months after it was published. The wild thing was, I had a ten-minute interview with Chris Wallace on *The Today Show*—and then there were no books in bookstores *[laughs]*!"

More recently, Francis has continued to act on stage and television, "and also to have fun with life as well." She much prefers looking ahead to looking back, and does not bother to collect her own movies or television appearances. "My movies are things that have been done; I'm through with them. I know what they are, and I move on to the next thing. Right now, I'm studying musical theater *singing*—and having a *lot* of fun with that. I'd love to do some musical work on the stage. I've sung in the past, but I've never *really* studied it for placement and endurance, which theater really takes. I've been working on it for a year now, and each lesson [my voice] gets stronger and stronger. And I love doing it, it's just great therapy."

She's heard the recent rumblings about a big-screen version of *Honey West*, but "nothing as far as *my* being involved with it! Actually, I really wouldn't have any idea where I would fit into something like that at this point. Yes, I'd be interested, but it would depend on what the role was. *Not* the Irene Hervey part, thank you very much!" She realizes that, for many people, she'll

According to Anne Francis, there *is* no down side to being a cult actress.

always be best remembered for her limited role in *Forbidden Planet*, but she takes the realistic stance that "I don't have much to say about that, really *[laughs]*! It's okay with me because I accept *life* as okay. To make it '*un*okay' would be spending time in a mood or an attitude that's not very beneficial."

According to Anne Francis, there *is* no down side to being a cult actress.

"I have fun; I sign posters and things that are sent to me; I answer letters from those who seem most sincere. Years ago I got a postcard which was just *crammed* with writing, how wonderful, how terrific, how great I was. 'Would it be possible, do you think, that I could ever meet you? I would love to marry you.' This was all squeezed onto the card, in tiny little letters. Then at the bottom, it said, 'P.S.: If you're not interested, would you send this to Debbie Reynolds?'"

ANNE FRANCIS FILMOGRAPHY

This Time for Keeps (MGM, 1947)
Summer Holiday (MGM, 1948)
Portrait of Jennie (Tidal Wave) (Selznick, 1948)
So Young, So Bad (United Artists, 1950)
The Whistle at Eaton Falls (Columbia, 1951)
Elopement (20th Century-Fox, 1951)
Lydia Bailey (20th Century-Fox, 1952)
Dreamboat (20th Century-Fox, 1952)
A Lion Is in the Streets (Warner Bros., 1953)
The Rocket Man (20th Century-Fox, 1954)
Susan Slept Here (RKO, 1954)
Rogue Cop (MGM, 1954)
Bad Day at Black Rock (MGM, 1955)
Battle Cry (Warner Bros., 1955)
Blackboard Jungle (MGM, 1955)
The Scarlet Coat (MGM, 1955)
Forbidden Planet (MGM, 1956)
The Rack (MGM, 1956)
The Great American Pastime (MGM, 1956)
The Hired Gun (MGM, 1957)
Don't Go Near the Water (MGM, 1957)
Girl of the Night (Warner Bros., 1960)
The Crowded Sky (Warner Bros., 1960)
The Satan Bug (United Artists, 1965)
Brainstorm (Warner Bros., 1965)
Funny Girl (Columbia, 1968)
Star! (Those Were the Happy Times) (20th Century-Fox, 1968)
Hook, Line and Sinker (Columbia, 1969)
More Dead than Alive (United Artists, 1969)
The Love God? (Universal, 1969)
Impasse (The Golden Bullet) (United Artists, 1970)
Pancho Villa (Challenge of Pancho Villa; El Desafio de Pancho Villa) (Bernard Gordon [Spanish/English], 1972)
Born Again (Avco Embassy, 1978)

My agent said, "Listen, you just do [the Lost in Space *pilot episode] and don't worry about it. Take the money. Because nobody's gonna see it and it'll never sell." I said okay.*

Mark Goddard

IT IS A COOL AUTUMN DAY on the boardwalk in Atlantic City, and inside one of the adjacent hotels, unnoticed by most of the slot-machine players, a small piece of television history is in the making. At the Taj Mahal, the entire surviving cast of *Lost in Space* is having one of their first full reunions in the quarter century since that CBS science fiction series disappeared from television airwaves in September of 1968, and followers from up and down the East Coast have congregated for the event. Most of these fans were still in school in the sixties, when the Space Family Robinson was at the height of their popularity. Now, in 1992, they are all grown up and surprised to find that costar Mark Goddard, Major Don West in the space series, has gone...

"Back to school!" He laughs, recognizing the irony in the situation himself. "Back when I was of school age, I went to Holy Cross College in Worcester, Massachusetts. I was in the dramatic society and I did some acting. I decided I wanted to try [to earn a living at it], so I left college in my junior year and I went to New York to study acting. Then I did stock in Florida and in New England, and I really enjoyed what I was doing, so I didn't go back and finish college. And that's something I always thought that I *should* do. I'm the youngest of five, my brother and my three sisters all graduated from college and I'm the only one who never did. I didn't feel too good about that, because we were all expected to go to college and finish. So, after I had my career as an actor, I began to think that I wanted to maybe get involved in education. I came back East and went to Bridgewater State College, and I've gotten a bachelor of arts in Communications and I graduated magna cum laude, which I'm proud of. Then I continued on and just last August ['92] got my master's degree in elementary school education. *Now* I'm going to school and starting my courses—it'll take me about a year and a half and I'll have my master's in special education.

"I'm committed to what I'm doing one hundred percent. It's a good life. I think that teaching is not only rewarding, but it takes a lot of time and effort, and it's very challenging. It's a growing process. I grew with the *Lost in Space* experience and I'm growing with the experience of teaching. I'm fifty-six years old and I'm still growing, and someday I'll decide what I want to do in life when I grow up!"

Obviously Mark Goddard has come a long way from the days of playing the two-dimensional Major West—piloting the *Jupiter 2*, dallying platonically with Marta Kristen's Judy Robinson and barking out the signature line, "Get back to work, Smith!" Born in Lowell, Massachusetts, July 24, 1936, the actor (real name: Charles Goddard) grew up in Scituate ("great little town") where his father owned a five-and-ten. He had been at Holy Cross three years when "Father Gallagher, who was my English professor and the head of the dramatic society, took notice of my acting and said, 'Hey, you've got something special.

Previous page: **During his three years *Lost in Space*, Mark Goddard wondered if he was not also Lost in Hollywood.**

It seems to come across the footlights.' Those were his exact words. And that was all the encouragement I needed—I was off to New York. That was 1958. James Dean died—when? '55?—and that was still a big influence. When I was doing dramatics in college, I felt like, 'Jeez, I'm gonna be the next Jimmy Dean.' And when I went to New York, there were about five hundred Jimmy Deans runnin' around *[laughs]*. We all had our red jackets and our little motorcycles. I lived at the Iroquois Hotel where Dean had lived, I got my hair cut by his barber, and it was like everybody was trying to be Jimmy Dean."

Goddard attended the American Academy of Dramatic Arts by day and worked at night as a floorwalker at a Woolworth's at 45th and Broadway. "I wasn't very successful at it," he recalls. "At Woolworth's I had to wear a suit—I had *one suit*, an old, funny-lookin' suit and tie. I remember taking my jacket off to help somebody move some cartons, and somebody stole my jacket. So I was the floorwalker and I didn't catch anyone stealing, but I lost my jacket *[laughs]*!"

Goddard soon moved from Woolworth's stock room to stock *companies*, where "basically what I was doing was running the lights or painting the scenery—I didn't get to do much acting. That was my apprenticeship. (I have a firm belief that you have to serve before you can *be* served, that you have to put that time in.) I got to Hollywood back in 1959. I was with the William Morris Agency, and the agency represented companies. They represented Dick Powell in Four Star Television, and while I was a client of theirs, they had *The Rifleman* with Chuck Connors. That was the first show I did—just a small part, I may have had one line. I was part of a posse and I got shot. I had to get on a horse for the first time and ride, and I didn't know how to do that, and the horse ran away with me. But, like I say, you learn as you go *[laughs]*. Acting or teaching or *any*thing is a process of learning as you're doing it."

The same agency also represented Aaron Spelling, who was at Four Star with Powell, and Goddard ended up with a costarring role in the first series Spelling produced, the CBS Western *Johnny Ringo*, in which Goddard appeared as lawman Ringo's (Don Durant) young deputy. "I did a pretty good job on that. It only lasted for one year, but in those days, we used to shoot 39 episodes a year. You'd be on the air for 39 weeks, and then in the summertime just 13 weeks of reruns. Nowadays, of course, they shoot 20 shows and then do 26 reruns—somehow *[laughs]*. In those days, we used to shoot more than we did reruns. I was on that show for a year, and when it went off the air, Dick Powell, who had become like a father figure to me, called me into his office at Four Star. He was a wonderful man and he had a generous heart, and his office door was always open. Actors, craft-service people, grips, *any*body that worked in his company could go into his office anytime they wanted and talk to him. He called me in and he said, 'Mark, *Johnny Ringo* is going off the air, but I have a new show coming on called *Michael Shayne* with Richard Denning, and there's also a part opening up on *The Detectives*,

Starring Robert Taylor.' (That show had already been on for a year.) 'Which one would you like to do?' I chose doing *The Detectives* because I really wanted to work with Robert Taylor, who I admired very much—I grew up watching movies like *Johnny Eager* and *Quo Vadis*, et cetera. I knew that he was the ultimate professional and that I would learn a lot from him. I was very happy and very fortunate to work with him for three years."

Joining the cast of the police drama in its second season, Goddard's sidekick character Chris Ballard was brought in to lure a younger audience to the ABC series (which until then was drawing mostly middle-aged viewers). "When I went into that show, it was like I was the star of the show and Robert Taylor was like the sidekick as far as the *publicity* was concerned. They threw a lot toward me during that first year. They wanted another 'Kookie' Byrnes; they wanted that 'look.' It wouldn't work today, but in those days it did." Of the experience of working opposite a major star like Taylor, Goddard recalls, "Let's say there was going to be a medium two-shot, Robert Taylor and myself. They'd spend about thirty-five, forty minutes lighting Robert Taylor *[laughs]*. I'd be just in back of him, my head over his shoulder. Then they'd say, 'Okay, let's go, let's shoot.' And they'd been lighting only Taylor all that time. I'd say to the cameraman Howard Schwartz, 'What about *me*? Do *I* get any light or what?' And Howard said, 'Mark, you just get all the leak light. All the light that's left over, that Robert Taylor doesn't use, *you* get!'"

After turning in his shield when the series wrapped up its caseload in 1962, Goddard continued to work in television, often in comedy: He guested on sitcoms like *Fair Exchange* and *The Beverly Hillbillies*, appeared in the unsold Desilu pilot *Maggie Brown* with Ethel Merman and was a regular on the short-lived *Many Happy Returns* (1964-65) with John McGiver. One of Goddard's infrequent film appearances was in Disney's *The Monkey's Uncle* (1965) with Tommy Kirk as the disaster-prone college whiz-kid Merlin Jones and Goddard in an unbilled supporting role as the head of a football-minded fraternity. "*The Monkey's Uncle* was fun because I was working at Disney—*everybody* wanted to work at Disney. It was just exciting to walk around the Disney lot because of its history."

Nowadays, of course, roles like these have become footnotes in Mark Goddard's career: In 1965 he was drawn (reluctantly!) into appearing in the pilot episode for a space-adventure series—a job the actor took only because he was assured that the show would never get off the ground. "I was with the General Artists Corporation agency and they represented Irwin Allen, who I didn't know at the time. My agent was named David Gerber, and David came to me one day and said, 'How would you like to do a pilot? A space pilot?' I said, 'I'm not really into space too much.' David said, 'Well, you've been everything else—you've been a detective, you've been a cowboy, you've done comedy. This is about a family going into space, and there's gonna be a lot of adventures, earthquakes—' I said, 'Gee, I don't know. I'm not sure, because of the subject matter.' And David said, 'Well, listen, you just do it and don't worry about it. Take the money. Because nobody's gonna see it and it'll never sell.' I said okay.

"It took about twenty-one days to shoot the pilot—that's a l-o-n-g time to shoot a pilot. It was a lot of earthquakes and water stuff, all physical—there wasn't really a lot of acting to do. I've always been athletic, so I enjoyed that part of it. *And they sold it.* So I went to find David Gerber, 'cause he'd said, 'I promise I can get you out of this if you don't like it.' But he wasn't around anymore. About six months had passed, and he had become a producer over at 20th Century-Fox, where Irwin was. So I just said to myself, 'Well, this is meant for me to do, so I'll just do it and I'll do the best job I can.'"

Goddard can joke about his early days on the show now, but he certainly was not laughing then. "The day that I went to wardrobe and they put the silver lamé space suit on me, I think I cried. I *cried*! My wife at the time put her hand on my shoulder and said, 'It's gonna be okay,' but I said, 'I don't know if I can do this.' She said, 'Yes you can, yes you can.' So I said to myself, 'Yes I can, yes I can!' I had realized that it was *not* going to be an acting challenge. It would be physical, and I wouldn't be getting the kind of direction that I wanted. I wouldn't be getting my teeth into material that had to do with [real] things, into the reality of emotional stuff. I just knew it had to do with outer space things and things that would be hard for me to relate to. I think I did okay, but—it's just different." (Coincidentally, one of Goddard's distant relatives is Robert Goddard, the professor and inventor known as "the father of modern rocketry.")

Unintentionally, Goddard almost *did* manage to avoid space duty aboard the *Jupiter 2*: a motorcycle accident nearly put the actor out of commission. "This was real early on in the show, maybe even just before the pilot. I used to drive motorcycles—Steve McQueen got me interested, 'cause he was also at Four Star. I was driving a bike back from the races and I hit an oil slick, and I went down on my left side. I skidded about forty feet. It took all the skin off the left side of my body ... took a piece of my thumb off ... cut a hole in my leg, stuff like that. (It also sheared practically all the metal off the left side of my bike—along with my skin!) There were four lanes of traffic and all these cars were just buzzin' by me. I was able to get up and cross the street and get to the side—and I went down there. The next thing I knew, I was in the ambulance.

"Later on, *months* later, I was at a party and an agent I knew said, 'I saw you that day you had your motorcycle accident.' I said, 'Oh?' He said, 'We were coming back from the races, too. God, you looked awful, you were all bloodied up there at the side of the road.' And then he said, 'We would have stopped to pick you up, but we didn't want to get any blood in the car.' How's that for a Hollywood story *[laughs]*?"

In costumes adjusted to allow for his bandages, Goddard began what would become a three-year stint on the 20th Century–Fox series, with every phase of the series (a popular part of CBS's Wednesday night lineup) supervised by veteran movie and television producer Irwin Allen (who also directed the pilot episode). "Irwin Allen was a good director when it came to 'vision,' and he knew what he wanted as an editor; he probably knew editing, he probably could envision things. But he wasn't a good director as far as actors were concerned, because he didn't *like* actors. And a director's *gotta* like actors, he's gotta *want* to work with them in some way.

"Doing a show like that is very difficult. I used to always put myself down, I'd say, 'Gee, I'm not very good. This is tough to do.' Then one day years later I was on the set of *The Towering Inferno* [1974] and I stood there and I watched Irwin directing Paul Newman and Steve McQueen in an office scene. Paul Newman is one of my favorite actors and one of the best actors who's ever been around, and one of the great things that you have to do as an actor is to be relaxed. That's very important. I was watching the scene being done, and I watched the tension in Paul Newman grow. I couldn't believe that *he* — even *he* — was having a hard time with this kind of dialogue, with this kind of directing, and what was happening. Of course, he was doing it because he was getting a million dollars or something. He did it for the money — he wasn't doin' it because he wanted to work with Irwin Allen *[laughs]*. But I saw that tension and I said, 'Boy, even with Paul Newman. Words that don't work are even hard for him. I guess I'm not doin' such a bad job after all!' That put things in perspective for me, in a way."

Goddard concurs instantly with the other *Lost in Space* veterans who have often described Allen as a man who considered his series regulars — and their performances — relatively low on his list of priorities. "With Irwin it was like, 'Get it all right technically, and if all the firecrackers go off, print it.' It didn't matter if I didn't get my line out right because a firecracker went off in the middle of it *[laughs]*, or if I just 'wasn't there with it' as an actor.

"I did a lot of series, and I found that the greatest support you get in a series usually is from the crew. When I did *Johnny Ringo* and *The Detectives*, I had great rapport with the cinematographer, the crew members, the writers and everyone that came down to the set, and everything was a pleasure. Everything fell in, everything was just nice, you know? We had our Friday afternoon parties, we all had a drink together and laughed about the week and had a good time, then went home to our families in a relaxed state. There was a whole family thing going on. With *Lost in Space*, there was tension all the time. There was tension with the cinematographer, there was tension with the writers coming down, there was always something going on. Tension with the actors, tension with the directors. *Always tension.* And, you know what they say, 'the fish stinks from the head'? This isn't fair to say because Irwin is dead and he can't defend himself, but I think that his kind of *perfection*, what he *wanted* and the *way* he wanted it, his very cold manner with everyone — this permeated right from him to the writers, to the directors, to the cast, to the crew. You could sense that.

"That was the three years on *Lost in Space* for me: 'Is the show good enough?' 'Is it getting the ratings?' And the cast was worried: 'Is this laughable?' (Especially after *Star Trek* came on—'Can we compete with this kind of a show?') Then we went up against *Batman* and *that* hit us—they got good ratings and we didn't, although we *did* come back later. '*Batman*'s a real camp show. *We're* not a camp show. Are we a real show? We're not a real show like *Star Trek*, and we're not a camp show like *Batman*...' Tension! We didn't know where we fit, we hadn't found an identity. An identity came near the end, when finally it was Dr. Smith [Jonathan Harris] and the Robot doing silly things, and that's what the show became. But that's not what it set out to be. I always wanted to do a comedy, but I never knew [while I was on *Lost in Space*] that I *was* in a comedy *[laughs]*! One day I said, 'Hey, I've been doin' all this method stuff—I didn't know we were doin' a comedy here!'"

Another sore point for Goddard was the fact that, during the show's run, he never knew who its audience was. "The show *had* an audience, but I didn't know that. The audience was kids from (say) six to ten—and I didn't run around with those kids *[laughs]*! I wasn't out playin' golf with those kids, I wasn't playin' tennis with 'em, they weren't on motorcycles, I didn't see 'em at the racetrack, they weren't at the parties that I went to. The people that I *was* dealing with, it was almost like they looked down at [*Lost in Space*]. They didn't ever watch it, unless they had little kids (which they didn't). So I didn't know who I was reaching. It's not until recently that I realized [who the fans were]—they're now in their thirties and so forth. As kids, they loved it and got off on it and wanted to play *Lost in Space*. That is what I missed. If I knew that we were reaching an audience, and that they were really looking up to Don West and Judy and the Robot and Dr. Smith, and they were having fun with it, I'd have said, 'Gee, I'm doin' something worthwhile.' But I didn't know that, I didn't know *what* I was doing.

"We had a couple of directors I liked, like Sean Penn's father, Leo Penn; he directed a show and he was cool, he was a good director. I don't know why he did it—maybe his agent said, 'Hey, do it,' maybe he was in between jobs or something. Bob Butler was good, Harry Harris was good, so we had, sporadically, some good directors. But we also had directors who were just going by the numbers most of the time. You could say anything you wanted to some of these guys, and it was in one ear, out the other. One director, Sobey Martin, used to fall asleep on the set a lot, *while* he was directing! One day I woke him up and I said, 'Hey, Sobey, Sobey! Can I do this scene in the nude?' He said *[in a groggy voice]*, 'Oh, yeah, yeah, yeah, go ahead, whatever.' *[Laughs.]* It was like this: 'Say the lines, take the money and run. *That* was what we heard every day: 'Hey, don't question it. If you analyze these scripts, you'll go crazy.' But take the money and run is *not* why I became an actor. If

The stoic smiles of the *Lost in Space* stars were the false face of what Goddard recalls as an "angry show." (*Left-right:* Marta Kristen, Goddard, June Lockhart, Guy Williams.)

I wanted to take the money and run, I would have been a teacher, because I would have made more money as a teacher in those thirty years than I did as an actor. Even though I made good money some years, my *average* was half of what I would have made as a teacher. That sounds astounding, but it's true."

Goddard went from $1,150 to $1,350 to $1,750 a week during the three years (83 episodes) of *Lost in Space*. He was third-billed below Guy Williams and June Lockhart in the weekly saga of a "space family" (and their pilot,

Giant footprints warn Guy Williams and Goddard that they are not alone on their new planet in the *Lost in Space* pilot.

Goddard) marooned on various planets in deep space. Williams was the ostensible star of the series, but when the decision was made to gear the series strictly toward kids, "special guest star" Jonathan Harris (who played the "reluctant stowaway" Dr. Smith) quickly moved to the fore. "It was a very difficult position for Guy," Goddard recalls of Williams' "demotion." "He was hired to be the star of this show, the father of the family, then all of a sudden he *wasn't* the star. Jonathan Harris was, Jonathan and the Robot. Hollywood has a way of 'getting' you: What they do is, they give you a lot of money, and *then* they say, 'Now that you've got all this money, now that you've got this lifestyle, *now* we're gonna tell you what you *can* do and what you *can't* do.' So Guy didn't have a lot of leverage, 'cause say he was making good money on this show; he had a family, he had a home — what was he gonna do? He needed to keep that money coming in, he had all that overhead. So when he wasn't the star of the show anymore, he'd get angry that Jonathan was getting most of the lines.

"And *one* time, Guy took some of *my* lines. I went in one morning to do a shot, and all of a sudden, when I was ready to do my lines, *Guy* had them all! So I got angry about that — of course. But Guy was havin' it pretty difficult. He'd come off *Zorro* [the 1957-59 Disney series] and that was a pretty big feather in his cap — he was a bigger star than *I* was, that's for sure, and probably the biggest star in the show, coming off of *Zorro*. And now he was being aced out by somebody nobody had ever heard of before, Jonathan Harris. (Maybe *some* people knew of Jonathan; I never had. But he wasn't like Guy.)

"So Guy was upset about that, and maybe some days he'd come in late, or maybe he'd walk off the set if something wasn't right. He was just angry about certain things and he threw his hands up in the air a few times. He never lost his temper about anything, at least not as far as I can remember; he was a gentleman. But he'd just *walk*, he'd just go. And so a couple of times, he and June were written out of shows, and I was written out of a show, for insubordination. It was like suspension time; it was like Irwin Allen was the headmaster of this co-ed school and we were getting our hands slapped if we didn't stay in line all the time."

Despite the discord brought on by the restructuring of the show, Goddard felt no rancor toward Harris other than *on*-screen, where pompous rascal Dr. Smith and hot-tempered Major West feuded incessantly. "Jonathan was the consummate professional. He did more than was ever asked of him, and you've gotta admire him. He developed that character, he worked on it, he came up with lines — he did *all* the kind of work that we as actors *want* to do, but we [other *Lost in Space* regulars] *didn't* do because we threw our hands up in the air. (At least *I* did.) If I had done the work that Jonathan did, maybe I would have come off better, but I really couldn't, my hands were tied. I'd get miffed at the Robot, because that was a piece of metal that was upstaging me *[laughs]*, but not at Jonathan; Jonathan deserved everything *he* got. He did the work and created a wonderful character."

Lost in Space was not a show that lent itself to big-name guest stars, but Goddard does remember a few favorites among the gallery of character actors who also did time on the Robinson family's galactic oasis. "Warren Oates and Albert Salmi were two of my favorites. Everybody has different favorites, but those were my two — those were *my* kind of actors, more than (say) a Michael Rennie or a Henry Jones. And I loved working with Kurt Russell. Kurt was

Goddard battles the out-of-control Robot (Bob May) in the initial *Lost in Space* episode, "The Reluctant Stowaway."

maybe 12 when he was on *Lost in Space*; his dad Bing I worked with a lot on *Johnny Ringo*. Kurt was a nice boy, a *great* kid, and a great *man* today—people say wonderful things about him. A lot of the *Lost in Space* guest stars I didn't get a chance to work with, because most of 'em worked with Jonathan.

"But, see, on *The Detectives*, I worked with Robert Taylor, with Edward G. Robinson—and I really *worked* with these people. On different shows, I *worked* with David Janssen, Chuck Connors, Myrna Loy, June Allyson, Tuesday Weld—a lot of people. So on *Lost in Space*, it wasn't like 'Oh, wow!' when they'd finally bring some guest star in." One unofficial *Lost in Space* semiregular was Dawson Palmer, who played many of the monsters during the series' three years, but "I don't remember him at all," admits Goddard. "See, by the time I'd get on the set, [the monster actors] were already in their outfits, and I wouldn't know Dawson Palmer if I *saw* him *[laughs]*. As a matter of fact, Michael Conrad was on *Lost in Space* once; in later years, he was the sergeant on *Hill Street Blues*. He played a monster in a show, made up like an ape kind of guy in a prison outfit. I had already worked with Michael at the Actors Studio, I *knew* Michael, but it wasn't until the last day that he finally told me it was him—I didn't know *[laughs]*. I *thought* the voice was familiar, but it was kind of muffled."

Remembering the *Jupiter 2* itself, Goddard reveals the actual layout of the (supposedly) two-level spaceship. "When we had scenes on the upper deck, we actually shot inside of the spaceship. Remember the big window that we looked out? The camera would just come up into there and shoot right in through the window at us, a big master shot. Then if they wanted to get close-ups, they could just set a camera up inside. They didn't cover close-ups too often, and if we were standing at the panels, they'd get our close-ups right there by shooting in through the view port. The elevator only went down about four feet, so to make it look like we were going down out of sight, we had to duck down and lie on the floor of the elevator. And if there were three or four of us going down, we'd be crammed down in there *[laughs]*. On another stage was the bottom floor, which we didn't shoot in as much."

After *Lost in Space* was canceled in 1968 at the end of its three-year run, Goddard found himself driven into what has been called "a seven-year sabbatical from acting"—a description he balks at initially, then admits, "Well, maybe it's *not* all that far from the truth. When I finished *Lost in Space*, I wasn't happy with the prospect of what I was going to do next, because I knew that I would be typed as a 'space show' actor and I didn't know how I'd get out of it. And I figured the best way to get out of it was to go back into studying acting. So I wasn't on a sabbatical from acting, it was a sabbatical from trying to get *jobs*, a sabbatical from hopping around and getting a lot of rejection. That's when I did a lot of serious acting; that's when I started becoming an actor. I knew that if I was going to have a career in acting, I couldn't just do *Lost in Space* and then go out and bounce around from interview to interview; I had to step back, get ahold of myself, reestablish myself in the craft and gain my confidence back as an actor. I'd lost my confidence as an actor 'cause I wasn't doing any real acting. That's my own fault, not the fault of *Lost in Space*. My fault."

Roles in the 1970s included a supporting part in the horror film *Blue Sunshine*, about people changing into bald-headed rampaging killers ten years after using an LSD-type drug in college. "I'm a straightlaced guy," Goddard explains, differentiating between himself and the drug peddler cum politician he played in the 1977 film. "I won't say I didn't inhale *[laughs]*, but I wasn't a smoker—you know what I mean?—and I wasn't into drugs and I've always been very straightlaced 'cause that's my generation. In *Blue Sunshine*, I played a character who had been involved in drugs and became a congressman. It was a good low-budget film, I thought. I liked the political part of it, because when I was young I thought that I would have liked to go into politics, and it gave me a chance to play a politician."

A far brighter high point in Goddard's career came a year later, when he costarred with Liza Minnelli on Broadway in *The Act*. "Doing that was the most exposure I ever had to stars," he recalls proudly. "Every night I knew that in the audience there'd be a star or a major person. It might be Jacqueline Kennedy, it might be Robert DeNiro, Sammy Davis, Henry Kissinger, Mia Farrow, Sinatra—'cause Liza was a draw, and anybody who was in New York was gonna see the show with Liza. So that was a wonderful year for me 'cause I thought, 'Wow, all these people I've been watchin' all these years, now they're gonna watch *me*.' Even if it's just for a few minutes, their eyes are going to be on *me* part of the time! I mean, they wouldn't remember watching me, they would watch Liza, but in *my* mind, they were watching me, too! That was a wonderful year." A *One Life to Live* casting director caught Goddard in *The Act* (so to speak) and lined up a role for him on the popular New York–based afternoon soap. "I enjoyed that year. I was working with a lot of good people and I did have the opportunity to get my teeth into something a little bit. My character was on for a year before he was killed—they wanted to keep me alive longer because I was really getting hot on that show. It was a good character and people loved it. But I had already made other plans to go back to California, so they killed me when they were supposed to. Then I went back to California and I did some writing—I wrote a couple of screenplays. I tested for a *General Hospital* part I *didn't* get, then I came back and tested again for a *different* part and I was signed to a two-year contract."

Between his two experiences in daytime drama, Goddard also added yet one more sci-fi credit to his filmography—albeit in a (very) supporting capacity. "I only did *Strange Invaders* [1983] because my daughter Melissa was an assistant on that movie. *Strange Invaders* was made by Orion, and Mike Medavoy, who was one of the owners of Orion, was my first wife's second husband. So my first wife was now married to him and my daughter was now his stepdaughter. (Are you following this?) She was up in Toronto, Canada, working as like an assistant director, just helping out, and I was in New York. I wanted to see her, so I flew up. And they had the part of a cop, and they asked me to do it, so I said yes. It was a one-day shoot. The same thing happened on *Play It Again, Sam* [1972] with Woody Allen. My second wife, Susan Anspach, was in that movie and I was there, and Woody asked me just to sit down in a scene. I sat down and said a line, and I've been getting residuals—every two years, I get a six-dollar check for *Play It Again, Sam [laughs]*!"

Throughout his acting career, in between jobs, Goddard worked with children, from Head Start programs in California to Sloan-Kettering Cancer Center in New York City; now, back in his home state of Massachusetts, he is turning his full attention to at-risk kids at the Longview Farm School. "These are kids who have come from broken homes, kids that don't *have* homes, kids who have been in foster homes, kids who have been abused in their infancy or in their early childhood, kids who have a learning disability but it's *really* based on economic factors or family problems, and they just haven't been able to get the learning that they should. These kids become the at-risk kids when they get into high school, kids who're going to drop out and kids that don't care about going to school and these kind of things. I love those kind of kids, I feel that they could be *me* except that I had a better break when I was a kid. I was able to go to high school and college because I had the family background. And because I *did* have a strong family background, I really have a lot of empathy and feeling for kids that didn't, and I feel I want to work with those kids. I think I'm pretty good with kids, so those are the kids that I want to work with in special education.

"At the Longview Farm School, I'm the behavioral specialist. 'My' kids come to me during the day when they can't make it in the classroom, and they pretty much spend the day with me. And it's probably the toughest job in education—*very* tiring. But I'm learning a lot, and I think I'm reaching some of them. They've certainly reached *me*. So it's challenging and it's wonderful, and I don't have a minute to think about, 'Why did I stop acting?'"

But it is not as though Mark Goddard has severed his showbiz ties: Daughter Melissa is now a producer (she produced *Poison Ivy* [1992] with Drew Barrymore as well as *Big Girls Don't Cry ... They Get Even* [1992], a film about her father's work with his at-risk kids). Between his school duties and other responsibilities, he also finds time to do the occasional science fiction convention. "I never realized, never *dreamed* that I would be talking to fans at conventions about *Lost in Space* twenty-seven years later. I never dreamed that people would be interested still. So I'm grateful for that in a way, because it's nice to know that there are people who still want to read about me. I appreciate it in retrospect, everything that's happened, but at the time—*Lost in Space* was *not* the joy of my life."

MARK GODDARD FILMOGRAPHY

A Rage to Live (United Artists, 1965)
The Monkey's Uncle (Buena Vista, 1965)
The Love-Ins (Columbia, 1967)

Play It Again, Sam (Paramount, 1972)
Blue Sunshine (Cinema Shares, 1977)
Roller Boogie (United Artists, 1979)
Strange Invaders (Orion, 1983)

The agonies that some people go through, waiting for the phone to ring, wanting that great public success, has not been part of my makeup ... because of what I saw my parents do and what their concerns were with life as it should be lived.

June Lockhart

JUNE LOCKHART AND HER EXTENDED FAMILY are well on their way to setting some sort of record, if they have not done so already. "My daughter Annie is an actress, and it's quite possible that *her* two children will be the fifth generation [of Lockharts in the acting profession]," she recounts, filled with the sort of exuberance we all instinctively *knew* she had to have in real life. "Annie's two children are Carly, who's six, and a baby boy, Zane. Their father is Adam Taylor, who is an actor and a *very* good director—as a matter of fact, he's the first assistant on a movie that's being made in Tucson now called *Tombstone*, about the shootout at the O.K. Corral. *Adam's* father is Buck Taylor, who was for 17 years on *Gunsmoke* and after that on *Dallas*, and *his* father is Dub Taylor. [Adam and Dub Taylor both died in 1994.] Annie added up all the years of the two families in show business and figured there's 287 years between us."

The voice—and the long, hearty laugh that punctuates the anecdote—is unmistakable, a voice that nearly all of us have grown up hearing. Those distinctive tones beseeched Lassie to find Timmy and sternly instructed Will and Penny to stay away from that mysterious cave. Movie fans know the voice from MGM classics of the 1940s, and folks who grew up during television's Golden Age have heard it on most of the top dramatic shows. Nowadays, of course, she is best remembered for the mothers (Ruth Martin and Maureen Robinson) she played on *Lassie* and *Lost in Space*, although it is a disservice that an actress who has essayed such a wide variety of roles should now be known mostly for that one facet of her work. "One of my favorites was an episode of *Gunsmoke* where I played an alcoholic nymphomaniac murderess with the mind of a twelve year old, and I 'offed' Wayne Morris," she enthuses, laughing that laugh again. "I wore a dress which was cut way low, with the boobs hanging out, and, oh, it was nifty—Crazy Beulah was the name of the character!

"I just take the roles as they come, and when you get a role in which you're able to do that sort of acting—and I *have* certainly done some of them—they're fun. But in the long run, because of what my image is, I think that playing the [maternal] roles has been far more remunerative for me. Dan Rather said, 'I can control my reputation, but not my image, because my image is how *you* perceive me.' And that's really true."

Maureen Robinson, *Lost in Space*'s understanding, brow-knitting mom, was one of those maternal (and "remunerative") acting stints, one in which Lockhart could show all the motherly concern she could muster—but none of the wifely affection. "Guy Williams [Professor John Robinson] and I *did* have scenes of intimacy in the beginning. Great affection was shown—hand-holding and kisses—in the pilot, it's all there. But the dictum came down from CBS that we were not to touch each other because, they said, it embarrassed

Previous page: "Born in a trunk," June Lockhart continued her family's acting tradition—often in "goody" roles that do not reflect her oft-outrageous personality.

children watching at home to see their parents kissing. Well, we could *not* believe it. We had a new network guy come on, and I said, 'Do you know what is going on here with these parts?' He thought it was preposterous when I told him about it — he said, 'My God, I can't believe it!' Guy and I had put in all these little things to try to give this family a *warmth* like that — being demonstrably affectionate was something I was raised with, as was Guy, being an Italian. In my family, I never saw my father *pass* my mother without touching her, patting her, hugging her."

The touchy-feely father she describes is, of course, Gene Lockhart (1891–1957), the veteran vaudeville and stage actor and writer, and her mom was actress Kathleen (1894–1978); the two were introduced by Thomas Edison. (It was Gene's father, John Coates Lockhart, a concert singer, who represented the first generation of the family in showbiz.) Born in New York City, only-child June made her professional debut at age eight in a Metropolitan Opera production of *Peter Ibbetson*, playing Mimsey in the dream sequence. In the mid-thirties, the Lockharts relocated to California, where father Gene enjoyed a long career as one of the screen's great character actors. Being the child of famous parents has frequently furnished Hollywood brats with an excuse for unproductive lifestyles, but June flourished rather than floundered in this unique environment.

"It was my parents, of course, because they were *in* but not *of* the business. It was how my father made his living — he was awfully good at it and he really loved it — but when he came home, he was concerned with his writing and his correspondence and what had happened in the house, and he was *always* outwardly motivated toward people and causes. And the people that they entertained at the house were journalists, physicians, publishers, singers, composers, columnists — they were there every Sunday, playing badminton *[laughs]*. Growing up in this sophisticated atmosphere was really an extraordinary thing to be able to do. And the *laughter* in the house, all the time, *such* laughter. My maternal grandparents lived with us, and a maiden aunt. We had just a neat time. So it was always kept in perspective, and I was *never* part of that Hollywood society that one read about in the movie magazines. It was quite well balanced, just a rich, wonderful education and family life."

She made her screen debut in MGM's 1938 version of Charles Dickens' timeless tale, *A Christmas Carol*, playing — appropriately enough — the daughter of stars Gene and Kathleen Lockhart. "It was lovely to be working with my mother and father, and it just seemed quite a natural thing to do because all my life we had always celebrated Christmas with a reading of *Christmas Carol*, done concert style. My father wrote a script and the dinner guests would take parts, and we would play it. I would play Tiny Tim until I got old enough to be one of the sisters, my mother and father were Mr. and Mrs. Cratchit, and Leo G. Carroll would play Scrooge, because he was *always* a dinner guest. So we had done this all my life and it was lovely, and then there we were doing it at MGM! And it certainly turned out to be a classic." The experience of setting foot in front of MGM's cameras was not at all daunting for the 13 year old "because I was with my parents. The thing I remember vividly is that, in my very first scene, we were all set and ready to go, the assistant said, 'Roll 'em' and I started to move — I was *that* eager. And the director, Ed Marin, said to me, 'No, June, you have to wait till *I* say *action.*' And *that* stayed with me a l-o-n-g time *[laughs]*!"

Two years later, while still in high school, June was offered a supporting role in Warners' *All This, and Heaven Too* (1940), a Bette Davis–Charles Boyer vehicle. "I was at Marlborough School, which was one of the two top schools at the time in Los Angeles. Daddy and I went to Miss Blake, the principal, and he said, 'June would like to do this part for the experience, regardless of whether she ever becomes an actress when she grows up. This is a really lovely opportunity for her, and a first-class production.' Miss Blake listened to all this. He went on, 'What I would like, please, is if you would arrange so that June can keep up with her class by doing the classwork *on* the set with the tutor.' At that point, Miss Blake said, 'Well, Mr. Lockhart, I personally would have no objection to June doing the film, but I *really* don't think the parents of the other girls would want *their* children going to school with anybody in the movies.' There was this *pause*, and then my father turned to me and said, 'June, go to your locker and get your books.' I went, and by the time I got back, I was no longer a Marlborough student.

"Daddy was an educated man — he was an author and a composer, and just the most marvelously gentle man. And the insult that she had slapped him with was really, really awful. As we drove home after that, he said, 'Well, Juney, today you had an experience of the disregard with which the acting profession is held in some circles.' Marlborough School was old Los Angeles money — which meant probably seventy years *[laughs]* — old *oil* money. So I went to an interim school, Immaculate Heart, which I'd been at before (and loathed), and then I went finally to Westlake, the *other* top school, which I adored, it was wonderful. Also there while I was were Shirley Temple and Elizabeth Montgomery." Around the time of June's eight-week acting stint in *All This, and Heaven Too*, Gene Lockhart authored the article "A Doting Father and His Talented Daughter." "He wrote in that that my acting training had consisted mostly of making signals to my mother behind the old man's back *[laughs]*!"

At no point during these formative years, June Lockhart insists, did she ever make a conscious decision to become an actress. "My opportunities came along so easily that there was never any sweating and striving and anxiety over it all. It was not until my first marriage [in 1951] that I really knew how much I enjoyed it, and that I really knew what I could accomplish with it." Other early forties movie roles that came her way included *Sergeant York* (as Gary Cooper's sister), *Miss Annie Rooney* with Shirley Temple, *Forever and a Day*, in a scene written by her father, and then in a succession of roles at MGM (among others, *Meet Me in St. Louis*, *The White Cliffs of Dover* and, portentously, *Son of Lassie*).

A different type of dog was at the center of the plot of her first costarring film. "Oh, *She-Wolf of London* was fun to do," Lockhart laughs about this mutt of a movie, found wagging at the tail end of Universal's monster cycle. "If I'm remembering right, I was just submitted for it by my agent. I did it, and—I was *not* very good in it. But the following year, I was *the* hot ingenue on Broadway in a wonderful comedy, so I guess what I needed [in *She-Wolf*] was good direction." Lockhart pauses, realizing she has just cast an aspersion, regroups and then adds, "Well, I guess the director of *She-Wolf* was a good one, but the film was of the genre that they did at Universal—I think it only took two weeks to shoot. That was so early in my experience, I was still learning the technique of film acting."

In the 1946 B movie, Lockhart is a woebegone English lass whose family, legend has it, was cursed by wolves; when vicious attacks occur in a nearby park, she convinces herself that she is the female lycanthrope responsible. "There were a lot of English people in it who were friends of my father's—people who would come around the house and play badminton *[laughs]*—so there again it was not strange or unusual or awkward. Don Porter was my leading man, and he was a dear." The shooting of some retakes necessitated that Lockhart, Porter, director Jean Yarbrough and a technical crew work on Christmas Eve (1945), with all concerned champing at the bit to get home to their families. "Don and I were in a horse and buggy, with rear-screen projection behind us. We finished the final take, and *before* Don could help me down out of the buggy, everybody was gone. Just *gone*! And we both laughed about it—there was no help with your costume or 'Merry Christmas' or anything. It was like an evacuation!" Other than this one incident, Lockhart insists, B studio Universal was as efficient and businesslike a workplace as "studio of the stars" MGM. "It was all the same—we broke for lunch and had toilets and dressing rooms *[laughs]*, and they treated you quite nicely. I was not aware of anything being less than most professional."

The following year, 1947, Lockhart made her Broadway bow, playing the ingenue in the comedy *For Love or Money* with John Loder. The play itself was mediocre by all accounts, but Lockhart got a standing ovation opening night and immediately became the toast of Broadway; one critic compared her debut to the first big hits of Helen Hayes and Margaret Sullavan. Soon played up in all advertisements as the main attraction of the production, she went on to win a Tony, the Donaldson Award, the Theatre World Award and the Associated Press citation for Woman of the Year for Drama.

When television's unblinking eye first opened on America, she was there, too, playing roles in many of the top dramatic programs (some of them live from New York). One was a 1951 *Robert Montgomery Presents* adaptation of

Lockhart admits to needing better direction on *She-Wolf of London*: "I was still learning the technique of film acting."

Nathaniel Hawthorne's *The House of the Seven Gables*—again opposite father Gene. "Daddy and I got the giggles in one scene—we always had trouble getting through it in rehearsal. The line that my father had to say to me was *so* convoluted that I remembered it forever: He was the villain and he was leaving the house, and the line was, 'Tell your cousin I will return betide, for the benefit of her and hers, to further discuss the matter of which we spoke.' He did it beautifully on the air, of course, but we knew that we had broken up and laughed hysterically all during rehearsal over it — and they never *changed* it. That's one thing wonderful about working with a relative — when you look deep into the eyes, you *know* there is all that subtext, and it's just Daddy there tryin' to get through a bad piece of dialogue *[laughs]*."

Lockhart worked steadily throughout the fifties, on television and the stage, and every now and then obeyed an impulse to branch out. She worked for a year or two on *Guideposts*, an interfaith religious magazine, in order to learn about the publishing business, and in the mid-fifties she was granted permission to travel with newspaper reporters covering the presidential candidates. Ever since then — except for a short break during the time that "people started shooting at our presidents" — she has attended Washington briefings every time an opportunity has presented itself. "Even today, whenever I'm in Washington, no matter *what* the administration or *who* the press secretary is, I call up and I'm invited to attend the briefing. April 1991 I was there and I was staying for over a week, so I got to a lot of briefings. This sort of filtered around town — nobody's ever made a fuss over this at all. The *Washington Post* wanted to run a little blurb about it, so they called different White House photographers to see if anybody had a picture of me in the briefing room. Finally one of the photographers said, 'A picture of *June*? Nobody takes a picture of June when she's here — she's just one of the guys!' And I thought that was the greatest compliment I'd ever had in my life — isn't that *terrific*?"

In sharp contrast to her busy, vivacious life was her role as the demure, gingham-clad, stay-at-home mom on television's *Lassie*, an acting stint that began in 1958. She remained with the show until 1964, but did guest shots on other series during those years, including the aforementioned *Gunsmoke* episode and a 1958 version of *Beauty and the Beast* on *Shirley Temple's Storybook*. "Oh, God, did we have a good time in that, with Chuck Heston as the Beast and Claire Bloom as Beauty. Barbara Baxley and I were the wicked and ugly sisters, and we had the most fun on that — it was neat."

It was a guest spot on ABC's *Voyage to the Bottom of the Sea* that led to Lockhart's *other* most-famous television role. Acting in the episode "The Ghost of Moby Dick," she met veteran producer Irwin Allen. "I had not met him before, to my knowledge. I was doing that *Voyage to the Bottom of the Sea* guest appearance in like maybe August or September [1964], and on the second day, Irwin saw the rushes of the first day. He came down and found me and he said, 'We're doing a series called *Space Family Robinson*. Would you like to do another series?' I said yes, and so he gave me the script and I called my agent and said, 'This looks interesting.' So we did it."

Rechristened *Lost in Space*, the original series pilot — at that time one of the most expensive in the history of television (over $600,000) — began shooting January 6, 1965, on the 20th Century-Fox Westwood lot. It starred Guy Williams as astrophysicist John Robinson and Lockhart as his biochemist wife, Maureen; accompanied by their children Judy (Marta Kristen), Penny (Angela Cartwright) and Will (Billy Mumy) and by Dr. Don West (Mark Goddard), the space pioneers set out aboard the *Gemini 12* to colonize the planet Alpha Centauri, only to be sidetracked by a meteor storm that sends them into the uncharted depths of outer space. Mark Goddard, who was not much interested in starring in a space show, has said that he accepted the role in the pilot when he was assured that the series would never sell, but Lockhart suffered under no such delusion. "Oh, I knew it would sell. Well, they already had an air date—this was set. CBS was part owner and I *knew* that it was going on the air for at least a year."

Before the series reached the airwaves, extensive changes were made, including the addition of Jonathan Harris as the saboteur caught aboard the spacecraft (renamed *Jupiter 2*) just before liftoff. Convoluted plots and intricate special effects caused delays, with the reported result that (for a time) the show was running only seven days ahead of air time. "Seven days ahead of air time in *Canada*," Lockhart corrects. "Sometimes we'd finish on Monday and it would be on the air in Canada the following Saturday night. And if the show wasn't ready, 20th Century-Fox or CBS would have been fined $50,000. But we made it every time, because Irwin kept everybody there working twenty-four hours a day, practically—the postproduction and everything."

Lockhart dismisses published accounts of a registered nurse visiting the set three days a week, and also denies another report that she took out a Lloyds of London policy against serious injury—but she admits that, early on, working on *Lost in Space was* a strenuous and often physical task. "The hours were very, very long. And there *was* a lot of physical stuff—there was less of that to do later in the run, because the story line changed—but, yes, the pilot was *very* physical, and all the flying on wires— *that* was an experience! And it was very hot, of course, in the silver lamé suits. However, we just accepted it all and did the job—you do your best to just keep yourself comfortable under those conditions. Bitching is not one of the things I do on a set, anyway, because *everybody's* doing the same thing. We had some very good directors on *Lost in Space* that first season, but they usually only did one or two shows, and then *probably* went to a halfway house *[laughs]*!"

The addition of Jonathan Harris to the cast would, of course, eventually take the series in a whole new direction; Lockhart is not certain whether the show would have been more successful had it stayed serious rather than going the "camp" route. "I don't know—it's hard to say what the length might have been. But *that* is what they chose to do with the show, to make it a comedy show about an old man [Harris] and a little boy [Mumy] in space. So there's still a lot of unmined area there, to have a *real* show about a family colonizing a new planet. That certainly would have been a different show! Would it have *run* as long—or longer—I don't know." Her role diminished in size the more the series concentrated on the misadventures of Harris and Mumy (and the

Robot, played by Bob May), but Lockhart does not admit to being disappointed by the change. "It took a while to realize that that was the direction they were going in. But I certainly would not agitate to leave the show. I believe in contracts, and certainly was happy to stay until the finish of it." Hers was also the only character who was never once the centerpiece of an episode. "Yes, I think that's right, and—you know—that *never* occurred to me before. That shows you about where my ego is, I guess!"

Other *Lost in Space* cast members have talked about the constant tension on the sets—caused, some say, by the influence of Irwin Allen—but according to Lockhart, "I wasn't aware of it. I went to work, I brought all the things I wanted to read, and I had a marvelous time with Guy. We used to play music in the dressing rooms, and people would come and join us and sit there and we'd listen to Tchaikovsky or Rachmaninoff or something. (Guy was a brilliant musicologist.) Then I'd go in and do my stuff, and come *back out* to my dressing room. So I wasn't aware of whatever was going on. I knew we were *always* under the gun, time-wise. (For example, if we were doing a scene with an explosion in it and you fluffed a line and the *explosion* was perfect and they had to do it over, you *really* felt bad *[laughs]*!) But about all that other stuff—I don't take that stuff on, because it can drive you nuts if you do."

Even if *Lost in Space* did represent long hours and an undemanding role, there were plenty of rewards, like the opportunity to bring her daughters Anne Kathleen (born 1953) and June Elizabeth (1955) to the set. "Oh, they loved coming to the set. But we *all* loved the set, it was just *amazing*—all that great silver hardware and lights blinking and things going up and down. It was really quite wonderful." The series was canceled at the end of its third season, but the "family" can still be found together at an occasional convention or—more regularly—gathered for lunch on the same Fox lot where they filmed their extraterrestrial adventures a quarter century ago. "We get together at least once every three or four months," Lockhart smiles. "In fact, we all had lunch together last week at Fox—Marta and Jonathan and Billy and myself, and even Bobby May was there for that one, the man in the robot suit. (Angela couldn't come this time, and of course Mark is back East.) But we're looking forward to us all being together again soon. We're all in touch all the time, we talk on the phone and we correspond and we've never ceased to be involved closely with each other."

The one absent "family" member is of course Guy Williams, who died in 1989, but Lockhart says that he's still "close to their hearts" as well. "This I think is quite unique in the business: I arranged a dinner with Jan Williams, Guy's widow, and her son and daughter and their mates and all of us [the remaining *Lost in Space* regulars], and Angela's husband and Marta's husband and Billy's wife. We all took them out to dinner, to a place in Santa Monica, and we all sat around and talked about Guy Williams. Talked about *Guido*, which is what we used to call him. It was the loveliest, sweetest, most senti-

The family created by the show (*Lost in Space*) is still one today, according to Lockhart.

mental evening—of course, we knew Guy's family through Guy while we were shooting. To be able to do this, to bring us all together like that, was really neat, and I *think* quite an original, unique idea. At no other time has a television family taken out the *real* family under those circumstances—for the sentimentality of it. It was a sweet evening."

As for the series itself, Lockhart has "a *few* of them on tape—I don't have them all—and I recently was given the original pilot, and that's grand to have.

I was given it by the Sci-Fi Channel prior to my hosting the premiere of it—it had never aired before. Hosting it and doing some interviews, that was great fun to do."

Retirement—or even just the thought of it—is apparently nowhere on the horizon for the actress, who says she cannot think of a single regret associated with her 50-odd-year career. "I never had a desire to be famous, I *never* had that driving force—gotta act! gotta get out there! It has just unfolded *so* naturally in my life. The agonies that some people go through, waiting for the phone to ring, wanting that great public success, has not been part of my makeup—again, because of what I saw my parents do, and what their concerns were with life as it should be lived." She has watched her own daughters grow, and now enjoys seeing acting daughter Anne's career develop. "She was Sheba in *Battlestar Galactica*. She's a very good actress, and has great potential still, I feel. She's awfully good on the stage—we did *Butterflies Are Free* and *Forty Carats* together. She's also a marvelous horseback rider—she appears at rodeos with her husband riding cutting horses, that's her particular favorite. She also is one of the busiest and most sought-after actresses for ADR work, which is postrecording of dialogue. You'd be very surprised at the number of films that you've seen in which you've heard Annie's voice on the sound track, often overdubbing dialogue for famous actresses." Mother and daughter both appeared in 1986 in *Troll*, with Anne playing the younger version of her white-wigged mother. The *Gremlins*-like film did not get a great reception from fans, but Lockhart—who *swears* in the movie (gasp!)—also swears by the experience. "God, I had the best time! We shot it in Italy, and on days when we weren't working, they made all the arrangements for the most fabulous sightseeing— off to Rome, off to Florence, off to Venice. Lordy me, it was wonderful and I'd go again in a New York minute!"

Obviously, the *real* June Lockhart is a very different person from many of the poised, serene, housebound women she has played in her long career. She still stands by her long-ago quote, "I really have no understanding or patience for people who won't expose themselves to the innovative"—although, asked to name something *she* would never have tried, she is quick to specify bungee jumping. A *TV Guide* article once called her a "happy nut," a description that might ruffle a lot of actresses, but Lockhart just laughs it off. "Well, I don't know if *nut* is quite the word now, because *nut* may have a different connotation these days than it did years ago, when that was written. But I certainly am ... *outrageous*! One of my greatest compliments in life was when Annie called me an eccentric, and I shouted, 'Hallelujah! I've been waiting for eccentric-hood all my life!' She didn't mean it as a compliment at all, but *by God* it was neat. Who wouldn't want to be an *original*?"

Lockhart has never had an acting lesson, nor the "gotta act! gotta get out there!" compulsion that drives many performers.

JUNE LOCKHART FILMOGRAPHY

A Christmas Carol (MGM, 1938)
All This, and Heaven Too (Warner Bros., 1940)
Adam Had Four Sons (Columbia, 1941)
Sergeant York (Warner Bros., 1941)
Miss Annie Rooney (United Artists, 1942)
Forever and a Day (RKO, 1943)
Meet Me in St. Louis (MGM, 1944)
The White Cliffs of Dover (MGM, 1944)

June Lockhart

Keep Your Powder Dry (MGM, 1945)
Son of Lassie (MGM, 1945)
Easy to Wed (MGM, 1946)
The Yearling (MGM, 1946)
She-Wolf of London (The Curse of the Allenbys) (Universal, 1946)
It's a Joke, Son (Eagle-Lion, 1947)
Bury Me Dead (Eagle-Lion, 1947)
T-Men (Eagle-Lion, 1947)
Time Limit (United Artists, 1957)
Lassie's Great Adventure (20th Century-Fox, 1963)
Just Tell Me You Love Me (1979)
Butterfly (Analysis, 1982)
Strange Invaders (Orion, 1983)
Troll (Empire Pictures, 1986)
Rented Lips (Cineworld, 1988)
The Big Picture (Columbia, 1989)
Dead Women in Lingerie (AFI/USA, 1991)
Sleep with Me (MGM, 1993)

*I was cast as a director of dinosaurs.
Like I was a lion tamer — but with dinosaurs!*

Eugene Lourie

They Fought in the Creature Features

EUGENE LOURIE ENJOYED A FASCINATING and wide-ranging career in movies. In 1919 Yalta, while still a teenager, he worked as a bit player in an anticommunist movie called *Black Crows*; in 1930s France he was a renowned production designer collaborating with legendary screen directors Jean Renoir, René Clair and Max Ophuls. Arriving in Hollywood in the early forties, he resumed his career as art director (often working with fellow émigré Renoir); designed films as diverse as Chaplin's *Limelight* (1952) and Clint Eastwood's *Bronco Billy* (1980); even returned to acting with a bit in Richard Gere's *Breathless* (1983). "And yet," Lourie added, with a touch of regret, "*The Beast from 20,000 Fathoms* typecast me as a director of science fiction."

Lourie (who died on May 26, 1991) became involved with the classic 1953 dinosaur-on-the-loose thriller when a trio of low-budget producers approached him to handle the art direction on their upcoming slate of films. "They were called Mutual Films. They had three pictures to do—very cheap pictures—and they asked me if I would be interested in [art directing]. Jack Dietz, Hal Chester and Bernie Burton—they were the three that headed the company. That *was* the company *[laughs]*! They told me, 'We don't have any scripts, we have short outlines.' One outline was amusing to me; it was a subject that very seldom was done. It was the dinosaur coming out of the water. And I told them, 'I am interested in this picture. Who would direct it?' They said, 'We don't know. We don't have anybody to direct it yet.' I said, 'I doubt that anybody will know how to direct this picture. But if you like, I feel capable to do it, and I will do it.'

"They said okay, and that was all. Two weeks later, the call came from these same people: 'Gene, were you joking when you spoke of directing this film for us?' I said, 'No, I wasn't joking. I really can do it.' And they said, 'Well, then, it's your picture. Now find a writer to write the script.' I said okay. I found a friend who worked with me, and we wrote the screenplay in a very short time, one or two weeks. And then we made the picture."

The Beast from 20,000 Fathoms was the first of three dinosaur movies that Lourie would eventually direct, and the film that would stamp the eminent production designer as "a director of science fiction"—an association he found limiting in later years. Born in czarist Russia in 1905, Lourie's first brush with the movie medium came in 1911 when a cinema theater opened in Kharkov ("It was an unforgettable moment in my life"). Lourie remained an ardent young moviegoer throughout those turbulent years; escaping Russia, he found himself in Istanbul, where he drew and painted posters for a local movie theater to earn money for his fare to Paris and (to cut expenses) slept in the theater, atop its grand piano. "I had a kind of an adventurous youth because I was raised and I lived through the First World War and the Russian Revolution," Lourie recalled. "Like many young people of my generation, I wished

Previous page: Director Eugene Lourie (seen here acting in *Krakatoa, East of Java*) grew to regret his reputation as a "dinosaur specialist."

to leave Russia, to find my own life. I escaped through Turkey, from Crimea to Istanbul, and I lived in Istanbul one and a half years without money, trying to earn money. And then finally I went to Paris. My idea was to become a painter."

After working as a painter and a ballet set designer in France, Lourie turned to films and began a long association with famed French director Jean Renoir (*La Grande Illusion* [Grand Illusion], *La Bête Humaine* [The Human Beast], *La Règle du Jeu* [The Rules of the Game]). In 1941, during the Nazi occupation, French filmmakers (including Lourie, Renoir, Clair, Ophuls and others with whom Lourie had worked) fled for Hollywood. "I was a very known art director in France, and when a lot of people escaped from France, I decided to go where the films are made. Jean Renoir came here [to the United States], and I came here. Hollywood was like a giant magnet."

Lourie quickly found employment in Hollywood: he reteamed with Renoir on his stateside films, and also art directed such forties fare as *The House of Fear* (a Basil Rathbone/Sherlock Holmes mystery) and Abbott and Costello's *In Society*. (He even vaguely remembered working on an Invisible Man film, presumably *The Invisible Man's Revenge* [1944].) One difference between making films abroad and churning them out in Tinseltown, according to Lourie, was the fact that he "didn't like the dictatorial power of the production office. The studio dictated many things. I remember working at Warners and being told, 'Listen, this scene takes place in France. You go to the back lot and shoot it in our Paris street.' Their Paris street was made by a German art director, and it looked like a Bavarian village *[laughs]*. But you had to accept it. This was a little surprising."

It was in 1952 that Lourie was offered the director's chair on *The Beast from 20,000 Fathoms* (titled *The Monster from Beneath the Sea* during production). "Chester, Dietz and Burton were going to produce three films and release them through regional distributors," Lourie remembered. "They knew of my work for Renoir, and they knew also that I was designing cheap TV pictures at the Hal Roach studios. They were of no help to me [in directing the movie]. The one who was *pretending* to [be helpful] was Hal Chester; he provided the money, but he didn't try to influence me in any way. He was at one time one of the East Side Kids. I did have a *little* help from Bernie Burton because he was a very experienced filmmaker and a film editor. Otherwise, I was on my own. It was shot in a studio [the Motion Picture Center]. The Arctic scenes were shot on the stage. The amusement park was Long Beach. That picture was extraordinarily fast; I had a very quick cameraman named [Jack] Russell and I think we did it in twelve days. It cost about $200,000."

Lourie also helped to write the movie, although he did not take screen credit for his writing contribution (credit went to Lou Morheim and Fred Freiberger). "I was not full of vanity as I am now," Lourie joked. "[A writing credit] was not important to me. It was important at that point for me to make an interesting picture. A friend worked with me on the screenplay, and he also did not want his name on the film. I still remember his name, but as he didn't want credit then, I don't know if it would be discreet to name him." Asked about Ray Bradbury's contribution, Lourie recounted, "Bradbury got a story credit because, as we were working on the story, we came across a short story of his where a dinosaur answers the call of a lighthouse. I told my producers, and they decided the name of Bradbury would be good to add, and they bought his story. That's why his name is on the prints."

Beast, directed by Lourie and animated by Ray Harryhausen, opens in the Arctic with a nuclear blast freeing a prehistoric monster (a "rhedosaurus") after countless centuries suspended in ice. The creature promptly begins to wend its way south, from the snowy wastes at the top of the world toward New York City, its ancestral breeding ground. *Beast*'s large-scale crowd scenes (New Yorkers fleeing in panic from the rampaging creature) "were shot partly on location in New York City and partly on the back lot of Paramount Studios — Paramount had a big New York set. I went to New York with Bernie Burton [to shoot process plates and some of the mob scenes]. We shot on a weekend when there would be not much traffic. We had hired extras to play stevedores and dockworkers, and when we saw them we saw that they were puny men, they did not look like a stevedore should look. So we hired some real stevedores. When we were done, they asked for me to pose with them in a photo. They wished to show the photo to their wives; this would prove that they were working [in the film], not getting drunk in a bar *[laughs]*.

"The next day we shot on Wall Street with a crowd of twenty-five people. There were supposed to be many more, but the production manager said that it was a Sunday and extras would have to be paid double, so twenty-five was all we could afford. But I knew that we would be shooting [additional crowd scenes] at Paramount, so it was unimportant. The largest amount of extras I remember at Paramount was four hundred for one day. [Producer] Bernie Burton was the editor on it, and as he was cutting the film he said, 'Gene, you don't give me any prerogative. You shot the scenes [in such a way] that I can only put them together the way you shot them.' I said, 'That was the idea!'"

The official stars of *Beast* were Paul Christian and Paula Raymond, but the *real* star was the monster itself, brought to "life" by Harryhausen. "Hal Chester, one of the producers, told me that they had investigated all means of animating the beast and they had the name of a young animator who had worked already with Willis O'Brien, who made *King Kong*. Chester said, 'I think it would be useful for you to meet him and speak to him and decide if he will be part of our crew.' So I met Harryhausen; at that time he was animating fairy-tale [shorts] for children. We spoke and I liked him very much, and I saw the pictures he made and the animation was usually without jerks. So I said, 'Let's do the picture together.' I was amazed how long it took, the frame-by-frame animation. The time it took to shoot the picture was twelve days; to animate it, it took two or three months! But I enjoyed working with Harryhausen very much."

On the subject of his "official" stars, Lourie recalled, "Paul Christian is a German actor; his real name was Hubschmid, and he was very known in Switzerland. He was a very charming man. I remember I had a photograph of me with him; as he is very tall and I am quite short, the photograph was of me using a stepladder to speak to him *[laughs]*. Paula Raymond was a mediocre actress; she was very rigid. But Cecil Kellaway was very, very charming; he gave the picture a little humor and a nice kind of tone."

When the film was completed, producers Chester, Burton and Dietz were all pleased—and a bit surprised—that *Beast* had exceeded their expectations. "They were all *extremely* happy with the picture," said Lourie. "But when Dietz saw that it was better than they expected, he didn't want to release it through a small organization. He went to Jack Warner and offered *him* the picture. But Warner didn't want to release the picture; he wanted to buy it outright. And he *did* buy it outright, for $450,000, and Warners changed the title to *The Beast from 20,000 Fathoms*. Then, when the returns started coming in, Jack Dietz was very *unhappy* that he had lost the rights, because it was number one at the box office. Each time he read about it in *Variety*, he said, 'Oh, I am stupid!'"

Harryhausen's amazing effects also exceeded the expectations of everyone involved—invluding Lourie. "He invented some scenes that were very good. The scene of the Beast in the burning roller coaster was like a big opera act, like a tenor who dies in a very dramatic scene. That roller coaster was another miniature, like the Beast itself. It was eight feet high. We put rubber cement on the roller coaster so it would burn and we had pieces precut so that they would fly off in flames. Then Harryhausen added the Beast into the scene, attacking the roller coaster, and it all fit together. I saw the film at a matinee; Jean Renoir came with me. The ending of it affected my daughter. She was about six years old when I took her to see the picture. And coming home, she started to cry and said, 'You are bad, Daddy! You killed the big nice Beast!'"

The huge success of *Beast from 20,000 Fathoms* instantly typed Lourie as a science fiction specialist. "It was very strange. Many people came with projects for me to do, and they all wanted copies of *The Beast from 20,000 Fathoms*. Finally a producer named Dave Diamond came to me; he had seen *The Beast* and he had a film project where, instead of one villain-beast, it would be strange radiation coming from the river. I started to work with his writer on the story; it was going to be a coproduction between Allied Artists and an English company called Eros Films. But Eros Films insisted that I use the same type of beast and the same type of tricks as I did in *Beast from 20,000 Fathoms*— they wanted a physical monster. My friend Daniel Hyatt and I spent ten days [putting together] a rough draft that was a copy of *Beast*, and I told Dave Diamond that after the contracts with Eros Films were signed, the script would

Armed with a radiation field (and obvious mold seams), *The Giant Behemoth* invades London.

have to be redone. That did not happen, and so the film *[The Giant Behemoth]* was a copy of *The Beast from 20,000 Fathoms*. I *did* resent this—but not *too* much. Visually, it's much easier to see the villain-beast than to see radiation *[laughs]*."

Obviously, minus the involvement of stop-motion genius Ray Harryhausen, *Giant Behemoth*'s prehistoric animal was strikingly inferior to the incomparable rhedosaurus seen in *Beast*; Lourie himself knew that *Behemoth*'s special effects did not begin to compare with Harryhausen's. "I think the beast itself was not interesting in *The Giant Behemoth*. It's a visual thing, and very difficult to explain; you *feel* that [something] is wrong, but you don't know exactly what it is. It was bad animation and a bad animal—the model itself, I mean. Originally, I was to do [the effects] myself together with Harryhausen or with Willis O'Brien. O'Brien was still alive, and he worked together with Pete Peterson on animating. Dave Diamond decided to give [the effects work] to an outlet on a contract basis. So they listened to me when I spoke, but what they did, they did what they wanted. Essentially *The Beast* and *The Giant Behemoth* were *both* cheap pictures anyhow. The difference was, one was cheap in dollars and the other, cheap in English pounds *[laughs]*." (Was Willis O'Brien, "father" of *King Kong* and the dean of stop-motion animators, an interesting man to get to know? "No," Lourie responded flatly. "He was a one hundred percent technician.")

The Giant Behemoth (released as *Behemoth, the Sea Monster* in England, where it was made) was redundant both in title *and* story line, a carbon copy of *Beast*, with the dinosaur (here spawned by radiation) leaving a wake of destruction between Cornwall and London. Remembering the English crews he worked with on *Giant Behemoth* and (later) on *Gorgo*, Lourie offered, "Basically, they were no different from a Hollywood crew. Different in the kind of personal relations you had with them, maybe, but I liked them very much. They're a little slower, and a little more *stubborn*—especially the special effects men. The special effects men worked like a group of engineers: They all wore white smocks, and they all had very definite ideas about what could be done and what could not be done." Unlike *Beast*, which included a conventional boy-girl subplot, *The Giant Behemoth* (which starred Gene Evans and Andre Morell) avoided that well-traveled lane. "I didn't see what love relations between two humans had to do with a dinosaur."

The seeds of Lourie's third dinosaur film, *Gorgo*, were sown the day the director's daughter complained that her daddy had killed "the big nice Beast [from *20,000 Fathoms*]." "That is why, in *Gorgo*, I tried not to kill the beast," Lourie explained. "Gorgo escapes alive back to the sea. My daughter should have a writer's credit *[laughs]*."

In *Gorgo* (based on a story by Lourie and Daniel Hyatt), a volcanic eruption at the bottom of the Irish Sea rouses a giant beast, who wanders onto nearby Nara Island before being driven off by villagers. Salvage divers Bill Travers and William Sylvester capture the 65-foot beast and deliver it to London, where it is placed on display at an amusement park. But the beast proves to be just an infant—one with a very angry 250-foot mother in close pursuit. Explaining his involvement on the film, Lourie reminisced, "I was called to meet the King Brothers [the producers]. They were two nice chaps and they made my life quite easy with *Gorgo*. We met, and they had a writer in mind to write the story, but I didn't like his idea. I told them I would write it with my friend Hyatt. The King Brothers liked our story. They were very attached to their mother, and I do believe that the project appealed to them because the mother comes to save her baby.

"At first the King Brothers wanted to destroy a big town. They said, 'Let's go to Paris. Let's have the beast climbing the Eiffel Tower!' I worked with a sketch artist who made numerous sketches with the beast climbing the Eiffel Tower and destroying the Notre Dame of Paris. I said to Frank King, 'The problem is, we don't have a sea in Paris. The beast would have to walk knee-high in the Seine River!' *[Laughs.]* Now we went with the King Brothers to Germany, because they said they'd shoot the picture in Germany. We met a man over there who had a studio in Berlin, but his studio was too small. At this time, they had an offer from an English company to make *Gorgo* with them,

The man-in-a-monster-suit idea for *Gorgo* originated with Lourie, who believed it would give him much more control.

in their English studio. Part of it was shot in Ireland, too, in a port near Dublin. That is how it happened."

Unlike *Beast* and *Behemoth*, *Gorgo* fell back on the economical man-in-a-monster-suit technique rather than employing time-consuming (and costly) stop motion. "The man in the suit was my idea," Lourie added. "I thought—wrongly—that I would have more control, and it would be much faster anyhow. It would not necessitate the long delay of frame-by-frame animation. I wanted to have a lightweight suit for Gorgo, so that the man inside could use his physical strength to move the thing. I did not want to rely [on remote controls]. But the King Brothers employed [effects engineers] whose idea was hydraulic. The man who played the beast had to carry enormous weight on his back. I would have preferred the other idea."

Other people—namely, the King Brothers themselves—had had other, even *worse* ideas. "In spite of being ex-gangsters, they were very naïve in real life. Frank King often said, 'Gee, why don't we do a monster in rubber, like Macy's parade? We could carry it through the London streets, this big beast passing by.' He wanted to use *that* for the monster!

"We put the stunt man who played the monster on miniature sets to give

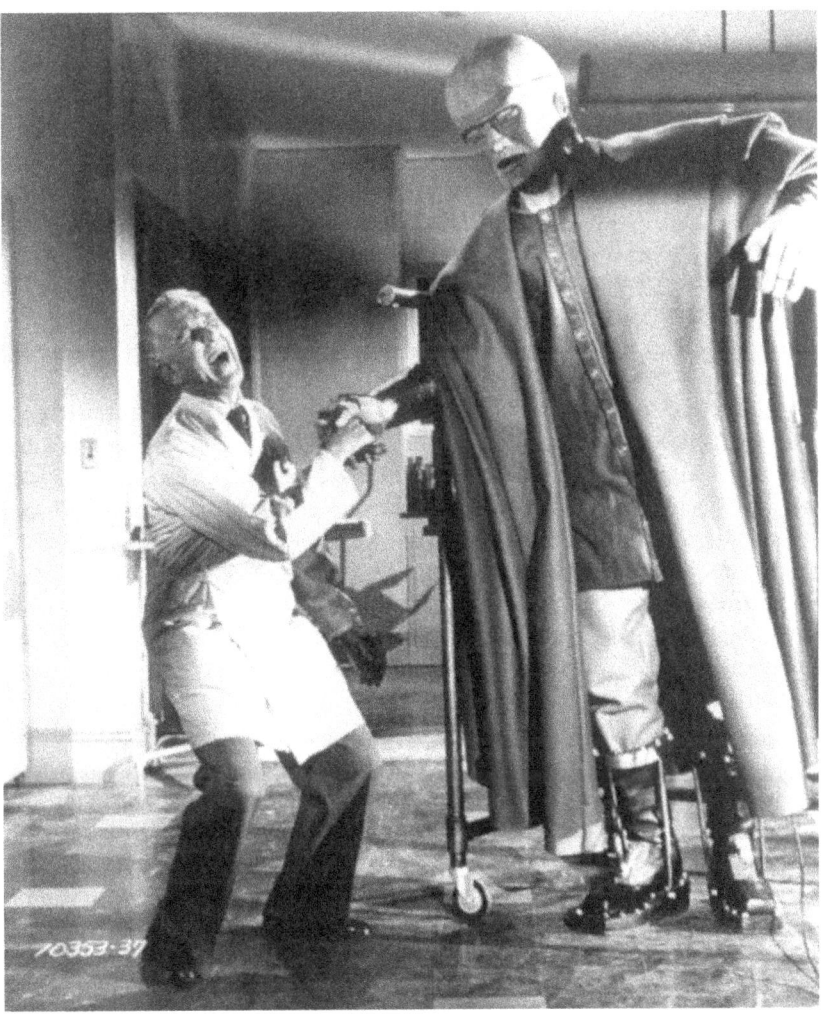

The Colossus of New York has the upper hand over creator Otto Kruger in Lourie's one nondinosaur directorial credit.

him the proportions," Lourie continued. "They cost a lot of money — and a lot of work! The biggest miniature set was the Thames River set, with the Bridge — it occupied MGM's biggest stage in London. The 'river' was not very deep, just knee-high water. It was a comical scene, because the stunt man who played the beast had trouble walking through the water with the big, clumsy dinosaur's feet. So we cut the costume, and from the knees down were human legs with tennis shoes. It was a very strange beast *[laughs]*!"

The filmmakers' ingenuity also came into play when it came time to shoot scenes of a flatbed truck carrying the supine Gorgo through London's bustling streets. "We had the problem of how to take through the streets of London a beast that we didn't have. We had only a [full-sized] head and the paws. King said, 'Let's put the beast under a tarpaulin on a truck. I will put a truck with an orchestra in front of it, and we will pass through Piccadilly and the streets will be full of people trying to see what it is.' We could get our shots of crowds that way and not have to employ extras for the scenes. On Sunday morning, we put the beast on a big platform truck—the head and the paws, and the rest was just tarpaulin. We hid the camera inside of the beast to shoot the reactions of people—and nobody came! This Sunday morning was very dismal—the scenes we got were of empty streets, and occasionally a few people *[Lourie made a scowling face]*, 'What the hell is *that*?'"

Lourie fondly remembered the stars (Travers and Sylvester), but held out reservations about Vincent Winter, who plays an Irish youngster throughout the film. "I was not very happy with the little boy. I had an idea to use another boy, but this boy Winter had a little bit of experience—and he was an old ham already *[laughs]*. I had a big pleasure to shoot the picture, especially making the crowd scenes in real streets, and then destroying the miniatures. But I was not so satisfied with Gorgo itself, because frame-by-frame animation makes the animal more alive than the stuntman in the rubber suit." Of his three dinosaur films, Lourie claimed that *The Beast from 20,000 Fathoms* remained his favorite.

Lourie remained active (as an art director again) throughout the 1960s and 1970s, working on a characteristically wide variety of projects, including director Sam Fuller's cultish *Shock Corridor* and *The Naked Kiss* ("Sam is a little crazy, but a very nice man"); he also worked as a miniatures and special effects unit director for such films as *Crack in the World*, *Battle of the Bulge* and *Krakatoa, East of Java*. His autobiography, *My Work in Films*, was published by Harcourt Brace Jovanovich in 1985, with full chapters devoted to the Renoir classics, *Limelight*, *Beast from 20,000 Fathoms* and many more. Toward the end of his life, largely incapacitated by strokes, he still kept busy, granting interviews and writing about his early life. "On my way from Russia to Paris, I had many experiences that would be good for interesting stories, and I am writing a series of short stories. I am contemplating sending them to New York. It will be great if they will accept them. If they do not accept them, I will be one more rejected writer."

With typical openness, he also admitted that—prior to *The Beast from 20,000 Fathoms*—he had no interest in science fiction films whatsoever, a fact which surely added to his discomfort with being typecast as a science fiction specialist. "I *was* very unhappy about that, because I was cast as a director of dinosaurs. Like I was a lion tamer—but with dinosaurs! All my life, *The Beast from 20,000 Fathoms* was hanging like an albatross around my neck."

*There are two different audiences for science fiction pictures:
One is made up of the kids ... and the other is made up
of older, intelligent, concerned people who are genuine
sci-fi fans. They're not what I call "the idiot Godzilla fan."*

Jeff Morrow

IT IS A LONG WAY FROM BROADWAY to Hollywood to Metaluna, but during the 1950s monster boom, actor Jeff Morrow made the transition in easy strides. An accomplished stage actor, Morrow made an indelible mark on science fiction history via his portrayal of Exeter in Universal's *This Island Earth* (1955). Other genre credits include a strong performance as the paranoid protagonist in the same studio's *The Creature Walks Among Us* (1956), director Kurt Neumann's *Kronos* (1957) and the notorious science fiction cheapie *The Giant Claw* (1957).

The New York–born Morrow developed an interest in the theater as a result of his studies at art school. As Irving Morrow, he made his stage debut in the 1930 production of *Penal Law*, and later appeared in such plays as *Once in a Lifetime*, *A Midsummer Night's Dream*, *Twelfth Night*, *Romeo and Juliet* and *Macbeth*, treading the boards opposite stars like Katharine Cornell, Maurice Evans, Katharine Hepburn, Luise Rainer, Mae West and many others. He also racked up an imposing total of three thousand airwave performances, including two years as radio's redoubtable Dick Tracy.

Morrow made his film debut in 20th Century–Fox's Biblical epic *The Robe* (1953), with Richard Burton and Jean Simmons. His effective portrayal of the scowling, scarred centurion impressed both viewers and critics, and the fledgling screen actor followed up on this early credit with supporting roles in Paramount's 3-D *Flight to Tangier* (1953), a contrived foreign intrigue drama, and Universal's clichéd jungle adventure *Tanganyika* (1954). Struck with Morrow's screen possibilities, Universal approached the actor with a two-picture-a-year contract.

Over lunch at DuPar's in Encino, California, a lanky, bearded Jeff Morrow recalled the genesis of his first role as a Universal contract player. "My contract went into effect some time in February 1954, and just prior to that date Universal suddenly decided they wanted me to play the lead in a science fiction picture, *This Island Earth*. They sent me the script, I read it and went in to talk with the producer, Bill Alland, who is a very nice chap, quite able and talented, and the writer, Franklin Coen."

Morrow was intrigued by Coen's script but disappointed to find that his character, Exeter, an interplanetary emissary, had been written as a one-dimensional heavy. "You had no idea why Exeter was doing any of this stuff, except that he was an ornery character. I didn't have to do the picture because it was going to start ten days before my contract went into effect, so this was one of the few instances in all the times I've signed for pictures that I had a little bit to say about it! I told them, 'I'm interested in doing it, but he's such a heavy. Can't we do something about it—show that he is, let's say, the epitome of a true scientist, and really concerned about the effect of what he does upon the world?' So we talked for about an hour, and there was a sort of

Previous page: Jeff Morrow immediately saw all the possibilities inherent in the role of the noble Exeter in *This Island Earth*. (Photofest)

general agreement that it wasn't a bad idea. And when we walked down the street to the parking lot, Frank Coen said, 'I'm so glad you were there, because I've been trying to sell them on that concept for a month!'"

As a consequence, the rewritten screenplay, which Morrow received a week or ten days later, depicted the Exeter character in a more favorable light. The screenplay revisions, combined with Morrow's larger-than-life performance, resulted in one of the most memorable film characters of fifties science fiction.

Special makeup designed for Morrow necessitated his arrival at the studio a full two hours before cameras rolled. "They gave me a slightly enlarged forehead, which had to be put on very, very carefully, and then a white wig over that. It was the kind of look where, if you walked down the street, people wouldn't notice you, but then twenty feet later they would suddenly stop, turn around and say, 'He looked a little odd, didn't he?'" Later, unfortunately, the white wigs worn by Morrow and others in his cosmic coterie presented some unforeseen difficulties. "The wigs we wore were so white that we were all very worried, especially the woman hairdresser, about how they would wind up looking on film. I did a test, and that was printed and delivered on a Monday — the same Monday that we started shooting the picture. And, as we predicted, when we saw the dailies, we saw that my hair came out pure white—it looked like cotton candy. It was terrible! Well, after the producers and executives all went into a bit of shock, they decided, 'We'll just print the film darker, and the hair won't look so white.' So they printed it darker, but then my skin looked as though I had been out in the sun all my life! The consequence was that every day, little by little, the hairdresser would twist and comb so that there was a wave in the white hair—not for any cosmetic appearance, but simply so there'd be a little light and shade, and it wouldn't look this ghastly pure white. They also softened the lights on the hair, and after a short time I looked fairly human."

Dazzling special effects provided most of the highlights of *This Island Earth*; *New York Times* critic Howard H. Thompson perceived this when he closed his review by acknowledging technical artists Clifford Stine, William Fritzsche, Alexander Golitzen, Richard H. Riedel, David S. Horsley, Russell A. Gausman and Julia Heron as "the real stars" of the picture. The film's story, with its male-and-female Earthling protagonists, trips through space, enthroned space despot (Douglas Spencer) and gratuitous monster, is a bit closer to comic book pap like *Flash Gordon* than to any sort of "serious" science fiction. Morrow's Exeter is the film's one intriguing character, much of his appeal deriving from Morrow's sympathetic performance; the Franklin Coen-George Callaghan script is otherwise weak in characterization, and Newman fails to draw anything but wooden, wonderstruck performances from most of the rest of his cast. But whatever the film's minor failings, *This Island Earth* has stood the test of time and is today regarded as a milestone of the genre.

Broadway actor cum B movie star Jeff Morrow took on monsters from outer space in the fifties films *This Island Earth*, *Kronos* and *The Giant Claw* (pictured).

Morrow looked back on *This Island Earth* with affection. "By and large, the film was quite good; as a matter of fact, I think it was slightly underrated by some of the New York critics. To the best of my knowledge, it cost about $750,000, the shooting schedule was about six weeks, and it had extremely good special effects, much in advance of most of the science fiction pictures of that time. It certainly had a lot more to say than practically any of the science fiction pictures that I've seen recently—ones that cost $25–$30 million—which are not only not-positive but extremely negative in their point of view. And,

Morrow and Leigh Snowden react to off-camera commotion in a posed shot from Universal's *The Creature Walks Among Us*.

oddly enough, I know I did get more fan mail from that picture than any other I ever did." The one jarring note that Morrow detected was the last-reel appearance of the Metaluna Mutants. "[Universal] felt they had to have the insurance of audience reaction on the part of the kids, and they wrote in a monster. That really could've been cut out of the script, but we lived with it."

Morrow's next role for Universal was in the lively costume adventure *Captain Lightfoot* (1955), a Rock Hudson starrer made on location in Ireland. Morrow cut a dashing figure as the Irish rebel leader Captain Thunderbolt in this Douglas Sirk–directed swashbuckler, and *Captain Lightfoot* remained his favorite filmland experience. Returning to science fiction, he was reteamed with his *This Island Earth* costar Rex Reason for director John Sherwood's *The Creature Walks Among Us*, third and last film in Universal's Gill Man trilogy. Morrow starred as a famous surgeon who organizes an expedition to track down the notorious Creature from the Black Lagoon, presently residing somewhere in the Florida Everglades. A certifiable neurotic, Morrow's Dr. William Barton is full of nutty notions on subjects ranging from the evolutionary process to his buxom blond wife's (Leigh Snowden) fidelity, and he receives just desserts for his on-screen unpleasantness in the film's roof-raising finale. "I had done all my dialogue scenes, and on what I believe was the last day of shooting they gave me a script of 'new scenes' for the day. I was a little horrified, thinking that they'd thrown a lot of new dialogue at me, but I opened it and there was not a single line. It was a map of the house that we were in—the stairs, the gallery, the balconies, the rooms where I am chased by the Creature, finally caught and thrown off the balcony—which, needless to say, was the end of my character." Asked about the stunt, Morrow explained, "They had me on a wire that led up to a pulley on the ceiling. When Don Megowan—the Creature—reached down and grabbed me, they pulled me up with the wire as he lifted me. Needless to say, he did not throw me over; he raised me up to the ceiling and then they stopped—thank goodness!—and put a dummy up there in my place."

Due to his roles in *This Island Earth* and *Creature Walks*, Morrow's name was now apparently linked with science fiction in some producers' minds. For Robert Lippert's Regal Films, Morrow starred with Barbara Lawrence in *Kronos*, the story of a giant extraterrestrial robot absorbing energy and growing in size as it stalks up the West Coast from Mexico. An unenthusiastic critic for the *New York World Telegram* hit the nail exactly on the head when he griped that *Kronos* "presents an electronic monster too complicated to be very terrifying," but Morrow was fond of the finished film. "*Kronos* was a very good little low-budget picture. We made it in a couple weeks. The concept, I thought, was interesting, and it made good sense. I did a little fast research beforehand so that when I wrote down on the blackboard the figures of the alphas and the betas and the gammas, I think I knew what I was talking about and I think I *sounded* as if I knew. That was a very good, simple little picture."

Morrow's keenest memory of *Kronos* centered around the type of embarrassing situation actors are often unable to avoid. "Barbara Lawrence and I were shooting a scene on the beach, and I was supposed to run into the water. I stripped off my slacks and shirt and started to run, and then they yelled *cut* and in came a double, in bathing trunks, who was going to go into the water for me. But as I was walking off, heading for another section of the beach for

Morrow, his actress-wife Ann Karen and their daughter, Lisa, behind the scenes on Universal's final Gill Man stanza, *The Creature Walks Among Us*.

my next shot, I happened to look back and I saw that he was terribly bow-legged. And of course, seen from the back, everyone would assume that that was me!"

Morrow visibly cringed at the mere mention of his next film. "The less that's said about *The Giant Claw*, the better" *[laughs]*! Actually, we had a very good cast, and the basic concept of the story was also good. It was based upon a new development in science: the concept of the mirror image in outer space." The Samuel Newman–Paul Gangelin screenplay took the antimatter principle and applied it to the film's story of a colossal prehistoric bird emerging out of the depths of space to wreak havoc on a helpless modern world. "We poor, benighted actors had our own idea of what the giant bird would look like—our concept was that this was something that resembled a streamlined hawk, possibly a half a mile long, flying at such speeds that we could barely see it. That was the way *we* envisioned it. Well, the producer, Sam Katzman, decided for economy reasons not to spend the $10–$15,000 it would take to make a really good bird—he had it made in Mexico, probably for $19.28! I went to a sneak preview in Westwood Village, and when the monster appeared on the screen it was like a huge plucked turkey, flying with these incredible *squawks*! And the audience went into hysterics. I shrunk down in my seat, hoping that no one would realize that I was that man up there on the screen. My only consolation was that, when the picture was over and the lights finally came up, I heard somebody in front of me say, 'And it's such a shame, too, because he's such a very good actor.'" Morrow laughed, "After hearing that, I walked out feeling a little more hopeful."

While Morrow appeared to have a certain regard for science fiction films, the actor looked back on the fifties brand of science fiction with a harsh critical eye. "There are two different audiences for science fiction pictures: One is made up of the kids, many of whom are not the brightest in the world at that period in their lives, and the other is made up of older, intelligent, concerned people who are genuine sci-fi fans. They're not what I call 'the idiot Godzilla fan.' I think at that time [the fifties] there were about five or six science fiction pictures that had considerable merit—*The War of the Worlds*, *The Day the Earth Stood Still*, *Forbidden Planet* and perhaps a few others. But by and large the rest were pretty junky pictures."

Morrow's film and television appearances grew less frequent in recent years, but in the early seventies he marked time in two low-budget genre productions. Writer-director Harry Essex's *Octaman* was a shoddy semiremake of Essex's *Creature from the Black Lagoon*, with Kerwin Mathews and Pier Angeli battling a ludicrous octopus man in a primitive Latin American fishing community. Fortuitously removed from the film's main action, Morrow was confined to a single dialogue scene with Kerwin Mathews. "The producer, Mike Kraike, and the writer-director Harry Essex contacted me and said that one of their actors was sick and that they were in a jam, and would I do this small part as a special favor? So I did that one scene in a half a day, and it's one of the few pictures of mine that I've never seen."

His last fantasy film credit was director Carl Monson's *Legacy of Blood* (1973), a lurid murder-in-the-mansion melodrama filmed on location on an estate in Pasadena. Despite a strong cast (Jeff, John Carradine, Faith Domergue,

John Russell, Merry Anders, John Smith, Rodolfo Acosta), the results were disappointing. "That was a real horror picture—no great ethical value to it. I attended a screening of it, and the horror shots, which should have been just a few frames, just a fraction of a second, were instead lingered upon for perhaps a beat of three—which ruined the picture. It was just that the director and the cutter, everybody connected with it, were quite devoid of any kind of artistic taste."

Although largely absent from films and television in his later years, Jeff Morrow remained active by working as a commercial illustrator and taking the occasional acting assignment (most notably, a recent *Twilight Zone* episode that teamed him with fifties standbys John Agar, Kenneth Tobey and Warren Stevens). Morrow was open and enthusiastic about his long, wide-ranging career, and while he had no overwhelming affinity for science fiction subjects, he recognized and appreciated the fact that many of his biggest fans were from that contingent of film buffs. As for a favorite among his own science fiction credits, Morrow was emphatic in his obvious choice.

"*This Island Earth*, very definitely. The thing that I felt was important about *This Island Earth* was the fact that there was a sense of hope—that if we *do* ever come to meet people from another planet, in some way we'll be able to communicate on a human level of understanding. At least, let's hope to!"

JEFF MORROW FILMOGRAPHY

The Robe (20th Century–Fox, 1953)
Flight to Tangier (Paramount, 1953)
Siege at Red River (20th Century–Fox, 1954)
Sign of the Pagan (Universal, 1954)
Tanganyika (Universal, 1954)
Captain Lightfoot (Universal, 1955)
This Island Earth (Universal, 1955)
Hour of Decision (Astor, 1955)
The Creature Walks Among Us (Universal, 1956)
World in My Corner (Universal, 1956)
Pardners (Paramount, 1956)
The First Texan (Allied Artists, 1956)
Copper Sky (20th Century–Fox, 1957)
Kronos (20th Century–Fox, 1957)
The Giant Claw (Columbia, 1957)
Five Bold Women (Citation Films, 1960)
The Story of Ruth (20th Century–Fox, 1960)
Harbor Lights (20th Century–Fox, 1963)
Octaman (Filmers Guild, 1971)
Legacy of Blood (Blood Legacy) (Universal Entertainment, 1973)

Clips of Morrow in *This Island Earth* are seen in *The Incredible Shrinking Woman* (Universal, 1981).

Morrow, 86, died December 26, 1993, in a Canoga Park, California, nursing home after a long illness.

To do science fiction in those days was like a step down, career-wise. You generally started with something like that — you didn't want to build up to it!

Lori Nelson

A LARGE NUMBER OF STARRING FILM ROLES may make a talented actress popular, but it is no guarantee of lasting stardom. Universal's youngest contract player in the early 1950s, pretty Lori Nelson, displayed considerable charm and ability in many of the studio's bread-and-butter pictures: Ma and Pa Kettle movies, Audie Murphy Westerns, a Francis the Talking Mule epic and even the 3-D *Revenge of the Creature*. But shortsighted studio execs perceived Nelson as an actress suited only to these colorless ingenue roles, and she broke with Universal to find more diversified work as a freelancer.

These days she is looking to make a comeback: going on interviews, taking acting workshops and carrying the other behind-the-scenes baggage fans never consider when they think about a movie star's lifestyle. A good dramatic role is what she would like to land; although still radiant, she thrives on the character roles she plays in her workshop, like the unhappy widow in *The Trip to Bountiful* ("gray wig, an old sweater, the oxford shoes and all") and the frumpy mom in *'night, Mother*. "Those are the kinds of things that I'd dearly love to do. But I'm finding it very difficult to get back into the business again because it's very difficult for women my age—there aren't enough parts. For me it's almost like starting all over. Not because I don't have the experience; my major credits speak for themselves, and whenever I go on an interview, they do remember the stuff I was in. But there are so many women in my category and so few roles for women of any age, character or glamorous. Roles are few and far between, and there's a tremendous amount of competition. It's almost a crapshoot. What we have to do is just keep going out on the interviews until it's your turn—until the roulette wheel stops at you."

Born Dixie Kay Nelson in Santa Fe, New Mexico, she began her showbiz career at the tender age of two and a half, dancing in a hometown show. She was voted Santa Fe's most talented and beautiful child, and toured the state billed as "Santa Fe's Shirley Temple." At the age of four, Dixie moved to Hollywood with her mother and father and there was named Little Miss America. With the continuing help and encouragement of her mom, she worked as a fashion and photographer's model and in the early forties made her first bid for a movie career, testing (unsuccessfully) for a role in Warner Bros.' *Kings Row* (1941). A second false start came a few years later, when Dixie caught the fancy of Arthur Landau, a well-known Hollywood producer and self-proclaimed discoverer of thirties star Jean Harlow. Landau expressed interest in casting teenage Dixie as Harlow in a movie account of the platinum bombshell's life and times; but Dixie was too young and Landau unprepared to go into production, and the project never got off the ground.

Finally it was Hollywood agent Milo Frank who helped the aspiring actress get her foot inside a studio door. Frank wangled a Saturday appointment with

Previous page: After years of regretting her starring stint in *Revenge of the Creature*, Lori Nelson has made peace with her one "cult" credit.

one of the casting people at MGM, but when the day of the interview arrived, they learned that their Metro contact had been whisked away for an emergency appendectomy. Undeterred, Frank hurried Dixie over to Universal, where she and the agent met with front office and casting people. Dixie trained with studio dramatic coach Sophie Rosenstein over the next several weekends, enacted a scene for the front office and ultimately was offered a seven-year contract, which was approved in court on her 17th birthday.

"In those days, the most ideal, the most wonderful situation to be in was to be under contract," the actress (quickly redubbed Lori Nelson by Universal) stresses. "Actors today just don't know what they're missing. Because it was real training, it was like being at a university for actors. I was 16-going-on-17 when I was signed at Universal, and in fact I finished high school at Universal—I went each morning to the little schoolhouse that was right on the studio lot. I was the only student in school, and it was like having my own private tutor. I learned more in the short time that I was there finishing high school at Universal than in all the years previous to that, when I was in 'regular' school. I graduated second year college grades when I graduated from high school.

"I would go to the studio early in the morning and go to school three hours a day in the schoolhouse. Then I would go up to the dancing class with Hal Belfer—we'd learn routines. Next I would go to the gym and work out a while. On certain days we'd go out to the back lot, and the wranglers would teach us how to mount, dismount and ride horses. Then we had voice and diction and singing lessons. Then to Sophie Rosenstein's class, to work on scenes with other contract players. Put on little shows, little skits. Do scenes with other prospective actors that were being considered for possible contracts. We would also go to the screening rooms and critique old movie classics and acting techniques. It was like going from one class to another. And then in between we'd make a picture *[laughs]*! It was just the greatest training you could have ever imagined."

Enjoying what she still calls "the most fun in all the world," Nelson was not about to fret that most of her early pictures were silly confections like *Ma and Pa Kettle at the Fair* (her debut film, as the Kettles' oldest daughter Rosie, 1952), *Walking My Baby Back Home* (1953) and *Francis Goes to West Point* (with future television stars David Janssen and Leonard Nimoy in small parts, 1952). "When I first went to Universal, I had never done movies before, and it was all new and exciting to me. So starring in a movie with Donald O'Connor, or with Marjorie Main and Percy Kilbride [Ma and Pa Kettle]—or with Francis the Talking Mule *[laughs]*!—was very exciting, especially since I had never done featured roles. Right from the very beginning I was put in starring and costarring roles."

Better parts eventually ensued, like her role as the daughter of Barbara Stanwyck in the heart-tugging period piece *All I Desire* (1953) or her romantic lead in *All American* (also 1953) with the up-and-coming Tony Curtis. Their acting stables swelling with young talent, Universal saw fit to loan Nelson out to RKO for the deep-sea diving adventure *Underwater!* Typical of the wasteful extravagance for which that studio's Howard Hughes regime is remembered, RKO retained Lori's services for a full eight months but used her in only the one film. When Nelson returned to Universal in the latter part of 1954, she found herself a veritable stranger on the lot. "Milton Rackmil and Capital Records had bought Universal while I was doing *Underwater!* over at RKO. When I came back after those eight months, I knew practically no one and practically no one knew me."

Hoping for strong roles as a sort of welcome-back present, Nelson was placed in *Destry* (a remake of the 1939 *Destry Rides Again*, with Audie Murphy and Mari Blanchard in the James Stewart and Marlene Dietrich roles) before being taken aback when Universal lined up as her next leading man a scaly, dark-green prehistoric beast hailing from the jungles of South America. "In the beginning I didn't want to do *Revenge of the Creature* because I felt like it was almost a comedown for me. Most of the other movies that I did at Universal were a much better caliber than that. To do science fiction in those days was like a step down, career-wise. You generally started with something like that—you didn't want to build *up* to it *[laughs]*! But then I did find while I was making the movie that I really enjoyed the experience, and that it was above the average, a very high-caliber science fiction film."

Announced (under the title *Return of the Creature from the Black Lagoon*) by Universal even before *Creature from the Black Lagoon* was released, *Revenge* picks up the story where *Creature* left off, with adventurous John Bromfield scouring the Amazon for the Gill Man. Captured, the Creature is transported to Florida's Marineland, where scientists John Agar and Nelson poke and probe the Devonian relic, and later track the rampaging beast after its inevitable breakout. Much of *Revenge of the Creature* was shot in Florida at Marineland, where Agar, Nelson and Ricou Browning (the Gill Man) descended into tanks filled with denizens of the deep.

"I had learned how to use an Aqualung while I was making *Underwater!* I didn't have to do any scenes in *Underwater!* ... underwater *[laughs]*, but because [stars] Richard Egan and Jane Russell were learning how to use the Aqualung, I got to learn how, also. I took all the lessons, never dreaming that it would come in handy when I did *Revenge of the Creature*! I did all my own diving in the Creature picture."

Being asked to swim amidst sharks would test any actress' mettle, but Nelson's hesitations were short-lived. "I had a little trepidation about it in the beginning. In the tank they had moray eels, stingrays, manta rays, bat stingrays, sharks—and of course all of the other various and sundry fish large and small. But the Marineland people told us that all those fish get fed every hour, and unless they're hungry, they're not going to bother you. And of course they made sure that they *were* fed just before any of us went in to do any underwater scenes. And therefore it was not dangerous, and it didn't bother me. It was a little scary the first time I went down, but after that I couldn't wait to get back in again. It was the most exciting thing in the world, to go down in those tanks with all those fish and see what was going on. As everyone else who has ever done it says, it's a fascinating world down there.

"Most of the time, the camera photographed us from an indoor viewing area that was below water level, through portholes that were designed for the tourists to see through. But there was also a professional diver with an underwater camera in the tank with us. He took close-up shots and so forth, and then also shots from the Creature's point of view, where he's looking out the windows at the people that are looking in at *him*. But most of the shots were shot from that viewing area outside. I remember that there were also a couple of professional underwater swimmers in the tank with us—off-camera, as protection, in case anything happened."

Nelson got wet not only in the tank scenes, but later in the picture as well, when the Creature abducts her from Jacksonville, Florida's, Lobster House and leaps with her in his arms into the St. Johns River. "There was a real strong current, and we had a hard time swimming back to the dock—a few times I didn't know whether I was gonna make it or not. Then we did another scene where John Agar and I dive off a boat and go for a swim, not knowing that the Creature has followed us. They had us swim way, way out, because they wanted us to be far away from the boat when the Creature came up underneath us—out so far that we couldn't conceivably be able to get back to the boat. That made it more suspenseful. John and I would swim way out and then cavort a while, and then we'd have to swim back, and a few times it got pretty hairy—I was awfully tired before I got back. I looked good in the water—I had good form—but I've never been a stamina swimmer *[laughs]*!"

Like John Agar, Nelson remembers the contribution of Creature portrayer Ricou Browning with awe. "He was a professional underwater swimmer, and he wore the suit and did all the underwater swimming. He was an incredible swimmer and a talented guy. He's the one that developed the Creature's way of swimming. There was an air tank off on the side—either another swimmer would be holding it or it would be stationed down there someplace. He would go off-camera and take a breath out of the tank using the mouthpiece, and then he would come back into the shot to do whatever business he had to do. Then back to the tank for another breath. They would just keep the camera rolling as he would swim off to take breaths, and then come back into the shot." Nelson recalls that the actor who played the Creature on land (Tom Hennesy) had a difficult time moving around in the heavy latex rubber suit, "so can you imagine swimming around in it underwater, like Ricou Browning did? And Ricou was not a big man. They had an actor who was very tall play the Creature on land."

Memories of her fellow cast members and of director Jack Arnold? "John

Location shooting at Florida's Marineland Studios gave Nelson and the rest of the *Revenge of the Creature* contingent some unique R & R opportunities.

Agar was probably one of the sweetest people I had ever met, a dear, dear man. His wife, Loretta, was on location in Florida with us; as a matter of fact, she had a bit part in the film. We had a lot of fun because I got along with both of them very well. And John Bromfield was a nice guy, too. I had a real crush on John Bromfield, but he was dating a dancer named Larri Thomas and they were quite close at the time. He was such a gentleman that nothing ever materialized between us; he was definitely true to Larri." And director Arnold "was another person I enjoyed working with, very much. Primarily because I thought he was quite a good director. I felt that he did very well with that film, with the shots and the angles, the suspense and the way he set everything up. And he was good with the actors, too."

Even though Nelson had fun making *Revenge of the Creature*, she remained slightly miffed at Universal for having assigned her to the type of role which she hoped she had outgrown. "I wanted to expand and move on and do bigger and better things. And I'd begun to figure that I probably wouldn't be able to do that at Universal, especially when I had done *Underwater!* and then I came back and they stuck me in *Revenge of the Creature*. So that was another reason why I decided that I wanted to leave Universal, and when my contract came up for renewal, I did. I'd been there for a number of years, and I wanted to move on. The movies that I did at Universal — they *were* good movies, but in those days they weren't top-notch, high-caliber motion pictures like some of the other studios were doing."

Revenge of the Creature is certainly no longer the sore spot it once might have been. "I'm much happier with it today than I was then," Nelson laughs. "In those days, I don't think I was terribly proud of the movie, but today I am. It really is one of the better science fiction movies."

Working as a freelancer kept Nelson bouncing from studio to studio: for Warners she costarred in a pair of remakes, *I Died a Thousand Times* (1955) with Jack Palance (a reworking of the Bogie classic *High Sierra*) and *Sincerely Yours* (also 1955) with Liberace (a second version of Warners' *The Man Who Played God*), and at Paramount she played Dean Martin's romantic interest in the next-to-last Martin and Lewis comedy, *Pardners* (1956). "After I left Universal, I had some good years when I did really good movies, and also some fantastic TV shows like *Climax!*, *Playhouse 90*, *G.E. Theater*, *20th Century-Fox Hour* and guest shots on lots of other shows. And then times began to get a little lean, for whatever reason, and I was not able to hold out for the plums. And so, as many actors do at some time in their careers *[laughs]*, they start doing what they consider schlock. And even though you're advised against it by whatever people are advising you, you wind up doing stuff that you wish you didn't have to do, in order to eat. And to keep your face in front of the public. Sometimes it's like that old adage, 'I don't care what you say about me, as long as you spell my name right.'"

Her name was spelled right in a variety of low-budget pictures, but Nelson remembers not all of them fondly. "*Untamed Youth* and *Outlaw's Son* [both 1957] I did for Howard Koch — Koch-Schenck Productions. *Outlaw's Son* was a pretty good movie, and I was not really unhappy with doing that; *Untamed Youth* I was kind of unhappy about. And *Hot Rod Girl* [1956] I was *very* unhappy about. And *Day the World Ended* was probably the thing that I was *least* happy about *[laughs]*!"

Day the World Ended is rich in B-movie significance: it was Roger Corman's first science fiction film as director as well as the picture that helped pull American International Pictures (then still calling itself American Releasing Corporation) back from the brink of collapse. Understandably, however, these historical niceties were lost on Lori Nelson at the time. "It was a very, very cheaply done, very low-budget movie. Roger Corman's movies in those days were not the caliber of the ones that followed — he later became quite the filmmaker. But in those days his pictures were not considered top-notch in any sense of the word.

"Roger and his brother Gene were two very, very nice guys; I can't remember now in what capacity Gene worked on *Day the World Ended*, but I met him at that time, too. Roger produced and directed that, and he was fun to work with. And working fast? Gosh, I think we did the whole picture in two weeks, maybe not even that long. It seemed like we had just barely started, and it was over *[laughs]*! And everything was so — *economical*! Even the monster costume that they used — the three-eyed mutant — was just not the caliber that the Black Lagoon Creature was. I'm sure I'm not offending Roger by saying that — surely that shouldn't be news to anyone *[laughs]*! He's a certain kind of filmmaker, and that is what he is famous for. He has a specialty, and nobody does it like he does."

In *Day the World Ended*, a ragtag assortment of survivors of an atomic war scurry to the comparative safety of a secluded valley shielded from the lingering radioactivity. Tensions flare among the survivors, and a three-eyed mutant spawned by the radiation (and played by AIP standby Paul Blaisdell) appears to menace the dwindling group.

"The actor inside the monster suit was very small, and not very strong. He was kind of wimpy-armed, not muscular at all, and not much taller than me. We were doing the scene by the lake, and he was carrying me down the bank. He was kind of staggering around — his knees were buckling. I think he stepped in a hole or tripped on a stick — he fell and I fell on top of him. I landed on his chest, and because the costume was made of rubber I started to bounce up and down. I started laughing, and I could hear the 'mutant' laughing, too — muffled — within the suit *[laughs]*! Luckily we fell down on the bank, right on the edge of the water; that was a good thing, because I don't know how well that monster suit would have stood up if it got wet. Also, he might have drowned, the suit was so heavy."

Stars Richard Denning and Touch (Mike) Connors were, again, "a couple of nice guys. It seems like I'm always saying that about these actors I've worked with, but they really were. I don't think there was anyone, in any of the films

Opposite: Nelson, who was unhappy with several of her mid-fifties roles, was *"least* happy about" the low-budget *Day the World Ended*. That is creature Paul Blaisdell on bended knee.

that I did, that was not a gentleman." Oh, come on—not even one? "I'm serious. Even Jack Palance [*I Died a Thousand Times*]—he had a terrible reputation for being kind of difficult to work with. Everybody worried how he'd get along with Shelley Winters, because they were both temperamental and that seemed like a lethal combination. But I never saw any of that in the scenes I did with Jack; he was always wonderful. I loved working with him, he's so good at what he does."

Television fans remember Lori Nelson best for her starring role in the syndicated series *How to Marry a Millionaire*. An extension of the 1953 20th Century–Fox movie, the 30-minute sitcom starred Nelson, Merry Anders and Barbara Eden as sexy New York bachelorettes waging a campaign to trap wealthy husbands. But Nelson quickly wearied of the day-to-day rut of a sitcom; her discontent mounted when her bosses insisted that the three actresses go without pay on their personal appearance tours. After 39 episodes, Nelson and the owners of the series, NTA, were not able to reconcile their differences, and Lori exited the show. Lisa Gaye replaced her, and the series expired after only 13 more episodes.

A guest shot on television's *Riverboat* led to romance and an engagement to series star Burt Reynolds, then at the beginning of his career. Six months after their breakup, Nelson married composer/conductor Johnny Mann in 1961 and gave birth to daughters Lori Susan (in 1962) and Jennifer Lee (in 1965). Picturemaking took a backseat to baby raising, although Nelson did little theater and a few workshops through the years to keep from losing her dramatic edge. After a series of separations and reconciliations, she and Johnny Mann divorced in 1971. Wanting to resume her career but realizing now more than ever how much her daughters needed her, she decided that show business would have to wait.

Encouraged by her new husband (since 1983) Joe Reiner, who is retired from the Los Angeles Police Department, Lori Nelson Reiner is determined to return to the acting fold, but roles for older women are depressingly scarce. "It is excruciatingly frustrating and anguish producing, because it's still predominantly a male-oriented business. There have been a few inroads, but just not enough and not fast enough. I feel that I am better than ever now, ten times the actress I was back then [in the fifties]. Through time and experience and through just living life, you get better at whatever you do. I think an actor or an actress very definitely gets better. So what a terrible time to find out that there are less roles for a woman, and that your hands are tied!

"I was starring in movies years before Barbara Eden ever came to Hollywood, and if I had hung in there like Barbara did, I would probably still be working today. But even *she* has to produce her own stuff now, to get any roles at all; Faye Dunaway, too. Meryl Streep talks about this every chance she gets. And it seems so unfair that this seems to be one of the only businesses in the world where you can have all the training and all the experience and all the

Looking to reenter the acting profession, Nelson is finding that the 1990s is "a terrible time to find out that there are less roles for a woman."

expertise, but if you stop working even for a while, they rarely make a place for you if you are a woman, especially an older woman. It's a hard pill to swallow."

Like it or not, for now, one of Lori Nelson's major claims to fame remains *Revenge of the Creature*—the one out of all her movies she was perhaps most reluctant to do. "I figured, okay, I might as well go ahead and do it, get it over with. There was no sense in fighting a studio like Universal because they had you under contract, and whatever film it was, they would have insisted that you do it. They never had to twist my arm very hard—I was pretty compliant in those days—but I'd have turned down *Revenge of the Creature* if I had been given a choice. Then time went on, of course, and I realized that it had become a cult film, and that it was considered by most science fiction people as quite an extraordinary and quite a good movie. *[Laughs.]* It just goes to show that actors don't always know what's good for 'em!"

LORI NELSON FILMOGRAPHY

Bend of the River (Universal, 1952)
Ma and Pa Kettle at the Fair (Universal, 1952)
Francis Goes to West Point (Universal, 1952)
All I Desire (Universal, 1953)
All American (Universal, 1953)
Walking My Baby Back Home (Universal, 1953)
Tumbleweed (Universal, 1953)
Destry (Universal, 1954)
Underwater! (RKO, 1955)
Ma and Pa Kettle at Waikiki (Universal, 1955)
Revenge of the Creature (Universal, 1955)
I Died a Thousand Times (Warner Bros., 1955)
Sincerely Yours (Warner Bros., 1955)
Day the World Ended (American Releasing [AIP], 1956)
Mohawk (20th Century–Fox, 1956)
Hot Rod Girl (AIP, 1956)
Pardners (Paramount, 1956)
Outlaw's Son (United Artists, 1957)
Untamed Youth (United Artists, 1957)

The Pied Piper of Hamelin (1957), a 90-minute television special starring Van Johnson, Claude Rains and Nelson, received limited theatrical release in 1961.

This Island Earth *has done a lot for me as far as giving me a little notoriety, keeping me alive in the minds of fans and giving me a feeling that my work in films had a little worth.*

Rex Reason

SOMETIMES AN ACTOR CAN TOIL in Hollywood for years without achieving recognition, and sometimes lasting fame can come from a single production. Rex Reason appeared in a score of fifties films, starred in two popular television series and guested in numerous television episodes, but film fans tend to remember him first and foremost as the staunch scientist-hero of 1955's *This Island Earth*. Reason does not resent the instant association, although he is quick to name other films and television appearances of which he is equally proud. The husky six-foot-four Reason now makes his living through real estate but is happy to reminisce about his stint as a Hollywood heavy/hero/he-man. Tanned, relaxed and affable, he settles into a favorite chair in the den/office of his Walnut, California, home and basks in science-fiction slanted memories of his film career.

Reason was born on November 30, 1928, in Berlin, Germany, while his family was in Europe on a business trip. He grew up in Los Angeles but, early on, his show business aspirations were nil. "I was never truly interested in the theater," the deep-voiced actor recalls. "It was my mother who had the interest and who was hoping that her two boys, my brother Rhodes and myself, would become interested." Maternal influences notwithstanding, Rex's acting career grew partly out of an inferiority complex that he developed during his high school years. A six-foot-three 15 year old with the voice of an adult, he frequently found himself the center of attention and became self-conscious as a result. His mother took him to a dramatic coach who, in working with Rex, recognized his stage and screen potential.

Apparently acting was in the cards for the teenage Reason: he transferred from Hollywood High to Glendale's Hoover High School, and on his first day in this new setting, the school dramatic coach spotted him in the hall and told him, "You are the one I want for the lead in my next play."

"The play happened to be *Seventh Heaven*, which my mother was in love with. She knew the role I was going to play, which was Chico — just the kind of romantic, dramatic part she was probably praying I'd get. She was very happy — tearfully happy — and she took ahold of me and said, 'Rex, you're going to *do* this play!' There were only two weeks to prepare, and she drummed those lines into my head, worked me until I was in bed, sick, and even *then* she kept at it!"

At 17, Reason enlisted in the army and used his time in uniform trying to figure out what he wanted to do with his life. His father's wish was that he become a civil engineer, while his mother kept after him to try for a career in acting. After his discharge, he opted for the latter, enrolling at the Pasadena Playhouse. Tiring of acting studies after a year and a half, he moved on and became involved in little theater. The big break came when an agent spotted him in a stage production of *Monserrat* and asked him whether he would like to try out for a picture.

Previous page: Actor Rex Reason turned his back on his movie and television career when he decided that it was not giving him "a chance to grow up."

Fantasy film fans remember Rex Reason exclusively for *This Island Earth* and *The Creature Walks Among Us*, tending to forget that his very first film, *Storm Over Tibet* (1952), also boasts mild supernatural overtones. Top-billed Reason played the role of an Air Transport Command pilot who, in preparing to be mustered out of the service and return home from the Himalayas, pilfers as a souvenir the skull mask of the Tibetan God of Death. When his copilot, Myron Healey, questions his right to steal the sacred symbol, the two tussle, Reason is slightly hurt, Healey takes over the flight and is killed in a crash. Reason becomes convinced that Healey suffered the fate the Death God had ordained for him. "From that point on, I did a search within my soul: I went back home, I saw Healey's wife [Diana Douglas], so on and so forth. In need of an answer, she and I took a trek back to the Himalayas, joined a UNESCO expedition and undertook the search. I climbed the mountains, got up to the top and challenged the Sinja god, and in the end I found my answer. That was the gist of it."

Directed by Andrew Marton, *Storm Over Tibet* was largely built around stock footage from a Himalaya-set feature that Marton had directed 20 years before (some of this stock had previously turned up in Columbia's *Lost Horizon*). Reason's mountain-climbing scenes were actually shot indoors, on a huge stage in a rented studio on Los Palmas in Los Angeles. "The snow in those scenes was corn flakes, painted. And I remember that when the wind machines started and those corn flakes were flying and we had to talk and react in the face of all of that, that these corn flakes got in our nostrils and got stuck [*laughs*]! So it was very difficult to cope with that." Reason also has fond memories of the film's producer, the late Ivan Tors. "Ivan, as I recall, was quite interested in animals at the time. In fact, he was studying a lot about porpoises, and as you know he later did a television series called *Flipper*. He and Laslo Benedek were the producers of *Storm Over Tibet*, and Marton was the director. They all were extremely interesting and helpful to me."

While at Columbia, Reason also played supporting roles in pictures such as *Salome* with Rita Hayworth, *Mission Over Korea* and *China Venture* (all 1953). Of his minor role in *Mission Over Korea*, the *New York Times* wrote, "In exactly two scenes, totaling approximately three minutes, a newcomer named Rex Reason wins top acting honors" over a cast that included veteran players John Hodiak, John Derek, Audrey Totter and Maureen O'Sullivan.

When Reason's tenure at Columbia reached its end, his agent talked him up at Universal. "Universal said they had a part which might get me a seven-year contract. It was the part of the Indian brother to Rock Hudson in *Taza, Son of Cochise* [1954]. They tested me, and they seemed to be very excited about the results. It was a rape scene with Barbara Rush—which, needless to say, was exciting to *me* [laughs]! And so, a few days later, they signed me to a seven-year contract and set up three pictures immediately for me to do; *Taza, Son of Cochise* and *Yankee Pasha* [1954] were the first two. And, although I didn't

The Flash Gordon and Dale Arden of the 1950s three-strip Technicolor era: Reason and Faith Domergue in *This Island Earth*. (Photofest)

know it at the time, for the third they had me penciled in as a possibility for *This Island Earth*."

In the latter half of the 1950s, Reason would become typecast as a movie and television hero, but early on, Universal heaped villainous roles on the stern, stentorian actor. In the 3-D *Taza, Son of Cochise*, he was Naiche, the hot-blooded Chiricahua savage who refuses to honor the peace his tribe has made with white men ("I want to live like an Apache warrior—by the lance, the arrow and the knife!"); and in the seriocomic costume adventure *Yankee*

Pasha, he was the bearded Islamic nobleman Omar Id-Din, who buys Rhonda Fleming for his harem and meets a gruesome impaling death that he had intended for hero Jeff Chandler.

Reason has fond memories of the early days when he dished out dastardly deeds as a Universal contractee. "It was wonderful there," he grins. "There were acting workshops where we would memorize a scene, do some improvisation; there was dancing; there was fencing—the whole grooming process. All the Miss Americas and Miss Universes would come out, and we would host all those lovely ladies, so on and so forth. I did love it because it kept us busy. Being a part of it and having roles in pictures and seeing your name up there on the screen is all very exciting, and I felt kind of blessed to be a part of that whole life." The one negative aspect of a contract player's life was that he was constantly subject to the whims of the front office. "Milburn Stone walked in on me one morning with a trade paper spread open in front of him, and he said, 'Hi, Bart.' I said, 'What do you mean?' and he read to me, '"Rex Reason's name now changed to Bart Roberts."' Well, that made me a little disturbed. So I went and talked to Ed Muhl, who was head of production at Universal, and I said, 'You know, if my name were Bart Roberts, I bet you'd change it to Rex Reason!' I told him Rex Reason was a good name and he didn't argue—he said, 'Fine, you can have it back.' However, as it ended up, those first two pictures [*Taza, Son of Cochise* and *Yankee Pasha*] went out with the Bart Roberts name on 'em."

It was by being in the right place at the right time that Reason won his best, and best-remembered, role as the hero of *This Island Earth*. Actress Piper Laurie was making a test for a Western picture and Reason was asked to play opposite her in a short scene set on a stagecoach. The scene belonged to the actress, Reason was relaxed and casual in his supporting part and today he cannot even recall what the picture was or if Piper Laurie got the part. "But Ed Muhl watched that scene and seemed to like it very much, and I think as a result of that he thought of me for the role of Meacham in *This Island Earth*. I read the script and I found it very interesting, I started testing and the rest you know."

Technicolor cameras rolled on Universal-International's most lavish science fiction production in January 1954. Reason and another screen newcomer, Jeff Morrow, starred respectively as hero and extraterrestrial tragic hero, sultry Howard Hughes discovery Faith Domergue assumed the female lead and supporting parts were filled by such fifties reliables as Russell Johnson, Lance Fuller and Robert Nichols. But it was the Universal special effects technicians who would emerge as the true stars of the film as *This Island Earth* began to grow in importance in the eyes of studio executives. "I know they put a lot of money into the special effects, and day after day the more it progressed toward getting ready for the screen, there was a lot more talk about it. It seemed to be a very important project at the time—important enough for them to put the money into it and make it as first-class as possible."

What Reason calls his "good vibes" over the picture and its possibilities were furthered bolstered as his relationships with cast and crew began to develop. "The producer, William Alland, had a lot of imagination. He was always fascinated with whatever it was he was doing, and he was always giving us his ideas regarding what we were going to do. He was quite an imaginative gentleman and always quite energetic. Joseph Newman I would call a comfortable director. A few of the directors I worked with did a lot of screaming and yelling, but Joe was very comfortable and easy to work with."

Regarding his costars, Reason is unstinting in his praise. "Jeff Morrow was, to me, *the* professional—he was very stimulating to watch and to work with. He was 'in' his part, and he had a lot of respect for his fellow actors. And as a result of this, I was better—he was 'high,' and this called forth every bit of my attention and involvement as an actor. His few remarks to me during the shooting of *This Island Earth* helped me. He said, 'You know, you have looks, Rex, but if you think that you do have looks, it's going to take away from your acting. You're the kind of person who's going to have to work a little harder.' I did the best work I knew how on *This Island Earth*, and I think I held up my end of the picture to his satisfaction. He is to be categorized as an 'actor's actor.'" And leading lady Faith Domergue "was quite a sport," Reason continues. "There was a scene where I had to dunk her down into some dirty water and a chase where I had to yank her along, and she didn't ever complain. She never once played the 'Hollywood Queen' with me—she did a good job, she was a lovely lady and she was real nice. I'm sorry I didn't get to know her better."

Production went smoothly over what Reason remembers as a six-week shooting schedule, with enthusiasm for the project continuing to grow and Reason enjoying the change of pace from his usual villainous roles. Questioned about reports that an uncredited Jack Arnold was partially responsible for the film's direction, Reason dismisses the rumor. "Jack Arnold was there, and he was very excited about being part of the picture," the actor allows, but to the best of his recollection, Arnold was in charge for only a few stray pickup or insert shots.

Reason continues to look back on *This Island Earth* with pride although he (like Jeff Morrow) regards Universal's decision to shoehorn monster scenes into the film's climax as an unhappy miscalculation. "I would say that those scenes definitely detracted from *This Island Earth*," he nods. "They didn't have the realism that the rest of the picture did—you could tell immediately that this was just a stuntman in a bug uniform, and that took away from the picture. If they had perhaps showed the monsters only in close-ups, if they had kept the camera up around their heads, it might have had more impact, but the long shots spoiled the moment. For the small kids it was all right, but *This Island Earth* was in some ways a rather thoughtful story, and I felt it was just too bad that they had to have those in there."

Metaluna mutants to the right of them, bogus backdrops to the left of them, Rex Reason, Faith Domergue and Jeff Morrow wish they were back on *This Island Earth*.

If Reason hoped that his heroic role in *This Island Earth* would change his screen image, Universal quickly dashed his hopes by returning him to deep-dyed villainy in pictures like *Kiss of Fire* (1955, as the ruthless governor of New Mexico) and the same year's *Smoke Signal* (as a conniving cavalry lieutenant). "But I enjoyed those villainous roles because I could lose myself. To my mind, I wasn't good looking enough to be a Rock Hudson or somebody like that, so I felt much more comfortable with some of those character roles. I knew how to act—I came off the stage, so to me acting was important. To know your job, do your job well. And I always did my job as well as I could. But I never really had any objective of getting to be a star or anything; I felt it was just part of the activity of growing up."

Asked what type of niche he had hoped to fill as a Hollywood actor, Reason pooh-poohs the question. When pressed as to what he would have considered an ideal role, he waxes metaphysical. "I've always had a philosophical attitude that I was hoping to find in a script: something that had a wonderful message, something that would fit my type and that I could carry. I like to say a few things about my relationship with Someone higher than I, Something divine. I don't want to use the word God because everybody uses it, misuses it and places it outside themselves where it shouldn't be. Once I really got into acting, I wanted to have that one certain role."

Neither Reason nor his Maker could have been overly pleased with the actor's next science fiction assignment, *The Creature Walks Among Us* (1956). Third installment in Universal's popular and profitable Gill Man trilogy, *Creature Walks* is notches below the earlier Creature films in quality, and to this day remains a slightly sore spot for its stalwart star. "If I had known that it would be shown on television and been around, I wouldn't have done it, to tell the truth. I did the film feeling it was just a job, but I really hadn't anticipated the possibility of it getting on television—there weren't too many movies of that type on television at the time, and I thought of it as a picture I'd be able to simply put behind me. I personally thought it was kind of corny."

Former assistant director John Sherwood assumed directorial duties on this final Creature outing while Reason was reunited with Jeff Morrow in the leading roles. A Gill Man–hunting expedition into the Florida Everglades is organized by Morrow, a slightly batty surgeon who spends most of his time bickering about evolution and casting fishy stares in the direction of his sorely tried bride, Leigh Snowden. Between verbal sparring matches, Morrow and fellow scientist Reason track down and capture the Gill Man, who is transformed by fire into an air-breathing, smooth-skinned Frankensteinian brute in a baggy sailcloth jumpsuit. Eventually the Creature rebels, kills Morrow and lumbers instinctively back to the sea and a presumed drowning death.

Like Jeff Morrow, Reason remembers precious little about his Creature encounter except that there were no opportunities for him in the picture and no challenges as an actor. "It was a comedown after *This Island Earth* and *Kiss of Fire*—a downer," he says, and once again wishes aloud that he had had the foresight to turn thumbs down on the assignment. Adding to his unhappiness is the fact that he still carries a scar from his Creature experience: "We had an accident while we were shooting the scene on the motorboat. There was a little lantern on board which fell over and started a fire. I jumped out, but there was a little piece of metal on the side of the boat that ripped open my left ankle."

Like John Agar, who quit Universal when he realized that science fiction roles were all the studio planned for him, Reason was becoming extremely wary of genre assignments. When Universal initially announced *The Deadly Mantis* in mid-1956, Reason and Mara Corday were slated for the leads and Rex finally put his foot down. "That was one picture when I finally spoke up and told them I didn't want to do it. To me it was very corny. I knew that the monster would be the star and I felt that I was worth a little more than just to support a praying mantis." As it turns out Reason need not have made a fuss over the proposed role: *The Deadly Mantis* was not shot until after the mid-fifties Universal shake-up in which most of the studio's contract players were dropped from the payroll. When the picture finally went into production in July 1956, Craig Stevens and William Hopper were sharing the top male slots opposite female lead Alix Talton.

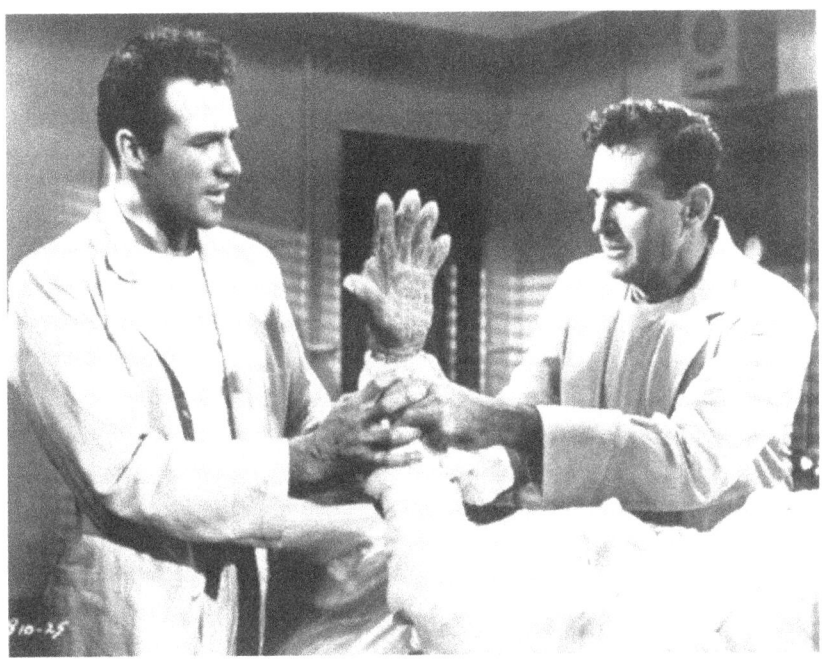

Scientists Reason and Jeff Morrow examine the injured Gill Man in the tawdry *The Creature Walks Among Us*, a film assignment Reason remembers as "a downer."

A freelancer after parting with Universal, Reason continued to work in pictures (mostly Westerns) and then in television. His first television series was the syndicated Western *Man Without a Gun*, which lasted 52 episodes, and his second, *The Roaring Twenties*, a Prohibition Era adventure series that ran on ABC-TV from 1960 to 1962. (He turned down the lead in television's *Maverick*, the show that established James Garner.)

After *The Roaring Twenties* wrapped up, Rex Reason, the man who once told an interviewer that "if I couldn't act, I wouldn't know what to do with my life," suddenly turned his back on acting. Reason explains his unexpected move: "At age twenty-two, I landed the lead in *Storm Over Tibet*, and I was considered a leading man in Hollywood all of a sudden, to some people a star. To me I was just a working actor, but the Hollywood life is very demanding and very magical. In those ten years I spent as an actor I didn't ever have a chance to grow up—to experience the normal processes of getting out, finding a job, working, dealing with people and so on. That was all sort of held in abeyance. If you're a leading man in Hollywood, that's all kept away from you: whether people like you or not, they *bow*. A few of my friends that I went to school with, who I would see from time to time during my acting career—I could see a growth, a *something* happening within them that was not happening within me. I didn't like not knowing or experiencing that growth. So that was part of the reason that I left and started really soul searching. It was very difficult to leave, and to try and find another profession. Three years it took me before I actually became receptive." His search for a new direction in life was complicated by the fact that many people still tended to look up to him as an actor and to associate him with the roles he had played in television. "At any time, if I ever got frustrated, I could have easily turned around and said, 'The heck with it' and moved back into acting. But I couldn't let myself do that."

Although his acting days are now permanently behind him, Reason recently has been talking to agents about the possibility of getting back into the business and doing some voice-over work. He made his last film in 1959, but occasionally he will pop up in a picture like *The Incredible Shrinking Woman* or *E.T. The Extra-Terrestrial*—in clips from *This Island Earth*. (Reason went to see *E.T.* because he had heard that he was in there somewhere, and missed the scene while buying popcorn.) Clearly *This Island Earth* has become and will remain the film for which the actor will always be best known, and Rex Reason has no qualms about the permanent link. "Well, you're here today!" he laughs. "I've done several interviews on the subject of *This Island Earth*, and I still get a lot of fan mail, believe it or not, from people who also mention *This Island Earth* constantly. So *This Island Earth* has done a lot for me as far as giving me a little notoriety, keeping me alive in the minds of fans and giving me a feeling that my work in films had a little worth. So, yes, I do have very fond memories and an appreciation of *This Island Earth* and what it's done for me."

REX REASON FILMOGRAPHY

As Bart Roberts:

Taza, Son of Cochise (Universal, 1954)
Yankee Pasha (Universal, 1954)

As Rex Reason:

Storm Over Tibet (Mask of the Himalayas) (Columbia, 1952)
Scaramouche (MGM, 1952)
China Venture (Columbia, 1953)
Salome (Columbia, 1953)
Mission Over Korea (Columbia, 1953)
Sign of the Pagan (voice only; Universal, 1954)
Smoke Signal (Universal, 1955)

Lady Godiva of Coventry (Universal, 1955)
Kiss of Fire (Universal, 1955)
This Island Earth (Universal, 1955)
Raw Edge (Universal, 1956)
The Creature Walks Among Us (Universal, 1956)
Badlands of Montana (20th Century-Fox, 1957)
Under Fire (20th Century-Fox, 1957)
Band of Angels (Warner Bros., 1957)
Thundering Jets (20th Century-Fox, 1958)
The Rawhide Trail (Allied Artists, 1958)

The Sad Horse (20th Century–Fox, 1959)

The Miracle of the Hills (20th Century–Fox, 1959)

This Island Earth clips featuring Reason are seen in *The Incredible Shrinking Woman* (Universal, 1981) and *E.T. The Extra-Terrestrial* (Universal, 1982).

Actors really don't retire in the usual sense, because there's nothing to prevent you from working until the day you die. If they need an old person and you're old, maybe you'll get the part. And another thing: At that point, your competition will soon begin to disappear!

William Schallert

246 They Fought in the Creature Features

FOR THE PAST 35 YEARS, he has occupied a comfortable niche as one of television's most avuncular family men/father figures; those twinkling eyes can be seen in hundreds of sitcom episodes, that friendly voice (heard in countless commercials) enthusiastically invites us to try/taste/test drive every product under the sun. Is this all there is to actor William Schallert?

Hardly. The easygoing on-screen personality he has perfected might be a reflection of Schallert the man, but it does not do justice to Schallert the actor, who takes his craft *very* seriously. Years before his lucrative stints as Patty Duke's television father and *Get Smart*'s tottering Admiral Hargrade, he honed his talents on the stage, studied British repertory theater in England, even lectured at Oxford. And during the early days of his career, he also turned up regularly in science fiction—the film genre that, in fact, gave him his first big-screen break, when Schallert played one of the leads in the low-budget science fiction favorite *The Man from Planet X*.

"I've always felt very beholden to [producers] Aubrey Wisberg and Jack Pollexfen for recognizing that I was a usable actor and putting me into several of their pictures," Schallert recalls. "The first time they used me was in *The Man from Planet X*, which we made in 1950. At that point, I'd been working on the stage for four years, and I'd built a *kind* of a reputation in town. I was starting to climb the ladder: I wasn't famous or well known or anything, but as a beginning character actor, a few casting directors knew who I was. And that's all that matters. It's not who you know, it's who knows you. They begin to think of you more and more regularly, especially if you're reliable. So somebody probably suggested me to Wisberg and Pollexfen, or maybe they had seen me work. At the time, I also had a beard, and maybe that helped; the guy I played in *Man from Planet X* was the villain of the piece. I was called over to Hal Roach Studios, read for them and got the part."

The moody film, set amidst the rising mists of Scotland's moors, found Schallert fourth-billed as a scientist who is on hand when a small space vehicle—manned by a single, dwarf-sized occupant—sets down in the nearby wilderness. Fellow scientist Raymond Bond and reporter Robert Clarke attempt to communicate with the seemingly friendly alien, but Schallert, obsessed with learning its secrets, antagonizes and abuses X, which then turns against the humans. The film, a cult favorite today, was the first production for writers Wisberg and Pollexfen, who were on the Hal Roach lot sets constantly, supervising their maiden effort.

"They were an oddly matched couple of guys. Jack Pollexfen was a really strange looking guy; we used to kid and call *him* the Man from Planet X *[laughs]*. Jack was American and Aubrey was British, and they cowrote the thing. They were primarily writers, and they were trying to leverage themselves

Previous page: From struggling bit player to television mainstay to Screen Actors Guild president: The William Schallert Story. (Photo from *Innerspace*.)

A villainous role in *The Man from Planet X* (with Robert Clarke, left) represented a big career step forward for Schallert.

up into the producing end, which they did on this thing. And of course Edgar Ulmer, who directed it, has quite a good reputation among cineastes as the King of the B Pictures, for doing film noir low-budget movies. Edgar was ... okay. I didn't think the picture was a particularly stylish film or anything like that, but I guess it accomplished what it needed to. We shot it in six days, all on a single soundstage at the old Hal Roach Studios, which are not there anymore."

Like many actors who have labored in this type of ultracheap cult picture, Schallert does not think as highly of it as its diehard fans do. "That's true. *The Man from Planet X* was exciting for me *at the time*, representing as it did a big step forward for me, but I didn't think it was a stunning picture or anything like that. Of its genre, it's probably okay. But I must say that Edgar Ulmer made the picture *look* quite interesting. I don't know how good he was with actors, to tell the truth; I think it was mostly that he was pretty good with the camera and with the lights, and could do things on the cheap." Schallert cannot clearly recall whether Ulmer ever attempted to guide his performance but "I'm sure he *must* have had ideas about what I should be doing and he probably communicated them to me. All directors, whether they're good with the actors or *not*, will let you know whether you're doing something that satisfies them or not. And if they can't tell you what to do, you just have to *invent* something else."

Third-billed, Schallert was acting in support of stars Robert Clarke and Margaret Field, who were paired in several B movies of that early-fifties era. "I knew Bob for a number of years after that; he later married one of the King Sisters," says Schallert. "Maggie I used to see once in a while; she later married Jock Mahoney, and of course she's Sally Field's mother. She was a *very* sweet person, I thought, and they were both nice to work with. I also remember working with Raymond Bond, who played the older professor. He and I once discussed how to make yourself cry, and he was describing what he did to do that."

The one burden shared by every one of *Planet X*'s leads was that of coping with their ornate, overwritten dialogue. "I'm afraid that's true, it *was* hard to make that dialogue your own, as we say in the acting profession. You always try to make whatever it is you have to say feel as though it's something that you are saying at the moment because you're responding to whatever the situation is. It's very difficult to make the kind of dialogue Wisberg and Pollexfen wrote 'your own.' Now, in a later picture of theirs [*Sword of Venus*, 1953], I played a drunken attorney in a jail cell. Somehow in *that* scene, the rather elaborately written, didactic, formal language was okay; it worked very well for that guy. But in some of the other pictures—oh, Jesus!"

"Cheap," according to Schallert, was the key word for *Planet X:* The $41,000 film was shot in less than a week, on reused sets from Ingrid Bergman's *Joan of Arc*, and with special effects which were primitive even by early 1950s standards. "When you shoot a whole feature film in six days, you don't have a lot of time to think about it. You just have to put in long days. And we were not paid handsomely, either. I think I got $225 for the week, and that was at a time when we had a six-day week. I also remember X himself. He [the actor] was a very small guy, kind of middle aged. He mostly just *looked* interesting; I don't know that he was much of an actor. In a way, you look back on pictures like *Man from Planet X* and you say, 'God, that whole thing was just a *joke*,' but it *has* lived on. It was made for less than $50,000 in six days, and Wisberg and Pollexfen sold it to Sherrill Corwin, who ran a chain of theaters. I guess Corwin got his money out of it okay; Wisberg and Pollexfen got enough money out of it to go on and make the next picture [*Captive Women*], with Albert Zugsmith."

Planet X capitalized on the big publicity push RKO was giving Howard Hawks' *The Thing from Another World*, insuring a warm box office reception. "*Planet X* didn't ride on the coattails of *The Thing*; it actually rode on the wave just ahead of it. *The Thing* had this enormous publicity campaign; it was the first really big, serious science fiction film in quite a while. (And a very stylish film, too, very well done.) *Planet X* took advantage of all *The Thing*'s publicity; we opened the week before *The Thing* did and gained a lot of benefit from all its publicity. *The Thing from Another World* and *The Man from Planet X*, they sounded vaguely alike to people, I guess. A friend of mine was in New York and he told me that there was a larger-than-life-sized head portrait of me in the lobby of one theater that was running *Man from Planet X*. 'There you were,' he said, 'a *star!*' *[Laughs.]* So, yeah, it *was* a big deal for me; I had good billing in the film and all the rest of that."

Encouraged by the success of *Planet X*, Wisberg and Pollexfen hustled to put a second science fiction film into production, reuniting Clarke, Field and Schallert in the postapocalyptic *Captive Women*. "That was originally called *3000 A.D.*," Schallert reminisces. "It was kind of a *dumb* film, but I thought that it had an interesting premise, the idea of people surviving after the Bomb and living in New York City subways. It was an unusual notion. The same plot was used later in one of the *Planet of the Apes* films [*Beneath the Planet of the Apes*]; *Captive Women* anticipated that. I don't know that Wisberg and Pollexfen ever had any *original* ideas, but they were very good at grabbing on to ideas that had some merit. I thought *Captive Women* had some possibilities. My wife [Leah — now Lia — Waggner] was also in that, incidentally, in a bit part. We played characters who were not called mu*tants* — we were called mu*tates*. I don't know whether that was just illiteracy or some perverse notion on the part of Wisberg or Pollexfen that that was a better word *[laughs]*."

In the film, the survivors of a devastating atomic war fight amongst themselves in and around the rubble of Manhattan. Schallert, a radiation-scarred member of the Mutate tribe, is banished after contesting Ron Randell's leadership and turns traitor, leading the warlike Up-river men against his own people. "The fellow who did the makeup was named Steve Clensos. He had invented a makeup remover which was called Clens *[laughs]*, so it was advantageous that his name was Clensos, I guess. Steve worked pretty quick: He would make up one side of my face with silver, to show the effects of radiation, and then he also added a scar to it. We probably shot that in ten days or two weeks, something like that." Production was hectic, with new scenes being written daily and an inexperienced director, Stuart Gilmore, having difficulty maintaining order. "Stuart had been an editor, and I don't know how much directing he'd done prior to this. *Captive Women*, I guess, was his break, but I *vaguely* remember Gilmore as being a man with not very much patience. He was under a lot of pressure. I don't have a lot of recollection of it, though, because we *all* had our problems with that picture. It was tough to make.

"Albert Zugsmith was one of the producers on that, along with Wisberg and Pollexfen. After I did *Captive Women* and a couple of other pictures for them, Zugsmith got the notion that I could do just about anything, and he became quite a champion of mine. He really did do his best to get me into everything he made, in one way or another. In fact, when he was at Universal, he tried to put me into his films, in parts that I was totally unsuited for. He tried to force me on Orson Welles in *Touch of Evil* [1958], to play the part that was played by Joseph Calleia, for God's sake *[laughs]*! Calleia was thirty years older than I, and he also was Mexican, which is what the character was *supposed* to be. It was just insane. Zugsmith used me in a thing called *The Girl in the Kremlin* [1957], and I played Joseph Stalin's brother. I remember trying to do this dumb Russian accent, and I must say that when I finally saw it, I thought to myself, 'Oh, God...!' (In it, I killed Stalin by driving off the road with him.) Well, all I can say is, a job is a job, and at a certain stage of your life, you just take what comes.

"You could almost say that Aubrey Wisberg and Jack Pollexfen were to blame for bringing Albert Zugsmith into the motion picture business—depending upon how you feel about Zugsmith's pictures. But he did make *Written on the Wind* [1956], which garnered Dorothy Malone an Oscar, and a couple of other things at Universal that might have been okay. In general, his pictures had a strong sense of schlock about 'em, but then *[laughs]*, Wisberg and Pollexfen were not exactly the top of the heap, either!"

One of Schallert's best-remembered small roles was his supporting part in Zugsmith's later *The Incredible Shrinking Man*. "*That* was a very good film, I thought. Jack Arnold directed that, and I thought Jack was a very stylish director. *The Incredible Shrinking Man* had an interesting story by Richard Matheson. *Shrinking Man* was a superior piece of writing; Matheson also did some very good writing for *Twilight Zone* and other shows. I played the doctor who diagnosed that Grant Williams was shrinking.

"It was nice that Albert Zugsmith used me so often, even though I used to end up playing roles that maybe I wasn't right for. But I was usually quite grateful, because I was trying to *survive* during that early- to mid-fifties period. The key thing about an actor who was in my position—the position I was in until I started to click in the late fifties in television—was staying alive without doing anything but acting. That's really tough to do, but I managed, partly because my wife was willing to tolerate it. But by 1954, we had three kids. You would step from one slowly sinking rock to another as you crossed the stream of life, and keep hoping for a new rock. It was always very dicey until about 1957, '58, when I began to work more, and especially in '59—that year I really worked a lot. From then on, I was okay."

Early on, before television typecast him as the affable sitcom dad, Schallert had a number of good heavy roles. Does he miss those opportunities? "I must say that I always found parts like that interesting. I continued to do that kind of thing in television a lot; I did a lot of interesting character work in TV even after *The Patty Duke Show*. But when it came to serious work, I was really typed for the warm, fatherly kind of guy. The 'heavier' parts do still come up from time to time: I've played a couple of sleazy lawyers recently on episodic television, so they haven't completely disappeared. So, yes, of course I've always enjoyed them; any actor does."

The son of Edwin Schallert, former drama editor of the *Los Angeles*

Times and the dean of West Coast critics, William became interested in an acting career while at UCLA in 1942. "I had been trying out various things while I was there—I worked on the newspaper, studied composing, did some singing, things like that. And I didn't feel that I was really very well suited to any of them. One night I was at a party, and there was an actress named Blossom Akst, whose father was Harry Akst, a well-known song lyric writer. She said, 'Listen, why don't you come down and audition for a part in a play I'm doing?' I had never thought about acting, but she kept at it: 'Sure, c'mon, you'd be very good for that.' (I used to kid around a lot, show off in various ways—typical actor's behavior.) So I went to the reading and tried out for the part; it was a play at UCLA, an adaptation of Ben Jonson's *Volpone*, and the role I was trying for was Corbaccio, an old miser and a lecher. A very interesting, fun character to do.

"I got it, and I guess I was reasonably good in it because they called me out to 20th Century-Fox about a week later. Ivan Kahn, who was the talent scout there, said it was a very interesting performance. He sent me into another room with a fellow who was their acting coach; I don't remember much about that except that we read together, and he kept saying to me, 'Don't move your hands so much!' *[Laughs.]* I guess I passed whatever minimal test they were laying on me, and Kahn said, 'So what's your status with the draft?' I said, 'Oh, I've probably got two or three months before the ROTC gets called up.' Kahn said, 'Well, be sure to look us up after the war.' I realized afterwards that they were lookin' for *any* warm male body in those days, with so many Hollywood actors off fighting the war! But, still, they *had* shown interest in me and I figured that was a good sign. So while I was in the service, I did start to plan on giving acting a shot.

"When I came back, I went back to UCLA to finish up, and I did two or three more plays there. I also got in a directing class—*why* I don't know; there was no acting class at the right time, I guess. Boris Sagal, who later became quite a well-known director before he was killed, was in the same class. And in the course of working in that class, I got cast in a lot of projects that other directors were doing. I would just play these little scenes, but in that one semester I did maybe ten or twelve scenes and I probably learned the fundamentals of how to act in doing that. Or, I should say, I found out what I could do. (You know, you really can't *learn* acting—you can either do it or you can't. You can get *better* at it, and training can certainly help, but you find out very quickly whether you can do it.) By the time that semester was over, I had a kind of a sense of myself, especially in comedy.

"Right after I got out of school, I got in with a group that had formed at UCLA, the Circle Theatre. I went down and read for them, and they took me on. I worked there for the next four years, and gradually became one of the owners of the place. By the time those four years were over, I had gotten into the Screen Actors Guild and AFTRA, and the year after we closed the

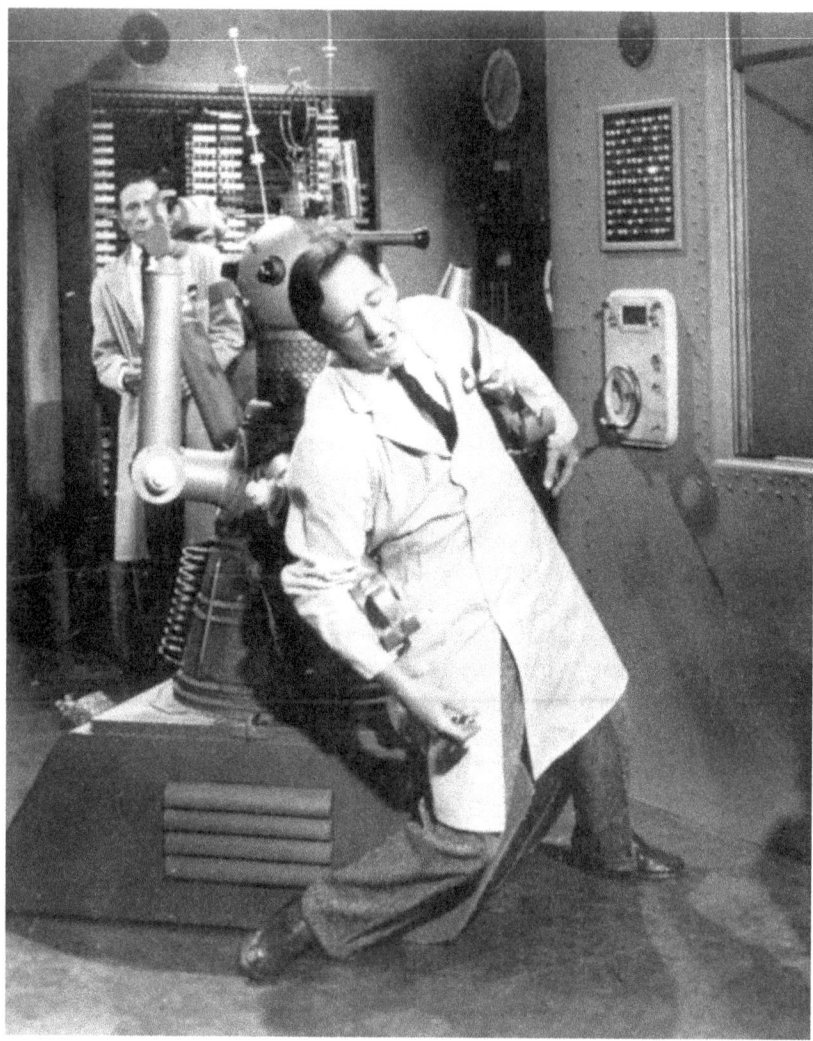

Being strangled by a robot is Schallert's main memory of playing a lab assistant in science fiction producer Ivan Tors' *Gog*.

theater, I joined Equity and did a lot of stage work. From then on, I was committed. By then I was married and had a child, so I had to work. I didn't have any choice *[laughs]*!"

The first of Schallert's approximately 80 movies was *The Foxes of Harrow* (1947), a period drama starring Rex Harrison. "William Bacher, the producer of *Foxes of Harrow,* and John Stahl, the director, each had one daughter who was part of our Circle Theatre; William Bacher's daughter talked to her father about the people at the Theatre. (We were doing *Ethan Frome* at the time, and people *were* rather impressed with the production.) Bacher and Stahl either came to see the play or they took their daughters at their word, because several of us were called out to Fox. I got a one-line bit, and *[laughs]* I still remember it: 'Gentlemen, gentlemen! The bank of the United States and Philadelphia has closed its doors.'"

During his early years, Schallert frequently played bit or supporting parts in science fiction and fantasy films, some of which he remembers (*Mighty Joe Young*, *Them!*, *Gog*), others of which he does not (*Port Sinister*, *Invasion USA*, *The Monolith Monsters*). Working in the genre suited him just fine, since "I was a big reader of *Astounding Science Fiction* from about the end of the war on up through the early fifties. I used to read it all the time; in fact, I remember when L. Ron Hubbard first appeared. The first advertisements for Dianetics appeared in *Astounding Science Fiction*, which really defined it for me pretty well *[laughs]*. I did read one of Hubbard's space operas, I think. I used to read *all* that stuff: I remember A.E. Van Vogt and Isaac Asimov, the *Foundations* stories in particular.

"I worked for [producer] Ivan Tors, who did a lot of that kind of thing; I did some stuff for him that was kind of junky, but it was good fun. *Gog* I remember, because I got strangled by a robot *[laughs]*. They had robot suits for that film, with people inside them. I don't remember the picture too well otherwise, except that I worked with a guy named John Wengraf, who was a very good Viennese actor; I'd already worked on the stage with him. I thought he was very stylish and had an interesting voice."

Schallert initially hooked up with Tors through the efforts of his then-agent Leon Lance — "who never really would sign me," he laughs. "I didn't ever have a signed contract with an agent until 1954, when I'd been in the business for seven years. That's not unusual for a character actor; it takes a long time to get off the ground. Leon was a very funny guy who had a rare way of speaking. He handled Jim Arness in (as Leon would say) *The Ting* and *Dem [The Thing* and *Them!]*; I once heard him say to an actress over the phone, 'Listen, you should do it, darlingk. It's a *fireproof* part!' ('Fireproof' being somewhere between surefire and foolproof, I suppose *[laughs]*!) Leon knew Ivan Tors — Tors was a European himself, so they kind of knew each other."

Working for Tors again, this time on television's *Science Fiction Theatre*, Schallert had his one chance to act opposite character star Edmund Gwenn. "We played Martians. He was a rather benign Martian and I was his assistant, trying to keep him under control and not let him do too much good. Edmund Gwenn was a really wonderful guy to work with. He'd already done all of his great movie stuff and had retired, but he had terrible arthritis in his knees from having played football when he was younger. He was a very distinguished actor — he'd been in the first productions of a couple of George Bernard Shaw's plays, besides winning the Academy Award for *Miracle on 34th Street*. And here he had to come out of retirement and work in this cheap *Science Fiction Theatre* thing because he needed the money—he needed arthritis treatment. It was really sad—his knees were killing him, he was having a really hard time. We [actors] didn't have a pension and health plan back then. Even in those days, if you got a really crippling disease, it could exhaust your funds."

A second robot movie, Republic's *Tobor the Great*, provided Schallert with a day's work at a very opportune time. "I was really having a tough time right about then. I'd been out of the country for a while—Lia and I had gone with two kids to England. I had a Fulbright Fellowship for a year, and I was studying British repertory theater. (*Why* I was doing that is beyond me; I was hoping I could work over there, I think.) Anyway, I'd come back and it was very slow. Leon Lance, my agent, called me one morning and said that a client of his named Charlie Wagenheim had gotten sick, and could I go to Republic to replace him? It was the part of a reporter, just a few lines or something like that, in *Tobor the Great*. It was probably a hundred, a hundred twenty-five dollars for the day, and I said, 'You *bet*, I'll be there!'—we could use that to pay the rent! Now, I've always suspected that maybe Charlie Wagenheim wasn't really sick, that Leon had simply said to him, 'Listen, I've got somebody who *desperately* needs the money. Would you mind?' and Charlie must have said okay. I've always had a feeling that it was just a good turn, but I've never known for sure and nobody would ever tell me. That's just a characteristic story of what it was like to be a struggling actor."

On television, Schallert was also briefly featured as a regular on the small-screen *Commando Cody*, playing sidekick to Judd Holdren, who wore Republic's familiar bullet-helmeted rocket suit. "I did a fair amount of work at Republic, which was a kind of a beginner's studio—they didn't have a lot of money. It was the bottom of the ladder, but they cranked out Westerns and serials. In 1952, they were still making serials, and they decided they would make a science fiction serial called *Commando Cody*. (Commander *Cory* was the star of a live television science fiction show called *Space Patrol*, and I used to play heavies on that on a regular basis—I must have worked for 'em a half a dozen times. Commander Cory was a well-known character, and I think Republic just ripped the name off for *Commando Cody*.) The fellow who played the lead in *Commando Cody*, Judd Holdren, had been a bookkeeper, and I bumped into him again years later when he was the bookkeeper at a commercial agency when I first began to do voice-over commercials. That was an interesting coincidence.

"*Commando Cody* was going to be done as a serial, in twelve episodes. But in the back of their minds, Republic also was thinking that they might release it as a television show. So it was kind of a hybrid, partially made as a theatrical serial and also partially made as a television series. It was kind of a Buck Rogers–type series about traveling in a spaceship. They had a big mock-up of a spaceship, split in half; we would climb up in there and do whatever we had to do. It was dumb writing. There was an actress named Aline Towne who was in it, too; she was actually quite a good actress, I thought. And Judd Holdren was okay; Judd was not a terrific actor, but he was a manly looking guy, the kind of guy you would cast in that. I played his sidekick/assistant; I did those types of 'other guy' roles at Republic, generally somebody with a sense of humor because I could do comedy pretty well."

Schallert appeared only in the first three segments of *Commando Cody* before he managed to pry himself out of the series. "I realized that, in order to continue to do it, I had to sign a term contract with Republic. Once I found out what they were going to pay me, and thought about it, I said to Leon Lance, 'We gotta get out of this.' I didn't think I could live on it — even though it was probably as much money as I was going to make that year anyway *[laughs]*. (Maybe it was just the fact that I didn't want to be trapped at Republic.) They were going to pay me $150 a week for 40 weeks, which was $6,000 for the whole year. I had one child and I knew what our rent was and all of that, and I didn't see how I was going to survive on that, especially since I couldn't do anything else. So I managed to get out of it — which was, in a way, insane. I don't know what I thought my prospects were that made me think I was going to make more money than that in the course of the year; in fact, I think I went to England later that year on the Fellowship. But it was one of those quickly sinking rocks that I managed to stand on for a short time. And after that, the casting director at Republic did not have a friendly feeling toward me for a while, because I had sort of reneged. I eventually went back to work for them."

Between jobs, Schallert often found time to take in some of his own movies; he attended the premiere of the John Wayne–starring *The High and the Mighty* [1954]. "I walked into the lobby of the Egyptian Theater in Hollywood, in a rented tux, with my wife. (We had driven up in our old Morris Minor that had a torn roof, and she had borrowed the formal dress she was wearing from a girl upstairs.) We came into the lobby, and there was a crowd of people there — premieres used to be that way. There was a rope holding the people back, and somebody cried out, 'There he is! There he is!' Some guy came under the rope and came *racing* toward me and held out something for me to sign, which I did. And as he was going back, the people who had been saying, 'There he is! There he is!' were now saying, 'Who *is* he? Who *is* he?' And the guy who got my autograph read it and groaned, 'Aw, it's *nobody*!' *[Laughs.]* I would say that that defines my situation in terms of the business, in terms of the general public, anyway, in those days, about as well as anything. I was really on the ragged edge, just eking out a living.

"One other thing about *The High and the Mighty*. I had one day's work on it, and again I was getting paid like maybe $150 for that one day. It was for William Wellman, a top-notch director, it was a very classy picture, and the scene was quite good — it was a brief scene, but I thought I'd done a good job in it. The same day that I worked on that, I had an offer to work at MGM for *two* days—in a nothing role, and not in a good picture, but it would have paid me $125 a day and I'd have made $250. And unfortunately (from *my* standpoint), I'd already committed to doing *The High and the Mighty*. I did not work for about two *months* on either side of it, and it was typical of the actor's struggle to survive that I would have a conflict on the same day I worked."

Other 1950s films roles included an early Roger Corman quickie (the switched-sex Western *Gunslinger*) and the notorious all-star Irwin Allen production *The Story of Mankind*. "In *Gunslinger*, I was the marshal, Beverly Garland was my wife, and once I got shot—in the first scene *[laughs]*—*she* became the marshal. That was the only time I ever worked for Corman, so I guess he was not impressed *[laughs]*. Beverly went on to do several things for him. She's a really good actress, and an intelligent person, too. And a good businesswoman—she's got a chain of hotels out here. I like Beverly a lot, she's a real down-to-earth person. And *The Story of Mankind*—God! I played the Dauphin in a scene with Hedy Lamarr, who was playing Joan of Arc. *[Laughs.]* I'm laughing, because Hedy Lamarr's reputation was as this sexpot, and here she was playing Joan of Arc. I made a lot of money on it, because I had to be in very early for makeup—I had a bald wig in that—and we did it all in one day. I worked until like eleven at night, *very* late; it was a long, long day and I got a lot of double time and overtime and all of that. So I was very happy with the film, simply because of the money I made on it."

While Schallert worked (somewhat) steadily in pictures throughout the fifties, he insists that he never sought any special niche in the movie business or tried to model himself after any other actor. "I don't think I ever approached the business that way. To tell the truth, I never thought about things like that, I was really very naïve when it came to thinking about myself in terms of a career. I felt like I could do almost anything that anybody asked me to do. That's *nonsense*, but that's what I thought. As to whether I ever tried to model myself after any other actor, *no*, although I have of course admired a great many actors for the kind of work they did. I guess if I saw *any*body who I thought it would be nice to be like, it would be Alec Guinness. When I was first starting, Guinness was also starting; I remember seeing *Kind Hearts and Coronets* [1949], in which he played eight roles, and thinking, 'Gosh, I would love to get a shot at something like that, because I think I could do it.' Actually, the thing that I had the most success with when I worked on the stage was comedy. There's a certain kind of comedy that I think I can do as well as anybody; if there was any way that I was ever going to be a star, it would have been from doing stuff like that."

From 1963 to 1966, Schallert played Martin Lane, the sorely tried but always patient father on television's *The Patty Duke Show*. The ABC half-hour sitcom remains, like it or not, Schallert's claim to fame, but action and science fiction fans probably prefer his shorter stints in other shows, *The Wild Wild West* and *Star Trek*, in particular. "I enjoyed working on *Wild Wild West*; there I got to play an assortment of different roles. When Ross Martin had a heart attack, he was out for about five episodes, and Charles Aidman and I replaced him serially. They offered that to me mainly because I had played such a variety of characters and they thought I could do almost anything; 'Okay, Schallert, we'll stick you in there and you can play all these wild characters the way that Ross did.'"

Asked about reported friction between stars Robert Conrad and Ross Martin, Schallert can offer little input. "There was never any evidence of that on the set; from what *I* saw, it seemed to me that they got along okay. Conrad's a kind of a prickly guy, and he would go through phases where he was doing what seemed to be rather foolish things, but actually he's a pretty good actor. People don't give him credit for very much, but I've seen him do some good things in movies of the week and that kind of stuff. He didn't have the technical resources of Martin, who was a very wide-ranging actor with a lot of facets to his personality and his skill, but Conrad does what he does very well. To tell you the truth, I always thought they got along pretty well, and seemed to have a lot of fun on the show. Maybe I missed some of the bad stuff."

Star Trek must be a subject about which Schallert is asked regularly, because he recalls the experience *and* the episode title without the slightest prompting. "'The Trouble with Tribbles'! I remember those little furry balls that they used for the Tribbles — they were all over the place — and you had to treat 'em as though they were alive in some way or another. Stanley Adams, who played the trader who sold them, was one of the funniest guys I'd ever met in my life. He was a comedy writer — I think he used to write for Red Skelton — and I enjoyed working with him always. He was a very funny guy on the set, and also a very good actor. And Charlie Brill, who's also a very funny fellow, played my lieutenant, who of course turned out to be the nasty guy who started all the trouble."

In the episode, a favorite among Trekkies, Schallert played Nilz Barris, official in charge of the delivery of a huge supply of grain to a distant planet. Some of the episode's humor derived from insults arrogantly tossed by Captain Kirk (William Shatner) at the uptight Barris; fans prefer to ignore the fact that Barris' misgivings about Kirk are well founded, since Kirk *does* in fact do a thorough job of bungling his important assignment.

Schallert recalls, "The character *I* played was characteristic of the way they sometimes cast me, which is as a stuffy sort of bureaucrat. Those are *not* rewarding roles, they're really not. It was okay, I played it, but it's not the kind of part I'd like to be remembered for, the rest of my life. (Unfortunately it *will* be, I guess *[laughs]*!) I probably saw an episode or two of *Star Trek* prior to working on there, but I was not a great devotee of science fiction shows; there are very few of 'em that I watch regularly. I was not a Trekkie. For whatever reason, that show never grabbed me."

Schallert even had his own shot at a starring role in a series in 1963, when Richard Donner directed him in the television pilot *Philbert*. "That was the first thing that Dave DePatie and Friz Freleng did together; they're the people who created the Pink Panther character. I played a cartoonist who drew a daily strip, and the character that I drew was Philbert—a little wiseass guy with a snap-brim hat and a perky attitude. He suddenly came to life and walked off the page, in the magical fashion of the sitcom, and entered my life. We had somewhat the same sort of relationship that Bill Bixby and Ray Walston did in *My Favorite Martian*: He would sort of mess up my life and then get me *out* of the mess. The problem with the show was that it cost about 50 percent more than anything else that was being done at the time, because of the animation. The average half-hour show in those days cost $50,000 an episode (roughly one-twelfth of what they cost today), and mine was going to be $75,000. Friz Freleng told me that that's what killed it; ABC just wasn't willing to spend that kind of money on it. I thought, when I saw it, that what I did was quite good, and if it had gone, who knows where it would have led."

The actor had the distinction of being assassinated with a hydrogen bomb in *Colossus—The Forbin Project*, 1970s entrant in the computers-take-over science fiction subgenre. "That was directed by a good friend of mine, Joe Sargent; I've worked for him a couple of times since. I thought Joe did a stylish job with that, and it was a very interesting idea, too. I don't think that picture made much money, which is too bad; it really deserved a better fate, because it was very well done. Speaking of that picture, I'm the only person I know of who was assassinated with an H-bomb—they usually don't go to that extent of overkill to get rid of one person *[laughs]*. Computers took over the world, and found out that I was the government official who was trying to defuse all the H-bombs that the computers were holding over us. I'm sitting there smoking a cigar when the computers unleash one of the bombs on us; the countdown starts and all the other people get up and start running away screaming, but I just sit there with a cigar in my mouth, knowing there's no point in running a few feet *[laughs]*. Then the flash comes. So there I was, assassinated by an H-bomb."

In a much lighter vein, Schallert played Professor Quigley in the Disney live-action comedy/fantasies *The Computer Wore Tennis Shoes* and *The Strongest Man in the World*. "Those were very satisfying. I thought, number one, that the films themselves were always very well done and a lot of fun to watch; you really could have a good time seeing them. Number two, the experience of working on 'em was very good. Disney was a pretty good quality lot to work on. It's a nice place, very democratically organized. I think because it was started as an animation studio, they didn't have much of a class system there. When they went to the commissary, there wasn't an executive dining room—Disney got in the line with everybody else, apparently. That tradition sort of carried over. It had a nice feeling, that lot. Also, I thought the writing on those shows was very good; in fact, I knew the writer, Joe McEveety, who went to school with my brothers. Joe had a bad heart; he was living on borrowed time when he was working at Disney, and he did die not long after that." Schallert adds that he definitely saw the "writing on the wall" for Disney's Kurt Russell, who starred in both movies (as well as in the Schallert-less *Now You See Him, Now You Don't*) as the accident-prone college whiz Dexter Riley. "He was my idea of an extremely talented young actor. I thought, 'This guy really can act'—and, God knows, that's really been proven with time. For a long time I didn't think he got his due, but he is now."

From 1979 to 1981, Schallert was the president of the Screen Actors Guild, an organization with which he is still affiliated. In the 1980s, three of the five features in which he appeared were helmed by fantasy filmmaker Joe Dante. "I like Joe a lot. I think he's a very inventive and creative director. I didn't want to do *Twilight Zone—The Movie* when they first approached me because they were paying minimum. At that stage in my life, I said, 'I'm not going to work for minimum. It's ridiculous.' And 'Why is Spielberg so cheap?' is what I *really* wanted to know *[laughs]*. But that's the kind of a shop they were running, because they didn't know how this picture was going to turn out and everybody was working on the cheap. Everybody in the cast was getting the same thing—everybody, that is, except the individual star of each episode; they were getting more. But anyone who was playing a supporting role got minimum—that included people like Patricia Barry and Kevin McCarthy. There was also a girl in it named Nancy Cartwright, who is the voice of Bart Simpson now. *Twilight Zone* was one of the first things she did here in town; she played the girl who got her mouth sealed up.

"It was a kind of wild experience working on that thing because the sets were all done like cartoons. They used forced perspective, and nothing was real looking. For instance, when you went up the stairs, the steps kept getting smaller the higher you went. So it was very difficult to go up 'em. Those sets were really fascinating, because I'd never worked in that kind of an environment; it had a very cartoonlike *feeling* that Joe did deliberately—that's what he was after. He had a real definite sense of style for this thing. And he wanted me, and some of these other people, in it because he's a great devotee of old films, and especially of old science fiction films. He particularly wanted to have people in it who were in those films; I *have* done my share of 'em *[laughs]*. I found working with Joe on that to be quite a good experience."

Working for Dante again in *Gremlins* (1984) was "kind of accidental. I had asked Joe for a favor: I was helping a group of people raise some money for the deaf, and they thought that if we could have a premiere showing of *Twilight Zone* someplace, they could raise some money. Joe provided the film, and then he said, 'Okay, now you owe me one. I want you to be in *Gremlins*.'

Schallert offers Cathy Moriarty a hand in the science fiction takeoff *Mant*, the movie-within-a-movie in director Joe Dante's *Matinee*.

It wasn't much of a part: He wanted me to play the kind of old guy I used to play on *Get Smart*. I played an old priest, spent most of a day doing a lot of stuff (some of it scripted, some of it invented right there). It was really funny stuff. All of it got cut, except for one event at a mailbox—that's all that's left of me in the picture. Joe told me that was all that was left, and he asked me if I wanted billing, and I said, 'Absolutely not!' *[Laughs.]* I'm just there for that one quick shot. I'm sorry that the other stuff didn't stay, but I understood why—it didn't advance the story. Obviously they knew what they were doing, because *Gremlins* did very, very well."

Schallert acted for Dante a third time in *Innerspace* (1987), in a scene reminiscent of his *Incredible Shrinking Man* doctor gig, examining hypochondriac patient Martin Short. "Working with Martin was terrific. He's such a funny guy and very inventive. And in addition, he's a very good actor; not just a funnyman, but also a very honest actor who's very much in touch with himself. Even though he does rather exaggerated things, I always *believe* him; he's got a good sense of *truth*, which some comics don't have."

Today, besides his work in front of the camera, Schallert keeps active with SAG-related projects: He's still the trustee of the Pension and Health Plan, and also one of the trustees of the Motion Picture and Television Fund. "Also, once a year for about six or eight weeks, I serve on the Allocations Committee of the Permanent Charities Committee, which is like the Hollywood version of the United Way. We in fact *give* money to the United Way, too, but we also fund a large number of projects of various kinds, mostly having to do with the health area. We've expanded now to deal with homelessness and in particular with AIDS."

William Schallert never gives retirement a thought. "Oh, no!" he scoffs, as if (at 69) he is surprised at the question. "I'm old enough to retire, but to tell the truth, I'm working so steadily that as long as people keep asking for me, I guess I'll keep working. Actors really don't retire in the usual sense, because there's nothing to *prevent* you from working until the day you die. If they need an old person and you're old, maybe you'll get the part. And another thing: At that point, your competition will soon begin to disappear *[laughs]*! Surviving is everything! And when you survive *long* enough, you do become a kind of an icon. I've been around long enough, and everything I've ever done in my life is being recycled on cable, particularly on Nick at Nite. Eventually, *all* of this stuff comes home to roost, and unless you were really ghastly, people are very fond of you for it. It's a nice feeling."

WILLIAM SCHALLERT FILMOGRAPHY

The Foxes of Harrow (20th Century-Fox, 1947)
Mighty Joe Young (RKO, 1949)
The Reckless Moment (Columbia, 1949)
Lonely Hearts Bandits (Republic, 1950)
The People Against O'Hara (MGM, 1951)
The Man from Planet X (United Artists, 1951)
Belle Le Grand (Republic, 1951)
Bannerline (MGM, 1951)
The Red Badge of Courage (MGM, 1951)
The Jazz Singer (Warner Bros., 1952)
Hoodlum Empire (Republic, 1952)
Paula (Columbia, 1952)
Storm Over Tibet (Mask of the Himalayas) (Columbia, 1952)
Captive Women (1000 Years from Now) (RKO, 1952)
Holiday for Sinners (MGM, 1952)
Rose of Cimarron (20th Century-Fox, 1952)
Just This Once (MGM, 1952)
Sally and Saint Anne (Universal, 1952)

Flat Top (Monogram, 1952)
Sword of Venus (RKO, 1953)
The Girls of Pleasure Island (Paramount, 1953)
Invasion USA (Columbia, 1953)
Torpedo Alley (Allied Artists, 1953)
Port Sinister (Beast of Paradise Isle) (RKO, 1953)
Down Three Dark Streets (United Artists, 1954)
Captain Kidd and the Slave Girl (United Artists, 1954)
The Raid (20th Century-Fox, 1954)
Them! (Warner Bros., 1954)
Riot in Cell Block 11 (Allied Artists, 1954)
The High and the Mighty (Warner Bros., 1954)
Gog (United Artists, 1954)
Tobor the Great (Republic, 1954)
Shield for Murder (United Artists, 1954)
Black Tuesday (United Artists, 1954)
Bobby Ware Is Missing (Allied Artists, 1955)
An Annapolis Story (The Blue and the Gold) (Allied Artists, 1955)

Smoke Signal (Universal, 1955)
Top of the World (United Artists, 1955)
Hell's Horizon (Columbia, 1955)
Glory (RKO, 1956)
Friendly Persuasion (Allied Artists, 1956)
Raw Edge (Universal, 1956)
Gunslinger (American Releasing [AIP], 1956)
Written on the Wind (Universal, 1956)
The Tattered Dress (Universal, 1957)
Band of Angels (Warner Bros., 1957)
The Story of Mankind (Warner Bros., 1957)
The Girl in the Kremlin (Universal, 1957)
The Incredible Shrinking Man (Universal, 1957)
The Tarnished Angels (Universal, 1957)
Man in the Shadow (Pay the Devil) (Universal, 1957)
The Monolith Monsters (Universal, 1957)
Man on Fire (MGM, 1957)
Torpedo Run (MGM, 1958)
Juvenile Jungle (Republic, 1958)
Cry Terror! (MGM, 1958)
Some Came Running (MGM, 1958)
The Beat Generation (This Rebel Age) (MGM, 1959)
Blue Denim (Blue Jeans) (20th Century-Fox, 1959)
Pillow Talk (Universal, 1959)
Day of the Outlaw (United Artists, 1959)
The Gallant Hours (United Artists, 1960)
Lonely Are the Brave (Universal, 1962)
Paradise Alley (Sutton, 1962)
Philbert (Warner Bros. featurette, 1963)
Shotgun Wedding (Pat Patterson Productions, 1963)
In the Heat of the Night (United Artists, 1967)
Hour of the Gun (United Artists, 1967)
Will Penny (Paramount, 1968)
Speedway (MGM, 1968)
Sam Whiskey (United Artists, 1969)
The Computer Wore Tennis Shoes (Buena Vista, 1970)
Colossus — The Forbin Project (Universal, 1970)
Tora! Tora! Tora! (20th Century-Fox, 1970)
The Trial of the Catonsville Nine (Cinema V, 1972)
Charley Varrick (Universal, 1973)
The Strongest Man in the World (Buena Vista, 1975)
Tunnelvision (World Wide Films, 1976)
The Jerk (Universal, 1979)
Hangar 18 (Sunn Classic, 1980)
Peege (USC/Phoenix Films short, 1982)
Twilight Zone — The Movie (Warner Bros., 1983)
Gremlins (Warner Bros., 1984)
Teachers (MGM/United Artists, 1984)
Innerspace (Warner Bros., 1987)
House Party 2 (New Line, 1991)
Matinee (Universal, 1993)

Schallert's scenes were cut from *Singin' in the Rain* (MGM, 1952) and *Bigger Than Life* (20th Century-Fox, 1956). *The Terminal Man* (Warner Bros., 1974) features the actor in a clip from *Them!* He narrated *Doomsday Chronicles* (1979).

*When I decided I wanted to direct, I couldn't even get
to first base; to get a half-hour show, I practically had
to kiss Dick Powell in the middle of Santa Monica Boulevard!*

Don Taylor

They Fought in the Creature Features

THEY ARE A DIME A DOZEN TODAY, but up until the 1950s, with the obvious exception of major names like Chaplin, Olivier and Welles, the actor-director was a genuine rarity in Hollywood. In the fifties, however, the floodgates opened, and in the forefront was a light leading man who remembers only too well the stumbling blocks that were once placed in the path of would-be directors.

"It took me quite a while, because in those days, nobody would let *any*body new direct," Don Taylor recalls. "Today, all you have to do is say, 'I wanna direct,' and the next thing you know, you got a movie. Back in the fifties, it was a hell of a lot tougher. Dick Powell, who was then one of the regulars on a television anthology series called *Four Star Playhouse*, gave me the chance to start directing.

"It started out slow, but I parlayed things. In other words, somebody would ask me to act in something, and I'd say, 'Sure, if you'll let me direct.' But after a while, that didn't work any longer because people weren't taking me seriously, and I had to really say, 'I'm a director.' I was a trailblazer. Paul Henreid, Ida Lupino, Dick Powell — we were the forerunners of actors becoming directors in that period. But it was very difficult — *very*. We really had to prove ourselves."

Of course, the days when Don Taylor had to prove himself as a director are long gone, with his list of features running to double digits and the roster of television directing jobs to the hundreds. Few directors that prolific have avoided dabbling in the science fiction and fantasy genres, and Taylor has done more than his full share in that field, helming such well-remembered science fiction titles as *Escape from the Planet of the Apes*, *The Island of Dr. Moreau* and *The Final Countdown* — not to mention the supernatural shocker *Damien — Omen II* and numerous episodes of television's *Alfred Hitchcock Presents*.

Born in Freeport, Pennsylvania, Don Taylor studied law, then speech and drama at Penn State University, where as a freshman he began taking part in college stage productions. ("There was never any question about it once I put my foot on a stage. I knew I was going to be an actor.") Hitchhiking to Hollywood in 1942, the youthful Taylor screen-tested at Warner Bros. but was rejected because of his draft status. MGM, not quite as fussy, signed him to a contract and immediately put him to work, assigning him the minuscule role of a soldier in director Clarence Brown's sentimental slice of Americana, *The Human Comedy* (1943). "They sent me downtown and put me on a train. I said, 'Where's my dialogue?' and they said, 'You don't have any dialogue. When the train stops in Pasadena, there'll be a family there. They'll shout, 'Don! Don!' and you'll greet them — you're coming home from the war.' So I got to Pasadena and got off and, boy, I kissed my 'family.' I had a merry old time! And then I suddenly heard Clarence Brown screaming: 'Get him out of

Previous page: Actor Don Taylor fought to turn director back in the days when it just was not done.

there! Get him the hell *out* of there!' The actor who they were really trying to photograph, John Craven, couldn't get off the train because I'd monopolized the whole area [laughs]!"

More minor roles followed before Taylor enlisted in the army, but even there he continued acting. Playwright/screenwriter Moss Hart chose him to play one of the leading roles in the Army-Air Force production of his play *Winged Victory*, which opened in November 1943. Amidst a bevy of rising stars (Lon McCallister, Jeanne Crain, Edmond O'Brien, Judy Holliday, Lee J. Cobb, Karl Malden, Gary Merrill, Martin Ritt), Corporal Don Taylor repeated his stage role in 20th Century-Fox's film version of the play, directed by George Cukor, in 1944.

Returning to civilian life, Taylor resumed his work in pictures with a top role in the trendsetting crime drama *The Naked City* (1948), which still stacks up as his favorite among his own films. "*Naked City* was a classic, one of the first of its kind. It was improvisational in many, many ways; now it's very ordinary to go and shoot anywhere, but *Naked City* we did long before anybody else." *The Naked City* was shot on actual locations throughout New York City with director Jules Dassin utilizing a hidden camera, although on at least one occasion all did not entirely go well. "I was walking down Fifth Avenue and keeping in view of the hidden camera — stepping around people, so forth and so on," Taylor recalls. "All of a sudden, a college fraternity brother of mine came along — 'Hey, Don, how are you?' I said [*firmly*], 'Get out of the way, I'm makin' a movie.' But he wouldn't leave me alone, and finally he even grabbed me!" The role for which he is best remembered remains the MGM comedy *Father of the Bride* (1950), as fiancé to Elizabeth Taylor ("That's still going strong — and so's Liz [laughs]!"). He reprised the character in 1951's *Father's Little Dividend* as well as playing other leading parts in fifties films at RKO (*Flying Leathernecks*, *The Blue Veil*), Fox (*Japanese War Bride*, *Destination Gobi*) and Paramount (*Stalag 17*, as the missing prisoner around whom the plot pivots).

Most actors have at least one skeleton in their closet of film credits, and Taylor has a dilly. "I was getting a divorce at the time, so I called my agent and I said, 'Listen, I've had it. I want to get out of the country. Do you have anything?' He said, 'Yeah, we've got a picture that's going in Brazil — ' I said, 'That's for me.' Turned out to be a thing called *Women of Green Hell*. I didn't even read it; when I got to Brazil, they gave me the script. And when I read it [*laughs*], I was ready to cut my throat!"

The notorious fantasy-adventure (written, produced and directed by Curt Siodmak) was shot under the title *Women of Green Hell* but released by Universal as *Love Slaves of the Amazons*. The top-billed Taylor was captured by a tribe of green-skinned warrior women in the unexplored jungles of South America. "Curt Siodmak — the brother of Robert Siodmak — had written a famous novel called *Donovan's Brain*, and he wrote a bunch of films. But this one—oh, God! *Terrible*! He was a good writer, but he didn't know how to direct. But there was a dear old actor down there, Eduardo Ciannelli, and he and I just had a great time together. We said, 'What the hell, let's do it.' We kidded each other and we got through it. I got along with Siodmak—almost—but Ciannelli was very rude to him—'Why don't you go back to school?' and comments like that *[laughs]*. And yet I was having a ball because I was 'out of commission'—really, that's all I was doing, hiding out."

He ended up hiding out a lot longer than he expected. "That damn movie never ended—shooting went on and on and on. For a cheap movie, it was amazing—I was down there in São Paulo for a long time. I swam in waters that I don't think I'd want to go in anymore; I remember a guy saying, 'Watch out for the piranhas' just as I was diving in *[laughs]*! Brazil uses the Portuguese language, and we had a crew from Argentina, which speaks Spanish. And the Brazilians didn't like the Argentineans anyway!"

In the film's one good scene, our heroes' boat, is boarded by a gang of cutthroats and a lively brawl ensues. "That scene, I think, was almost an ad-lib. We'd been out all day and we were coming home, and the unit manager (an American out of Universal, there to protect the money) said, 'Shoot something.' Siodmak said, 'What do I shoot?' and the unit manager said *[sharply]*, 'Put the camera there and turn it on!' Then he yelled at some guys, 'Hey, *you* guys start chasing *these* guys.' That's why that was probably the best scene: Siodmak didn't direct it!" Temple scenes for *Love Slaves* were shot in the Vera Cruz Studios in São Bernardo ("It didn't have any soundproofing, so when I came back here I think I had to loop most of the picture!").

"I believe Universal did *Love Slaves* because they had 'frozen funds' in Brazil, just sitting there, and so when somebody said, 'I can make a film in Brazil,' they said right away, 'Sure! Go ahead!' I told myself that nobody would ever see it—a movie like that would never make it. Then television bought it, and that son of a gun's on all the time! God, I have people call me at four or five o'clock in the morning, laughing so hard they can barely get the words out. They say, 'Guess what! *Love Slaves of the Amazons* is on!'" The *Love Slaves* experience had a happy ending when Taylor was asked by the Johnston Office to travel through South America on a goodwill tour upon completion of the picture. "I flew to almost every country, and there was a mob waiting for me every time. I really felt like I was back to being a star. It was fun, and I had a good time."

His acting career in a slump thanks to pictures like *Love Slaves* and Hammer's drecky *The Men of Sherwood Forest*, Taylor's desire to switch career gears and direct continued to grow. "I'd been in about two dozen films, and starred or costarred in most of 'em. But the creative forces that I was not feeling as an actor were all in the director's path. That's really why I did it. I had spent a lot of time watching directors, and I knew a lot more about directing than I thought I did." With Dick Powell's help, he made his directorial debut with an episode of *Four Star Playhouse* and soon branched off into other shows such as *Telephone Time* and *Alfred Hitchcock Presents*.

"I'd known Mr. Hitchcock because I had been up for a couple of his films. *Rope* [1948] was one of them; I had just finished *Naked City* and I went to see Hitchcock about *Rope*. We just talked—he had just seen *Naked City* and he wanted to know how they made this shot, that shot and the other shot. He marveled at the fact that we shot on Fifth Avenue.

"Anyway, I didn't get *Rope*, but I'd been interviewed by him. And once I got to do that first *Hitchcock* episode, then I used to sit and watch him direct—he was taking all the good scripts. My first year, he and Arthur Hiller and myself were among those directing. Arthur and I were way down at the bottom—if Hitch didn't want to do it or couldn't do it, then Robert Stevens got it, and if he'd already had one, then it came down to Arthur or me. Once in a while we'd get a good one; a lot of times we were struggling. But basically those were good scripts—when I think of the stuff that goes by me today, those were *excellent* scripts. The only thing that was wrong with them was what was wrong with most of the shows at that time—there was absolutely no production. They'd put up two walls and put a picture on the wall, a chair and a table and say, 'Shoot.' No books, no magazines, no papers, no frills. You couldn't get any production worth a damn."

The CBS show yielded another dividend for Taylor, one far more important than the directing jobs and the experience of working with Hitchcock: Directing the 1958 episode "The Crocodile Case" brought him in contact for the first time with red-haired actress Hazel Court, reigning scream queen of British horror films. Romance eventually blossomed; Taylor and Court tied the knot in 1964 and the happy marriage endures to this day.

After several years of directing in television, Taylor made his behind-the-scenes feature bow with the fantasy-comedy *Everything's Ducky* (1961), starring Mickey Rooney and Buddy Hackett as sailors who team up for a series of adventures with a talking duck. The film could hardly have been more minor, but Taylor was still happy to get the assignment. "It was a big step at that point. I was directing a TV series called *Hong Kong* with Rod Taylor when Mickey Rooney called me and said, 'Would you please direct this?'—I'd directed him four or five times in television at that point. I was hesitant, but Hazel said, 'Oh, go ahead and do it,' so I did. I got Arthur Hiller to direct the *Hong Kong*s so I could get released.

"*Everything's Ducky* was too tough—we had to do it in eleven days. Mickey and Buddy were good in it, but they were clowning and I had a terrible time—I couldn't stop 'em from clowning, and yet I didn't have the time for it. Mickey was the producer—it was his company making the film—so what could I do? And the duck didn't work—they finally tied his beak with a rubber band and made him eat cigarettes, that's the only way we could get him to open and close his mouth as though he was speaking. Talk about cruelty to animals *[laughs]*!"

Directing for television was not always a pleasure, either, especially when working with a series star who had definite ideas of his own. "That was always one of the difficulties of directing a series," Taylor grimaces. "Richard Boone had a TV series *Have Gun, Will Travel* that I had been asked to direct. At one point during an episode I said to him, 'Why don't we do such-and-such?' Boone said, 'Nope.' *[Pause.]* I said, 'Then, how 'bout so-and-so?' 'Nope.' About five 'nopes' later, I asked, 'Well, what do *you* want to do?' He said, 'I'll just walk over here and sit down.' And I said, 'Okay!' *[Laughs.]* He's directing — I'm only directing traffic, a stop-and-go director. There's no joy in that. I was supposed to do four *Have Gun, Will Travel*s, but I think I only did one — that was enough of that."

More to Taylor's liking were his two episodes of Rod Serling's *Night Gallery*, "They're Tearing Down Tim Riley's Bar" with William Windom (Taylor was Emmy-nominated for his direction) and "The Messiah of Mott Street" with screen great Edward G. Robinson. "'Messiah of Mott Street' was tough — I couldn't get Eddie Robinson to be Jewish. And he *was* Jewish! As a matter of fact, he was my technical adviser, because he was a Levitical student at one point — he helped me a tremendous amount. But he'd spent years being an Italian gangster, and now he wouldn't give me the Yiddish flavor. He was very sweet, but he wouldn't bend at all."

Taylor's other sixties films as director were *Ride the Wild Surf* (1964), a *Beach Party*–inspired surfing romp (Taylor replaced the original director Art Napoleon, who was injured in a fall) and the U.S./German *Jack of Diamonds* (1967) with George Hamilton. He directed one of his best and most popular films in 1971 when he signed on to handle the second sequel to Fox's profitable *Planet of the Apes*.

"*Escape from the Planet of the Apes* was just glass all the way, smooth as silk," Taylor reminisces. "Good script (no, a *beautiful* script), the actors were divine, everything went right. It was one of those instances where I just couldn't wait to get to the studio every day. There should be more pictures like that, but you don't get 'em anymore. In those days, all the people hadn't gotten in the act. Today, you do a picture like that and you have twenty people wanting to get their hands in, wanting to be creative, wanting to have a say. In the old days, it was easy — there'd be a producer and maybe one other person. You can handle two or three or four people, but you can't handle 15, 20."

Taylor had not seen either of the first two *Apes* films when he was approached to direct *Escape*. "When they suggested I do *Escape*, [producer] Arthur Jacobs, who I knew for years, said, 'Well, we can set it up for you to run at the studio, or you can come to my house tomorrow night for dinner and I'll run it for you.' So we ran *Planet of the Apes*, and I thought it was marvelous. Eventually I saw the second one, *Beneath the Planet of the Apes*; Ted Post directed that. It was a real bastardized version of the first one and it didn't really work, didn't have a story. But *Escape* was one of the best scripts—Paul Dehn was a good writer. I liked our script for *Escape* as much as I liked the first *Apes* script; in fact, ours was more humane."

Aside from the strong story, Taylor's job was facilitated by cooperative stars who knew their characters inside and out. "They were so pro, Kim Hunter and Roddy McDowall, and they knew their characters—I never *told* them what to do, I always *asked*. Sometimes Roddy'd say, 'No, I don't think our characters would do (whatever it was),' and how could I disagree? This was their second, third time out! Makeup-wise, though, Kim and Roddy had a terrible time — they had to get in about three o'clock in the morning for makeup, and then when they were done for the day it took an hour and a half to get it off. They'd be sitting there at night after they were finished, having the makeup taken off, and I'd go in and talk to them about the next day's work. With little drops of alcohol, the makeup men were able to dissolve the glue that held the makeup on and, inch by inch, they'd peel it off. It was painful."

Escape had its share of lighter moments—more so than any other film in the five-film series—but it also posed some interesting philosophical questions. "That's right, the profundity suddenly came through at one point. It was a plot where Somebody Had to Be Dumb, and in this case it was the human beings. In this film it worked. But that gets boring after a while; in almost every television show today, Somebody Has to Be Dumb—say something or do something that's so stupid, because that's the only way the show can develop or progress. It's true of a lot of movies, too."

Extensive makeup played an even larger role in Taylor's next science fiction film. "I had just done *The Great Scout and Cathouse Thursday* [1976] for American International, and they wanted me to do *The Island of Dr. Moreau* for them. But I inherited something that I couldn't do anything about, and that was the appliances that had been made—chin, nose and forehead for all these man-animals. The idea was that these animal men should have been grotesque—half-human and half-beast. But they weren't—they were all Disney. Cuddly. You wanted to kiss 'em *[laughs]*. I couldn't make any grotesquerie out of 'em at all! We had about eight makeup men, with John Chambers and Dan Striepeke in charge; they created all the stuff for the *Planet of the Apes* films. They made it in their cellars *[laughs]*—it was one of those things. And again, you couldn't reuse the appliances; by the time they came off, that was it, you just threw 'em away."

AIP's *Dr. Moreau* got an added box office boost from the casting of Burt Lancaster as the vivisectionist, even though Lancaster was far from the first choice for the role. "We were going for an English actor—the fact that it was based on an H.G. Wells story and all, we thought an Englishman should play the part. [Richard] Burton and [Peter] O'Toole and people like that were considered; we never got turndowns from any of them, they just weren't available.

Burt was available. Back in the days when I made *Naked City* and he made *The Killers* [1946] for Mark Hellinger, Burt and I were very close, but even so, when he was brought up in connection with *Dr. Moreau*, I said, 'Jeez, I don't think this is a part for Burt.' Somebody turned to me and said, 'You wanna make the picture?' and I said, 'Yeah.' He said, 'Well, don't turn down *every*body.'

"Right around that point, Burt showed up in Cannes, and he tore the place apart just walking down the street—the people went ape, because he's an old star, and I guess they don't get many old stars there anymore. That convinced us that we should use Burt. But even he had some hesitation, so I went and I talked to him. He said, 'You got a problem with the script.' I said, 'Yeah, but what picture have you done lately that didn't?' We did have a problem with the script, and we did a serious rewrite on it that ... didn't work, unfortunately. But Burt was very good, because he was secure with me; I took care of him, watched him. That's my whole theory of directing; security. Give the actor security and, to a great degree, let him go. Sometimes you're able to do that completely, like I did with Burt, and sometimes you're not—that's when you get into trouble. Burt worked very hard, and we had a good relationship."

Hero Michael York, Taylor opines, also did a good job in the film, but "he was out there on a wing and a prayer. And when it came time for him to start wearing the [man-animal] makeup, was he scared! 'What are you doing to me? Christ, I'm a leading man! I don't wanna be a bear'—or whatever it was. We had to hold his hand!" And Barbara Carrera "was about fourteen feet off the ground in those days—she was swingin' somewhere that I wasn't *[laughs]*. But she's so gorgeous, she was perfect casting for it."

Shot in the Virgin Islands and costing far more than the average AIP exploitation item, *Island of Dr. Moreau* "was a big picture for Sam Arkoff, and it didn't do that well. Sam had a good little company, a family-oriented kind of company. I saw letters that went out to his distributors, and they were like, 'Hi, Joe. How's Mrs. Doakes this week? Hope she's feeling better.' It was like a high school newspaper *[laughs]*, but it was very sweet, the way that company worked. And they made money—a *lot* of money. On small investments—they didn't make big money, but for the investment, they made three hundred, four hundred percent. That's not bad. AIP movies generally ran in drive-in theaters, and I remember when the rushes on *Dr. Moreau* got to Sam, he started sending cables saying, 'More light! More light! It's too dark!' He was afraid they couldn't run in at the drive-ins."

Taylor is nothing if not consistent on the subject of *Dr. Moreau*: He doesn't think the Wells story was much good ("Wells wrote it, I think, on a weekend *[laughs]*"), nor was the 1932 Paramount version ("It's terrible! But critic after critic saw ours and said it wasn't as good"), nor his own AIP effort. "But I've seen it now a couple times on television, and it looks better now than

Taylor on location in the Virgin Islands for AIP's *The Island of Dr. Moreau*.

it did when I made it — I don't know how to explain *that* one, but it's true. For what it was, it worked. But there wasn't enough horror in it."

There was no shortage of horror in *Damien — Omen II*, 20th Century-Fox's sensationalistic follow-up to their 1976 box office winner *The Omen*. That li'l devil Damien (Jonathan Scott Taylor), no worse for wear after the bloodbath of *Omen*, was back, this time in the charge of William Holden and Lee Grant, and all Hell was breaking loose once again in a picture that seemed determined

to outgruesome its predecessor. "That's one thing that I think was wrong with the script, the idea that More Is Better. There was too much gore—every time you changed a reel, there was another character that you knew was gonna get it. I inherited all that—I would have eliminated at least two of those killings. All the stuff that I did (the kid being killed by the train, the doctor cut in half in the elevator, and so on) was good—I just thought it was too much. Then it got really gruesome at the end. Suddenly Bill is stabbed to death, and Lee Grant gets burned up—Jesus! More is *not* better."

Replacing British director Michael Hodges, who had worked on the film for about two weeks ("He and the producer just weren't seeing eye to eye as to what was being done, and he was fired"), Taylor shot the film in Chicago and on location in Wisconsin, with many interiors also shot on the Fox lot. "I had to redo quite a bit—I would say out of the two weeks work Michael Hodges did, I augmented or reshot about a week."

Star Holden had been offered the lead in the first *Omen*, but turned up his red nose at the idea of doing a horror film. This all changed, of course, two years and an offer of $750,000 later. "Getting Bill for *Omen II* was a plus value; we had made two movies together [as actors: *Submarine Command* (1951) and *Stalag 17* (1953)] and we were old friends. Bill and I used to drink like it was going out of style. *Everybody* used to drink in the business." All Holden did during *Omen II* was complain about it ("...sick-sick excesses... unhealthy ambience..."), leaving Taylor a bit mystified. "He thought it was pretty good when we did it—I ran it for him about three times, so I don't know why he complained."

A *Twilight Zone*-ish type of science fiction story, Taylor's next, *The Final Countdown*, was set aboard the *U.S.S. Nimitz*, an ultramodern aircraft carrier that passes through a time warp and winds up in the Pacific on the eve of the December 7, 1941, Pearl Harbor attack. Should Captain Kirk Douglas and the men of the carrier prevent the Day of Infamy and change the entire future history of the world? "When my agent sent me the script and I read it, my first thought was that it was going to be difficult. And it *was* tough—it was a big picture. It was a good picture, except we had no ending—it just went nowhere, the air came out of the balloon. Everything was interesting getting *into* it; I thought it was just dreary getting *out* of it. About halfway through, you knew that Pearl Harbor was such a historical entity, that it had to happen." *Escape from the Planet of the Apes* had posed the same type of hypothetical science fiction question, but Taylor is quick to point out that "the thing about *Escape* is that both Roddy McDowall and Kim Hunter are killed—at least there's an ending. The ending in *Final Countdown* had nothing to do with the whole

---

Opposite: Taylor's complaint with *Damien—Omen II* is that "every time you changed a reel, there was another character that you knew was gonna get it." (Pictured: Lew Ayres.)

Don Taylor and Hazel Court Taylor today.

picture, of being in a time warp. Suddenly they're just back in their own time period, sailing blithely along!"

Shot aboard the *Nimitz*—a privilege the filmmakers paid a quarter million dollars for—*Final Countdown* bears a producer credit for Peter Vincent Douglas, "but it turned out to be Kirk. Kirk was great for about two-thirds of it, and then Peter was getting kind of in the way and in trouble, and so Kirk exercised his muscles. Of which he has quite a few. He made a lot of noises. Kirk was very difficult. As an actor, he's superb; as a producer, he's a pain in the ass. That's meant nicely *[laughs]*. He's a good actor, easy to direct, no problems."

In 1987 Taylor directed the made-in-Toronto television movie *Ghost of a Chance* with Redd Foxx and Dick Van Dyke, a *Here Comes Mr. Jordan*–type fantasy that was meant to spark a series. Taylor admits that it was a film that probably shouldn't even have been made, at least not under the circumstances. "We didn't have a [workable] script, and it was the start of a writers' strike. We should have never started. We were rewriting the whole time."

Taylor is not as busy with directing as he once was, often turning down television directing offers and devoting more and more time to writing; he and

Hazel Court Taylor also will not watch television or new movies the way they used to, subsisting instead on a video diet of PBS. "Outside of a movie here and there, most of the new stuff is just terrible," Taylor says. "There is a great need—a *cry* is the word for it—for something different, especially in TV. But when you go and give 'em something different, they say, 'Oh, no, we can't make this.'"

Right now his wish is to return to his first love, the stage. "I know I'll direct a couple more pictures—as a matter of fact, I'm contemplating doing one right now—but I feel like acting again and I'd like to do a play. But I haven't found a play that I particularly want to do." For a writer/director like Taylor, the solution is simple: "I think I'm gonna write myself a part!"

And he is equally happy with his acting and directing careers. "I love seeing some of those movies that I was in, but I would have died not directing. As I told you, I broke into it when it wasn't easy. It upsets me now that Kevin Costner, for God's sake, has gone and done a twenty-five million dollar picture *[Dances with Wolves]*—he's starring, he's producing, he's directing.... When I decided I wanted to direct, I couldn't even get to first base; to get a half-hour show, I practically had to kiss Dick Powell in the middle of Santa Monica Boulevard! But at least I helped to break that barrier down, in a way. It *is* a director's medium."

DON TAYLOR FILMOGRAPHY

The Human Comedy (MGM, 1943)
Girl Crazy (MGM, 1943)
Thousands Cheer (MGM, 1943)
Swing Shift Maisie (MGM, 1943)
Salute to the Marines (MGM, 1943)
Winged Victory (20th Century-Fox, 1944)
Song of the Thin Man (MGM, 1947)
For the Love of Mary (Universal, 1948)
The Naked City (Universal, 1948)
Battleground (MGM, 1949)
Ambush (MGM, 1949)
Father of the Bride (MGM, 1950)
The Blue Veil (RKO, 1951)
Father's Little Dividend (MGM, 1951)
Flying Leathernecks (RKO, 1951)
Submarine Command (Paramount, 1951)
Target Unknown (Universal, 1951)
Japanese War Bride (20th Century-Fox, 1952)
Destination Gobi (20th Century-Fox, 1953)
The Girls of Pleasure Island (Paramount, 1953)
Stalag 17 (Paramount, 1953)
Johnny Dark (Universal, 1954)
I'll Cry Tomorrow (MGM, 1955)
The Bold and the Brave (RKO, 1956)
Ride the High Iron (Columbia, 1956)
Love Slaves of the Amazons (Universal, 1957)
Men of Sherwood Forest (Astor Pictures, 1957)
Everything's Ducky (director, Columbia, 1961)
The Savage Guns (MGM, 1962)
Ride the Wild Surf (director, Columbia, 1964)
Jack of Diamonds (director, MGM, 1967)
The Five Man Army (director, MGM, 1970)
Escape from the Planet of the Apes (director, 20th Century-Fox, 1971)
Tom Sawyer (director, United Artists, 1973)

Echoes of a Summer (director, Cine Artists, 1976)
The Great Scout and Cathouse Thursday (director, AIP, 1976)
The Island of Dr. Moreau (director, AIP, 1977)
Damien — Omen II (director, 20th Century-Fox, 1978)
The Final Countdown (director, United Artists, 1980)

I think [Radar Men from the Moon] *is a gas. It's hard to relate it to the science fiction films of today—we didn't have the equipment, didn't have the knowledge of a lot of things. But I think that what we did, for that time, was good. The dialogue was hokey, but back then, it fit. And if people liked it, that was the important thing.*

George Wallace

HE IS ONE OF THOSE ACTORS who has seen both ends of the success ladder and all the rungs in between. At the age of 13, George Wallace was working in a West Virginia coal mine; years later, he was up for the New York Drama Critics Award for playing the male lead in Broadway's *New Girl in Town*. In between, in the guise of Commando Cody, he saved our Earth from devastating conquest and lunar invasion in the serial *Radar Men from the Moon*. A veteran of stage, television and almost 50 movies, Wallace is more than happy to look back on his days in the flying suit, his adventures on the Moon and on Altair-4, and the pitfalls of being an action hero in the days of Republic serials and Saturday matinees.

The New York City–born Wallace, who played the inventor of the flying suit (as well as an interplanetary spaceship) in *Radar Men from the Moon*, does not hesitate to talk about his upbringing during the Great Depression or the fact that as a kid he did not get the chance to go to high school. "I started to go to high school in Far Rockaway, Long Island, but that was right after the Depression, 1933 or '34. I just couldn't afford to finish going through school, because I had no dad—my dad left when I was six months old. I never saw my father—it was just my mother and me, so I had to go to work. I finished maybe three months of high school, and that was it. Then my mother remarried when I was thirteen, and the man she married was a coal miner from West Virginia. As soon as she married him, he packed us from Far Rockaway and we moved to outside of Wheeling, a place called McMechen, which is a sort of coal mining town. At thirteen, I started to work in the coal mines, and I've been workin' ever since."

Wallace joined the navy in 1936 and got out by 1940, although when World War II got underway he was right back in again. ("I was chief bosun's mate in the navy, which is like a master sergeant in the army. In the navy, they claim a bosun's mate is like a sea gull—all he does is eat, shit and squawk all day *[laughs]*!") Beaching himself in Los Angeles after a total of eight years in the service, Wallace supported himself with an array of odd jobs: working for a meat packer ("knockin' steers in the head"), as a lumberjack in the High Sierras, a truck driver, a bouncer, et cetera. "Finally I became a bartender here in Hollywood. In the navy, I always liked to sing, so when I would tend bar, I used to sing along with the jukebox. That was always good for a tip: Some guy would say, 'Hey, George, sing "Heartaches,"' he'd put down 15, 20 cents, and I'd sing 'Heartaches' with the jukebox. One day a guy came in and had a drink, and when he left, he gave me his card and said, 'Call me tomorrow.' I looked at the card the next day, and it was a man called Jimmie Fidler. Fidler was a famous Hollywood columnist, like the Walter Winchell of the West Coast. I

Previous page: Commando Cody (George Dewey Wallace) patrolled America's imperiled skies in Republic's *Radar Men from the Moon*. (The actor's great-grandfather/ namesake, George Dewey, was the U.S. naval commander whose victory over the Spanish fleet at the Battle of Manila Bay in 1898 led to the U.S. acquisition of the Philippines.)

went to see Fidler, and he said, 'How would you like to sing in a Jewish benefit?' I said, 'I'm not Jewish.' He said, 'Who cares?'" *[Laughs.]*

Fidler introduced Wallace to Mickey Katz (the father of Joel Grey), who played the clarinet. "I started with Mickey Katz, singing at Jewish benefits, but after a while somebody said, 'You better take lessons—you don't know how to sing.' So I started to study with an instructor, 'paying' her for my lessons by taking care of her yard and her house. Her husband was kind of sick, so I got two lessons a week by doing all that kind of stuff. Then after a while I went to dramatic school on my G.I. Bill of Rights, to help my singing, and that's how I got in the business."

Wallace enrolled in drama school while earning his living during the day tending the greens at MGM at the time of movies like *The Sea of Grass, Green Dolphin Street* (1947) and *The Kissing Bandit* (1948). His first television role was as an army sergeant in an episode of one of television's earliest filmed dramatic shows, *Fireside Theatre*—a performance that won him the Sylvania Television Award. Small parts in movies (*The Sun Sets at Dawn, Up Front, The Fat Man*) followed before Wallace landed what has come to be known (by science fiction fans, at any rate) as his "signature" role: the two-fisted super-scientist Commando Cody in the Republic serial *Radar Men from the Moon*.

"I was with a little English agent, and she sent me out to Republic for a role as a heavy in *Radar Men from the Moon*," the actor recalls. "I went out in the morning around ten o'clock and spoke to the producers, and they said, 'Do you have any film on yourself?' I said, 'Yes, a *Fireside Theatre*, which won me an award.' They said, 'We'd like to look at it. Just hang around.' So they sent for the film, and in the meantime, I was getting very upset, hanging around—they kept me there all afternoon, just to get a crummy part in *Radar Men* as a heavy. They called me in again about three o'clock and said, 'We saw the film. How would you like to be Commando Cody?'"

Seizing the starring role, Wallace and the rest of the *Radar Men* company began production on the 12-chapter serial October 17, 1951, with Wallace as Cody (no first name, not even among his on-screen friends), Aline Towne as loyal Girl Friday Joan Gilbert, and William Bakewell as lab assistant Ted Richards. Furnishing the film's requisite villainy, Roy Barcroft climbed back into his old Purple Monster tights as Retik, ruler of the Moon, bent on waging war with the Earth and beginning a mass migration of Moonmen from Luna's barren, sunlit(!) surface to our greener world. Clayton Moore took fifth billing as Graber, an earthling ex-convict in the employ of the Moonmen (the part for which Wallace was being considered before he landed the role of Cody).

"Aline Towne and Billy Bakewell were such nice people," Wallace remembers. "We did a lot of stuff that actors today just wouldn't *do*; in those days, you just *did* it, it was part of the job. (In the old days, if you went in for a Western, the director would say, 'Do you ride?' You'd say, 'Yeah.' 'Do you fight?' 'Yeah.' That was *it*!) So we became a unit, a group, and we got

Wallace doffs his helmet to take on Earthbound crooks in *Radar Men from the Moon*.

along just wonderfully. Roy Barcroft had been well known as a Western heavy for so many years, and he was a big, lovable bear, a sweetheart of a guy. And Clayton was just fine, except in one of the fight scenes, he broke my nose accidentally! It was a good group, we all had fun in those days."

Scenes of Cody and Ted (Wallace and Bakewell) fighting the Moonmen's agents in their own Earthly backyards were shot at or around the area of Republic Studios, but scenes set amidst the rocks and cliffs of the Moon surface were shot at Red Rock Canyon, a rugged area in the desert miles from Los Angeles. "Up in Red Rock Canyon, it was 112 degrees in the day, and running around in that hot weather with the heavy leather jacket and all this other stuff on, you sweated quite a bit. We had to stay out there all week to shoot. We'd start first thing in the morning, as soon as the sun came up, and work until the sun went down that night. Of course, I didn't know anything about the business then, because it was like the second thing I ever did. Up at Red Rock Canyon, we stayed in some little dinky motel right alongside of a freight yard. And every night we'd hear the boxcars being changed around for different destinations—clanging and banging all night long. We didn't get much sleep [*laughs*]!"

A highlight of *Radar Men from the Moon* is, of course, the flying scenes, most if not all of them culled from the earlier serial *King of the Rocket Men*. Some new close-up shots of Wallace's Commando Cody in airborne action, however, were filmed in front of a rear-projection screen. "For the scenes of Cody flying through the clouds, they sent a plane up and they took shots of clouds going by. Then they rear-projected this footage onto a screen, and I'd work in front of the screen. They built a platform just off-camera and they attached a two-by-four to it, extending it out into camera range maybe three feet. Very easily, I would crawl out onto this two-by-four, on my belly, and then they'd close my jacket around the two-by-four. And there I'd be, 'flying' in front of these clouds. But sometimes—quite a *few* times!—I'd lose my balance and I'd flip, and I'd be hanging upside-down by my jacket, off this two-by-four!" Wallace laughs.

"Then there were my takeoff scenes. They had a trampoline just in front of the camera, and I would jump and hit the trampoline and go sailing past the camera—and land in a big heap on a couple of mattresses. Then the director [Fred Brannon] said, 'George, you're not flying straight up, you're flying level. We want you to get more straight up.' So they put up a sort of high bar, like eight feet off the ground, and now I would be bouncing off the trampoline and jumping up past the camera for the high bar—which was a good shot. But being so hot and sweaty, I'd grab the high bar and my feet would swing free, 'cause I was clear of the ground, and every so often I'd lose my grip and fall from it *[claps hands together]* down onto my back!"

Radar Men's futuristic props, simplistic by 1990s high-tech standards but still effective, included Cody's bus-sized spaceship and a compact tank in which the evil Moonmen pursued Cody across the rocky lunarscape. "The first time you see the rocketship is in Chapter 1, where Aline, Billy and I drive up to it with a couple of cops who are seeing us off. The thing was probably twenty feet long and maybe eight feet high. It was just a front, a facade, not circular all around. Then they had a smaller rocketship, like maybe ten feet long, that they put on a wire which they had strung up between a couple of cliff rocks. They'd stick a sparkler in the rear end of it, give it a shove and down it would go. For the scenes on the Moon where Retik's henchmen were chasing after us in their tank, they took an old Chevy or something and built a plywood silhouette of a tank around it."

No Republic serial would be truly complete without a fistfight (or two) in every chapter, and in these once-a-reel brawls, Wallace was generally doubled by stunt ace Tom Steele while Dale Van Sickel replaced William Bakewell in the fisticuffs. "The thing that helped me was the fact that in the navy, before the war, I was a boxer—I fought light heavyweight in the Pacific Fleet, 1939–40. For the movies, I had to learn how not to hit somebody when I threw the punch, and also how to telegraph the punch. In a real fight, you throw the punch maybe six or eight inches, but in films or on television, you have to reach back and throw the punch, like maybe three *feet*, so it really shows."

Wallace (as Commando Cody, left) and William Bakewell, poised for action in *Radar Men from the Moon*.

Two of *Radar Men*'s fistic encounters were set in a restaurant, with Wallace and buddy Bakewell taking on baddie Clayton Moore and his criminal companion, Bob Stevenson. "Because it was one of the fights in the restaurant, I didn't have the Commando Cody flying helmet on. It was about five minutes to twelve as we were doing the fight scene, and all of a sudden *[Wallace punches palm of left hand]* Clayton Moore whacked me, and I heard a crack. We kept right on going, finished the scene. They called lunch, put me in a car and took me to St. Joseph's Hospital out in the Valley, where a doctor set my nose and gave me a shot so it wouldn't swell. Then we came back to the set, they had a coffee and a sandwich for me, and at five minutes to one, they said, 'Places!' I had a towel that I'd hold up to my nose, because it was dripping blood a little bit. They'd say, 'Action!' and I'd take the towel down and start the dialogue, until it started to bleed again. But, so that we wouldn't lose five minutes on the show, we kept right on going, me with a broken nose *[laughs]*!"

Less than four months after the filming of *Radar Men*, the character of

Cody was back in front of the cameras for the Republic television series *Commando Cody—Sky Marshal of the Universe*—with not Wallace but Judd Holdren, once serialdom's *Captain Video*, playing the role (Wallace was not offered the part).

Wallace does not try to put lesser screen credits behind him or to ignore the older films altogether. "I saw *Radar Men* again maybe a year ago—every so often, I have somebody over and they want to look at a chapter or two. I think it's a gas. It's hard to relate *Radar Men* to the science fiction films of today—we didn't have the equipment, didn't have the knowledge of a lot of things. But I think that what we did, for that time, was good. The dialogue was hokey, but back then, it fit. And if people liked it, that was the important thing."

Most of Wallace's other early fifties roles were in Westerns, with Wallace generally siding with the bad guys in such outdoor adventures as *Destry*, *Drums Across the River* and *The Lawless Breed* (in which Wallace's character, Bully Brady, climactically shoots star Rock Hudson in the back). Asked if he enjoyed playing these villainous roles, Wallace turns on his darkest look as he hisses a sinister *yes-s-s*. "When you're an actor, you're almost like a kid in a way. Like a little kid in the backyard in a cardboard box, and the mother says, 'Willie, come in the house,' and Willie says, 'I can't,' 'cause he's driving that cardboard box a hundred miles an hour and he can't go in right now! Being a heavy, you can bring to it a limp, an eyepatch; you can snarl, you can grow a beard; you can do all type of things that maybe you always wanted to do as a kid. It's almost sort of fun to hide behind the character, the makeup. I did a film called *Six Black Horses* [1962], with Audie Murphy and Dan Duryea, in which I played a *real* mean heavy. I was so mean, I scalped Indians, and I had Indian scalps hangin' from my belt! Heavies are fun to do."

What Wallace really wanted to do, however, was sing, an opportunity he had never had in films, so when Broadway beckoned, he was right there to answer the call. He debuted in Richard Rodgers' *Pipe Dream*, replaced John Raitt in *Pajama Game*, and was award-nominated for his leading role in *New Girl in Town*, a musical version of *Anna Christie* with Gwen Verdon (all in the fifties). Other stage roles have included *The Unsinkable Molly Brown* opposite Ginger Rogers in Dallas, *Jennie* with Mary Martin, *Most Happy Fella* (during production of which he met his present wife, Jane A. Johnston), *Camelot* (as King Arthur), *Man of La Mancha*, *Company* and more.

"Stage is wonderful because you get the audience reaction right as it's happening. Film or TV, all you get is *cut*, *print* and that's it, and you don't know what has happened. Then, too, you're torn because of money—after all, that's what we *all* work for. The theater, unfortunately, does not pay the type of money films and TV do. It does if you're a big name star—like when I did *Molly Brown* with Ginger Rogers. Ginger was getting I think $5,000 a week, plus a percentage, plus an apartment, plus an automobile, plus, plus, plus.

For playing Johnny Brown, which was the male lead opposite her, I was getting $1,250, paid for my own car, paid for my own apartment, paid for everything. So you're torn between making an existence and doing what you like to do. A lot of the stars today will go back and do off-Broadway stuff because they can afford it, and they *like* to do it. I've been offered many off-Broadway shows, but I can't afford it because I don't live in New York anymore. They only pay a couple of hundred dollars a week—I couldn't get a hotel *room* for that, let alone food and live there!"

Wallace never played Commando Cody a second time, but he did take a second trip into space in 1955 when he joined the crew of the United Planets Cruiser *C-57-D* on their trip to MGM's *Forbidden Planet*. "A man named Leonard Murphy was casting *Forbidden Planet*, and I went in for an interview. He said, 'George, when you were here several years ago [as a greensman], I heard that you were a bosun's mate in the navy.' I said, 'That's right. Why?' He said, 'Well, there's a bosun's mate in this rocketship. I thought of you, and that's why you're here.' That's how I got the part, because he remembered I was a bosun's mate and they needed a bosun's mate!" Wallace laughs.

"The spaceship and the planet surface were built on Stage 15, which was the largest stage at Metro. Way at the end of the stage, they had the backdrop, the skies in the distance. I was very aware of the bushes and things because years before that had been my job. Near the spaceship, the few little bushes they had were maybe two-and-a-half, three-feet high, and as you looked out in the 'distance,' across the stage, the bushes were smaller and smaller and smaller, to give the set more depth. And then they had a couple of midgets in space suits back there, too, to complete the illusion. You would swear that you were looking out for miles.

"Inside Robby the Robot, they had a guy who used to be a child actor, Frankie Darro. In the old pictures, he used to play jockeys, little tough guys, roles like that, but as years went on, he couldn't get a job and he ended up inside Robby the Robot. During lunch, I guess, Frankie would belt down a few, and after lunch, two, three o'clock in the afternoon, we'd go back to working. Robby would come walking into a scene and stop, then start to waver back and forth a little bit. And then all of a sudden, Robby would fall over backwards *[laughs]*, 'cause Frankie got a little drunk and he would fall over under the weight of the costume. So they fired him and they got somebody else and put him into the robot."

Wallace's opinion of science fiction in general is that "it's great, because all the stories have a futuristic theme to them. When I was a kid, we'd look at the comic books and they'd be full of rays and rockets and this and that, all beyond our scope at that time. Today, here they are: We *go* to the Moon, we *have* lasers, we *have* this and that. Look at the [Persian Gulf] war that just finished: a tank shooting another tank thirty miles away. So I think science fiction is great, very inventive, a terrific look ahead at things that could be in the future. I enjoy it."

Wallace's career was stalled in 1960 when the horse he was riding on television's *Swamp Fox* series reared and fell on him, breaking his back. After a painful seven-month recovery, film and television offers were slow to come in, Wallace now being considered a risk. He returned to the theater and to driving a cab in order to make ends meet while the incident passed from memory.

More recently, science fiction credits for Wallace have been scarce outside of television, where he has played a general in the 1973 television movie *The Six Million Dollar Man* and a captured human in the seventies teleseries *Planet of the Apes*. "The poor people playing the apes were constantly sweating because they were under all that makeup and wardrobe. Roddy McDowall had to stop shooting every day about 12:00 because he was allergic to the makeup and the spirit gum and all that stuff, and a heavy rash would break out if he played any longer than till about noon. That was interesting to do, though."

These days he calls himself George D. Wallace, to avoid confusion with the comic George Wallace (not to mention the ex-governor of Alabama). His eighties films have included *The Stuntman*, *Protocol*, *Just Between Friends*, *Punchline*, the fantasy-comedy *Defending Your Life* and the horror film *Prison*; on television he was most recently featured as a regular on *Sons and Daughters*. Less was seen of Wallace's character (Grandpa Hank) when the CBS series moved from an early evening, family oriented time slot to ten P.M., and adult themes ("all the young people in bed and having sex and this and that") began to prevail. Frequently preempted by Gulf War coverage and other special events, viewership dwindled and the show was axed.

Despite Wallace's work in the business for over 40 years and his rather impressive stage credits, die-hard science fiction fans continue to think of him, in knee-jerk style, as Commando Cody, protector of America's endangered skyways. Is our somewhat lowbrow orientation an annoyance to him? "No, I think it's just fantastic," Wallace grins. "A few years ago I went to Knoxville, Tennessee, for the annual Riders of the Silver Screen Western convention. It was amazing—they get this big convention hall and there must be two hundred, three hundred dealers selling memorabilia. So much from *Radar Men*, things that I never knew even existed. And the people are just as nice as can be.

"I was at an autograph table and I looked up and I saw two big guys in line, about six-three, big beards, dirty T-shirts, just staring at me. *Staring*. Gradually they came closer and closer in the line, looking like they're going to tear me in half. They finally got up to me and leaned forward onto the table, looked me in the face and one of 'em said, 'You've *always* been our hero.' I just wanted to kiss these guys, they were so sweet, I wanted to hug 'em! They told me that, as kids, they wanted to make Rocket Man helmets out of coat hangers and things like that! I'm awed and very pleased that after that long a time, people still remember, still care. I think that's just great."

George Wallace poses with a familiar photo.

GEORGE WALLACE FILMOGRAPHY

The Sun Sets at Dawn (Eagle-Lion, 1950)
Up Front (Universal, 1951)
Submarine Command (Paramount, 1951)
The Fat Man (Universal, 1951)
Man in the Saddle (Columbia, 1951)
We're Not Married (20th Century–Fox, 1952)
Sally and Saint Anne (Universal, 1952)
Million Dollar Mermaid (MGM, 1952)
Meet Danny Wilson (Universal, 1952)
Japanese War Bride (20th Century–Fox, 1952)
The Big Sky (RKO, 1952)
Kansas City Confidential (United Artists, 1952)
Radar Men from the Moon (Republic serial, 1952)
The Lawless Breed (Universal, 1952)
The Lusty Men (RKO, 1952)
Back at the Front (Willie and Joe Back at the Front) (Universal, 1952)
Arena (MGM, 1953)
Francis Covers the Big Town (Universal, 1953)
The Star of Texas (Allied Artists, 1953)

The Homesteaders (Allied Artists, 1953)
Vigilante Terror (Allied Artists, 1953)
The Great Adventures of Captain Kidd (Columbia serial, 1953)
Pardon My Wrench (RKO short, 1953)
The French Line (RKO, 1954)
The Human Jungle (Allied Artists, 1954)
Border River (Universal, 1954)
Drums Across the River (Universal, 1954)
Destry (Universal, 1954)
Rage at Dawn (RKO, 1955)
Soldier of Fortune (20th Century-Fox, 1955)
Man Without a Star (Universal, 1955)
Strange Lady in Town (Warner Bros., 1955)
The Second Greatest Sex (Universal, 1955)
Forbidden Planet (MGM, 1956)
Slightly Scarlet (RKO, 1956)
Six Black Horses (Universal, 1962)
Dead Heat on a Merry-Go-Round (Columbia, 1966)
Texas Across the River (Universal, 1966)
Caprice (20th Century-Fox, 1967)
Skin Game (Warner Bros., 1971)
Clay Pigeon (MGM, 1971)
The Swinging Cheerleaders (Centaur, 1974)
The Towering Inferno (20th Century-Fox/Warner Bros., 1974)
Lifeguard (Paramount, 1976)
The Private Files of J. Edgar Hoover (AIP, 1977)
The Stuntman (Melvin Simon Productions, 1980)
Protocol (Warner Bros., 1984)
Just Between Friends (Orion, 1986)
Prison (Empire, 1988)
Punchline (Columbia, 1988)
Defending Your Life (Geffen Film Co./Warner Bros., 1991)
Diggstown (MGM, 1992)

Fans were first introduced to Amanda during a "Journey to Babel."

My agent called up and said, "Do you want to be on Star Trek?" *and I said, "What is it?"*

Jane Wyatt

SHE IS BEST REMEMBERED TODAY as the mom on the long-running television sitcom *Father Knows Best*, but every movie buff worth his salt knows there is a lot more to her than the Emmy-winning role of Margaret Anderson: First came several seasons of Broadway and a contract with Universal Pictures, followed by years of freelancing in movies and television. So it is odd, and not entirely fair, that her second-best-known role should spring not from one of her many movies or celebrated stageplays, but from a single television episode that she herself has not seen since it was first broadcast. The show is *Star Trek*; the role, that of Sarek's earthling wife; and the actress, it goes without saying, is Jane Wyatt. The mother of Spock and Starman (and the First Lady of Shangri-La), Wyatt has enjoyed a career in fantasy and science fiction that has spanned a full half-century.

Born in Campgaw, New Jersey, Jane Waddington Wyatt came from a New York family of social distinction (her father was a Wall Street investment banker and her mother a drama critic). Jane was raised from the age of three months in New York City, attended the fashionable Chapin School and later Barnard College. After two years of college she left to join the apprentice school of the Berkshire Playhouse at Stockbridge, Massachusetts, where for six months she played a varied assortment of roles. One of her first jobs on Broadway was as understudy to Rose Hobart in a production of *Trade Winds*—a career move that cost her her slot on the New York Social Register. "It didn't bother me being dropped, but I hated being bracketed with whoever else was being dropped at the same time because of scandal or something," she laughs.

Making the transition from stage to screen was an easy step for a photogenic actress in the early thirties, but at first Wyatt resolutely resisted the move. "In those days, if you made any sort of little splash you were asked to go into the movies. And we'd all say, 'Oh, no, no, we couldn't stand it!' Leave the theater? We wouldn't *think* of it! I was kind of the little white hope of the ingenues in New York, and I was in demand for all these studios. But I stayed with the stage for quite a little while, and then one year I had kind of a bum year. This was the time of the Great Depression and it was a very bad year in New York, so I thought, 'Oh, well, I might as well try [Hollywood].'"

Wyatt landed a berth at Universal, but the circumstances of her deal at the studio were highly unconventional. "I made a stupid arrangement—at least, my agent did. I'd come out to Hollywood but only for the summer months; Universal would use me in the summer and then I'd go back to the Great White Way. And of course that was ridiculous; it was not realistic at all. Movie studios don't operate that way—they can't have a picture ready for a minor person. It's absurd!"

The arrangement would not work for long, but Wyatt did get some valuable filmland experience under her belt and began to learn some of the ways that working in films differed from working in the theater. "When you're

Previous page: Star Trek fans were introduced to Spock's (Leonard Nimoy) mother (Wyatt) in the episode "Journey to Babel."

in the theater you make yourself up, there's no makeup man or anybody. I came out to Hollywood and I went into makeup at Universal for the first time, and the makeup man was little Jack Pierce, who was quite celebrated (which I didn't know at the time). Ugly as sin, you know, and he had the worst breath—that's what I'll always remember about poor Jack Pierce *[laughs]*! And he started pulling out all my eyebrows! I cried out, 'Stop! Stop! I don't *want* you to pull out my eyebrows!' He said, 'Listen, little girl: I have made up the greatest. Don't you tell Jack Pierce what to do. Look!' And he waved his arm toward all the pictures he had up on the wall. Well, they were not glamour pictures, they were Boris Karloff and Bela Lugosi and I don't know who else *[laughs]*! He was a wonderful little guy and I got to be very, very fond of him."

Wyatt made her film debut in *One More River* (1934), a "veddy British" drawing-room drama directed by James Whale, Universal's prime purveyor of classic thirties horror. "Diana Wynyard and I played sisters, and in the picture Diana was divorcing her husband, Colin Clive. And in the courtroom scene, when she got up on the stand, they asked her why and she said *[in a stage whisper]*, 'Because he did ... *unmentionable* things to me!' *[Laughs.]* I *still* remember that line! We had a marvelous cast. We had Mrs. Patrick Campbell as our aunt and Sir Aubrey Smith as our father, Colin Clive, Lionel Atwill, a whole lot of very good people."

Wyatt made a favorable impression with viewers and critics alike despite a mild case of first-picture jitters. "I did have the jitters, I'm sure, but everybody was very helpful. James Whale was the most charming man—he wasn't a warm man, he was kind of austere. But he was great with Mrs. Patrick Campbell, who *did* have the jitters—she *really* had the jitters! He was wonderful with her, and he did beautiful things with the picture—he was a real artist. The interiors of the houses were just beautiful because they spent hours lighting them and getting the flowers just right. I thought *One More River* was a very good picture, but they shouldn't have paired Frank Lawton and Diana Wynyard [for romantic scenes] because she looked like she could have been his mother. In fact, they had just finished *Cavalcade* [1933], where I think she *did* play his mother *[laughs]*! She was never an ingenue, she was always a tall, wonderful-looking woman. And Frankie was *tiny*! So there wasn't any romance, there wasn't any tension. Frankie Lawton could be very good, but in *One More River* he was so wimpy and Colin Clive was so much more attractive! He was strong and very masculine, a macho kind of guy."

Wyatt wrapped up her first two-picture summer with Universal's adaptation of the Dickens classic *Great Expectations*, starring (as Estella) with Henry Hull (Magwitch) and Phillips Holmes (Pip). "You know what's interesting about *Great Expectations*? There were two girls that tried out for the part of Estella—I was one, the other one was Valerie Hobson. And for whatever reason, I got the part—I think it was because Valerie was so imperious looking that she really wouldn't have been right for it. And then years later, in the great

Great Expectations, Valerie Hobson finally got the part. And Francis L. Sullivan was in *both* pictures, playing the lawyer." Of course the film that Wyatt calls the great *Great Expectations*, the classic David Lean version of 1946, has dwarfed Universal's rendition to the extent that many film fans are unaware that Wyatt's earlier version even exists. "But, you know, ours really isn't a bad picture, not bad at all. But that was the first time I ran into drugs—Phillips Holmes. He wasn't showing up and there were all sorts of whisperings about him going on, that the trouble was that he was on some kind of drugs. He was so attractive and so good looking."

Still an exile from the New York Social Register, Wyatt got another reminder of the social status of actresses during the making of *Great Expectations*. "The director was Stuart Walker. I met Walker's son and I went out with him. He asked me one weekend to go with him to the Bel-Air Bay Club—have lunch and go swimming and so forth. We got within about five miles of the place and all of a sudden he said, 'Oh, darn it!' I said, 'What's the matter?' and he said, 'I just remembered you can't take *actresses* to the Bel-Air Bay Club.'"

Back and forth between Universal and Broadway Wyatt hopped; one of the films Universal planned to place her in was *Dracula's Daughter* (1936), but delays and problems with the script caused a cast shake-up and Wyatt was dropped in favor of Marguerite Churchill, lent to the studio by Warner Bros. The Universal deal began to collapse entirely during the summer of 1936. "That particular summer they didn't have anything for me, absolutely nothing. On the advice of my agent I had a big brouhaha with Universal, because there was nothing for me in the future at Universal either. So they said, 'All right, you can make *one* outside picture. You just find the picture.' And I was lucky enough to get *Lost Horizon*. They were having auditions of some kind; and I-don't-know-how-many other people tested. There was an awfully nice Englishman who stood in for Ronald Colman and played these various scenes. And then I was chosen, I think because I was not well known at all and I was very young."

Was it the Frank Capra name that attracted her to *Lost Horizon*? "Oh, listen, I was attracted to anybody who would *hire* me, what are you *talking* about?"

Based on the 1934 novel by James Hilton, the Columbia production of *Lost Horizon* still remains a high-water mark in the careers of everyone involved, from director Capra, photographer Joseph Walker and maestro Dimitri Tiomkin to the superb cast, which included Ronald Colman, Wyatt, John Howard, Margo, Thomas Mitchell and Edward Everett Horton. Wyatt first read the Hilton book when it was recommended and sent to her by actor Walter Connolly, who tried out for the role of the High Lama in the picture. "It was really a charming book. Of course, my part wasn't in the book, and that's what made my part difficult to act. They just manufactured this character, and she really had no connection with anything. She was just someone for the star [Colman] to be able to talk to and have a romance with. I was used to playing parts in plays where I was part of the plot, and my role in *Lost Horizon* wasn't anything like that. I was just wandering through there. But I was thrilled to get the part, obviously."

Even after more than 50 years, Wyatt's memories of director Capra are warm and respectful. "Oh, Frank Capra was just a love. Isn't it remarkable to think that his mother never learned how to read, and *he* graduated from Cal Tech? Frank was lovely; he let you pretty much have your way; he's not a director like Elia Kazan, who has brilliant ideas and then says something to you that lights up the whole thing for you. Frank more or less let you do what you wanted and then told you what was wrong, or 'Why don't you do it *this* way?' Capra was very sweet; he wrote me a letter many years later, and in it he said, 'I just want to tell you I admired so much what you did in *Lost Horizon*.'"

An opulent production by any yardstick (and particularly by the tatty yardstick of Columbia, then Hollywood's least-prestigious major studio), *Lost Horizon* was shot on the Columbia ranch where an elaborate Tibetan lamasery was constructed for the film. "Those sets were quite stark, and there was a lot of criticism that they didn't look like a lamasery," Wyatt recalls. "But I've seen pictures in books, and they certainly *did* look like lamaseries — but the lamaseries were more dilapidated looking!"

One of the many famous scenes in *Lost Horizon* featured Wyatt's character taking a nude dip in a lake as Ronald Colman watches from a distance, a scene that you would think must have taken the actress aback when she first read the Robert Riskin script. "I just didn't think it was going to happen — but it *did*!" Wyatt laughs. A nude double was used in extreme long shots and Wyatt did her swimming in a strapless, flesh-colored suit. "They got a girl to do the dive, and she was really starkers standing up there. And she dove in, and it was flat. I was really quite a good swimmer and I always resented that *[laughs]*!"

While Wyatt did not do her own diving in *Lost Horizon*, she prides herself on having done her own horseback riding. "I may not have been much of an actress, but I was an awfully good horseback rider," she bubbles enthusiastically. "My sister saw the picture in New York at some sort of big opening. There were two men behind her and one of them said, 'Look at that girl! What a wonderful seat!' They meant my seat on the horse [manner of riding], but it doesn't sound very flattering *[laughs]*! But Ronnie Colman didn't like horses at all, he was terrified. He had a double who did most everything."

Working on *Lost Horizon* also brought Wyatt in contact with James Hilton himself, who hung around the sets as the film version of his best-selling novel was being produced. "He was around quite often. Little, thin guy, very nice. My husband [investment banker Edgar B. Ward] had broken his leg in Switzerland, very badly — it was a compound fracture with the bone sticking

"Ronnie was really a thoroughly charming man, very, very intelligent," Wyatt recalls of her *Lost Horizon* co-star Ronald Colman.

out. This was in the days before penicillin, before any kind of antibiotics. The doctors thought they'd have to cut off the leg—they didn't, but he was two months in that clinic. And when he read *Lost Horizon*, the descriptions were exactly the view he had from the clinic in Switzerland. So I asked Hilton, and he said yes, that was the very valley he described in writing about Shangri-La!"

Another visitor to the set of the film was Columbia chief Harry Cohn, legendary film mogul/tyrant and (according to Hedda Hopper) the man you had to stand in line to hate. "The way Frank handled him was, Harry Cohn would come on the set and Frank would say, 'Cut.' And we'd all gather and we'd all talk to Harry Cohn and just stand around. And Harry Cohn would get more and more nervous—it was costing him a thousand dollars every half a second—until he left the set. And then we'd begin again *[laughs]*."

Conversely, Wyatt (and Capra) had nothing but the highest regard for star Ronald Colman. "Ronnie was really a thoroughly charming man, very, very intelligent; he was well cast when he did *The Halls of Ivy*, his television series. I don't know whether he wrote poems but he *read* poems all the time (he would read aloud); he had a beautiful sense of humor. And it was always so entertaining when you think that he married Benita Hume later on, because she was really bouncy and open, she played in music halls and she was none of the things *he* was *[laughs]*. She was just wonderful, and they were such an entertaining couple."

According to Edward Bernds, who was sound man on *Lost Horizon* and other classic Capra films of the thirties, the director and Colman got along well, even though Capra regretted the fact that once Colman prepared for a scene, he was not open to last-minute suggestions or line changes and inflexibly stuck to the material he had memorized. "Colman also wasn't very happy in great, huge dramatic scenes," Wyatt adds. "When he had to make up his mind to leave Shangri-La, it was done in silence—no background music, nothing. He did the whole thing with his eyes, those wonderful, marvelous eyes. And I think Frank really admired that because it was an amazing scene. Of course, Ronald Colman had started his career in silents; in a way, that added a lot to some actors' stature, because they could do things that other actors couldn't.

"Tommy Mitchell and Eddie Everett Horton I liked very much, and they were good actors, but it seemed such routine casting to us then because they had both played those two parts over and over and over *again* in a million different things. But seeing the picture now, I like them, because Tommy was the quintessential businessman and Eddie was the quintessential ... whatever-he-was *[laughs]*, with the double takes and everything. They were wonderful."

While *Lost Horizon* put a new word (Shangri-La) into the English language, the film itself was treated with less than reverence during World War II, when it was reissued with many pacifist references excised. Other cuts were also made over the years until eventually the film was a shadow of its former 132-minute self. Much of the footage was (and still is) missing, but the American Film Institute and the UCLA Film Archives managed to piece *Lost Horizon* back together: finding scenes, locating the entire sound track and using stills to illustrate scenes where sound but no picture exists. In an odd postscript, the man who restored *Lost Horizon* then admitted that "some of the new footage just slows things down," and Wyatt agrees: "I think it *is* a little bit too long now, but I don't know where they should cut it. Not *my* scenes again, I hope *[laughs]*. But those are the ones they had cut, and quite rightly so. Those scenes weren't in the book; they were just jammed into the film. And it's not a very interesting character, really and truly."

One of the best-restored scenes depicts the first meeting of Colman and Wyatt in the Shangri-La apiary, where amidst the flutter of pigeons Wyatt tells Colman that it was her notion to shanghai him to the mountain retreat. "Ronnie had been to Bali, and he said that in Bali they had whistles tied onto the back legs of the pigeons, so that when they went up in the air and the wind came through, you'd hear this wonderful whistling sound. So that idea of his was incorporated into the film. Of course, Columbia nearly died after they brought the pigeons, because they never have been able to get *rid* of the pigeons out on that ranch *[laughs]*!"

After having frequently confessed that she is less than pleased with her performance in the film, Wyatt is finally beginning to mellow: "When I see it at the august age I am now, I see exactly why I was right and what was good about what I did. I just didn't feel when I saw it initially that I was any good." Her negative reaction to the remake, however, is unchanged. "Oh, I don't even *think* of that!" she scoffs, taken slightly aback. "I was working at Universal at the time when that was being made, and someone said to me, 'Wouldn't you like to go out and see the sets?' Now, I had nothing against them doing a musical remake, but I knew it wasn't going to be any good when I saw the sets. We had all real flowers in our *Lost Horizon*; they had fake flowers. And they had fuchsias and sweet peas blooming at the same time that they had all the autumn flowers like dahlias. I thought, 'This is just plain fake and it's gonna be awful.' I felt terribly sorry for Liv Ullmann—there was nothing for a great actress like her to dig her teeth into in any way, shape or manner. At least I had the horse—she didn't have *any*thing! And Peter Finch—a fine actor, but no good in that. He looked soft, and he couldn't possibly have fought his way back to Shangri-La like Ronnie Colman did. Ronnie was trim and taut, and you knew he could return. But poor Peter Finch, there was no way he was gonna march back! That was really a disaster."

The secret of *Lost Horizon*'s ongoing popularity? "Oh, I think it's the message, don't you?" Wyatt smiles. "Everybody's looking for Shangri-La."

Wyatt took a few years off from films after *Lost Horizon*, returning in 1940 to do a series of fluffy comedies and minor Westerns. Roles in major pictures like Clifford Odets' *None but the Lonely Heart* (1944) and Elia Kazan's *Boomerang!* and *Gentleman's Agreement* (1947) helped to raise her stock in Hollywood once again. For director Fritz Lang she appeared opposite Louis Hayward and Lee Bowman in Republic's *House by the River* (1950), an atmospheric and morbid suspense story. "Fritz Lang was a great director, no question about that, but *House by the River* wasn't one of his great pictures," Wyatt recalls. While Wyatt liked Lang and got along well with him, she saw

Jane Wyatt

Wyatt in the 1950s.

firsthand his legendary bullying of actors, and got a taste of it herself. "When he started treating Lou badly, Lou would just go into a fit — he'd really begin to twitch. He was awfully nervous through that picture, but I think he would do this *[Wyatt shakes and twitches]* just to protect himself from Fritz Lang! Then Fritz started with Lee, and *[gritting her teeth]* Lee planted his two feet down and gave Fritz the gimlet look and wouldn't do a *thing* Fritz asked him to do. So Fritz had to give up on that. So then he started on *me*! One day I was in a rocking chair and I was rocking, and I was crocheting, and I was also doing something else. And he just kept after me and after me and *after* me. I had never in my life done this before, but in the middle of a take I got up and walked out of the shot."

From 1954 until 1960 Wyatt co-starred with Robert Young in *Father Knows Best*, the classic television sitcom chronicling the life and times of the Anderson family in the midwestern town of Springfield. After a slow start, *Father Knows Best* hooked viewers with its homey charm and remained a ratings champion throughout the fifties. A 1959 episode commissioned by the U.S. Treasury Department, *24 Hours in Tyrant Land*, showed how the Anderson children (Elinor Donahue, Billy Gray, Lauren Chapin) attempted to cope with a make-believe dictatorship. The episode was never aired but circulated to schools, churches and other organizations "to show the importance of maintaining a strong American democracy."

Today, squeaky-clean, idealized-family fifties sitcoms like *Father Knows Best* and *The Donna Reed Show* are being looked back upon by cynics more as camp than for their human or comic elements, but Wyatt (who won three successive Emmys for her *Father Knows Best* role) feels differently. "I travel around an awful lot for the March of Dimes, and I've been to every little place in the country. And right up to today people are looking at it and telling me, 'Gee, we want our children to look at it' or 'I just wish it was like that today.' No, I'm amazed at how solemnly they take it and, truly, I don't think that it's looked upon as camp. Of course, I don't like to be bracketed with *The Donna Reed Show*, because I don't think it compares *[laughs]* — but then I don't think *any* of the family shows compare to *Father Knows Best*."

Among the several television appearances Wyatt made during the sixties was a stint on *The Alfred Hitchcock Hour*, in the classic episode "The Monkey's Paw — A Retelling." An updated but otherwise faithful reprise of the well-known tale, it starred Wyatt and Leif Erickson as a married couple whose wish for wealth results in the insurance money they receive from the fiery death of their son in a race car accident. "Oh, I loved doing that, that was really fun. And my son in that was Lee Majors — he had never been before the camera at all, and was he nervous! He was always holding his little Bible *[laughs]*."

The television guest shot for which she is most frequently remembered is as Amanda, wife of Vulcan Sarek (Mark Lenard) and mother to Spock (Leonard Nimoy) in the *Star Trek* episode "Journey to Babel." "My agent called up and said, 'Do you want to be on *Star Trek*?' and I said, 'What *is* it?' I had a look and they sent a script and I thought it would be fun. I went there the first time thinking, 'Well, we'll all have a good laugh over this,' but not at all. Everybody in makeup, having their ears put on and everything else, was so serious. That's what made it so good, they were dead serious."

Although that serious attitude was maintained on the set, Wyatt says she enjoyed the *Star Trek* experience. "Oh, it was great fun. Mark Lenard [Sarek] was very good — I see he's going to be in the new TV series *[The Next Generation]*. He's going to be two hundred years old, but they've killed Amanda off — she was human. Mark is so good looking when he gets his *Star Trek* clothes on, and his ears are so good looking! And I think my 'son' [Leonard Nimoy] is better looking with his ears, too — I think all men ought to wear pointed ears; they're very becoming, aren't they?"

Wyatt is no Trekkie: She has not seen "Journey to Babel" since it was first aired, she could not tell you the first thing about the current state of Vulcan-Klingon race relations and she did not even know her name was Amanda in the show until fans started yelling it at her at a *Trek* convention. "No, I'm no Trekkie, but I have a grandson who is, so if I ever have any doubt about anything, I call him up and he tells me over the phone." She had little contact with series creator Gene Roddenberry, but shortly before his death attended a function where Roddenberry was honored as Humanitarian of the Year of the March of Dimes. "The party turned out very well, and Roddenberry was an awfully nice guy. He was so moved by this whole thing, he could hardly speak at the end. I was there and I introduced Ray Bradbury, the great science fiction writer. I had great fun with Ray — he was very entertaining and funny.

"I remember years ago going to UCLA to hear Ray Bradbury and Aldous

Huxley and somebody else talk—I guess it must have been about science fiction. I went to hear what Mr. Huxley was going to say, but the only thing I remember now is Ray Bradbury, because among the things he said was that the science fiction writers were writing about things to come—but it all comes true. And you see they *do*—the astronauts, when they walk on the Moon, look just the way the science fiction people said they would. And the Moon itself looks just the way it was described. And the rockets and all the other things that they dreamed up beforehand. Ray's feeling was that they had given the great scientists some good ideas to pursue *[laughs]*—which might be true! He's a very witty guy."

Wyatt also enjoyed working with series regulars Nimoy and William Shatner, either on the "Babel" episode or in the more recent *Star Trek IV: The Voyage Home*. "Shatner I'd seen in New York in several plays, and he was a very nice, light comedian, and very good. I don't know how good he is now in it, but he was a very good actor on the stage and he'd been trained in classic things. He did light comedy very well—it was the time of the drawing room comedy, and he was really entertaining. I had great fun with him on the set. My 'son'—he was more dour. I've gotten to know him since then and like him very much, but at that time he didn't really talk much. He was always busy on the telephone with a new deal or something or other *[laughs]*!"

Wyatt reprised the character of Amanda in *Star Trek IV*, 1986's popular installment in the continuing series of *Trek* films. "[Producer] Harve Bennett called me up to ask me to do *Star Trek IV*—they called it a cameo and I called it a bit, but never mind. I said, 'Oh, I'd love to.' But then it turned out they wanted me to do it at the time that I was going with my husband fishing at Christmas Island in the Pacific, and I said, 'I'm sorry, I couldn't.' Harve said, 'Oh, no, no, we can rearrange it'—which they did. And when I walked on the set after coming back from Christmas Island, Harve Bennett wasn't there but I had a telegram from him that said, WELCOME HOME, MOMMIE DEAREST!"

Wyatt's cameo/bit in *Star Trek IV* reunited her with Nimoy, who was directing the film as well as costarring. "I liked Leonard very much on that. He was an extremely good director and I thought the picture was good. But I don't really like acting with somebody who's also directing, because you're talking to them and in your close-up he's looking to make sure the lights are all right, et cetera, and he's not concentrated. When he did his close shots, he did it with so much more intensity; if I'd known he was going to do it like that, I would have done mine a little differently. But he was thinking about other things. I think that's always true if you're directing and acting in the darn thing, unless you have a stand-in that acts for you." Wyatt worked two days on *Star Trek IV*: the first day on the scene in which Amanda is reunited with Spock, and the second day on a silent shot of Amanda and Saavik (Robin Curtis) waving good-bye as the *Enterprise* crew heads back toward Earth.

More recently, Wyatt has attended a pair of *Star Trek* conventions; not being a Trekkie, did she really enjoy the offbeat experience? "Not very much." She smiles apologetically. "I did them because the young fellow who runs these things was so nice on the telephone. I've only been associated with *Star Trek* twice, and I honestly don't understand what's going on. Leonard was with me at one out here, and when we stood up together the place went wild, absolutely wild. He had a whole script—he reads his script and he reads his poems, and he has a whole routine that's been written for him to do. I just get out there and the fans ask these questions and so forth. The question they asked me in New York really threw me for a loop: 'What is it like making love to a Vulcan?' Oh, I just didn't know what I was going to say, and then all of a sudden I heard myself answering, 'Well, I'm not the kind of girl that kisses and tells!' They know everything, those people! In New York, there was a delegation from Paris that came, and they had the *Star Trek* clothes on! It was jam-packed, it was really extraordinary! But I doubt if I'd ever do another one."

One extraterrestrial son would be enough for most actresses, but Wyatt went beyond the call of duty playing Stella Forrester, mother to television's *Starman* (Robert Hays)—or, rather, mother to the human photographer whose identity Starman assumed. "I saw one or two episodes before I shot my *Starman*—when they asked me to do it, I made an effort to see the show and I saw an awfully good one. I thought Robert Hays was very good in it and I liked the series. We shot on location in Northern California, in an old mining town—it's a tourist place now, a very attractive town, and it was wonderful. We had a good time on that."

Jane Wyatt obviously is not one to dwell in the past; maintaining her beautiful gardens means more to her than cultivating a collection of videotapes of her own films, which in most cases she will not bring herself to watch. "I have more trouble looking at myself...!" she sighs with an emphatic shake of the head. "Like with *Father Knows Best*—I looked at each one as they came out, but the idea of sitting down and looking at them again *[laughs]*—well, the garden calls, or something else calls! I'm not terribly interested in seeing [my work] and I'm always disappointed in myself, so there you are." *Task Force* (1949) is still her favorite from among the 33 films in which she appeared ("We started in young and then grew old, and Gary Cooper was so marvelous").

She's still swamped with fan mail and autograph requests ("Hundreds of pictures from *Star Trek*!") and there's always work to be done in the garden (she rattles off the names of her exotic plants with a horticulturalist's zeal) and she just can never manage to remember her anniversary ("We've been married since 1935 and never once remembered—except our 50th!"); there just do not seem to be enough hours in Jane Wyatt's day. But this still-lively, still-lovely septuagenarian is not complaining.

John Howard and Jane Wyatt, the two surviving stars of *Lost Horizon*, reunited for the first time in 50 years at a 1986 Hollywood screening.

JANE WYATT FILMOGRAPHY

One More River (Universal, 1934)
Great Expectations (Universeal, 1934)
The Luckiest Girl in the World (Universal, 1936)
We're Only Human (RKO, 1936)
Lost Horizon (Columbia, 1937)
Girl from God's Country (Republic, 1940)
Kisses for Breakfast (Warner Bros., 1941)
Weekend for Three (RKO, 1941)
Hurricane Smith (Double Identity) (Republic 1941)
Army Surgeon (RKO, 1942)
The Navy Comes Through (RKO, 1942)

Buckskin Frontier (United Artists, 1943)
The Kansan (United Artists, 1943)
None but the Lonely Heart (RKO, 1944)
The Bachelor's Daughters (United Artists, 1946)
Strange Conquest (Universal, 1946)
Boomerang! (20th Century–Fox, 1947)
Gentleman's Agreement (20th Century–Fox, 1947)
No Minor Vices (MGM, 1948)
Pitfall (United Artists, 1948)
Bad Boy (The Story of Danny Lester) (Allied Artists, 1949)
Canadian Pacific (20th Century–Fox, 1949)
Task Force (Warner Bros., 1949)
House by the River (Republic, 1950)
My Blue Heaven (20th Century–Fox, 1950)
Our Very Own (RKO, 1950)
The Man Who Cheated Himself (20th Century–Fox, 1950)
Criminal Lawyer (Columbia, 1951)
Interlude (Universal, 1957)
The Two Little Bears (20th Century–Fox, 1961)
Never Too Late (Warner Bros., 1965)
Treasure of Matecumbe (Buena Vista, 1976)
Star Trek IV: The Voyage Home (Paramount, 1986)

Index

Page numbers in **boldface** *indicate photographs.*

Acosta, Rodolfo 219
The Act (stage) 185
Adam Had Four Sons (1941) 158
Adams, Don 128, 129
Adams, Julie ii, 1–11, **1**, **3**, **6**, **8**, 100, **154**
Adams, Stanley 257
Adler, Luther 92
Adventures of Captain Marvel (1941 serial) 62–64, **63**, 65, 132, 134–37, **138**, 139, 142
An Affair to Remember (1957) 155, 158
After the Thin Man (1936) 65
Agar, John 13–24, **13**, **19**, **22**, 103, 163, 224, 225–26, 219, 240
Agar, Loretta 226
Aherne, Brian 87
Aidman, Charles 257
Airplane! (1980) 86
Akst, Blossom 251
Akst, Harry 251
Aldrich, Robert 126, 127
Aldridge, Kay 65, **66**
The Alfred Hitchcock Hour (TV) 31, 166, 298
Alfred Hitchcock Presents (TV) 166, 264, 267
Ali Baba and the Forty Thieves (1944) 74, 77
All American (1953) 223
All I Desire (1953) 223
All This, and Heaven Too (1940) 190
Alland, William 5, 99, 105, 212, 238
Allen, Irwin 176, 177, 178–79, 182, 193, 195, 256

Allen, Judith 42
Allen, Woody 185
Allyson, June 183
The Amazing Mr. X (1948) **80**, 81
Anders, Merry 219, 230
Anderson, Eddie "Rochester" 39
Anderson, Richard 25–36, **25**, **28**, **32**, **35**, 165
Anderson, Warner 43, **44**, 45
Andrews, Dana 127–28, 166
Angeli, Pier 218
Ankers, Evelyn 77, 148, 149–50, 151, 153, 154, 155, 156, 157, 158
Anspach, Susan 185
Antosiewicz, John xi
Apache Woman (1955) 92
The Ape Man (1943) 139–40, **141**
The Aquanauts (TV) 106
Arabian Nights (1942) 75–6
Archer, Anne 40
Archer, John 37–49, **37**, **41**, **44**, **47**
Arkoff, Samuel Z. 21, 270
Arnaz, Desi 151
Arness, James 112, 120, 121, 253
Arnold, Jack 5, 18, 98, 100, **154**, 225, 227, 238, 250
Arnow, Max 52
Around the World Under the Sea (1966) 93
Arthur, Johnny 137, 139
Arvan, Jan **32**
Asimov, Isaac 253
Assignment Redhead (1962) 155
"Astounding Science Fiction" 253
Attack of the Puppet People (1958) 14
Atwater, Barry 57

303

Index

Atwill, Lionel 67, 291
The Avengers (TV) 168
Away All Boats (1956) 7
Ayres, Lew 148, **272**

Bacher, William 252, 253
Back from the Dead (1957) 57
Backlash (1947) 141
Bacon, David 137
Bacon, Rod 137
Bad Day at Black Rock (1955) 163, 165, 166
Bakewell, William 279, 280, 281, 282, **282**
Ball, Lucille 18, 151
Bandit xi
Barcroft, Roy 279, 280
Bard, Ben 38, 74
Bari, Lynn **80**, 81
Barker, Clive 15
Barnett, Buddy xi
Barry, Don "Red" 3
Barry, Gene 123, **125**
Barry, Patricia 259
Barrymore, Drew 186
Barrymore, Ethel 163
Bates, Jeanne 51–60, **51**, **55**, **56**, **59**
Batman (1989) 15
Batman (TV) 127, 128, 179
Battle of the Bulge (1965) 210
Battlestar Galactica (TV) 197
Baxley, Barbara 193
The Beast from 20,000 Fathoms (1953) 202, 203–5, 206, 207, 208, 210
Beaumont, Hugh 39
Bedelia, Bonnie 60
Beery, Noah, Jr. 88
Behemoth, the Sea Monster see *The Giant Behemoth*
Belfer, Hal 223
Ben Casey (TV) 52, 57
Ben-Hur (1926) 54
Bend of the River (1952) 4
Beneath the Planet of the Apes (1970) 249, 268–69
Benedek, Laslo 235
Benedict, Billy 61–72, **61**, **63**, **66**, **68**, 134, 136, 137
Bennett, Harve 299
Benny, Jack 39

Bergman, Ingrid 158, 248
Bernds, Edward 295
Bernstein, Morey 31
The Best Man (1964) 33
Bester, Alfred 42
La Bête Humaine (1938) 203
The Beverly Hillbillies (TV) 176
Bey, Turhan 38, 73–83, **73**, **76**, **80**, **82**
Beyond the Blue Horizon (1942) 146, 158
Big Girls Don't Cry ... They Get Even (1992) 186
Big Jake (1971) 21
The Big Trees (1952) 48
Bill Haley and His Comets 48
Bionic Ever After? (1994 TV movie) 36
Bionic Showdown: The Six Million Dollar Man and the Bionic Woman (1989 TV movie) 35
The Bionic Woman (TV) 34, 35, 108
Bissell, Whit 5
Black Roses (1988) 9
The Black Scorpion (1957) 146, 152, 155–56
Blackboard Jungle (1955) 163
Blaisdell, Paul **228**, 229
Blanchard, Mari 47, **47**, 224
Blithe Spirit (stage) 121
Bloom, Claire 193
Blue Hawaii (1961) 48
Blue Sunshine (1977) 184–85
The Blue Veil (1951) 265
Bogart, Humphrey 116, 227
Bond, Raymond 246, 248
Bond, Ward 18
Bonestell, Chesley 43, 45
Boomerang! (1947) 296
Boone, Richard **22**, 268
Booth, Adrian see Gray, Lorna
Borst, Ron xi
Bourneuf, Philip 113
Bowery at Midnight (1942) 39, 40, **41**
Bowman, Lee 296, 297
Bowman, Ralph see Archer, John
Boyer, Charles 190
Bradbury, Ray 204, 298, 299
Braeden, Eric 129
The Brain from Planet Arous (1958) 14, 20
Brainstorm (1965) 166–67
Brannon, Fred 281

Breathless (1983) 202
Brenda Starr, Reporter (1945 serial) 66
Brice, Fanny 170
Bride of the Atom see *Bride of the Monster*
Bride of the Monster (1956) 69
Bridges, Beau 93
Bridges, Dorothy 86
Bridges, Jeff 93
Bridges, Lloyd 46, 85–96, **85**, **89**, **90**, **94**, 106
Bridges, Lucinda 93
Bright Victory (1951) 4
Brill, Charlie 257
Bringing Up Baby (1938) 65, 126
Brocco, Peter 69
Broccoli, Albert "Cubby" 108
Bromfield, John 20, 224, 226–27
Bronco Billy (1980) 202
Brophy, Rick 14
Brown, Clarence 264–65
Brown, Courtney 92, 106
Brown, Johnny Mack 38
Browning, Ricou ii, 5, 20, 97–109, **97**, **99**, **102**, **104**, 224, 225
Bruce, David 77
Bruce, Lenny 20, 163
Bruce, Nigel 40
Brunas, John xi
Brunas, Mike xi
Brunas, Ruth xi
Buchanan, Larry 21
Buono, Victor 57
Burke, Paul 9
Burns, Bob 120
Burton, Bernard W. 202, 203, 204, 205
Burton, Richard 212, 269
Bus Stop (TV) 31
Butler, Bob 179
Butterflies Are Free (stage) 197
Byrd, Ralph 67
Byrnes, Edd 176

Caddyshack (1980) 108
Cagney, James 43
Cahn, Edward L. 31, 153, 154
Callaghan, George 213
Calleia, Joseph 250
Camelot (stage) 283

Campbell, John W. 122
Campbell, Mrs. Patrick 291
Capra, Frank 292, 293, 295
Captain Lightfoot (1955) 215–16
Captain Video (1951 serial) 283
Captive Wild Woman (1943) 77, 150
Captive Women (1952) 248, 249
Career (1939) 39
Carlson, Richard 4, 5, 100, 152, **154**
Carney, Art 128
Carol, Martine 126–27
Carol, Sue 133
Carpenter, John 122
Carpenter, M. Scott 93
Carradine, John 140, 218
Carrera, Barbara 270
Carroll, Leo G. 189
Carson, Jack 38, 39
Cartwright, Angela 194, 195, **196**
Cartwright, Nancy 259
Case, Tom 98
Castle, Peggie 57
Castle, William 48
Cavalcade (1933) 291
Chambers, John 269
Chandler, Jeff 237
Chaney, Lon, Jr. 75, 87, 150
Chaney, Lon, Sr. 87
Chapin, Lauren 297
Chaplin, Charles 202, 264
Chapman, Ben 1, 3, 5, **154**
The Charge of the Light Brigade (1936) 54
Chester, Hal E. 202, 203, 204, 205
"Child Star: An Autobiography" 16
China Venture (1953) 235
Chisum (1970) 21
Christian, Paul 204, 205
A Christmas Carol (1938) 189–90
Churchill, Marguerite 292
Ciannelli, Eduardo 266
Citizen Kane (1941) 120, 132, 133–34, 135, 137
Clair, René 202, 203
Clarke, Richard 137
Clarke, Robert 246, **247**, 248, 249
Clensos, Steven 249
The Climax (1944) 78–79
Clive, Colin 291
Cobb, Lee J. 92, 265
Coburn, Charles 124

Index

Cocchi, John xi
Coe, Peter 57
Coen, Franklin 212, 213
Coghlan, Frank, Jr. xi, 62, 63, 64, 134, 136, 137
Cohen, Herman 152
Cohn, Harry 18, 30, 52, 87, 133, 294–95
Colman, Ronald 292, 293, **294**, 295, 296
Colorado Territory (1949) 43
Colossus — The Forbin Project (1970) 129, 258
The Colossus of New York (1958) **209**
Commando Cody — Sky Marshal of the Universe (TV) 254–55, 283
The Commish (TV) 60
Company (stage) 283
The Computer Wore Tennis Shoes (1970) 258, 259
Conan Doyle, Arthur 40
Connery, Sean 108
Connolly, Walter 292
Connors, Chuck 175, 183
Connors, Mike 155, 229
Conquest (1937) 123
Conrad, Michael 184
Conrad, Robert 257
Conrad, William 166–67
Cooper, Gary 91, 147, 190, 300
Corby, Ellen 57
Corday, Mara 155, 156, 240
Corman, Gene 229
Corman, Roger 92, 154, 155, 229, 256
Cornell, Katharine 212
Cornthwaite, Robert 111–130, **111**, **119**, **125**, **128**
Corwin, Sherrill 248
Costner, Kevin 275
Court, Hazel 267, **274**, 275
Cowden, Jack 106, 108
Crack in the World (1965) 210
Crain, Jeanne 265
Craven, John 265
Crawford, Joan 48, 127
Crazy Over Horses (1951) 67
Creature from the Black Lagoon (1954) ii, 1, **1**, 2, **3**, 4–7, **6**, 9–10, **97**, 98–103, **99**, **102**, **104**, 108–109, 146, 152, **154**, 218, 224

The Creature Walks Among Us (1956) 105–6, 212, **215**, 216, **217**, 235, 240, **241**
Creature with the Atom Brain (1955) **145**, 146, 152, 153
The Crimson Key (1947) 141
Cronenberg, David 15
Cukor, George 265
Cummings, Robert 42
Cummins, James 14
Currie, Louise 63, 131-143, **131**, **138**, **140**, **141**
Curse of the Faceless Man (1958) 31, **32**
Curse of the Swamp Creature (1966 TV movie) 14
Curtis, Billy 120
Curtis, Donald **80**
Curtis, Robin 299
Curtis, Tony 20, 223

Dallas (TV) 188
The Dalton Gang (1949) 3
Damato, Glenn xi
Damien — Omen II (1978) 264, 271–73, **272**
Dan August (TV) 34
Dances with Wolves (1990) 275
Daniel, Dennis xi
Dante, Joe xi, 259, 260
Danton, Ray 7, 9
Darro, Frankie 164, 284
Dassin, Jules 265
Daughter of Dr. Jekyll (1957) 20
Davidson, John **63**
Davis, Bette 127, 190
Davis, Sammi 23
The Day Before Spring (stage) 42
The Day of the Dolphin (1973) 108
The Day the Earth Stood Still (1951) 218
Day the World Ended (1956) 146, 154, 227–29, **228**
Deadly Game (1954) 92
The Deadley Mantis (1957) 240
Dean, James 175
de Brulier, Nigel 134
Decision at Sundown (1957) 40
Defending Your Life (1991) 285
DeHaven, Gloria 116

Dehn, Paul 269
DeJarnatt, Steve 15
de Laurentiis, Dino 21
DeMille, Cecil B. 147
Denning, Pat 148, 152, **158**
Denning, Richard 5, 100, 145–160, **144**, **153**, **154**, **158**, 175, 229
DePatie, David H. 258
Derek, John 235
Destination Gobi (1953) 265
Destination Moon (1950) 37, 38, 43–47, **44**, 88
Destry (1954) 224, 283
Destry Rides Again (1939) 224
The Detectives, Starring Robert Taylor (TV) 175–76, 178, 183
Devlin, Joe 53
Dewey, George 278
Diamond, David 205, 206
Diamond, I. A. L. 117, 124
Dick Tracy (TV) 67
Dick Tracy Returns (1938 serial) 38
Dickens, Charles 189
Dickinson, Angie 93–94
Die Hard 2 (1990) 60
Dieterle, William 163
Dietrich, Marlene 224
Dietz, Jack 202, 203, 205
Dillinger, John 147
DiMaggio, Joe 124
Disney, Walt 259
Domergue, Faith 218–19, **236**, 237, 238, **239**
Donahue, Elinor 297
The Donna Reed Show (TV) 297, 298
Donner, Richard 258
"Donovan's Brain" 69, 266
Douglas, Diana 235
Douglas, Kirk 33, 48, 273, 274
Douglas, Peter Vincent 274
Dracula's Daughter (1936) 292
Dragon Seed (1944) 74, 78
Dream Girl (stage) 42
Drums Across the River (1954) 283
Drums of the Congo (1942) 75
Duke, Patty 246
Dukesbery, Jack xi
Dunaway, Faye 230
Dunne, Griffin 186
Durant, Don 175

Duryea, Dan 283
Dwan, Allan 18

E. T. The Extra-Terrestrial (1982) 242
Eason, B. Reeves 53, 54
Eastwood, Clint 103, 202
Eaton, Shirley 93
Eden, Alice 39
Eden, Barbara 230
Edison, Thomas 189
Edwards, Anthony 15
Edwards, Elaine **32**
Edwards, James 88
Egan, Richard 224
The Egg and I (1947) 40
The Elephant Man (1980) 58
Ellison, James 3
Emery, John 88, 91
English, John 88, 91
Eraserhead (1978) 58
Erickson, Leif 298
Ericson, John 168
Escape from the Planet of the Apes (1971) 264, 268–69, 273
Essex, Harry J. 218
Evans, Gene 207
Evans, Maurice 212
Everything's Ducky (1961) 267–68
The Exorcist (1973) 9

Fair Exchange (TV) 176
Falk, Lee 52
"Fangoria" xi
The Fat Man (1951) 279
Father Knows Best (TV) 290, 297–98, 300
Father of the Bride (1950) 265
Father's Day (stage) 2
Father's Little Dividend (1951) 265
Faulkner, William 116, 117
Fear (1990 TV movie) 21–22
Fenneman, George 118, 119, 122
Fermi, Enrico 117–18
Fickling, Forrest E. 168
Fickling, Gloria 168
Fidler, Jimmie 278–79
Field, Margaret 248, 249
Field, Sally 248

The Final Countdown (1980) 264, 273-74
Finch, Peter 296
Finders Keepers (1951) 4
Fireside Theatre (TV) 279
Flaming Frontiers (1938 serial) 38
Flash Gordon (1936 serial) 53
Fleming, Rhonda 237
Flight to Tangier (1953) 212
Flipper (1963) 106, 107
Flipper (TV) 106, 107, 235
Flipper's New Adventure (1964) 106, 107
The Fly (1958) 88
The Flying Doctor (TV) 155
Flying Leathernecks (1951) 265
Flynn, Errol 54, 74, 147
Fonda, Henry 18
Footsteps in the Dark (1941) 74
For Love or Money (stage) 191
Forbidden Planet (1956) 26-27, 28-29, **28**, **161**, 162, 163-65, 166, 171, 218, 284
The Forbin Project see *Colossus—The Forbin Project*
Ford, Glenn 148, 149
Ford, John 18
Forever and a Day (1943) 190-91
Forrest, Sally 29
Fort Apache (1948) 16-17
Forty Carats (stage) 197
Foster, John xi
Foster, Susanna 78, 79
Foulger, Byron **68**
Four Star Playhouse (TV) 264, 267
Fowley, Douglas 69
The Foxes of Harrow (1947) 252
Foxx, Redd 274
Francis, Anne 27, 161-72, **161**, **167**, **169**, **171**
Francis Goes to West Point (1952) 223
Francis Joins the Wacs (1954) 7
Frank, Milo 222-23
Frankenheimer, John 33, 34
Franz, Eduard **119**
Frazer, Alex **125**
Frees, Paul **119**
Freiberger, Fred 203
Freleng, Friz 258
Fresco, Erin Ray xi
The Frozen Ghost (1945) 150

The Fugitive (TV) 32
Fuller, Lance 237
Fuller, Sam 210
Funny Girl (1968) 170
Futureworld (1976) 129

Gangelin, Paul 218
Garbo, Greta 123
Gardner, Erle Stanley 33
Garland, Beverly 156, 163, 256
Garner, James 241
Gaye, Lisa 230
Gemini Rising (1970 short) 170
General Hospital (TV) 9, 185
Gentleman's Agreement (1947) 296
Gerber, David 176, 177
Gere, Richard 202
Get Smart (TV) 128-29, 246, 260
Ghost of a Chance (1987 TV movie) 274
Ghostbusters II (1989) 15
Ghosts on the Loose (1943) 67
The Giant Behemoth (1959) 205-7, **206**, 208
The Giant Claw (1957) 212, 214, 217-18
Gilmore, Stuart 249
Gingold, Mike xi
Giradoux, Jean 60
The Girl in the Kremlin (1957) 250
Girls in Prison (1956) 155
Goddard, Mark 173-86, **173**, **180**, **181**, **183**, 194, 195, **196**
Goddard, Melissa 185, 186
Goddard, Robert 177
Gog (1954) **252**, 253
The Golden Mistress (1954) 20
Goldfinger (1964) 93
Goldwyn, Samuel 30
Gomez, Thomas 79
Gone with the Wind (1939) 54, 136
Good, John 142
Gorcey, Leo 67
Gordon, Alex xi, 154, 155
Gordon, Richard 155
Gorgo (1961) 207-10, **208**
Grand Canyon (1991) 60
Grand Illusion see *La Grande Illusion*
La Grande Illusion (1937) 203
Grant, Cary 124, 126, 155

Grant, Lee 271, 273
Gray, Billy 297
Gray, Lorna 65
Great Expectations (1934) 291–92
Great Expectations (1946) 292
The Great Scout and Cathouse Thursday (1976) 269
Green Dolphin Street (1947) 279
Greene, Angela 129
Greenhalgh, Jack 57
Greenway, Lee 116, 120
Gremlins (1984) 259–60
Grey, Joel 279
Grey, Virginia 151, **153**
Grippo, Jan 67
Gudegast, Hans see Braeden, Eric
Guideposts 193
Guillermin, John 21
Guinness, Alec 256
Gunslinger (1956) 256
Gunsmoke (TV) 121, 188, 193
Gwenn, Edmund 253–54

Hackett, Buddy 267
Hackett, Joan 166
Hailey, Oliver 2
Hall, Jon 76, 93
The Hallelujah Trail (1965) 166
The Halls of Ivy (TV) 295
Hamilton, George 268
Hancock, Lou 15
Hand of Death (1961) 21
Harlan, Russell 117, 119
Harlow, Jean 222
Harris, Harry 179
Harris, Jonathan 179, 181, 182, 194, 195
Harrison, Rex 252
Harryhausen, Ray 204, 205, 206
Hart, Leon 4
Hart, Moss 265
Haskin, Byron 123
Hathaway, Henry 116
Have Gun, Will Travel (TV) 268
Havens, James C. 5, 100
Hawaii Five-O (TV) 146, 157
Hawks, Howard 112, 113, 116–17, 118–19, 120, 121, 123, 124, 125–26, 248
Hayden, Russell 3
Hays, Robert 300

Hayward, Louis 31, 296, 297
Hayward, Susan 42
Hayworth, Rita 235
Healey, Myron 235
Healy, Bill 137
The Heavenly Kid (1985) 108
Hecht, Ben 117, 119
Heinlein, Robert 43
Hellcamp see *Opposing Force*
Hellinger, Mark 269
Hennesy, Tom **19**, 103, 105, **221**, 225
Henreid, Paul 264
Hepburn, Katharine 74, 78, 212
Here Comes Mr. Jordan (1941) 87
Hervey, Irene 168, 170
Heston, Charlton 193
The High and the Mighty (1954) 255–56
High Noon (1952) 91
High Sierra (1941) 43, 227
Hill Street Blues (TV) 184
Hiller, Arthur 267
Hilton, James 292, 293, 294
The Hindu see *Sabaka*
Hitchcock, Alfred 267
Hobart, Rose 54, 290
Hobson, Valerie 291–92
Hodiak, John 235
Hogan, Ben 16
Hogan, James 78
Holden, William 271, 273
Holdren, Judd 254, 255, 283
Holliday, Judy 265
Holliman, Earl 27
Holmes, Phillips 291, 292
Home of the Brave (1949) 88
Homebodies (1974) 69
Honey, I Blew Up the Kid (1992) 86
Honey, I Shrunk the Kids (1989) 86
Honey West (TV) 167–70, **169**
Hong Kong (TV) 267
Hopper, Hedda 295
Hopper, William 240
Horton, Edward Everett 64, 292, 295
Hot Rod Girl (1956) 227
Hot Shots! (1991) **90**, 94–95
Hot Shots! Part Deux (1993) 94
House by the River (1950) 296–97
The House of Fear (1945) 203
How to Frame a Figg (1971) 48
How to Marry a Millionaire (1953) 230

How to Marry a Millionaire (TV) 230
Howard, John 292, **301**
Hubbard, L. Ron 253
Hubschmid, Paul Christian, Paul
Hudson, Rock 7, 20, 33, 215, 235, 283
Hughes, Howard 113–14, 224, 237
Hull, Henry 291
The Human Beast see *La Bête Humaine*
The Human Comedy (1943) 264–65
Hume, Benita 295
Hunter, Jeffrey 166
Hunter, Kim 269, 273
Hunter, Neith 60
Huston, Walter 23, 87, 163
Hutton, Jim 9
Huxley, Aldous 298–99
Hyatt, Daniel 205, 207

I Died a Thousand Times (1955) 227, 230
I Dream of Jeannie (TV) 69
I Love Lucy (TV) 151
I Saw What You Did (1965) 48
In Society (1944) 203
The Incredible Hulk (TV) 69
The Incredible Shrinking Man (1957) 250, 260
The Incredible Shrinking Woman (1981) 242
Indiana Jones and the Last Crusade (1989) 27–28
Indusi, Jeff xi
Indusi, Joe xi
Initiation: Silent Night, Deadly Night 4 (1990) 60
Innerspace (1987) **245**, 260
The Invaders (TV) 31, 166
Invasion USA (1953) 253
Invisible Invaders (1959) 20
The Invisible Man's Revenge (1944) 203
Island Claws (1980) 108
"The Island of Doctor Moreau" 269, 270
The Island of Dr. Moreau (1977) 264, 269–71, **271**
Island of Lost Souls (1933) 270
Island of the Lost (1967) 108

It Came from Outer Space (1953) 152
It Conquered the World (1956) 21

Jack of Diamonds (1967) 268
Jacobs, Arthur P. 268
James, Brion 58
Janssen, David 32, 183, 223
Japanese War Bride (1952) 265
Jennie (state) 283
Jesse Lasky's Gateway to Hollywood (radio) 38–39
The Jimmy Stewart Show (TV) 9
Joan of Arc (1948) 248
Joe Forrester (TV) 93
Johnny Ringo (TV) 175, 178, 183
Johnson, Bill 42
Johnson, Russell 237
Johnson, Tom xi
Johnston, Jane A. 283
Johnstone, Bill 42
Jones, Henry 182
Jones, Morgan **28**
Joseph, Allen 58
Judas Was a Woman see *La Bête Humaine*
Jungle Woman (1944) 150
Junior "G" Men of the Air (1942 serial) 67
Just Between Friends (1986) 285

Kahn, Ivan 251
Kane, Joe xi
Karen, Ann **217**
Karen (TV) 156
Karloff, Boris 57, 78–79, 133, 291
Kasdan, Lawrence 60
Katz, Mickey 279
Katzman, Leonard 151
Katzman, Sam 18, 39, 40, 66–67, 74, 81, 151, 155, 218
Kazan, Elia 293, 296
Kellaway, Cecil 205
Kelly, Jack **28**
Kerr, Deborah 155, 158
Kevan, Jack 4, 98, 103
Kilbride, Percy 223
The Killers (1946) 269
Kind Hearts and Coronets (1949) 256
King, Frank 207, 208

Index 311

King, Maurice 207, 208
King Kong (1933) 204
King Kong (1976) 21
King of the Rocket Men (1949 serial) 281
King of the Zombies (1941) 39–40
Kings Row (1941) 222
Kirk, Tommy 176
The Kirlian Force see Psychic Killer
Kiss Me Deadly (1955) 126
Kiss of Fire (1955) 239, 240
The Kissing Bandit (1948) 279
Kleiser, Randal 86
Knight, Fuzzy 3
Knotts, Don 48
Koch, Howard W. 227
Kraike, Michael 218
Krakatoa, East of Java (1969) **201**, 210
Kramer, Stanley 91
Kristen, Marta 174, **180**, 194, 195, **196**
Kronos (1957) 88, 212, 216–17
Kruger, Otto **209**
Kubrick, Stanley 31
Kyser, Kay 133

Ladd, Alan 38, 133
Lady in the Dark (stage) 162
Lamarr, Hedy 256
Lamour, Dorothy 146, 158
Lancaster, Burt 33, 269, 270
Lance, Leon 253, 254
Land of the Giants (TV) 32, 69
Landau, Arthur 222
Landers, Lew 54, 57
Landis, Carole 147
Lane, Sara 48
Lang, Fritz 296–97
Lansworth, Lew X. 52, 53, 55, 57, 58
Larch, John 23
Larsen, Keith 106
Lasker, Edward 115
Lassie (TV) 188, 193
Last of the Redmen (1947) 151
Laurie, Piper 237
Law of the Lawless (1964) 21
The Lawless Breed (1952) 283
Lawrence, Barbara 216
Lawton, Frank 291
Lean, David 292
Lebedeff, Ivan 123

Lederer, Charles 116, 117
The Left Hand of God (1955) 116
Legacy of Blood (1973) 218–19
Leifert, Don xi
Leigh, Janet 116
Lenard, Mark 298
The Leopard (1963) 33
Lerner, Alan 42
Lewis, Jerry 227
Liberace 227
The Lieutenant (TV) 31
Lights, Camera, Action (TV) 29
Limelight (1952) 202, 210
Lindon, Lionel 43
Lippert, Robert L. 46, 88, 91–92, 216
The Lives of a Bengal Lancer (1935) 146
The Lloyd Bridges Show (TV) 93
Lockhart, Anne 188, 195, 197
Lockhart, Gene 189, 190, 191, 192–93, 197
Lockhart, John Coates 189
Lockhart, June 180, **180**, 182, 187–99, **187**, **192**, **196**, **198**
Lockhart, June Elizabeth 195
Lockhart, Kathleen 189, 190, 197
Loder, John 191
Loewe, Fritz 42
The Lone Wolf Takes a Chance (1941) 87
The Loner (TV) 93
Long, Richard 155
The Looters (1955) 7
Lord, Jack 157
Lord, Marjorie 40, 46, 48
Lorre, Peter 133
Lost Horizon (1937) 114, 235, 292–96, **294**
Lost Horizon (1973) 296
"Lost Horizon" 292, 293, 294
Lost in Space (TV) **173**, 174, 176–84, **180**, **181**, **183**, 186, 188–89, 193–97, **196**
The Lost Moment (1947) 42
Lourie, Eugene 201–10, **201**
Love Slaves of the Amazons (1957) 265–66
The Love War (1970 TV movie) 93–94
Loy, Myrna 183
Lubin, Arthur 74, 79, 80
Lucas, George 27

Luce, Greg xi
Lugones, Alex xi
Lugosi, Bela 38, 39, 40, **41**, 52,67, 133, 139, 140, **141**, 291
Lundigan, William **8**
Lupino, Ida 264
Lydecker, Howard 135, 136
Lydecker, Theodore 135, 136
Lynch, David 58

Ma and Pa Kettle at the Fair (1952) 223
McCallister, Lon 265
McCallum, David 93
McCarthy, Kevin 259
McClory, Kevin 108
McDevitt, Ruth 69
MacDonald, Kenneth 53
McDonnell, Dave xi
McDowall, Roddy 269, 273, 285
McEveety, Joseph 259
McGavin, Darren 34
McGiver, John 176
McLaglen, Victor 18
MacLane, Barton 151, **153**
MacMurray, Fred 40
McQueen, Steve 177, 178
Macready, George 54
The Mad Ghoul (1943) 77–78
Maggie Brown (unsold TV pilot) 176
The Magic Carpet (1951) 18–19
The Magnetic Monster (1953) 67–69, **68**
Maharis, George **169**
Mahoney, Jock 7, 248
Main, Marjorie 223
Majors, Lee 31–34, **35**, 298
Malden, Karl 265
The Male Animal (stage) 40
Malibu Run see *The Aquanauts*
Malone, Dorothy 250
The Man from Planet X (1951) 246–49, **247**
The Man from the Alamo (1953) 4
The Man from U.N.C.L.E. (TV) 31, 166
The Man in the Iron Mask (1939) 31
Man of La Mancha (stage) 283
The Man Who Played God (1932) 227
Man Without a Gun (TV) 241

The Manchurian Candidate (1962) 33
Mangean, Teddy 120
Mank, Greg xi
Mann, Johnny 230
Manning, Irene 42
Mannix (TV) 155
Man's Favorite Sport? (1964) 126
Manson, Charles 26, 53
Many Happy Returns (TV) 176
Margo 292
Marin, Edwin L. 190
Mark of the Renegade (1951) 113
Marshall, George 64
Martin, Dean 227
Martin, Dewey 114, 122
Martin, Mary 283
Martin, Ross 257
Martin, Sobey 179
Marton, Andrew 93, 235
Martucci, Mark xi
The Mask of Diijon (1946) 54–57
Mask of the Himalayas see *Storm over Tibet*
The Masked Marvel (1943 serial) **131**, 134, 137–39, **140**
Massen, Osa 88, **90**, 91
Master Minds (1949) 67
Matheson, Richard 34, 250
Mathews, Kerwin 218
Matinee (1993) **128**, **260**
Mature, Victor 147
Maverick (TV) 241
May, Bob **183**, 195
Mayer, Louis B. 27, 30
Meador, Joshua 165
Medavoy, Mike 185
Meet Me in St. Louis (1944) 191
Megowan, Don 106, 216
Merman, Ethel 176
Merrill, Gary 93, 265
Michael Shayne (TV) 146, 148, 155, 175
Middleton, Charles 67
Mighty Joe Young (1949) 253
Miller, Ann 116
Million Dollar Manhunt see *Assignment Redhead*
Minnelli, Liza 185
Miracle Mile (1989) 14–15
Miracle on 34th Street (1947) 253
Miss Annie Rooney (1942) 190

The Missing Head see *Strange Confession*
Mission: Impossible (TV) 69
Mission Over Korea (1953) 235
Mr. and Mrs. North (TV) 146, 155
Mitchell, Thomas 292, 295
The Mole People (1956) 20
Mom (1991) 52, 58–60
Monkey Business (1952) 118, 123–26
The Monkey's Uncle (1965) 176
The Monolith Monsters (1957) 253
Monroe, Marilyn 124–25
Monson, Carl 218
Montez, Maria 76, 77
Montgomery, Elizabeth 190
Moore, Clayton 65, **66**, 279, 280, 282
Moore, Gar **32**
Moranis, Rick 86
Moreland, Mantan 39
Morell, Andre 207
Moreno, Antonio 5
Morheim, Lou 203
Moriarty, Cathy **128**, **260**
Morris, Chester 52
Morris, Wayne 188
Morrison, Bret 42
Morrow, Jeff 106, 211–19, **211**, **214**, **215**, **217**, 237, 238, **239**, 240, **241**
Morrow, Lisa **217**
Most Happy Fella (stage) 283
Muhl, Edward 99, 237
The Mummy's Ghost (1944) 75
The Mummy's Hand (1940) 75
The Mummy's Tomb (1942) 75
Mumy, Billy 194, 195, **196**
Murder, She Wrote (TV) 9
Murphy, Audie 222, 224, 283
Murray, Forbes **66**
Murray, Will xi
My Favorite Husband (radio) 151
"My Work in Films" 210

The Naked City (1948) 265, 267, 270
The Naked Kiss (1964) 210
Naked Paradise (1957) 155
Nance, John 58
Napoleon, Art 268
Nayfack, Nicholas 26, 164
Neill, Roy William 41

Nelson, Lori 2, 7, **19**, 20, 103, 221–232, **221**, **226**, **228**, **231**
Neumann, Kurt 88, 212
Never Say Never Again (1983) 108
New Girl in Town (stage) 278, 283
Newland, John 57
Newman, Joseph 238
Newman, Paul 178
Newman, Samuel 218
Nichols, Mike 108
Nichols, Robert 116, 125, 237
Nielsen, Leslie 27, **28**, 164, 165
Night Gallery (TV) 268
Night in Paradise (1946) 76, 79–80
'night, Mother (stage) 222
The Night Strangler (1972 TV movie) 34
Nightbreed (1990) 15–16
Nimoy, Leonard 223, **289**, 298, 299
Nobody's Perfekt (1981) 108
None but the Lonely Heart (1944) 296
North West Mounted Police (1940) 147
Now You See Him, Now You Don't (1972) 259
Nyby, Christian 112, 113, 117, 119, 122
Nyoka and the Tigermen see *Perils of Nyoka*

Oates, Warren 182
O'Bannon, Rockne S. 23
Oberon, Merle 79
O'Brian, Hugh 88, **90**, 91
O'Brien, Edmond 265
O'Brien, George 18
O'Brien, Willis H. 204, 206–7
O'Connor, Donald 7, 223
Octaman (1971) 218
The Odds on Mrs. Oakley (stage) 42
Odets, Clifford 296
O'Donnell, Cathy **80**
O'Feldman, Ric 107
The Oklahoma Woman (1956) 155
Olivier, Laurence 264
The Omen (1976) 271, 273
Ondine (stage) 60
One Desire (1955) 7
One Life to Live (TV) 185
One Million B.C. (1940) 147
One More River (1934) 291
One Step Beyond (TV) 57

1000 Years from Now see *Captive Women*
Ophuls, Max 202, 203
Oppenheimer, J. Robert 117
Opposing Force (1986) 108
O'Sullivan, Maureen 235
Othello (stage) 87
O'Toole, Peter 269
The Outlaw Gang see *The Dalton Gang*
Outlaw's Son (1957) 227
The Ox-Bow Incident (1943) 69

Pajama Game (stage) 283
Pal, George 38, 43, 45–46, 88, 123
Palance, Jack 227, 230
Palmer, Dawson 184
Pardners (1956) 227
Parla, Donna xi
Parla, Paul xi
Parsons, Lindsley 39
Paths of Glory (1957) 31
The Patty Duke Show (TV) 250, 256
The Pearl of Death (1944) 150
Pembroke, George **63**, 66
Penn, Leo 179
Penn, Sean 179
The Perfect Bride (1991 TV movie) 21, 23
Perils of Nyoka (1942 serial) **61**, 64, 65–66, **66**, 67
Perry Mason (TV) 31, 32–33
Peters, Jean 124, 125
Peterson, Pete 206
The Phantom (1943 serial) 52–54, **55**, **56**
Phantom of the Opera (1943) 78
Philbert (1963 TV pilot) 258
Pichel, Irving 43, 45, 46
Pidgeon, Walter 27, 164
Pierce, Jack P. 76, 79, 291
The Pinto Kid (1941) 133
Pipe Dream (stage) 283
Pivar, Ben 78
Planet of the Apes (1968) 268, 269
Planet of the Apes (TV) 285
Play It Again, Sam (1972) 185
Poison Ivy (1992) 186
Pollexfen, Jack 246–47, 248, 249, 250
Port Sinister (1953) 253

Porter, Don 191
Portrait of Jennie (1948) 163
Post, Ted 268–69
Powell, Dick 175, 264, 266, 275
Powers, Tom 43, **44**
Pratt, Jim 99, 105
Presley, Elvis 7, 9, 48
Preston, Kelly 21, 23
Price, Vincent 156
Prison (1988) 285
Prisoners of the Casbah (1953) 74, 81
Protocol (1984) 285
Psychic Killer (1975) 9
Psycho (1960) 9
Punchline (1988) 285
Purcell, Dick 39

Quaid, Dennis 14
Quick as a Flash (radio) 42
Quiet Please, Murder (1942) 149

Rackmil, Milton 224
Radar Men from the Moon (1952 serial) 277, 278, 279–83, **280**, **282**, 285
Raiders of the Desert (1941) 75
Rainer, Luise 212
Raise the Titanic! (1980) 108
Raitt, John 283
Ralston, Vera 136
Rand, Patrick 58
Randell, Ron 249
Randolph, John 33, 34
Rathbone, Basil 40, 203
Ray, Fred Olen xi
Raymond, Paula 204, 205
Reason, Rex 216, 233–43, **233**, **235**, **239**, **241**
Red, Hot and Blue (1949) 3
Reed, Philip 151, **153**
La Règle Du Jeu (1939) 203
Rennie, Michael 182
Renoir, Jean 202, 203, 205, 210
Return of Captain Marvel see *Adventures of Captain Marvel*
The Return of the Six Million Dollar Man and the Bionic Woman (1987 TV movie) 35
The Return of the Vampire (1943) 52
Revenge of the Creature (1955) 2, 14,

17, 18, **19**, 20, 101–5, **221**, 222, 224–27, **226**, 231–32
Reynolds, Burt 34, 164, 230
Reynolds, Debbie 30, 172
Rich Man, Poor Man (TV) 48
Ride the Wild Surf (1964) 268
The Rifleman (TV) 175
Riskin, Robert 293
Ritt, Martin 265
Rivas, Carlos 156
The Road Back (1937) 65
Road House (1989) 15
The Roaring Twenties (TV) 241
The Robe (1953) 212
Robert Montgomery Presents (TV) 191–93
Roberts, Judith Anna 58
Robinson, Ann **125**
Robinson, Edward G. 183, 268
Rock Around the Clock (1956) 48
The Rocket Man (1954) 20, 163
Rocketship X-M (1950) 46, 88–91, **89**, **90**, 93
Roddenberry, Gene 298, 299
Rodgers, Richard 283
Rogers, Ginger 124, 126, 283, 284
Romero, Cesar 81
Rooney, Mickey 163, 267
Root, Elizabeth **68**
Rope (1948) 267
Rosenstein, Sophie 223
The Rules of the Game see *La Règle Du Jeu*
Rush, Barbara 235
Russell, Bing 183
Russell, Jack 203
Russell, Jane 224
Russell, John 219
Russell, Kurt 182–83, 259
Ryan, Meg 14

Sabaka (1953) 57
Sagal, Boris 251
Salmi, Albert 182
Salome (1953) 235
Salty (1973) 108, 109
San Francisco International Airport (TV) 93
Sanders, George 164
Sands of Iwo Jima (1949) 16, 18

Santa Fe (1951) 45
Sargent, Joseph 258
The Satan Bug (1965) 166, **169**
Scapperotti, Dan xi
The Scarlet Coat (1955) 164
Schallert, Edwin 250–51
Schallert, William **128**, 245–62, **245**, **246**, **252**, **260**
Schary, Dore 30, 164
Schiller, Norbert **119**
Schow, David xi
Schwartz, Howard 176
Science Fiction Theatre (TV) 47–48, 253–54
Scrivani, Rich xi
Sea Hunt (TV) **85**, 86, 91, 92–93, 94, 106
The Sea of Grass (1947) 279
The Search for Bridey Murphy (1956) 31
Second Chance (1947) 141
Seconds (1966) 33–34
Selznick, David O. 16, 18
Selznick, Joyce 21
Sergeant York (1941) 190
Serling, Rod 33, 48, 57, 93, 166, 268
Seven Days in May (1964) 33
The Shadow (1994) 48
The Shadow (radio) 38, 42, 48
Shadows on the Stairs (1941) 75
Shakespeare, William 28
Shannon, Frank 53
Sharpe, Dave 63–64, 135, 136, 139
Shatner, William 257, 299
Shaw, George Bernard 253
She Devil (1957) 47, **47**
She-Wolf of London (1946) 191, **192**
She Wore a Yellow Ribbon (1949) 16
Sheedy, Ally 21–22
Sheridan, Margaret 122
Sherlock Holmes in Washington (1943) 40–41
Sherwood, John 216, 240
Shirley, Anne 39
"Shirley Temple: America's Princess" 16
Shirley Temple's Storybook (TV) 193
Shock Corridor (1963) 210
Short, Martin 260
Simmons, Jean 212
Sincerely Yours (1955) 227

Siodmak, Curt 67–69, 153, 265, 266
Siodmak, Robert 265
Sirk, Douglas 216
Six Black Horses (1962) 283
The Six Million Dollar Man (1973 TV movie) 285
The Six Million Dollar Man (TV) 26, 31, 34–35, **35**, 108
16 Fathoms Deep (1948) 92
Skal, David xi
Skelton, Red 257
Slaughter on Tenth Avenue (1957) 7
Smith, C. Aubrey 291
Smith, John 219
Smoke Signal (1955) 239
Snowden, Leigh 7, **215**, 216, 240
So Young, So Bad (1950) 163
Son of Lassie (1945) 191
Sonnenberg, Gus 42
Sons and Daughters (TV) 285
The Soul of a Monster (1944) 54
Space Patrol (TV) 254
Spelling, Aaron 175
Spencer, Douglas 119, 125, 213
Spielberg, Steven 27, 259
The Spiritualist see *The Amazing Mr. X*
Spook Busters (1946) 67
Stack, Robert 148
Stage to Thunder Rock (1964) 21
Stagecoach (1939) 136
Stahl, John M. 252, 253
Stalag 17 (1953) 265, 273
The Stand at Apache River (1953) 4
Stanley, Ginger 5, 100
Stanwyck, Barbara 168, 223
Star in the Dust (1956) 20, **22**
Star Trek (TV) 179, 257–58, **289**, 290, 298, 299, 300
Star Trek: The Next Generation (TV) 298
Star Trek IV: The Voyage Home (1986) 299, 300
"Starlog" xi
Starman (TV) 300
Starrett, Charles 52, 133
Steel, Bob 42
Steele, Tom 137, 139, 281
Stemple, Frank 38, 39
Stepkids see *Big Girls Don't Cry ... They Get Even*

Stern, Leonard 128–29
Stevens, Craig 240
Stevens, George 116
Stevens, Robert 267
Stevens, Stella 59
Stevens, Warren **28**, 219
Stevenson, Bob 282
Steward, Don 117
Stewart, Gloria 9
Stewart, James 9, 224
Stockwell, Dean 162
Stone, Andrew 126
Stone, Milburn 237
Stone, Virginia 126
Storm Over Tibet (1952) 235. 241
The Story of Mankind (1957) 256
Strange, Glenn 667
Strange, Robert **63, 66**
Strange Confession (1945) 87
Strange Invaders (1983) 185
The Strangler (1964) 57
Streep, Meryl 230
Streisand, Barbra 170
Striepeke, Dan 269
The Strongest Man in the World (1975) 258, 259
The Stuntman (1980) 285
Sturges, John 166
Sturges, Preston 29
Submarine Command (1951) 273
Sudan (1945) 77
Suicide Battalion (1958) 21
Sullivan, Francis L. 292
Summer Holiday (1948) 163
The Sun Sets at Dawn (1950) 279
Suppose They Gave a War and Nobody Came? (1970) 58
Suzanne, George **140**
Svehla, Gary xi, 14
Svehla, Sue xi, 14
Swamp Fox (TV) 285
Sword of Venus (1953) 248
Sylvester, William 207, 210

The Tall Texan (1953) 92
Talton, Alix 240
Tanganyika (1954) 212
Tarantula (1955) 14, 18, 20
Target Earth (1954) 146, 152–53
Task Force (1949) 300

Taylor, Adam 188, 197
Taylor, Buck 188
Taylor, Don 263–76, **263**, **271**, 272, **274**
Taylor, Dub 188
Taylor, Elizabeth 162, 265
Taylor, Jonathan Scott 271
Taylor, Kent 141
Taylor, Robert 176
Taylor, Rod 267
Taza, Son of Cochise (1954) 235, 236, 237
The Tempest (stage) 28
Temple, Shirley 16, 190
$10 Raise (1935) 64
Ten Seconds to Hell (1959) 126–27
Them! (1954) 253
The Thing (1982) 122
The Thing from Another World (1951) 112, 113–22, **119**, 123, 125, 129, 248–49, 253
Third Party Risk see *Deadly Game*
This Island Earth (1955) **211**, 212–15, 216, 219, 234, 235, 236, **236**, 237–239, **239**, 240, 242
Thomas, Frank 65
Thomas, Frank, Jr. 65
Thomas, Larri 226, 227
Thriller (TV) 31, 127, 128
Thunder Over Hawaii see *Naked Paradise*
Thunderball (1965) 7–9
Tickle Me (1965) 7–9
Tidal Wave see *Portrait of Jennie*
Tigger xi
Tighe, Virginia 31
Tightrope! (TV) 155
Tim Tyler's Luck (1937 serial) 65
Timpone, Tony xi
Tiomkin, Dimitri 115, 292
Tobey, Kenneth 112, 114, 115, 116, 118, 121, 122, 219
Tobor the Great (1954) 254
The Today Show (TV) 170
Tombstone (1993) 188
Tone, Franchot 146
Tors, Ivan 47, 48, 67, 92, 93, 106, 107, 108, 235, 253
Totter, Audrey 235
Touch of Evil (1958) 249–50
Tough Guys (1986) 33

The Towering Inferno (1974) 178
Towne, Aline 255, 279, 281
Tracy, Spencer 163
Trade Winds (stage) 290
Travers, Bill 207, 210
The Trip to Bountiful (stage) 222
Troll (1986) 197
Tuttle, William 34
Twelve O'Clock High (1949) 29
Twice-Told Tales (1963) 156
The Twilight Zone (TV) 48, 57, 69, 127–28, 166, 250
Twilight Zone – The Movie (1983) 259
Twins (1988) 23
Two Tickets to Broadway (1951) 116
Tyler, Tom 52, 53, **55**, 62, 63, 134, 136–37, **138**

Ullmann, Liv 296
Ulmer, Edgar G. 247
The Undefeated (1969) 21
Underwater! (1955) 224, 227
The Underwater City (1962) 7, **8**
Union Pacific (1939) 147
Unknown Island (1948) 151–52, **153**
The Unsinkable Molly Brown (stage) 283, 284
Untamed Youth (1957) 227
Up Front (1951) 279

Van Dyke, Dick 274
Van Patten, Vincent 34
Van Ronkel, Rip 43
Van Sickel, Dale 281
Van Vogt, A. E. 253
Verdon, Gwen 283
Vernac, Denise 55
Victor, Henry 39
Visconti, Luchino 33
"Voices from Home: An Inner Journey" 170
von Stroheim, Erich 54, 55, 57
Voodoo Man (1944) 139, 140
Voodoo Woman (1957) 21
Voyage to the Bottom of the Sea (TV) 127, 128, 193

Waco (1966) 21
Wagenheim, Charles 254

Waggner, George 78, 79
Waggner, Lia 249, 254, 255
Wagner, Lindsay 34
A Walk in the Sun (1945) 88
Walker, Joseph 292
Walker, Stuart 292
Walking My Baby Back Home (1953) 223
Wallace, Chris 170
Wallace, George 277–87, **277**, **280**, **282**, **286**
Walsh, Raoul 42, 43
Wanger, Walter 42
The War of the Worlds (1953) 122–23, **125**, 129, 218
Warner, Jack L. 205
Wayne, John 16, 18, 21, 120, 124, 136, 255
Weaver, Jon xi
Weaver, Julie xi
Webster, Ferris 166
Welbourne, Charles "Scotty" 4–5, 98
Weld, Tuesday 183
Welles, Orson 42, 116, 133, 134, 249, 264
Wellman, William A. 69, 255
Wells, H. G. 269
Wengraf, John 253
Wessel, Dick **153**
Wesson, Dick 43, **44**, 46
Wesson, Gene 46
West, Mae 212
Westmore, Bud 4
Westworld (1973) 129
Whale, James 65, 291
What Ever Happened to Baby Jane? (1962) 126, 127
The Whistle at Eaton Falls (1951) 163
The White Cliffs of Dover (1945) 191
White Heat (1949) 43
White Savage (1943) 77
"Who Goes There?" 122
Whodunit? (radio) 52
Wilcox, Fred McLeod 26, 28, 164–65
The Wild Wild West (TV) 31, 257
Wilder, Billy 29, 116

Williams, Grant 250
Williams, Guy 180, **180**, 181–82, **181**, 188, 189, 193, 195, 196, **196**
Windom, William 268
Windsor, Marie 92
Winged Victory (1944) 265
Winged Victory (stage) 265
Winningham, Mare 15
Winstrom (unmade movie) 14
Winter, Vincent 210
Winters, Shelley 230
Wisberg, Aubrey 246–47, 248, 249, 250
Witney, William 64, 135, 136
Wolfe, Ian 69
Wolff, Ed **209**
Wood, Edward D., Jr. 69
Wood, Natalie 162
Woodbury, Joan 66
Worth, Harry **63**
Written on the Wind (1956) 250
Wyatt, Jane 289–302, **289**, **294**, **297**, **301**
Wyler, William 170
Wynn, Keenan 93
Wynyard, Diana 291

Yancy Derringer (TV) 7
Yankee Pasha (1954) 235, 236–37
Yarbrough, Jean 40, 191
York, Michael 270
You'll Find Out (1940) 133
Young, Gig 38
Yust, Larry 69
Yuzna, Brian 60

Zamba (1949) 93
Zamba the Gorilla see *Zamba*
Zanuck, Darryl F. 163
Ziker, Dick 34
Zinnemann, Fred 31
Zorro (TV) 182
Zucco, George 77, 140
Zugsmith, Albert 248, 249–50

www.ingramcontent.com/pod-product-compliance
Ingram Content Group UK Ltd.
Pitfield, Milton Keynes, MK11 3LW, UK
UKHW041923140426
5217IPUK00014B/291